Electoral Dynamics in the Philippines

Electoral Dynamics in the Philippines

Money Politics, Patronage, and Clientelism at the Grassroots

Edited by
Allen Hicken, Edward Aspinall, and Meredith Weiss

NUS PRESS
SINGAPORE

Published by:

NUS Press
National University of Singapore
AS3-01-02, 3 Arts Link
Singapore 117569

Fax: (65) 6774-0652
E-mail: nusbooks@nus.edu.sg
Website: http://nuspress.nus.edu.sg

ISBN 978-981-3250-52-9 (paper)

National Library Board, Singapore Cataloguing in Publication Data

Name(s): Hicken, Allen, editor. | Aspinall, Edward, editor. | Weiss, Meredith, editor.
Title: Electoral dynamics in the Philippines: money politics, patronage, and clientelism at the grassroots / edited by Allen Hicken, Edward Aspinall, and Meredith Weiss.
Description: Singapore: NUS Press, [2019] | Includes bibliographical references and index.
Identifier(s): OCN 1090691401 | ISBN 978-981-32-5052-9 (paperback)
Subject(s): LCSH: Elections--Philippines--21st century. | Elections--Corrupt practices--Philippines. | Politics, Practical--Philippines--21st century. | Philippines--Politics and government--21st century.
Classification: DDC 324.709599--dc23

Cover: Photo by Richard Ian Mark T. Necosia

Typeset by: Ogma Solutions Pvt Ltd
Printed by: Mainland Press Pte Ltd

Contents

List of Tables and Figures

Acknowledgements

This volume would not have been possible without the support of a large number of individuals and institutions. Funding for the larger project, which focused on electoral dynamics in Malaysia, Indonesia and the Philippines,[1] came from a Discovery Project grant from the Australian Research Council (DP140103114). Our work in the Philippines was supplemented with grants from the Australian Department of Foreign Affairs and Trade and De La Salle University.

The highlight of this project has been collaborating with a large number of outstanding researchers in each country, and the Philippines was no exception. We could not have asked for a better partner than De La Salle University, and a better champion than Dean Julio Teehankee, who was an enthusiastic participant in the project from its very inception. At DLSU, Allen Surla, with the assistance of Glenn Teh, had the herculean task of managing the logistics for a team of more than 50 researchers scattered across the archipelago and somehow managed to keep the trains running on time. We also benefitted from our interactions with and support from faculty and staff at the University of the Philippines-Diliman and Ateneo de Manila University. Ronald Holmes and Pulse Asia were also critical partners. At the local level special thanks go to Grace Labalan who organised and managed our team of researchers in Sorsogon, cheerfully adapting to a number of unforeseen challenges and difficulties, and to Nico and Ditas Ravanilla for facilitating our research in Sorsogon. Joel Rocamora generously shared his time and insights with us on multiple occasions, providing both a bird's-eye and ground-level view of electoral dynamics. Finally, Paul Hutchcroft, who co-wrote the introduction to this volume with us, has been a wonderful collaborator and continued to be so during this study, even while other duties demanded much of his time.

Our biggest thanks go to an amazing team of researchers from across the Philippines. Only sixteen are represented in this volume, but each of

---

[1] Other publications in connection with this project include Weiss 2015, Aspinall and Sukmajati 2016, and Weiss and Puyok 2017.

them did incredible work in what were often challenging circumstances. They are: Lord Byron Abadez, Banni Paul Alli, Tetchie Aquino, Cleve Kevin Arguelles, Aries Arugay, Mary Pauline Balmes, Carmina Bayombong, Marvin Bernardo, Mary Joyce Bulao, Cleo Calimbahin, Menchie Ann Canlas, Gladstone Cuarteros, Duke Thomas Dolorical, Gerardo Eusebio, Jan Robert Go, Neil Steven Holmes, Georgeline Jaca, Acram Latiph, Kristoffer Daniel Li, Ladylyn Lim, Raph Limiac, Regina Macalandag, Roland Macawil, Francisco Magno, Jazztin Jairum Manalo, Armida Miranda, Louie Montemar, Marilou Nanaman, Richard Iam Mark Necosia, Margie Nolasco, Ella Oplas, Allan Hil Pajimola, Neil Pancho, Aldrin Pelicano, Allan Quiñanola, Michele M. Rocela, Jose Aims Rocina, Chonilo Saldon, Chanda Pearl Simeon, Michelle Sta. Romana, Diana Taganas, Phylis Marie Teanco, Donabel Tumandoa and Jonalyn Villasante. We also express our thanks to the candidates, brokers, journalists and academics who agreed to meet with our researchers and provide them information and access.

We also benefitted from our interactions with a number of scholars outside of the Philippines. We were fortunate to work with two skilled research assistants: Michael Davidson, who helped us design all aspects of our work in the Philippines, and Dotan Haim, who worked on this volume. Along the way we also benefitted from feedback from numerous scholars, including Paul Hutchcroft, Erik Kuhonta, Steven Rood, Julio Teehankee, Ward Berenschot, and participants in a workshop at Kyoto University. Thanks also to Maxine McArthur of the Department of Political and Social Change, Coral Bell School of Asia Pacific Affairs, Australian National University for her copy-editing. We are also grateful for the feedback from two anonymous reviewers.

Finally, we express our gratitude to our loved ones, who gave us the time and support needed to carry out this project.

Allen Hicken, Edward Aspinall, & Meredith Weiss

chapter **1**

Introduction: The Local Dynamics of the National Election in the Philippines

Allen Hicken, Paul Hutchcroft, Meredith Weiss,
and Edward Aspinall

The Philippines general election of 9 May 2016 gained global attention largely for the president who came to office, the unusually coarse and controversial Rodrigo Duterte.[1] Along with a slogan proclaiming that "change is coming", Duterte used novel techniques and new types of appeals to win the election handily (garnering a plurality of 39 per cent of the vote, some 15 percentage points more than his nearest challenger). In order to overcome a lack of resources, most apparent in the early months of his candidacy, the campaign introduced innovations with heavy reliance on the use of social media: highly sophisticated and well-coordinated messaging not constrained by norms of veracity (Ressa 2016; Hofileña 2016). Duterte's appeals had strong authoritarian underpinnings, as he promised to combat the problems of drugs, crime and corruption with the same coercive approaches that had won him widespread popularity as mayor of Davao City. As he proudly proclaimed before becoming president, "You will see the fish in Manila Bay getting fat" from all the executed criminals that he planned to dump there (HRW 2017).

---

[1] Parts of this introduction draws on Edward Aspinall, Allen Hicken, Meredith L. Weiss and Michael W. Davidson, "Local Machines and Vote Brokerage in the Philippines", *Contemporary Southeast Asia* 38 (2) (2016): 191–6.

Duterte's new techniques and shocking appeals should be viewed as part of the long-term evolution of national campaign strategies—going back at least to the innovation of more direct candidate appeals in the 1950s and the expansion of radio and television coverage in subsequent decades (Hutchcroft and Rocamora 2012: 105). There have also been many innovations in local-level campaigns, reflecting major shifts in local politics and political economies. Contributing factors include the long authoritarian interlude of Ferdinand Marcos (1972–86), significant devolution since 1991, and the automation of elections in 2010. Rapid urbanisation and a growing urban middle class, along with diversification of local economies connected with industrialisation, tourism, initiatives in agriculture and fisheries, and inflows of capital from overseas migration were also significant. Particularly in areas with the most dynamic economies, local patrons no longer enjoy the same degree of socio-economic dominance over their clients as that described and analysed in Carl Landé's classic 1965 work on patron-client relations.

Amidst such sweeping changes, however, there has been substantial continuity in how money and patronage politics continue to play a central role in local political contests throughout the Philippines. This continuity was on full display in the nationally synchronised 2016 election, which involved not only the notorious presidential contest but also thousands of other national and local races, from the Philippines Senate to the House of Representatives to gubernatorial and mayoral contests to provincial, city and municipal boards. The chapters in this volume detail and analyse the electoral dynamics in a subset of localities nationwide in order to shed light on how electoral campaigns were organised across regions of the Philippines. We are particularly interested in how candidates and their campaigns choose to appeal to and mobilise voters, the kinds of political networks used in campaigns, and how voters respond to different kinds of electoral appeals.

The research upon which this volume is based is part of a larger investigation into political networks and patronage flows across electoral regimes in Southeast Asia.[2] The Philippines portion of this project involved a team of more than 50 local and international researchers, spread throughout the Philippines. Researchers interviewed candidates, campaign staff, and vote brokers (termed locally *liders*); shadowed

---

[2] This research has been funded by a Discovery Project grant from the Australian Research Council (DP140103114) and was carried out in partnership with De La Salle University.

campaign sorties; observed campaign events; and scrutinised both the messages and gifts that candidates and their teams distributed. The aim was to develop a coherent sense not only of how campaigns work on the ground, but also of how that ground varies (or not) across areas and communities throughout the Philippines.

The chapters in this volume draw on some of the best work of these 50 researchers to present a picture of electoral dynamics at the grassroots level in the Philippines. The focus on local electoral dynamics sheds light on two key dimensions of Philippine elections: (a) the nature of political alliances and machines and (b) the role of money in greasing the wheels of those machines and mobilising voters. These two dimensions come together to produce a distinctive pattern of electoral mobilisation that pervades Philippines politics. The common pattern, fleshed out in more detail below, is that of a *local political machine* (or, just as often, competing local machines). It is our contention that the local political machine constitutes the foundation of contemporary Philippine electoral politics. Such local political machines are typically built around a leading local politician or family and incorporate connections with lower-level politicians. They also crucially include a multi-tiered brokerage structure connecting the political leader not only downward with voters but also upward with national-level politicians and parties.

Indeed, even national-level politics depends on such machines. For example, consider President Duterte. His rise to power and prominence was built on the foundations of a tightly knit local machine, centred on him as mayor of Davao City, Mindanao.[3] While he may be unusual in how he managed to propel himself from his local base to the highest office in the land—the first politician ever to do so—the pattern of strong local machines is one that we observe again and again in the Philippines.

Local machines bring with them a degree of local stability (and sometimes stagnancy) that belies the electoral volatility common at the national level of electoral politics. The same local machines, often family-based, tend to endure from election to election, even as the offices they hold and their national partisan loyalties can vary. However, while local machines are ubiquitous, they are not uniform. The contributors to this volume analyse the varied ways these local machines recruit loyalists, distribute resources, and seek to mobilise a winning number of voters

---

[3] This is not to suggest that Duterte's local machine is the sole reason for his success. Duterte's campaign stood apart from other campaigns, past and present, for a host of other reasons, from the nature of his rhetoric to his campaign's use of social media.

on election day. Amidst many commonalities across cases, notably the critical role of local machines and the centrality of patronage politics, the chapters also describe interesting and important elements of diversity— reflecting not only the differential importance of coercion but also a few locales where alternative forms of electoral politics have developed or are emerging.

The rest of this introductory chapter proceeds as follows. We first describe the setting, scope and goals of this volume and the underlying project as well as the questions, methods and research design at the heart of this study. Next, we situate our study within the rich literature on electoral dynamics and clientelism in the Philippines, and then provide a brief introduction to the political and institutional context to the 2016 election. We next turn our attention to the resources that flow across the electoral cycle but that increase to a heavy volume around election time. These resources range from pork barrel expenditures to jobs (whether plum appointments or lowly positions) to payments handed out to voters in the lead-up to the election. They enable candidates to construct and maintain their electoral machines, and help candidates build lasting relationships of loyalty and trust among some voters. After focusing on electoral resources, we turn to the machinery of electoral politics in the Philippines—the networks on which candidates rely, the organisations they build, and the alliances they form. The final two sections provide comparisons across locales and examine the weakness of national-level (as opposed to local-level) political machines.

SCOPE AND DESIGN OF THE RESEARCH

Our work in the Philippines around the 2016 election was part of a larger research project on electoral dynamics and money politics in Southeast Asia, and followed similar efforts centred on recent elections in Malaysia (2013) and Indonesia (2014).[4] The original conceptual foundations of our study untangled two closely-related but distinctive terms: patronage and clientelism. While the two terms are sometimes treated as synonymous (for example, in the influential work of Kitschelt & Wilkinson 2007), we utilise clear definitions in order to overcome longstanding conceptual confusion (building on Hutchcroft 2014a). Patronage is a *material*

---

[4] This volume complements Weiss 2015; Aspinall and Sukmajati 2016; and Weiss and Puyok 2017.

resource, disbursed for particularistic benefit for political purposes and generally (but not always) derived from public sources. Shefter's (1994: 283) seminal work offers a foundational definition: "Patronage ... involves the exchange of public benefits for political support or party advantage", and is given out by politicians to "individual voters, campaign workers, or contributors". This definition should be amended to reflect the fact that a great deal of patronage also flows among politicians, typically from higher levels (for example, the presidential palace and congresspersons) down to lower levels (for example, governors and mayors).

Clientelism, on the other hand, describes a *personalistic relationship of power*. In its classical definition, persons of higher social status (patrons) are linked to those of lower social status (clients) in face-to-face and enduring ties of reciprocity that can vary in content, purpose and direction across time. As James Scott (1972: 93) explains, "there is an imbalance in exchange between the two partners which expresses and reflects the disparity in their relative wealth, power, and status". Clientelist relationships are thus typically hierarchal and involve ongoing, iterated personal interactions where the behaviour of each party is contingent on the behaviour of the other (Hicken 2011).

Using these definitions, patronage, as an adjective, modifies resources and flows, and clientelistic, as an adjective, modifies relationships, linkages and ties. Untangling the definitions of patronage and clientelism allows for greater analytical precision. Not all patronage involves clientelism, as some patronage flows are impersonal and others are personal. And not all clientelism involves patronage, as the exchange of goods and services (as described by Scott) may or may not involve the "exchange of public benefits" (as described by Shefter). Indeed, the classic clientelistic tie, between landlords and tenants, can exist largely outside the state.

Our core research questions centre on candidate strategies, organisation and networks, as well as voter behaviour. An underlying theme motivating the research is the role of money in the electoral process. Starting with candidate strategies, we are interested in the kinds of appeals candidates rely on to mobilise voters. Do they emphasise policy differences, or ethnic or religious or class identities, or do they primarily rely on material appeals? If material appeals are important, what forms do these take? Do candidates rely on pork barrel and patronage to supply local public goods or more narrowly targeted club goods?[5] Do they target funds to

---

[5] Club goods are goods or benefits directed at groups of individuals that can be withheld from other groups but not withheld from individuals within the group.

social, political or religious leaders in wholesale vote buying efforts, or to individual voters in retail vote buying strategies? How important is everyday patronage during or between campaign periods (for example, money for medicine, cement for a new floor, bags of rice)?

From the voters' perspective, we focus on the factors that guide their decision about who to support. What are they thinking about when they enter the polling place? To what extent are they motivated by ethnic or religious affinities? Do party labels or policy platforms influence their decisions? Are personal or family ties an important consideration? Are voters embedded in ongoing clientelist relationships that shape their voting decision? Are they swayed by offers of cash or goods prior to the election?

Finally, we are interested in the networks and organisational machinery that connect candidates and voters. To what extent do candidates rely on existing social, religious or partisan networks/organisations, or do candidates create their own distinctive electoral machines from their personal networks? Are candidate electoral machines permanent or ephemeral organisations? To what extent do candidates rely on intermediaries (brokers) in their mobilisation efforts? What are the characteristics of these brokers and what is their relationship with the candidate and with the voters they target? Are brokers tied to particular parties or machines, or is there a market for hiring brokers? How do candidates and brokers decide which voters to target for mobilisation? What types of organisations, networks and relationships are used to distribute patronage and to facilitate other forms of money politics?

In seeking answers to these questions a primary goal of the project is to map the terrain of electoral politics in each of our three countries and document the broad patterns and similarities within and across country cases. At the same time we also explore the causes and consequences of variation across countries, across local contexts within particular countries, and across different sorts of offices as they are found at different levels of the polity.

This is an ambitious research agenda, and answering these and related questions is obviously beyond the scope of any single researcher or single research method. As a result, our research strategy involves the use of multiple methods and dozens of locally-based researchers (Figure 1.1).[6] Specifically, we conducted a national survey in which we studied voters'

---

[6] The research design was similar for our projects in Malaysia and Indonesia, including a comparable numbers of researchers.

attitudes toward and experience with money politics. Included in the survey was a set of survey experiments to address concerns about voter responses to sensitive items and potential social desirability bias. The national survey and survey experiments are useful for giving us a macroview of the general patterns. In order to get a better sense of electoral dynamics on the ground, and how they vary by local context, we also carried out local surveys and a set of experiments involving voters and vote brokers in two municipalities in the Philippines.

Figure 1.1
Research strategy

National Surveys	Survey Experiments	Field Research	Local Surveys/ Experiments
• 1,200 voters • Views on candidates • Attitudes and experiences with money politics • Voting behaviour	6 survey experiments embedded in the national survey	• 50 researchers • 2 weeks in field • ~1,200 interviews • Event reports • Final reports	• Broker surveys • Voter surveys • Field and survey experiments

As useful as these survey and experimental methods are, the centrepiece of our research strategy, and the basis for this volume, was an extensive field research effort. In partnership with De La Salle University in Manila, we recruited a group of 50 researchers who were mainly academics or graduate students from universities across the Philippines. After undergoing training on research methods, interview techniques, and research ethics, they were deployed to electoral constituencies throughout the country. Figure 1.2 displays the locations. Field researchers spent between two and four weeks in the field with the responsibility to interview candidates and campaign staff, shadow candidates as they carried out their day-to-day campaigning, and attend campaign events. Altogether the researchers carried out more than a thousand interviews, produced hundreds of pages of event reports, and wrote final analyses about what they observed. Sixteen of the field researchers were then invited to develop their analyses into chapters for this volume.

The result of this effort is a detailed and nuanced view of electoral dynamics across the Philippines. This is a ground-level view that provides a snapshot of the richness of local context, but one which is also motivated and informed by a common set of research questions guided by the

Figure 1.2
Field research locations

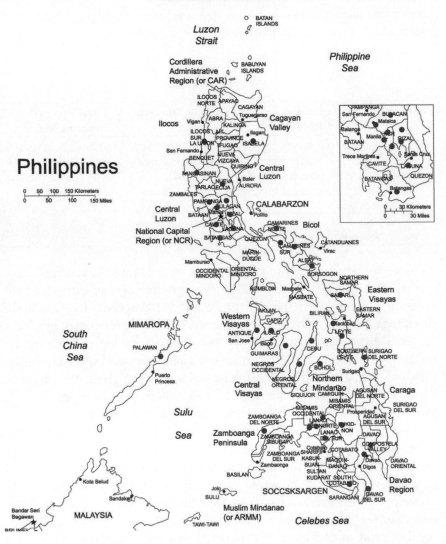

common framework already applied to our previous research in Malaysia and Indonesia.

A focus of all of the researchers was the use of patronage resources in political campaigns and the networks and organisations through which the resources flow. The researchers tracked several types of patronage that were deployed in the election campaigns they observed. These resources could be directed at groups of voters [for example, a barangay (neighbourhood or *barrio*) women's association, or farmers' cooperative] or they could be targeted to individual voters, whose party affiliation may or may not be a factor. Resources targeted at groups included things like *local public goods* (including those dispersed to entire communities through pork barrel mechanisms) and *club goods,* and were often completely legal.[7] Resources targeted at individuals included personal patronage (for example, school scholarships, medical care, employment), as well as election-related patronage, such as *vote buying* (giving undecided or opposing voters money in exchange for their vote) and *turnout buying* (giving money to tepid supporters in order to encourage them to come to the polling booth and cast a vote on election day).[8] Patronage could, as the patron-client framework would anticipate, be distributed to a significant extent through affective and enduring personalistic ties. Just as plausibly, however, the distribution of patronage could be influenced by relations that are thoroughly instrumentalist and short-term in character.

As the chapters in this volume demonstrate, various forms of election-related patronage, many of them illicit, are ubiquitous in the Philippines. That much reinforces the conventional wisdom about Philippine politics, but we go a step further to investigate the networks through which the patronage flows and the broader electoral dynamics of the Philippine patronage system. We argue that the foundational building block of the Philippine patronage system, created and sustained to support the

---

[7] Hutchcroft (2014a) cuts the pie in a slightly different way, distinguishing between meso-particularism (targeting everything from entire congressional districts and cities down to villages and neighbourhoods) and micro-particularism (where the beneficiaries are households and individuals). The former is the locus of impersonal patronage and the latter is the locus of personalistic or clientelistic patronage.

[8] The literature commonly refers to this type of resource distribution as electoral clientelism (see Gans-Morse et al. 2013), but in our framework—as noted above—we differentiate between patronage as a material resource, and clientelism as personalistic relationships of power. Given the ubiquity of clientelist ties, they are of most interest to the present analysis when they serve as mechanisms through which patronage resources flow.

political ambitions of a politician or a clan, is a *local political machine* able to articulate upward to the national level and downward to lower-level politicians and the voters. Local machines are built from a combination of clientelist (including familial) ties and short-term instrumentalist arrangements. This clientelist-instrumentalist combination also shapes the machine's upward relationships with allies at the national level, its downward relationships with allies in lower-level posts (for example, city or municipal councilors) and ultimately its relationship with the voting public. Lurking in the background, to varying degrees, is the coercive force the local machine may mobilise in support of its goals. Given the centrality of family and clan ties to these local machines, they are generally more durable and organisationally capable than the weak national political parties to which they belong.

The contributions to this volume provide what is to our knowledge the most comprehensive analysis ever undertaken of electoral dynamics across a range of localities in the Philippines. The volume's unique strength, therefore, is the opportunity to compare the local dynamics of this single yet pivotal election, as reported by scholars who conducted research in diverse parts of the archipelago. Just as importantly, we must emphasise what it is that the local-level studies did *not* focus upon. Unlike some of the work surveyed in the next section,[9] the researchers were not expected to produce in-depth longitudinal analysis of local politics and local political economies, for example, the economic basis of each clan's local power (whether it be some combination of agriculture, agro-industry, commerce, favourable ties to national politicians or such illicit activities as gambling and drug-dealing), the origins and potency of local private armies, and the extent of interaction between local politicians and whoever in the vicinity has significant coercive power (whether military, police, communist insurgents, or erstwhile Muslim secessionists). Rather, the chapters provide a snapshot of local dynamics prior to and including the election that was held on 9 May 2016. Similarly, it must be emphasised that the focus of the studies is on the disbursement of patronage resources and not on where those resources come from in the first place (whether, for example, from politicians' private wealth, contributions from higher-level politicians, corruption, proceeds from gambling networks or drug traders, and/or collusive ties with wealthy local allies who may expect to be given lucrative public contracts in return). The often shadowy world of

---

[9] Notably Kervliet and Mojares (1992), McCoy (1993), Sidel (1999), Abinales (2000) and Lara (2014).

campaign finance is a vitally important subject of study but not the focus of this project.

PATRONAGE, CLIENTELISM, LOCAL POLITICS AND ELECTIONS IN THE PHILIPPINES

No country in Asia has more experience with democratic institutions than does the Philippines, and through its colonial heritage the country also has long experience with electoral politics that are deeply imbued with patronage practices.[10] Unlike most colonial powers at the turn of the 20th century, the United States, motivated in large part by the desire to win over elites who were giving their support to the Philippine revolutionary movement for independence, took on a project of "political tutelage". Restricting the franchise to a narrow slice of the elite at the top of society, American colonialists began with the creation of elective local governments (municipal and then provincial) before proceeding to the 1907 opening of a national assembly heavily dominated by provincial elites from throughout the lowland Christian portions of the Philippines. They further encouraged the emergence of political parties, certainly not a normal activity for colonial rulers, while at the same time nurturing the leadership of a collaborationist elite. The model of politics was, not surprisingly, the patronage-oriented system that predominated at the time in the United States (which was of course very familiar to Governor-General William Howard Taft, himself a practised Ohio politician).

What came to be the leading party of the colonial era, the Nacionalista Party was, in the definition of Martin Shefter, an "internally mobilized" party "founded by elites who occupy positions within the prevailing regime and who undertake to mobilise a popular following behind themselves in an effort either to gain control of the government or to secure their hold over it" (1994: 30). In Shefter's framework, most "internally mobilized" parties will be patronage-oriented: because the parties occupy prominent roles *within the regime,* they have ready access to the patronage resources necessary to build a large following. There is one significant exception to the rule that an internally mobilised party will base its support on patronage resources, and that is the case of parties that have been established *after* the emergence of bureaucratic systems strong enough

---

[10] This discussion draws on Hutchcroft and Rocamora (2012: 99–101).

"to resist the depredations of patronage-seeking politicians".[11] Such a bureaucracy did not exist in the American Philippines, nor has it emerged since independence in 1946. Indeed, one can say that the "depredations of patronage-seeking politicians" have evolved over the decades in strikingly robust and creative ways.

This volume, and the project that underlies it, is part of a recent renaissance in the study of patronage and electoral clientelism involving the study of politics in many regions across the world—from Africa to Asia to Latin America (for example, Stokes et al. 2013; Kitschelt and Wilkinson 2007; Diaz-Cayeros et al. 2016; van de Walle 2007; Mares and Young 2016). Given the long and rich history of patronage and electoral clientelism in the Philippines, it is not surprising that some of the foundational work on clientelism and patron-client relationships in the social sciences came from scholars working exclusively on the Philippines (most importantly Landé 1965) or on the Philippines within a comparative perspective (Scott 1972).

Landé put his focus on "mutual aid relationships between pairs of individuals" or "dyadic ties", as they extend from the local level up to the national level (1965: 1). Even if they may have tried to claim programmatic and organisational coherence, each of the two major post-war Philippine parties were in practice "a multi-tiered pyramid of personal followings, one heaped upon the other in which [e]ach link in the chain of vertical dyads is based upon personal assurances of support and conditional upon the downward flow of patronage and spoils" (Landé 1977b: 86). A key building block of Philippine politics, in his analysis, was the family-based local faction. The core of this "family constellation" is with the more prosperous parts of the clan, and it extended outward to poorer relatives as well as to those who may be affiliated on the basis of marriage, fictive kinship (including compadre ties), and "ties of patronship and clientship" (Landé 1965: 17). As he explains further:

> Strong local roots and an ability to survive independently give the factions considerable bargaining power in their dealings with the national parties. . . . Candidates for national offices need votes, which local leaders with their primary hold upon the loyalty of the rural electorate can deliver. Local leaders in turn need money to do favors

---

[11] Shefter (1994: 28). In Shefter's second major category, "externally mobilized" parties are established by those outside the regime who do not have access to patronage and instead rely on ideological appeals in their quest for a mass following. Examples, he explains, are "socialist parties in Europe and nationalist parties in the Third World" (1994: 30).

for their followers, and this the candidates for high offices can supply [e.g.,] . . . public works projects and . . . influence with the agencies of the central government. . . . The result is a functional interdependence of local, provincial, and national leaders which promotes a close articulation of each level of party organization with those above and below it. (1965: 24, 82)

The relative bargaining power of the local faction, however, varies across the electoral cycle. This leads Landé to conclude that "[t]he balance of power between higher and lower levels of party organization is an unstable one" (1965: 82).

A friendly amendment to the patron-client framework came first in the work of Kit Machado on local political machines (1971 and 1974). This work is of obvious relevance to our own observation of the centrality of local machines in the Philippine politics, and is thus worthy of particularly careful attention here. Machado began his two major articles by explaining that his analysis of local factionalism "follows that of Landé" (1971: 1182; 1974: 524). A further strong and obvious influence in Machado's work is modernisation theory, which imbues the analysis with an almost teleological tone. Despite the latter, Machado did nevertheless offer at least two valuable insights. First, he observed that local political factions had become less multi-purpose and were instead transforming themselves into "quite specialized political organizations" (1971: 1183). Second, he saw a new type of "cement that binds" individuals to these organisations with the rise of "[i]nstrumental reasons for participation" (1971: 1183–4).[12] Both of these conclusions, part of Machado's attempt to project trends into the "modern" future, are broadly consistent with subsequent analyses of Philippine local politics (including our own).

At least four other elements of Machado's analysis, however, seem not to have stood the test of time. First, Machado asserted that "[i]ncreasingly, provincial and national considerations are shaping the actions of local faction leaders" as they respond to the "heavier constituent demands" that have arisen in the midst of "increasing social mobilization" (1971: 1183, 1193). This broad-brushed conclusion, unfortunately, lacks Landé's more nuanced view of the "unstable" nature of ties as they shift across the electoral cycle. There continue to be points in that cycle in which local politicians can exercise a significant degree of leverage over their national-

---

[12] Yet, as Kerkvliet points out, Landé's patron-client framework does acknowledge that there may be "monetary inducements to support or oppose particular candidates or factions" (1995: 403).

level counterparts. Second, Machado anticipated "further transformation [of local factionalism] into patterns more consistent with the demands of stable party organization" (1971: 1199). Nearly five decades on, this is not a type of party organisation that the Philippines has yet to experience with any degree of consistency. Third, Machado asserted that within "the more specialized organization" of the local political machines, kinship ties are reduced in importance because the extended family has ceased to be the central element (1971: 1184). Quite powerfully to the contrary, a large body of scholarship on Philippine politics across subsequent decades has continued to emphasise the centrality of the local clans. Fourth and finally, while in the (pre-modern) past "family prominence was traditionally the chief criterion for recruitment to positions of political leadership", Machado wrote, within a modernising Philippines there was supposedly "a tendency for notables from old leading families to be replaced in positions of leadership by upwardly mobile 'new men' from less prominent families" (1974: 524). In addition, he saw the emergence of "more professional criteria for recruitment" to local leadership positions and the rise of "the professional politician" (1974: 525). From the standpoint of subsequent trends in Philippine politics, Machado was correct to note high levels of social mobility but incorrect to assert the *replacement* of "notables from old leading families". Given the sheer number of elective posts in post-Marcos Philippine politics, there is ample room for both old faces and new entrants (the latter including, of course, movie stars, famous athletes, newscasters and the like). Some make politics a profession while others move effortlessly between political and other ventures. What is more, "professional criteria" are regularly trumped by a range of other factors, including the name recognition enjoyed by those from well-known families and/or highly public professions, the heft of personal campaign war chests, and the valuable linkages that can be forged with well-heeled patrons (whether higher-level politicians or business magnates).

A second amendment to the patron-client framework came much later in the work of David Wurfel on "development and decay" in Philippine politics (1988). The framework continues to be present in his work, but it is supplemented by attention to such pressing national concerns as agrarian reform and opposition to the Marcos regime. Writing as he was in the days in which so-called "cause-oriented groups" were instrumental in bringing down the Marcos regime and enjoying the post-Marcos "democratic space", it is not surprising that his major work would display much broader scope—not to mention a very different tone—than that found in Landé two decades earlier.

While Landé's work can still be regarded as the starting point for analysis of post-war Philippine politics, his framework of patron-client ties came under very direct challenge in the 1990s. One important line of critique, from Mark Thompson (1995), highlighted the failure of the framework to account for the anti-corruption and anti-electoral fraud movements that emerged episodically in post-independence Philippine politics—albeit most commonly at the national level. This was followed soon after by another strong challenge from Ben Kerkvliet, highlighting how the patron-client framework "leaves out and obscures a great deal about Philippine politics" by treating other "values, ideas, organizations, and conflicts" as marginal and "unimportant" (1995: 401).

A third convincing critique, particularly relevant to the study of local politics, came from John Sidel. Through his richly textured comparison of local politics in Cebu and Cavite, he attacked the patron-client framework for its general failure to examine the role of violence and local monopolies. In many parts of the archipelago, he demonstrated, local bosses have enjoyed "monopolistic personal control over coercive and economic resources in their territorial jurisdictions or bailiwicks" (1999: 141).[13] The most dramatic example of the coercive power of a local political machine came in the first decade of the 21st century, with the Ampatuan clan's terrifying dominance over Maguindanao province and nearby areas on the island of Mindanao (see Latiph's chapter in this volume). The Ampatuans were nurtured by powerful politicians in Manila keen to reap the national-level benefits of local-level electoral manipulation; in effect, local abuses were tolerated as long as the Ampatuans kept delivering implausible vote totals from their tightly-controlled bailiwick. The Ampatuans' bloody reign only came to an end in 2009, due to public outrage against the clan for the election-related massacre of nearly 60 persons by its private army (ICG 2009). (To date, the perpetrators of the massacre have yet to be convicted.)

Scholarship on Philippine electoral politics continues to put a major focus on patronage, clientelism, and other forms of money politics, with most observers finding ample evidence to indicate that material exchange remains central to Philippine electoral politics. Take, for example, the

---

[13] See also Anderson (1988) on the 20th-century origins of what he terms "cacique democracy". Hutchcroft (2003) applauds Sidel for focusing new attention on the importance of coercion and bosses but wishes there was greater clarity in differentiating between bosses and patrons—the latter are less reliant on coercion and lack a monopoly of local power, but are highly adept at distributing material resources to achieve their ends.

extensive literature on the strategic deployment of pork, or government resources distributed by politicians on a discretionary basis to discrete geographic areas or constituencies. Numerous studies find evidence that politicians distribute pork in such a way as to further their political and personal fortunes (Coronel and Balgos 1998; Balgos et al. 2010; Hicken et al. 2015). Other work focuses on the prevalence of vote buying[14] in Philippine elections (for example, Schaffer 2007) and the factors that affect its ubiquity, including political information (Cruz et al. 2016), socio-economic status (Coronel et al. 2004), the nature of anti-vote buying campaigns (Hicken et al. forthcoming), dynastic politics (Mendoza et al. 2015), social networks (Cruz 2013), and political culture (Abocejo 2014).

In addition to delving into the varieties of clientelistic exchange that can be found in the Philippines, another class of studies examines how features of the Philippines political system shape electoral dynamics, including the prevalence of money politics. These include the nature of the party system (discussed in more detail below) (Hutchcroft and Rocamora 2003, 2012; Kasuya 2008; Hicken 2009), the capacity of civil society (Hedman 2006; Quimpo 2008), election administration (Schaffer 2008; Calimbahin 2008), and electoral rules (Hicken 2016). A major theme in much of this literature is the ongoing central role of families and clans in Philippine electoral politics. An earlier generation of scholars focused broadly on prominent families and their influence in local and national politics (for example, McCoy 1993, 2009; Gutierrez et al. 1992; Gutierrez 1994). A new generation of scholars, led by Teehankee (2001) and Mendoza et al. (2015) have catalogued the prevalence of family dynasties across all levels of elected office.

Most of the work cited above adopts a national view of elections— looking to identify broad patterns and trends across the whole of the Philippines. As valuable as these studies are, equally important is work that provides highly textured accounts of political and electoral dynamics in specific locales, including the range of essays found in both Kerkvliet and Mojares (1992) and McCoy (1993), Kimura's (1997) work on elections in Lipa, Sidel's comparative analysis of Cebu and Cavite (1999), Abinales' historical account on "Making Mindanao" (2000), Kawanaka's study of politics in Naga City (2002), and the work of Lara on "shadow economies" in Mindanao (2014). A focus on the importance of local context also defines Labonne's work on the electoral impacts of conditional cash

---

[14] We define vote buying simply as the offer of material benefit in expectation of electoral support. More will be discussed below.

transfers (2013), while Hutchcroft's work on patronage and territorial politics examines the broader context of relations between national and subnational levels in both comparative and historical perspective (2012, 2014a, 2014b).

This volume contributes to this rich set of literature by painting a broad but nuanced picture using a deliberately local approach, structured to facilitate comparative analysis. The contributors devote little space to discussing national political contests in favour of a deep dive into the intricacies of the 2016 political campaigns at the local level. Some of the contributors focus on a single province, but most focus on a single congressional constituency, or part of a constituency, in an effort to build a picture of how electoral politics is organised and conducted at the grassroots. The chapters highlight the multiple means and methods candidates devise to curry favour with voters. At the same time, there are clear patterns and themes that emerge as we take a step back and look across the 45 local constituencies that were a part of this study. Before turning to those patterns, however, we first survey the context of the election that is the focus of this study.

THE CONTEXT OF THE 2016 ELECTION

The research for this project was carried out in the weeks prior to the 2016 synchronised national election. On 9 May 2016, voters selected candidates for a dizzying array of national, provincial and local offices (Table 1)—all told, more than 18,000 national, provincial and local positions were up for election. Officially, campaigning began in February for candidates for president, vice-president, and Senate as well as for parties competing for party-list seats. Campaigns for the remaining races kicked off in March. The election was largely a peaceful affair, with incidents of election-related violence fewer than in 2013. Still, the Commission on Human Rights reported 72 incidents of violence or harassment, including at least 30 deaths (Sauler 2016). Turnout for the election remained high, as is the historical pattern in the Philippines, at just under 82 per cent of registered voters.

The electoral system used in 2016 was unchanged from previous elections. For all executive offices (president, vice-president, governor, vice-governor, mayor, vice-mayor) the Philippines uses the common single member district plurality system, in which the candidate with the greatest number of votes in the relevant electoral district wins the position.

Unusually, however, voters cast a separate vote for each executive and vice-executive position. Single member district plurality is also used to elect 80 per cent of the members of the House of Representatives. The remaining 20 per cent are elected via a very unusual and complicated national party list that is an odd distortion of a proportional representation system: each voter casts a vote for a single party, and each party gets one seat for every 2 per cent of the vote they obtain, with a maximum of three seats per party. The electoral system employed for the Senate, provincial boards, and municipal or city council contests is multi-seat plurality.[15] Under this system electoral constituencies have multiple seats, voters can cast as many votes for individual candidates as there are seats, and seats are awarded on a plurality basis. For example, for the Senate election, voters can vote for up to 12 candidates, and the 12 contenders with the most votes each wins a seat. As explained below, the particular features of the Philippine electoral system combine to foster the perpetuation of weak political parties.

Table 1
Races contested in 2016

Races	District Magnitude (# of seats)	Electoral System
President	1	SMD plurality
Vice-president	1	SMD plurality
Senate	12	Multi-seat plurality
House of Representatives	1	SMD plurality
Party List	59	Distorted PR
Governor	1	SMD plurality
Vice-Governor	1	SMD plurality
Provincial Board	6–14	Multi-seat plurality
Mayor	1	SMD plurality
Vice-mayor	1	SMD plurality
Municipal or City Council	4–12	Multi-seat plurality

---

[15] Also known in the electoral systems literature as the block vote (not to be confused with how the term is commonly used in the Philippines, as a synonym for straight-party voting). The same system is used for barangay elections, but those elections follow a different calendar.

A notable feature of Philippine elections is the relatively high rate of turnover for elected offices. This is largely a function of term limits. The president is barred from immediate re-election, the vice-president and senators are limited to two six-year terms, and all other elected offices are limited to three consecutive three-year terms. In practice this means that, on average, around a third of electoral contests are "open", with no incumbent running. Those in favour of term limits hoped that they would hamper the ability of politicians to establish political dynasties. In fact, term limits have had precisely the opposite effect, amplifying incentives for investing in political dynasties (Teehankee 2001; Mendoza et al. 2015). A common practice in the Philippines is for term-limited incumbents to tap a family member (such as a spouse, child, or sibling) to stand in their place, while the incumbent seeks another elected office. For example, a term-limited mayor might run her son to replace her while standing herself for vice-governor. Exhibit A for this pattern is the career of President Duterte. Elected mayor of Davao in 1988, Duterte served three full terms. At the end of his third term he ran and won a seat in Congress while his vice-mayor and deputy became mayor. After serving one term in Congress, Duterte ran again for mayor of Davao in 2001 and won, serving three more full terms. Forced to step down in 2010 due to term limits, he ran for vice-mayor and supported his daughter Sara as his replacement. Since Sara had been serving as vice-mayor, they simply traded places. In 2013, Duterte ran again as mayor, tapping his son Paolo as his vice-mayoral running mate. In 2016, Duterte again stepped aside, this time to run for president; his daughter Sara stood in his place for mayor, with Paolo staying on as vice-mayor.

The combination of the Philippines' formal institutions and the emergence of family-based political dynasties has had profound consequences for the character of the Philippines' party system. Put simply, national parties are generally weak and ephemeral, while local party machines, built around individual politicians and their families, have emerged as the stable core of modern electoral politics in the Philippines.

Weak national parties

The Philippines party system is characterised by multiple parties—in the 2016 election, 17 parties captured seats in the district plurality election for the House, joined by another 46 parties that won representation via the party list. Parties in the Philippines tend to be short-lived alliances of convenience, built around key personalities, without much in the way of distinctive ideology. National party labels mean very little to voters or candidates, electoral volatility is high, and party switching (termed *turncoatism*) is common (Hicken 2014).

Four features of the Philippine electoral system tend to undermine the strength and cohesion of political parties (Hicken 2016). First, the use of multi-seat plurality for the Senate and provincial, municipal and local boards pits co-partisans against one another. This encourages candidates to develop personal networks of support that are distinct from parties, and encourages voters to discount party labels as guides to voting. Second, separate elections for executive and vice-executive positions undermine the value of parties for voters and candidates. Together, these first two features of the electoral system encourage candidates to eschew party strategies in favour of personal strategies. Elections are first and foremost personality contests and candidates generally exhibit little in the way of party loyalty. Multiple votes also allow voters to split their votes between candidates from different parties—something that Filipino voters frequently do—and there is no option on the ballot for straight-party voting (Hicken 2016). Third, the peculiar features of the Philippines party list electoral system previously discussed limit the influence of more party-centred strategies and effectively ghettoise smaller, more programmatic parties. And finally, the presence of term limits in an environment where parties are already weak undermines incentives for incumbents to invest in party-building. This is particularly true of the presidency, where term limits have contributed to "less party discipline, more factionalism, and to a larger number of short-lived parties" (Hicken 2014: 322).

Philippines elections involve a series of horizontal alliances between aspirants for national office as politicians sort themselves under different party banners. While this national-level manoeuvring by politicians tends to draw more attention, alliances between national candidates and parties on the one hand and local politicians and their machines on the other are actually more crucial. National candidates need access to the local mobilising power of the local machines, while national office provides access to resources, meaning that national politics often takes the form of ever-shifting realignments among both local and national politicians. In presidential election years like 2016, the strongest/largest parties tend to be those associated with the leading presidential contenders. Presidents control significant resources and their discretion over how those resources are distributed produces a pattern of president-centred turncoatism.

Candidates for both national and local offices commonly seek to ally with the person they judge to be the leading presidential candidate prior to the election. Once the election is over, most politicians in losing parties either switch to or ally with the party of the new president in order to increase their chances of receiving government largess.

The 2016 election saw a repeat of this pattern in the fortunes of the Liberal and PDP–Laban parties. The Liberal Party (LP) is one of the oldest parties in the Philippines but it had struggled since the return of democracy in 1986. In 2007, for example, the party won only 8.6 per cent of the seats in the House. Its fortunes improved dramatically in 2010. Propelled by the popularity of its winning presidential standard bearer, Benigno Aquino III, the party almost doubled its seat share, with 16.4 per cent. Almost immediately after the election, turncoats from across the political system flocked to the party, making LP the largest party in the legislature. In the 2013 mid-term election, the party solidified its status, winning nearly 38 per cent of the seats and control of most governorships and mayoral posts nationwide. Like his predecessors, however, President Aquino did little to build a strong, national party machine.[16] As Holmes describes in his chapter, LP's control of national and local government proved temporary. The party was not able to leverage this control into support for the party's presidential candidate in 2016, Manuel "Mar" Roxas II, who lost decisively to Rodrigo Duterte, though the party did succeed in capturing a plurality of House seats. But almost as soon as the election concluded, we witnessed the usual massive rush to the party of the incoming president. President Rodrigo Duterte's party, PDP–Laban, won only three seats in the House in 2016. Once the party-switching dust had cleared, however, the party was the largest party in the house, boasting 93 members (out of a total of 297), plus the support of several smaller parties (Porcalla 2016). By contrast, LP lost 80 representatives to turncoatism after the election, falling to 35 members from an immediate post-electoral high of 115 (Porcalla 2016).

---

[16] The government's decision to reduce its reliance on presidential patronage in favour of a less politicised public goods programme improved the efficiency of government spending, but weakened the ruling party's claim on local politicians' loyalty. In fact, more than one candidate we interviewed noted that the president's relatively even-handed distribution of government resources had placed LP at a disadvantage. Candidates learned that they didn't have to be aligned with the party to receive benefits.

The failed liberal party machine

One question going into the 2016 election was the extent to which LP had successfully built a national party machine. It was not uncommon to hear party leaders and political commentators espousing the belief that the party machinery could overcome the lack of enthusiasm for the party's presidential candidate, Mar Roxas. The LP, for example, boasted that 67 of the country's 82 incumbent governors were allied with the party (Ramos 2016). And, in fact, the national LP appeared to be more active at the local level than other national parties—LP "foot soldiers" worked the ground in some areas, and national and provincial party headquarters provided at least some funds to support them. Elsewhere, however, party support was fairly minimal, while in some areas "LP bailiwicks" were essentially the strongholds of local allies who had questionable loyalties to the national party. In Siquijor and Pangasinan, for instance, key local figures and families form the core of a well-oiled local LP machine. Many of the governors and mayors allied with the LP were hoping to be first in line for government pork and patronage. However, as discussed earlier, LP's push for programmatic delivery of non-contingent programmes—that is, *not* requiring that one be a party member to access state services and funds—won plaudits from some but in the end weakened the incentives of local politicians to aggressively mobilise for the party.[17] Ultimately, as Holmes's chapter describes, the vaunted LP machine failed to deliver on its promises. The incipient movement toward stronger institutionalisation heralded by the party's prospects in the lead up to the 2016 election may appear, in retrospect, as yet another example of the tendency for party energies to cluster, however briefly, around an incumbent president, only to dissipate when the next president assumes office.

PATRONAGE PATTERNS IN THE 2016 ELECTION[18]

Within the context of the broader 2016 election our focus is on the dynamics of electoral politics at the local level. Key to our investigation is consideration of varying forms and quantities of electoral patronage. Elections in the Philippines are especially costly affairs, given the money

---

[17] We heard this sentiment in interviews, but see also Vitug 2016.
[18] This section and the next draw on Weiss 2019.

distributed. The contributors describe a dizzying array of patronage strategies employed by candidates. These include the distribution of a mix of individual gifts and collective goods, the organisation of activities and provision of services, reminders of local "pork barrel" projects supplied, and claiming credit for programmatic policies, such as disbursements under the national conditional cash transfer scheme, Pantawid Pamilyang Pilipino Program (Bridging Program for the Filipino Family, dubbed 4Ps).

Vote buying,[19] largely in the form of cash payments to voters, was endemic in all but a few areas, particularly in connection with local rather than national contests.[20] Labelled "allowances" in Pampangan, *uwan-uwan* (rain showers) in Bohol, "banquet" or *salo-salos* in parts of Laguna, or by an array of other euphemisms, the practice of offering cash to voters extends nationwide. While not new, vote buying appears to have increased in scale and scope over recent elections. One explanation lies in decentralisation under the Local Government Code of 1991, which has raised the stakes—and, arguably, the expense and violence—of elections, as local officials have gained access to more substantial financial and other resources (including enhanced employment for themselves and favoured relatives or allies). These assets are all the more valuable where income and opportunities are otherwise scarce. The introduction of electronic voting offers another explanation, and one which better addresses *recent* shifts. Because electronic voting has reduced opportunities to secure victory through bribing electoral officials to engage in wholesale ballot-box manipulation, it seems plausible that candidates invest more in retail vote buying—targeting individual voters with offers of cash.[21]

Vote buying follows a similar pattern nationwide—echoing the pattern our earlier research found across Indonesia.[22] A pyramidal campaign structure is near-universal, with a local political figure at its apex (generally a candidate for mayor or governor) down to the sub-barangay

---

[19] We use vote buying colloquially as a shorthand for various kinds of election-related patronage.

[20] Electoral malpractice, too, is generally also tied more to local contests than national ones. Carter Center 2016: 10.

[21] Survey data tell a mixed story on this point. According to PulseAsia, 22 per cent of respondents reported being offered money or goods for their vote in 2016. This is the same percentage as 2013, but it is up substantially from 2010 (16 per cent), 2004 (11 per cent) and 2001 (8 per cent), but only marginally higher than what was reported in 2007 (21 per cent).

[22] On the Indonesian pattern, see Aspinall et al. 2017.

(*purok*), block, and even household level. (More on that network structure below.) Members of the team generally receive only a small honorarium, meals and allowance for expenses, supplemented with the lure of post-election jobs or access to services. However limited the remuneration for individual campaign workers, our researchers found that meals and transportation expenses for campaign staff and campaign meetings are among candidates' largest campaign costs, across constituencies.

These campaign teams, or local machines, do the work of mobilising voters at the grassroots level, including drawing up lists of voters prepared to vote for the candidate and his or her ticket, as well as delivering cash payments to voters. In most cases, funds are distributed via specially recruited barangay-level brokers, either in one payment—via "special operations" the night before polling day, or during the *oras de peligro* (hour of danger) or "end-game" of the final two days of the campaign—or in several tranches, starting a couple of weeks before election day. Some regions present variations. In Lanao del Sur, for instance, in what is termed "vote squatting", voters receive an initial deposit from a candidate they promise to support; if they then accept a larger deposit from a challenger, they will return the deposit received from the first candidate (see Latiph's chapter). Teams worried about their margins as the campaign proceeds will pay a higher price for these "squat votes" than for the votes of their solid supporters. In Leyte, one candidate distributed pseudo-bank cards, to be handed over to a campaign *lider* after voting in exchange for cash (see Mangada's chapter). The terms used are themselves evocative: for instance, the *gapang* (crawl) of discreet, final-days door-to-door vote buying, with opponents "stalking" rival campaign workers in hopes of catching them in the act.

Campaign strategists think carefully about how much to distribute to each voter, taking several factors into consideration. These include: how much their opponents will likely give (by estimating not only the extent of the total resources at the disposal of opponents but also how much their opponents will be ready to invest in the campaign), how confident they are of a given voter's support, how heated the contest is, what they expect their "mortality rate" (the rate of voter defection) to be, and the depth of their own pockets. Most aim to wait until the rival team has released its payments, then adjust as needed. Some candidates choose to distribute payments in tranches, allowing them to gauge the distribution of cash by rival candidates and respond in kind with a "last touch" (see Mangada's chapter). Loyalty and general preference may be enough to outweigh a difference of a few pesos, but once the other side ups the ante, even voters inclined toward a candidate may shift their vote (see chapters by Espia and Macalandag).[23] Nationwide, cash distributions to voters ran the gamut, from token PhP 20 payments from municipal-council candidates to 1,000, 1,500, or (more rarely) several thousand pesos from a would-be mayor, often inclusive of that candidate's local council slate and perhaps some parts of the broader national ticket.

Currency notes are typically stapled or clipped to sample ballots or candidate handbills or cards, often in an addressed envelope to ensure that only voters listed as likely supporters receive payments. Teams generally target their own supporters first. Given that candidates and voters rarely share a partisan or ideological bond, the support of any voter, even those who might be deemed "core supporters", cannot be taken for granted. As one candidate reported: "blood is thicker than water; but money, especially if it's a bundle of 1,000 pesos, is much thicker than blood" (quoted in Latiph's chapter). If funds permit, candidates may also extend their reach to swing voters or even less promising efforts among their opponents' supporters. Illustrative of the opportunistic alliances common across the Philippines—and the weakness of party loyalty— sample ballots frequently cross party lines. For instance, virtually all slates touted in the vicinity of Davao City had Duterte in the presidential slot, regardless of party affiliation. Most candidates in the area who were ostensibly part of party slates backing rival presidential candidates chose not to campaign for their party's actual candidate, lest they hurt their own chances.

Campaigns face the challenge of distributing resources in a way that is discreet yet not impersonal. For instance, one team in Bulacan reportedly brought voters to a resort where they distributed funds, as going for a swim would not seem unusual. In the Rinconada section of the province of Camarines Sur (see Dolorical's chapter), the majority of voters in a precinct were employed as poll-watchers, to conceal the payments made to them. Moreover, campaigns have to worry about security: an opponent may attack (or tip-off the police or New People's Army, NPA, troops to intercept) campaign staff carrying large sums of cash for distribution, or may themselves stop rival campaign workers from distributing payments within their own bailiwick. For example, one campaign consigliere reported tracking the movements of the rival campaign and alerting the

---

[23] In areas where welfare services are critically undersupplied, however, a candidate who has previously and reliably provided medical or other assistance is more likely to lock in that voter's support, regardless of the payments of others; more on that aspect below.

police when he knew money was being distributed so that the police would temporarily detain the rival *liders* and, more importantly, confiscate the cash. Campaign strategists developed creative plans to deal with such security challenges. These plans could include contracting or colluding with the police or NPA, and having personal strongmen and guns on hand in some areas.

Campaign resources come primarily from the upper-middle-range candidates on the ticket: mayor, governor, and sometimes congressional representative. Presidential candidates generally lack the funds for ground campaigns, especially vote buying, throughout the country. At lower levels of the political system, local council candidates are often themselves too poorly resourced to fund lavish campaigns of their own, and thus essentially become clients of a mayoral or gubernatorial candidate. The candidates who do fund the campaigns, in turn, derive their resources from proceeds from government contracts, kickbacks from government projects, personal wealth, family members, and wealthy or supportive friends. Businesses may donate in kind, and less often in cash, at the local level. Where provision of infrastructure is key to building support, contractors are often key campaign financiers, receiving project contracts in return. Incumbents benefit, too, from being able to draw on local government staff as campaign workers—even though other networks may be more central to their team (see Dolorical's chapter).

Consistent with patterns in other countries, poorer voters (Classes D and E, in the Philippines' categorisation) tended to be the most common targets of vote buying. In most cases poorer voters would wind up on a vote buying list drawn up by a broker who knew them personally (more on this process in the next section). However, in some cases, voters were more proactive (collectively or individually) in seeking funds from candidates (see chapters by Rocina, Sta. Ramano and Pancho). For example, in Antique Province (see Espia's chapter), intermediate brokers committed a number of votes in a bundle to the highest bidder. There were also cases of voters directly approaching a mayoral candidate's headquarters with an offer to sell their vote to that candidate, and then moving on to an opponent in the event that the first candidate approached was not willing to make a bid. We heard discussions, too, of abstention buying— of campaigns' paying voters, including entire families, not to vote, then sequestering them on polling day or marking their fingers with indelible ink to prevent their reneging—though these descriptions seemed more often discussed than actually pursued (see Aquino's chapter).

On election day in the Philippines, party monitors at the polling place do the work of assessing voter compliance.[24] Monitoring turnout or abstention is straightforward, and some campaigns did actively monitor which of their supporters had voted throughout the day, and attempted to mobilise those who had not yet voted as the day proceeded. Monitoring vote choice is much more difficult. The Philippines uses a secret ballot with automated counting, cameras are banned in the polling place, and voting receipts are to be deposited in a box before leaving the polling place. However, in some cases it is conceivable that party poll watchers could determine how voters were casting their vote. In at least some polling stations, voters sit within view of the party witnesses as they shade the ovals on their ballots (sometimes at nearly Lilliputian school desks rather than in private polling booths, for example) and not all voters used the cardboard folder supplied to veil their ballot as they brought it to the vote-counting machine (some of which broke down, leaving voters standing in a queue with their ballots). Party monitors were sometimes close enough to scrutinise at least some of the preferences shaded on the ballot as the voter fed it into the machine.[25] And in some cases voters reportedly retained their voting receipts in order to demonstrate their loyalty to vote brokers (Latiph's chapter). Even so, verification of vote buying is more difficult with the new automated voting system than under the previous manual counting system.[26] At the end of the day, according to our survey results, most voters believed their vote to be secret, and most candidates and brokers reported they could not be sure how voters voted.

Given the difficulty of monitoring voter behaviour, campaigns designed other incentives to encourage voters to vote the way they pledged. Some respondents, for example, reported that canvassers asked them to sign a contract promising not to vote, or to vote for a certain candidate, while others emphasised a moral obligation to follow through once they had accepted funds, trading on the cultural idea of *utang na loob*, or debt of gratitude. In some constituencies, campaigns offered bonus bloc payments to barangays if they "voted straight"—that is, if the full slate won the barangay.

Apart from money, candidates also distributed various goods: t-shirts, food, fans, alcohol, cigarettes, coffins, uniforms, and more, either in the

---

[24] It is in large part the right to appoint these poll watchers that makes registering as or with a party appealing—and the party headquarters generally covers the cost of polling agents, and little else.

[25] Our own observations, as well as the Carter Center 2016: 7.

[26] Carter Center 2016: 14.

course of canvassing and campaigning or in response to voters' requests. Provision of these items requires advance preparation and coordination, including selection of targeted beneficiaries (particularly for larger, costlier items). In some cases, distribution is at high-profile rallies, including as coveted door prizes; these are not illicit hand-offs, but public displays, intended to excite the crowd (see Dolorical's chapter). Candidates may also provide direct services during the campaign; in Laguna, for instance (see Sta. Romana's chapter), both sides offered such assistance as medical aid and meals, as well as *tulong* (financial help) from their headquarters, while in Muntinlupa city candidates supplied water or notary services to voters (see Rocina's chapter).

Beyond direct payments made during the campaign, however essential these were, forms of patronage distributed over longer time scales could also be important, and seem to have been more pivotal in some areas.[27] Ongoing contributions we observed included ceremonial items like gongs, chickens and black pigs for upland rituals in Baguio City, alongside more common services such as scholarships, transportation assistance, medical aid, casual jobs and disaster relief. In Bohol (see Macalandag's chapter), such practices are termed "sowing the seeds": preparing the ground for elections via prior sponsorship, gifts, and other patronage to build reputation and accumulate debts of gratitude. In Muntinlupa, one incumbent quite literally provided seedlings and gardening implements, to allow constituents to grow their own food and market the surplus (see Rocina's chapter).

In this vein, scholarship programmes were especially prevalent (see, for example, Espia's chapter). In many locations, we encountered candidates who expected scholarship recipients to campaign for them in return for their scholarship; such youths and their parents often formed a particularly reliable pool of volunteers. Promise of employment, particularly in poor, rural areas, performed a similar function. Incumbents were also expected to have invested in poverty alleviation, health and livelihood programmes—for instance, helping with hospitalisation and doctors' fees, burial assistance, or water connection costs. Whereas incumbents could point to, and promise to continue, the projects they had previously delivered to a constituency, well-resourced challengers could fund similar projects themselves prior to the campaign, to lay the groundwork with

---

[27] For instance, according to members of our research team in Baguio City, upland volunteers eschew payment lest they then be unable to request assistance in the future; there and in Benguet, Cordilleran voters tended toward clan voting, obviating most individual vote buying.

voters. In at least some cases, these projects helped to build up the reputation of the candidate and forge a personal connection with voters (see Tumandao's chapter).

In addition, candidates sometimes directed funds not only to voters but also towards fellow candidates. Our team encountered reports of "splitter" candidates (the term used in Antique Province; see Espia): candidates paid by one side to run for election in order to split the opposition vote. There were also many instances of candidates being paid *not* to run. Lastly, the New People's Army also collects payments from candidates in the form of permit-to-campaign fees, with the amount increasing from around PhP 40,000 to 150,000 (using Dolorical's estimates from the Rinconada area) depending on the stature of office sought.[28] However, these payments granted only access to voters, not assured support.

PATRONAGE, CLIENTELISM, AND THE LOCAL MACHINE

As discussed above, national political parties in the Philippines are comparatively weak, oriented at election time around leading figures (primarily the presidential and vice-presidential candidates, and secondarily a slate of senatorial candidates that commonly includes "guest" candidates from other parties). They typically lack both a minimal mass base as well as a clear, national public image and programme. Compared to Indonesia, where regional parties are disallowed by law (except at the local/provincial level in Aceh), or in Malaysia, where state-based or regional parties are dwarfed by deeply rooted national parties, the connections between the central and local levels in the Philippines are more complex. While central-local alliances bring critical mutual benefit there are also frequent shifts in these alliances within and across electoral cycles (that is, it is not uncommon for today's allies to become tomorrow's opponents who then become the following day's allies once again). At the core of these alliances, though, is the *local political machine*. Often branded with its own team name and logo, the local machine is the dominant form of political organisation at the local level and the most stable building block of Philippine politics. These machines are usually centred around a locally powerful family,

---

[28] These fees appear to be somewhat negotiable. A city council candidate in the Compostela Valley noted that their council slate was able to negotiate a lower group rate with the NPA.

but extend beyond this family core via personal/clientelist as well as instrumentalist relationships to incorporate layers of brokers or *liders* who do the candidates' campaign work. For example, voters who have been recipients of assistance in the past (such as parents of scholarship students) may be expected to canvass for the machine. Incumbents also use the activities and resources of government to gather reliable vote brokers and build their machines by, for example, courting barangay leaders through the targeted distribution of government resources. Furthermore, a distinct feature of the Philippine framework is its emphasis on participatory budgeting and the inclusion of non-governmental and people's organisations in governance. This structure not only opens communication channels between citizens and politicians, but can also provide rich vote banks and reliable, loyal campaign structures for political leaders able to incorporate such organisations into their local machines (Borromeo-Bulao, this volume). In short, in building their machines, local politicians are on the lookout for community-level leaders who wield social influence, are clued-in to local concerns, and who, when effectively compensated, can serve as loyal brokers for the party machine.

Most local machines strategically ally with a national party during election season, but the ties between local and national parties are often unstable and coordination minimal.[29] The national parties generally provide little apart from a weak brand, money for sample ballots, and resources for poll watchers. The costs of campaigning and voter mobilisation fall almost entirely on the local machine, and, not surprisingly, local races receive the most attention. For example, a would-be mayor typically selects a slate for city council, then the team's machinery urges voters to "vote straight" or support the "full slate". Voting for a full slate facilitates enactment of campaign promises, including provision of the sorts of projects and jobs essential to extending and sustaining support. Canvassers may also encourage voters to support the upper echelons of the ticket—such as the presidential candidate or district congressional candidates—but typically do so less consistently or forcefully.

---

[29] Even where the presidential candidate is connected directly with a local machine, the national party still may fade to the background: as Calimbahin explains in her chapter, incumbent vice-president Jejomar Binay's Team Binay ran as a "family brand" to secure their long-time stronghold in Makati, rather than emphasise the larger party (United National Alliance, UNA), even as patriarch Jejomar headed up the ticket to contest the presidency.

The primary task of the local machine is mobilising a sufficient number of voters. To do this, the machinery extends from the provincial or municipality level down to individual households. Figure 1.3 shows the structure of a typical local party machine, though the names and number of layers will vary from machine to machine. At the apex of the machine is a candidate, typically a mayor or governor. Below are the candidate's closest lieutenants—central-level brokers who are usually family members or individuals with longstanding ties of loyalty to the candidate. The next level down consists of village/barangay-level brokers or *liders*. Although officially non-partisan, the barangay captains (who are elected functionaries) often fill this role, coordinating campaign efforts for a given area. Where the barangay captain is allied with a rival campaign, or otherwise unavailable, candidates rely on other local leaders, such as barangay council members, a sub-barangay or *purok* leader, or a local-association leader. These relationships are held together by expectations of reciprocity: for example, when barangay elections come around, a barangay captain will typically turn to the higher-level candidate (who will now often be an elected official) for support. Other *liders* will receive other forms of assistance—patronage jobs in the local administration, for example, or financial or administrative assistance during some moment of need.[30]

Finally, within each barangay will be several local (*purok*) *liders*, brokers who interact directly with voters. Again, the most prized grassroots brokers are those who have strong ties with the candidate or one of the higher-level brokers, although campaigns may also need to rely on brokers with more tenuous ties to the machine (that is, brokers for hire). These grassroots brokers are responsible for generating lists of names for targeting and passing those lists up to the central campaign. In Bohol, for instance, campaigns divide voters among "ours" (loyal supporters); swing voters who will accept cash from both sides but not reveal their preference; *palitunon*, or undecided, whose votes may be bought; and those clearly inclined toward an opponent, but who can be "shot" with money in hopes of changing their mind (see Macalandag's chapter). The money then flows down the machine and it is the grassroots brokers who approach voters prior to the election with offers of cash.

---

[30] Politicians go to great lengths to maximise the reach of this kind of assistance. For example, one informant in Sorsogon explained that a single patronage job working for the local government was divided among 24 people, with each working for one-half a month.

A striking feature of these local machines, compared to those in Indonesia, is their durability. While these machines are politically promiscuous when it comes to national party alignment, the internal make-up of the team and their network of relationships are often relatively stable from election to election. In some cases, *liders* and candidates are bound together by ongoing clientelistic relationships of mutual loyalty, in which a *lider* receives personal assistance from a local political figure and in return helps that figure in repeated elections. In these cases, regardless of whether the *liders* are elected or unelected, their primary qualification is ties of loyalty to the candidate or one of his or her lieutenants. These ties may or may not be familial in nature, but even where kinship ties are absent, Philippine society has ample scope for forging new relationships and making mutual claims through "fictive kinship" (Abinales and Amoroso 2005: 20). Of course, such relationships sometimes break down, but they can and often do last a lifetime, and may even be passed on to subsequent generations of *liders* and politicians.

Alongside these more enduring clientelistic ties are ties that are clearly instrumentalist in character: brokers willing to sell their services to the highest bidder. And, of course, it is only natural that a particular relationship may combine both clientelist and instrumentalist elements. It is also possible that these ties shift in character over time: that is, instrumental ties develop into a more robust clientelist relationship, or the clientelist relationship weakens and fades. Finally, it must be noted further that when the relationship breaks down altogether (as, for example, when brokers abscond with the funds) coercive elements may also come into play. This will be most likely when the local politician has armed elements that can readily be mobilised for strong-arm appeals (see Latiph's chapter).

Figure 1.3 provides a schematic diagram of the local machine, as described by many of this volume's authors. At first glance it may look like a Landé-style patron-client pyramid. In fact, it is not. First, while personal relationships infuse this local machine, these relationships are not solely or necessarily dyadic. Second, local machines combine not only clientelist but also instrumentalist and brokerage arrangements. In addition, although not included in the diagram, our analysis gives full recognition to the fact that there will in some cases be coercive elements ready and able to back up the *liders*.

Campaign machines typically check the ground during the campaign period, starting with an initial mapping as well as surveys to gauge potential candidates' "winnability", then conducting what is sometimes termed "straw voting" (see Espia's chapter) or surveys to gauge voter support

Figure 1.3
The Structure of the Local Machine

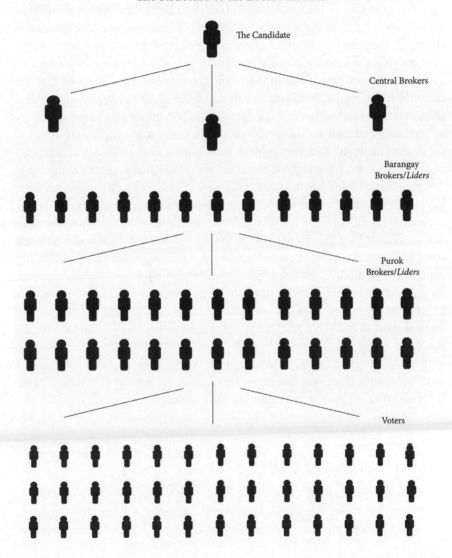

and "troubleshooting" worrisome areas, often starting well in advance of elections and proceeding through several stages. New technologies for surveys, compiling results and checking voters' registration status have refined procedures previously done through traditional clan or other networks.[31]

Given the size of the teams assembled, joining a candidate's campaign apparatus is a fairly common way to earn a bit of extra income (see Miranda's chapter). However, a common concern for candidates is the commitment of their *liders*. These local team members can shirk in a variety of ways, including defecting to a political rival, misrepresenting support for the candidate, failing to distribute funds to voters, and generally giving less than full effort in support of the campaign. For many *liders*, the memory of past support and the lure of jobs during and after the election helps them remain loyal and committed. Being found to be disloyal will end their access to such patronage in the future. Nonetheless, some campaigns described strategies for cross-checking or monitoring the work of their *liders* and releasing or sidelining those suspected of shirking. These tactics include scrutinising lists of "pledged" voters submitted by *liders*, sending teams to distribute payments rather than a single individual, and fielding complaints from voters who did not receive the expected payment. Some candidates or their close associates went so far as to personally present payments to voters (even if doing so problematically signalled their lack of trust in their machines), while others gathered supporters together for mass distributions. That said, machines tend to be fairly enduring for all but brand-new candidates; disloyalty was less a concern for candidates with prior campaign experience (especially incumbents) and established local machines than was the case with less-experienced candidates with more short-term and purely opportunistic or mercenary teams.

ISLANDS OF EXCEPTION

What we have described above is the modal pattern across the Philippines, but there are interesting and important departures from this pattern. For example, in most locations our researchers reported an electoral

---

[31] Some machines also make use of "consultants"—professionals hired on a contract basis to provide services for the campaign (for example, polling). These consultants operate outside the main machine structure. Our researchers also describe an apparent trend toward professionalisation of at least lead campaign staff, reflected in the increasing use of technology for surveys and creating voter-targeting strategies.

environment that was largely free of violence and intimidation. At first blush this may seem surprising given the reputation for the deployment during elections of the "3 Gs": guns, goons, and gold. It is striking that most of the case studies in this volume found little evidence of the first two Gs in 2016, though "gold" was very much in abundance. This is consistent with the national decline in election-related violence cited earlier. Our national and local surveys also bear this out—relatively few respondents report being victims of or concerned with violence or intimidation. Coercion, it appears, did not cast as big a shadow as it once did during the 2016 campaign.

However, while most of our field researchers observed little evidence of coercion, and while most of our survey respondents reported the same, it is important to not over-claim based on the relative lack of violence we observed in 2016. First, there are significant exceptions—areas where electoral politics still look very much like what Sidel described in his work on bossism and coercion. Latiph's chapter on politics in Lanao del Sur is the clearest example (see also Eusebio's chapter). Latiph describes how violence between rival campaigns as well as threats to voters continue to be defining features of elections in parts of the Autonomous Region in Muslim Mindanao. In fact, he notes that as many as two-thirds of the election-related deaths reported nationally in 2016 occurred in Lanao del Sur. Second, in some areas even though 2016 was largely free of violent incidents, past experiences with election-related violence continued to loom large in the memory of candidates and voters, and thus may have shaped their behaviour (see the chapters by Eusebio on Pangasinan and Espia on Antique). Finally, in some locales the *capacity* for and, therefore, the *threat* of violence remained very real. Thus, for some voters coercion existed even in the absence of visible displays of intimidation or violence (see Macalandag's chapter).

Another of the modal patterns we have described is that of the local party machine using money and patronage to mobilise votes. The fact that we see this same model in locality after locality should not mask the interesting variations on this modal pattern. For example, some machines are clearly linked to longstanding political dynasties, while others supplement money and patronage with coercive capacity. Across machines we also saw variation in the mix of clientelist versus instrumental ties. Compared to incumbents, the machines of challengers tended to have a greater ratio of brokers for hire to loyalists. And in general, our researchers noted a movement towards a greater reliance on professional or outside campaign staff, often working in parallel to the traditional machine.

In other areas, alternative kinds of appeals and alternative forms of local political competition have emerged or appear to be emerging. Both Eusebio and Rocina, for example, describe the beginnings of a shift to more programmatic competition. Patronage politics still dominate, but they are increasingly supplemented with more programmatic appeals. The most radical departure from the standard model is found in Naga City, as outlined in Borromeo-Bulao's chapter. The well-documented "Naga City" model represents a movement away from contingency-based patronage politics towards an emphasis on the provision of public services and mass-based politics.

The contributors also describe other networks and groups besides local machines that can be important for vote mobilisation. The Iglesia ni Cristo (INC) is the best-known of such groups—purportedly able to deliver 80 per cent of its members' votes—and appears among the key networks activated across our sample constituencies. Other networks that perform similar roles include transport groups (for instance, Tricycle Operators and Drivers Associations[32]), fisherfolk organisations, student and youth groups, and organisations representing women, farmers, or the lesbian, gay, bisexual, and transgender (LGBT) communities. However, these latter organisations seem less reliable than INC at delivering blocs of votes. Perhaps for this reason, we saw comparatively little in the way of a phenomenon that is very widespread in Indonesia and Malaysia: club-good distribution, for example, grants or donations, to organisations or targeted communities. However, there were exceptions. One campaign offered groceries for members of a pedicab drivers' association in Naga City (see Bulao's chapter). Moreover, certain areas saw donations for things like basketball court repairs, village signage, and so forth, and candidates wooed some local *liders* with "a little extra" for *merienda* (snacks), as in Laguna (see Sta. Romana's chapter). While in some areas, distribution of resources may have mattered for endorsement by religious or other groups (including INC), we saw far fewer election-time grants or promises to congregations, schools, or comparable entities than in Indonesia or Malaysia. That said, at least one candidate in Camarines Norte characterised middle-class voters as swayed by "collective benefits" rather than individual favours (see Nolasco's chapter).

---

[32] These groups are especially valuable allies since their members interact with, and can influence, so many voters as passengers, and can post stickers on or play jingles from their vehicles.

CONCLUSION AND PLAN OF THE BOOK

This book presents a series of sketches of how electoral politics works at the grassroots in the Philippines. While the chapters that follow capture much regional variation, and considerable heterogeneity in the appeals offered and networks relied upon by candidates, they also demonstrate numerous common features across far-flung locations. Indeed, a standard Philippine pattern of local electoral politics emerges through the following pages, characterised by two long-observed features of Philippine politics. The first is patronage distribution: our case studies demonstrate, if there could ever be doubt on this score, that the Philippines is a patronage democracy, in which material exchange is imprinted deeply into the fabric of most election campaigns. Cash distribution has long been a feature of electoral politics, but our study demonstrates wide variation— and considerable inventiveness—in the forms of patronage delivered.

The second feature, as we have stressed in preceding pages, is the centrality of the local party machine. Local machines constructed around powerful candidates, factions and clans are the basic building blocks of Philippine politics, operating alongside weakly institutionalised parties at the national level. Amidst the very sweeping changes that one can observe in Philippine politics and political economy, as highlighted at the outset, there has been substantial continuity in the degree to which money and patronage politics continues to play a central role in local political contests throughout the Philippines. And within this ubiquitous game of money and patronage politics, the most stable building block is the local political machine, itself constructed on a combination of clientelist, instrumentalist, and sometimes coercive foundations.

In fact, the local machine is a key distinguishing feature of Philippine politics: while many countries can be classified as patronage democracies, their organisational features vary widely. In Southeast Asia—bringing our attention back to the region studied in the broader research project that generated this book—the Philippines' pattern of resilient local party machines combining and recombining in continually changing opportunistic alliances with national politicians is certainly distinctive. In Malaysia, though patronage delivery remains a central feature of political life (see Weiss 2014), this patronage is for the most part channelled through remarkably resilient and stable national and state-based ruling parties. In Indonesia, local patronage politics is in some respects more fragmented than is the case in the Philippines, with Indonesia's open-list proportional representation system requiring legislative candidates to establish their own competing brokerage structures. The Philippines' single-member congressional districts, in contrast, produce less fragmentation and more coordination among candidates who are part of the same local political machine. There is, at the same time, more coordination with national structures in Indonesia as compared to the Philippines, given that every Indonesian local legislative candidate must be nominated by only one of a limited number of national political parties (Aspinall and Sukmajati 2016). In the Philippines, as explained above, the linkages between local machines and national parties are dynamic and ever-shifting. Further contrasts between the two archipelagic states must also be noted: the deep links that local executive candidates in Indonesia often have with the local state bureaucracy (vs extremely weak linkages in the Philippines) and the longstanding importance of local dynasties in the Philippines (vs their relative weakness in Indonesia, even as they do seem to be growing in importance over time).

The closest cognate to contemporary Philippines politics is perhaps Thailand in the 1980s and 1990s, a time when electoral politics in that country was dominated by local bosses, families, and factions. But this period was later superseded by the dramatic political polarisation produced by the prime ministership of Thaksin Shinawatra, a popular politician with authoritarian inclinations who helped radically transform the nature of political and party competition in the country. For all his strong-arm tactics, Thaksin, one must readily acknowledge, understood the importance of strong institutions, most obviously reflected in how he built a national political party machine but also in how he worked through the bureaucracy to institute major reforms in social policy (Kuhonta 2012).

By contrast, the prospects for a similar transformation in the Philippines seem dim. Duterte has not yet demonstrated the capacity to move beyond his *ad hoc* mayoral style of governance, and he has shown little if any appreciation for the value of institutions—even for the strengthening of his own political party, which has re-emerged from relative obscurity and is likely to return to relative obscurity at the end of his time in office. Duterte is far more adept at tearing down than building up, displaying exceptional skills in both intimidating the political opposition and accumulating more power—albeit without any clear strategic vision as to what he wants to do with it. His populist appeals and authoritarian inclinations pose major threats to the already weak political institutions of the Philippines, not to mention the future of Philippine democracy. Thus, while Duterte has innovated new appeals and new techniques—including the aggressive use of social media to mobilise support for the administration and cow potential opponents—he has not created the institutional foundations to enable him to lead and preside over his own transformation of Philippine politics (except through the steady deterioration of existing political institutions and constitutional protections). As a result, we can expect on-going continuity in practices at the local level: the dominance of money and patronage politics, combined in some places with varying degrees of coercion, and centred around local political machines that exhibit remarkable resilience and durability despite the many changes in their midst.

The remainder of the volume is organised by region. Chapter 2 gives us a national view, after which we shift our focus to local dynamics. Chapter 2 offers a bird's-eye perspective by Holmes of the 2016 contest, focusing on the role (or lack thereof) of national party machines in support of the leading presidential candidates. Chapters 3–10 then focus on local races on the island of Luzon. Chapters 3–7 present cases of local-level electoral dynamics that are fairly typical of the Philippines in 2016. Dolorical (Chapter 3) describes the importance of incumbency and patronage for contests in Rinconada, Camarines Sur. He notes that term limits, rather than limiting dynastic politics, have fuelled office-hopping by term-limited incumbents, who continue to rely heavily on patronage resources and credit-claiming to boost their candidacy. Nolasco explores the dynamics of patronage in Chapter 5, emphasising how socio-cultural conditions in Camarines Norte undergird patronage politics. She reports that while candidates feel bound to respond to patronage requests, they are also savvy and strategic in their deployment of patronage—for example, adapting their patronage approaches for different social classes.

Chapters 5 and 6 offer views from two different districts in Laguna province. In Chapter 5 Sta. Romana describes how election campaigning reflects the clientelist networks and flows of patronage that exist in between elections. She describes how candidates work to build a sense of comradery (*pakikisama*) with voters and a reputation for good character through large campaign events, smaller group meetings, house-to-house campaigning, and positive responses to requests for assistance. She also notes the difference in mobilisation strategies between incumbents and their party machines versus non-incumbents with their more personalised, promiscuous organisations. In Chapter 6 Miranda describes the connection between patronage in the periods between elections (where the electoral seeds are sewn) and campaign-related activities during election season (when the fruit is harvested). She details how campaigns strategically target a mix of groups and individuals in an effort to win supporters or, in some cases, to discourage opponents, and notes that voter demands are an important driver of money politics at the local level.

Moving to Metro Manila, Calimbahin's Chapter 7 focuses on the Binay clan in Makati and explores the advantages and limits of family dynasties. These dynasties award decided advantages to allied candidates, but can prove difficult to coordinate and maintain, particularly in the wake of scandals that damage the family brand. Calimbahin's chapter demonstrates some of the limits and vulnerabilities local dynasties face when trying to expand their power base horizontally (throughout a municipality or province) or vertically (to national-level office).

Chapters 8–10 describe new forms of electoral competition and voter mobilisation that are growing up alongside traditional patronage politics in some areas, and even supplanting local patronage machines in some cases. In Chapter 8 Rocina provides what on the surface appears to be a fairly standard account of patronage politics in Muntinlupa City, including the contingent provision of goods and services such as health, education, or water. However, Rocina notes that candidates also work to develop reputations as reliable providers of needed goods and services (including investing in the appropriate moniker, for example, "Mr. Water") and this potentially offers a form of programmatic accountability (voters rewarding politicians for public service provision) that goes beyond traditional forms of patronage politics. Eusebio in Chapter 9 draws on research from an electoral district in Pangasinan in which traditional local machines have begun to transform into what he dubs "developmental machines". While these emerging political vehicles continue to use the traditional tools of patronage politics, including the offer of goods, services and cash in exchange for votes, they also differ from their more traditional counterparts in at least two ways. First, they actively recruit participation and input from grassroots stakeholders. Second, they work to build reputations as effective providers of local public goods. Finally, Borromeo-Bulao describes electoral politics in the oft-studied Naga City—home to the late Jesse Robredo. In Chapter 10 she describes an alternative form of machine politics that regularises and systematises the distribution of government services through close consultation and coordination with grassroots societal groups. This "Naga City Model" still makes use of feelings of reciprocity among grateful voters and groups, but the model departs from the traditional machine model in two respects. First, government services are not contingent on support for the machine. Second, the local government does not target *individuals* for assistance, but rather partners with societal *groups*, which take a hand in identifying needs and distributing resources and services. These groups then become key vote mobilisers during the campaign. The consultation with societal groups and the mass electorate is systematic, from designing policy, to providing assistance, to selecting candidates. Though it is showing signs of strain, this alternative style of politics has thus far proved robust amidst competition from more traditional forms of money politics.

Chapters 11–14 examine electoral dynamics in the Visayas. We begin with a look at two congressional districts in Leyte. Mangada in Chapter 11 looks at how competition between two dominant clans shapes electoral politics in Leyte's 1st District. Emblematic of dynastic politics, term-limited politicians turn their offices over to family members as a matter of course. However, while the competition between these clans is fierce, in 2016 they appeared to have negotiated a non-compete pact—dividing up the elected positions between the two clans prior to election day. Despite this non-compete pact, most candidates recognised that voters still expected cash and so were active in distributing cash in the run up to election day. Mangada details how candidates deploy the resources at their disposal—money, political machinery and image-branding— to varying effect. Next door, in Leyte's second district, dynastic politics are also the norm. However, Tumandao (Chapter 12) investigates how it was that two outsiders were able to defeat dynastic candidates within the district in 2016. She ascribes the success of these outsiders to their ability to beat dynastic candidates at their own game (mobilising money and building local machines) while also mobilising voters around a few key issues, particularly issues of corruption.

In Chapter 13 Macalandag describes the pattern of the patronage politics observed in Bohol, taking special note of how these patterns have evolved over time. Through *"pamugas-pugas na daan"* (sowing seeds) and *pangulitaw* (courtship) politicians work to build long-term clientelist relationships with voters that they can turn into support during elections. She focuses on the under-studied issue of gender in patronage politics, looking specifically at the experience of female candidates. She finds that while female candidates may make greater use of gendered networks and campaign messages than their male counterparts, they are also forced to engage in the standard practices of patronage politics if they want to be competitive.

From Bohol we move west to the lone district in the province of Antique where Espia (Chapter 14) investigates the case of an incumbent who lost his first election in 30 years. The case suggests that while money is necessary to compete in an election, it is not enough. When other candidates are similarly resourced, other factors, particularly the quality of the campaign machinery, the effective use of media and candidate image, can tip the balance.

Finally, Chapters 15–17 focus on electoral dynamics in Mindanao. Chapter 15 tackles electoral politics in Compostela Valley. While most of the chapters in this volume focus on *voter mobilisation* by candidates, Pancho details the practice of *candidate solicitation* by voters. Though rooted in on-going relationships, solicitations for assistance increase exponentially around election time and how candidates respond can determine whether they win or lose. In Chapter 16, Aquino describes a bitter contest for mayor in nearby Tagum City. The election pitted two well-resourced allies-turned-enemies against each other, and featured established local machines that mobilised in support of the two rather controversial candidates. Chapters 15 and 16 make for an interesting comparison. Both Compostela Valley and Tagum City feature branches of the same family machine—the Uy political machine—but with different outcomes. The Uys lost their election bid in Tagum City, but were victorious in Compostela Valley—pointing, in part, to the continued advantage of incumbency.

As discussed previously, one striking theme that emerged from the case studies in this volume is the lack of two of the three traditional "Gs" of Philippines electoral politics (goons and guns) relative to past elections. The glaring exception to this pattern is the case of Lanao del Sur in the Autonomous Region in Muslim Mindao. In Chapter 17, Latiph describes the by-now-familiar reliance on money and clan networks in 2016. However, he argues that in Lanao del Sur, those resources were not enough to secure victory. Campaigns also employed violence and intimidation in order to prevent voter defection and discourage support for rival campaigns. In the end, elections were both a reflection of ongoing struggles between and within clans, as well as the catalyst for new conflicts.

chapter **2**

The Myth of the Machine

Ronald D. Holmes

In the run-up to the 2016 national election, two candidates, Manuel "Mar" Roxas of the Liberal Party (LP) and then Vice President Jejomar "Jojo" Binay of the United Nationalist Alliance (UNA), pinned their electoral hopes on what they believed were dominant electoral machines. Less than a month before election day, Roxas expressed confidence that the LP's machinery of local officials would ensure victory for him and his party (Yap and Cabacungan 2016). Binay, on the other hand, predicted that he would win by four million votes, asserting that the election was "a battle of organization, field work" and claiming that he had an organisation and network that had been in place since 2010 (Mallari 2016).

The election results told a different story. When the official results came out, Roxas landed second to Rodrigo "Digong" Duterte. Duterte had more than 16.6 million votes (39 per cent of the total votes cast for the presidential race), while Roxas garnered fewer than 10 million votes (23.4 per cent). Binay came in fourth, with only 5.4 million votes (12.7 per cent). The loyalists consistently claimed that pre-election polls did not take into account the party's machinery and yet Roxas's final vote share was only marginally higher than the 22 per cent he obtained in the last pre-election poll conducted by *Pulse Asia Research Inc* (PAR Inc). In the case of Binay, his final vote share was significantly lower than the 17 per cent posted in the same PAR Inc. 26–29 April 2016 survey. These figures suggest that the organisation, network, or machine that these two contenders thought would secure voting support eventually failed to churn out the numbers they expected. Thus, Roxas and Binay join the presidential contenders of yore, Ramon Mitra of the Laban ng Demokratikong Pilipino in 1992 and Jose de Venecia of the Lakas ng Tao-National Union of Christian Democrats in 1998, who boasted of a vaunted machinery that ultimately failed to deliver.

Compared to Mitra and De Venecia, Roxas and Binay appeared to have better chances to showcase how a political machine works. Roxas could draw strength from the anointment by a president who continued to enjoy majority approval at the end of his term. The Roxas team also claimed that they had the support of a significant majority of incumbent national and local officials. Aside from a large number of LP members, legislators and local officials belonging to other parties (for example, the National Unity Party, the Nationalist People's Coalitions, or even local parties, such as Kabalen of incumbent Governor Lilia Pineda in Pampanga) endorsed Roxas for the presidency. Among the governors, 67 of the 80 incumbent were reported to back Roxas. The endorsement of these officials was not surprising as many had benefitted from the programmes implemented by the Aquino administration. These included an expanded conditional cash transfer and health care coverage for their constituents as well as additional funding for provincial roads under the *Kalsada* (road) programme.

Binay, on the other hand, built up an "organisation" from the time he successfully vied for the vice-presidency in 2010 and had nurtured that organisation during his time in office. This organisation included sister cities of the town that Binay led for more than two decades, Makati. There was also his fraternity, the *Alpha Phi Omega* network, as well as the civic organisation, Boy Scouts of the Philippines (BSP), which he headed. Other organisations, so-called parallel groups supportive of Binay, were organised under the Victory for Binay Election Summit (VIBES), a network of volunteer groups established in January 2016 (Cepeda 2016). Given the extent of the network, Binay's chief campaign adviser, Ronaldo Puno, predicted that Binay would garner 30 per cent of the votes (Cayabyab 2016).

Roxas and Binay's "machineries" were more than just organisations on paper. Each machine had access to significant resources gleaned from both candidates' connections with government and supplemented with additional funds from campaign contributors. Indeed, their respective machines had the potential to mobilise support. However, as this chapter argues, the share of votes of each candidate in each province makes clear that the purported "machines" of the presidential candidates failed to deliver the expected votes. The disaggregation of the presidential votes by province supports the view that the results of the presidential race were determined more by the spatial, ethnolinguistic, and communication strategies employed by the contenders than by electoral machinery.

THE GUBERNATORIAL RACES OF 2016

One way to gauge the effectiveness of these party machines is to start by looking at the provincial level. The 2016 election included races for 81 provincial government seats. (This was one more than the 2013 election as a new province had been created—Davao Occidental.) A total of 267 candidates vied for the 81 positions. More than two-thirds (53) of the incumbent governors were running for re-election. Fourteen of the incumbent governors were uncontested in their re-election bids. Only two of the governors who sought re-election lost in their re-election bids. In 17 other provinces, a candidate who was a member of the incumbent governor's clan vied for the provincial chief executive position. Four of these contenders related to the outgoing governor lost in tightly contested races. For the 10 remaining provinces, the competition was among politicians who occupied other elective positions (for example, congressman, vice-governor, mayor) prior to the May 2016 election.

Table 2.1 shows the number of candidates fielded by the parties and the number of winners in the gubernatorial election of 2016.

As reflected in the table, the LP, Roxas's party, fielded the largest number of candidates and won nearly half of the gubernatorial seats in the 2016 election. On the other hand, Binay's new party, UNA, fielded a candidate in only a quarter of the gubernatorial seats in contention with only three of its candidates winning. These numbers would suggest that LP had a foundation of a formidable electoral machine. Moreover, even beyond the official LP members, a significant number of non-LP gubernatorial candidates had reportedly thrown support behind Roxas (for example, NUP and many independents).

Most of the gubernatorial races involved incumbency advantage or were virtually uncontested, with the average margin between the winner and the second placer at over 40 per cent of the total votes cast (Table 2.2). There were only 12 gubernatorial races where the margin between the winner and second-placed candidate was a single digit. These results were expected by strategists of a number of national candidates. It was for this reason that national candidates worked towards forging alliances with strong gubernatorial candidates with the hope that they could mobilise votes for the presidential contender, given that they did not have to worry about their own election bids.

Table 2.1
Candidates and winners by party affiliation, 2016 gubernatorial election

Political parties	Number of Candidates	Number of Winners
Kilusang Bagong Lipunan (New Society Movement)	12	0
Lakas-Christian Muslim Democrats (Lakas-CMD)	1	0
Laban ng Demokratikong Pilipino (Fight of Democratic Filipinos, LDP)	1	0
Local parties	14	7
Liberal Party (LP)	50	40
Nacionalista Party (NP)	15	8
Nationalist People's Coalition (NPC)	21	8
National Unity Party (NUP)	17	10
Pilipino Democratic Party-Laban ng Bayan (PDP-Laban)	3	0
Puwersa ng Masang Pilipino (PMP)	1	0
United Nationalist Alliance (UNA)	19	3
Independents	113	5

Source: Commission on Elections, tabulated by the author.

THE PERFORMANCE OF PRESIDENTIAL CONTENDERS AT THE PROVINCIAL LEVEL

To determine whether the alliance between presidential contenders and gubernatorial candidates benefitted the presidential hopefuls, I examine the share of the provincial votes of the presidential contenders in each province. These alliances, in the first place, constitute what has been presented as part of the presidential contender's "machine". If these alliances worked, we should expect the share of the presidential contender backed by the alliance to increase in the provinces concerned. As mentioned earlier, Roxas and Binay made claims that their "machines" would deliver the votes. Thus, I examine how these two fared in provinces where they had leading gubernatorial allies.

Among the provinces where Roxas had an incumbent ally running as governor, there was only one province, Camiguin, where the Roxas "machine" clearly worked. In this province, Roxas got almost 75 per cent of the votes for president. The dominant political family in Camiguin, the Romualdos, once more delivered support for their favoured presidential candidate, repeating their feat from 2010 when then LAKAS-CMD candidate Gilbert "Gibo" Teodoro edged out his more popular rivals due to the support of the Romualdos.

Beyond Camiguin, Roxas did very well in the provinces connected with his home regions of Negros Island and Panay. In these regions his share of the presidential votes ranged from a low of 41 per cent in Antique, to a high of 77 per cent in Capiz. If the much-vaunted machine had performed as hoped we might expect similar levels of support in provinces with allied governors. Roxas did top the presidential contest in 13 other provinces, but with vote shares below what we would expect from a party machinery actively working to turn out votes for him. These 13 provinces were: Agusan del Sur (52.14 per cent), Misamis Occidental (49.63 per cent), Siquijor (47.9 per cent), Masbate (44.32 per cent), Romblon (42.05 per cent), Batanes (40.37 per cent), Zamboanga del Norte (39.3 per cent), Occidental Mindoro (38.73 per cent), Palawan (38.59 per cent), Albay (36.77 per cent), Northern Samar (34.84 per cent), Eastern Samar (34.73 per cent), and Samar (33.82 per cent). Clearly, the Roxas "machine" failed to deliver the votes the party expected, even in areas where he won, and even in the provinces where his provincial allies were uncontested or trounced by their opponents. For example, in the provinces of Apayao and Quirino, where the LP gubernatorial candidates were uncontested, Roxas obtained only 17 per cent and 27 per cent of the presidential votes, with Jojo Binay garnering plurality shares (45 and 30 per cent, respectively), possibly due to his ethno-linguistic connections to those areas.

Binay performed creditably only in the regions where he traces his roots: Regions 1 (Ilocos), 2 (Cagayan Valley) and CAR (Cordillera Administrative Region). Specifically, he garnered a higher than average share of the votes in the provinces of Isabela (52 per cent), Cagayan (45.65 per cent), Apayao (45 per cent), Quirino (29 per cent), Kalinga (40 per cent), Abra (39 per cent), Nueva Vizcaya (30 per cent), La Union (28 per cent), Aurora (28 per cent), and Ifugao (24 per cent). In two other provinces with which Binay had connections he had a slightly higher share of the votes (Batangas 24 per cent and Nueva Ecija 22 per cent). Perhaps most damning is the fact that in the three provinces where the gubernatorial candidate from his own party won, Dinagat, Catanduanes and Cavite, Binay's vote share was lower or only marginally higher than his national average, at 7.24 per cent, 14.52 per cent and 14.48 per cent, respectively. At the end of the day some of Binay's provincial allies proved fickle. The Remullas of Cavite, for example, severed their ties with Binay towards the tail-end of the campaign and shifted their support to Duterte. Another ally of Binay, the Garcias of Cebu, also broke with the vice-president earlier, partially accounting for his dismal showing in the province, with a mere single digit share (4.7 per cent) of the Cebu presidential votes.

One thing that stands out in the preceding discussion is the effect of family and ethno-linguistic ties on voter preference. This is consistent with Landé's (1996) analysis of the 1992 presidential election. In more than a third (29 of the 81) of the provinces, the vote shares of the top four presidential contenders corresponded to a candidate's ethno-linguistic or geographic ties to the province, rather than his machine. In the case of Duterte, his win could be largely attributed to his significant majority support (averaging 69 per cent) in 19 of the 25 provinces of his home island, Mindanao. Duterte also drew sizeable plurality to slight majority support among his fellow Bisayan voters in Cebu (50.66 per cent), Bohol (49.49 per cent) and Dinagat Islands (63.07 per cent). The ethno-linguistic/geographic connection is further affirmed by Grace Poe's plurality victory (41.27 per cent) in Pangasinan, the home province of her late adoptive father, Fernando Poe Jr.

WHY DID THE ROXAS AND BINAY MACHINES FAIL?

A political machine is defined as "a party organization within which power is highly centralised and whose members are motivated and rewarded by divisible material incentives rather than by considerations of ideology or long-term goals of public policy" (Johnston 1979: 395). Information from key sources reveal that the Roxas and Binay machines did not meet one criterion of this definition, centralised control. After I made repeated requests for information about the structure of the Roxas campaign organisation, a key informant admitted that the structure to secure local allies and ensure vote mobilisation by these allies was compartmentalised.[1] Key individuals supportive of Roxas were tasked with taking charge of

---

[1] Interview with a member of the campaign team of the Liberal Party candidates, 8 April 2016, Manila.

certain areas/provinces to ensure that allies in these areas would be able to mobilise support. The informant revealed that these "coordinators" were provided with resources to disburse to their allies so that these could be used to finance projects or provide inducements to voters.

Binay's campaign organisation was initially described as a "'flat' organization, with several committees and point persons", but in which the candidate, Binay, had the final say (Cepeda 2016). An informant revealed that it was only in late 2016 that the organisation developed a relatively more centralised structure.[2] This was after Ronnie Puno, the campaign strategist of three former presidents—Ramos, Estrada and Arroyo—was tapped by the Binay camp to serve as campaign manager. Puno's primary task was organising local allies for vote mobilisation and approving all external communications (that is, advertisements). These "operations", one informant revealed, were financed by diverting resources initially allocated to parallel groups (that is, VIBES). However, as he came late in the campaign and drew primarily on his prior connections, rather than building upon the long-standing network of Binay, Puno failed to deliver on the promise of 30 per cent of the presidential votes for Binay.

Binay's organisational problems were reflected in the withdrawal of support of two erstwhile allies, the Garcias and Remullas, political families that dominated politics in the country's top two vote-rich provinces, Cebu and Cavite, respectively. The Garcias withdrew their support from Binay after the latter's team failed to coordinate local rallies in Cebu, alleging that "UNA members have been cavorting with local opponents, thereby sowing disunity, discord, and confusion" (Quintas et al. 2016). In Cavite the Remullas decided to shift their support from Binay to Duterte just a few weeks shy of the May 2016 election. News reports indicate that the Remullas came to this decision with their local leaders after recognising that Duterte was the favoured candidate of their constituents (Cinco 2016). However, an informant revealed that the Remullas withdrew their support after a series of differences with Binay came to the fore, including over how Binay should have responded to serious corruption allegations in early 2015, the appointment of Puno as "campaign manager, and the treatment of former Binay spokesperson, then incumbent Cavite Governor Jonvic Remulla, after the second presidential debate held in Cebu".[3] Remulla was alleged to have been censured by Binay in Cebu after

---

[2] Interview with Binay campaign team member, 20 April 2016, Manila.
[3] Interview with a member of the Binay campaign team, 4 May 2016, Manila.

Remulla failed to relay to the debate organisers Binay's intent to bring documents that he would refer to during the debate.

The failure to create a highly centralised structure is also a reflection of the multi-layered nature of Philippine elections. It is difficult to ensure that local allies will keep to their commitments when their own political fortunes depend on securing support for themselves and their local allies first. While it is the case that many of the governors were uncontested or easily trumped by their opponents, these governors also had to support the re-election or election campaigns of their allies running for various positions—single member district candidates for Congress, provincial board members, mayors, vice-mayors and councilors. In a few provinces where resources were handed down by national candidates to sub-national allies to mobilise support, an informant privy to the dynamics of national-local alliances in provinces in Muslim Mindanao revealed that the monies received were used primarily to boost the chances of local allies rather than to secure voting support for the national candidate. In some cases the resources were pocketed for personal gain.[4]

FAR REMOVED FROM THE PUBLIC

The failure of Mar Roxas to mobilise the "party machinery" could also be rooted in the fact that the administration party failed to build a connection for voters between the palpable individual benefits from projects or reforms and the party behind those benefits. With an aversion to credit claiming, former President Aquino prohibited agencies of government from putting up the usual placards that carry his photo or name alongside the details of the project. Moreover, when it came to the flagship project of the administration, the conditional cash transfer called the *Pantawid Pamilyang Pilipino Program* (4Ps), the other candidates vowed to sustain, expand or improve the programme, nullifying whatever advantage was enjoyed by Roxas, the administration's candidate. A study of the electoral effects of such programmes also indicates that CCTs are not likely to create a devout following for parties or particular politicians (Zucco 2013). With national politicians far removed from the voting public, even the strongest Roxas local ally would find it difficult to "sell"

---

[4] Interview with a senior bureaucrat from the Autonomous Region of Muslim Mindanao, 24 May 2016, Cebu, Philippines.

a politician when such candidate is not recognised for having delivered clear personal benefits.

An interview of a long-time politician reveals the difficulty that local patrons confront in delivering votes to their national allies. This informant, a veteran elected official from Luzon who belongs to one of the longest ruling political clans, recalls an experience he had in the election of 2004.[5] Tapped to secure support for the presidential bid of then incumbent president, Gloria Macapagal Arroyo (GMA), this politician used resources obtained from the central government as well as personal resources to provide monetary inducements to voters. On election day, he proceeded to the polling booth early. Observing the behaviour of voters who were writing down their preferences on the ballot, the politician was perplexed as to why the voters took a long time to complete their ballots. Suspecting that voters may have opted to vote for GMA's opponent, Fernando Poe Jr. (FPJ), he waited until the voters dropped their ballots in the ballot box and had an informal conversation with each of them.

When the voting was over, the politician asked the Chair of the Board of Election Inspectors (BEI) to open the ballot box and retrieve the ballots to see who the voters chose for president. The Chair initially refused, arguing that doing so would be a violation of the Election Code. But he eventually relented after being given the assurance that the politician's only intention was to see the presidential preference and that these indicated preferences would not be altered. The politician's suspicion was affirmed: every one of those who voted opted for FPJ.

The politician then asked the voters whether they received the PhP 300 distributed the night before the election. He claimed that two-thirds of the money given came from the national campaign headquarters; the remaining third was from personal funds. All affirmed that they did, prompting the politician to curse the voters, saying that "*kung alam ko lang na hindi ninyo iboboto si GMA, eh di sana hindi ko na kayo binigyan ng pabuya*" (had I known you will not vote for GMA, I would not have given you the incentive). One voter, replied with confidence but also respect: "*Sa loob ng isang taon, isang araw lang naman ang hiling namin sa iyo. Pagbigyan ninyo na po kami ngayon. Idol lang talaga namin si FPJ.*" (For an entire year, we only ask for a single day. Please just allow us. FPJ is our idol.) Hearing this, the politician could only smile and nod in agreement, realising that indeed the voters had been faithful to their local political machine and clan, constantly re-electing their members. He agreed they

---

[5] Interview with Northern Luzon politician, 1 May 2016, Makati, Philippines.

should be given the liberty to choose freely who they wished to elect as president (and for other national positions).

The same politician revealed that in the 2016 election, despite their governor's being sworn to support Mar Roxas, they did not commit to deliver votes inasmuch as another national candidate, a native of their place was bound to get much of the popular vote in their province. Moreover, the political clans in the province were also divided over whom to support for the presidency, with one group formally committed to support Roxas, and a second group to support Grace Poe. This pattern of members of the same family supporting different national candidates was not uncommon and was often done in order to ensure that the family or clan retained a connection with the eventual winner.

CONCLUSION

The results of the 2016 election show that the machines faltered due to a number of factors. First, indicative of what Pitkin (1967) refers to as "descriptive representation", voters supported candidates who shared the same ethno-linguistic attributes as themselves. Roxas and Binay drew majority voting support from their respective home provinces/regions. However, these were matched by Duterte's significant majority electoral support from his home island, Mindanao, as well as sizeable support from fellow Bisayan speakers in Cebu and Bohol. Thus, regional/ethno-linguistic ties trumped political alliances.

Second, and more importantly, the failure of attempts to build and employ national machines testifies to the continuous weakness of political parties, specifically the superficial direct link they have with citizens/voters. This is evidenced by Roxas' fate, as he failed to convert the resources distributed by the Liberal Party throughout its six-year dominance into votes for his own candidacy.

Finally, one can conclude that there were really no machines that operated at the national level. The so-called machines of Roxas and Binay were weakly organised, without the clear central control that was necessary to ensure the seamless implementation of vote mobilisation strategies and secure the compliance of sub-national politician brokers with their vote commitments. What were obtained were loose alliances between national candidates and sub-national politicians, propelled by the need of the latter to maximise their access to patronage resources to boost their own bids for re-election.

Table 2.2

2016 gubernatorial election results, margin between winning and second-placed contender

Province	Winner	Party	Vote share, winner (%)	Second-placer	Vote share, second-placer (%)	Difference (%)
Ifugao	Mayam-o, Pedro	LP	25.23	Balitang, Eugene (IND)	24.20	1.03
Cebu	Davide, Hilario	LP	47.79	Garcia, Winston (Cebu)	46.03	1.76
Camarines Norte	Tallado, Eduardo	NPC	47.25	Barcelona-Reyes, Cathy (LP)	45.04	2.21
Compostela Valley	Uy, Jayvee	LP	51.13	Amatong, Bobong (Aksyon)	48.42	2.71
Masbate	Kho, Tony	NP	35.03	Lanete, Dayan (NPC)	31.81	3.22
Cagayan	Mamba, Manuel	LP	38.20	Antonio, Tin (UNA)	34.68	3.52
Batangas	Mandanas, Dodo	IND	29.40	Mendoza, Dong (NPC)	25.57	3.83
Abra	Bernos, Maria Jocelyn	NUP	52.18	Bersamin, Ruby (LP)	46.50	5.68
Batanes	Cayco, Marilou	LP	37.37	Castillejos, Telesforo (NPC)	30.18	7.19
Davao del Sur	Cagas, Douglas	NP	51.21	Latasa, Arsenio (NPC)	43.99	7.22
Agusan del Norte	Amante-Matba, Angel	LP	53.95	Garcia-Tomaneng, Sadeka (NP)	46.04	7.91
Aklan	Miraflores, Joeben	LP	54.27	Maming, Antonio (UNA)	45.72	8.55
Catanduanes	Cua, Joseph	UNA	41.43	Wong, Jardin Brian (LP)	31.40	10.03
Tawi Tawi	Matba, Rash	NUP	55.94	Sahali, Nurbert (LP)	44.05	11.89
La Union	Ortega, Pacoy	IND	47.82	Ortega, Mario Eduardo (KBL)	35.77	12.05
Benguet	Pacalso, Cresencio	IND	40.13	Dangwa, Nelson (LP)	27.86	12.27
Guimaras	Gumarin, Samuel	LP	56.19	Nava, Nene (UNA)	43.80	12.39
South Cotabato	Avance-Fuentes, Daisy	NPC	56.15	Miguel, Fernando (IND)	43.53	12.62

(cont'd overleaf)

Table 2.2 (*cont'd*)

Province	Winner	Party	Vote share, winner (%)	Second-placer	Vote share, second-placer (%)	Difference (%)
Surigao del Norte	Matugas, Sol	LP	56.55	Romarate, Guillermo (NP)	43.44	13.11
Zambales	Deloso, Amor	IND	56.35	Ebdane, Jun (SZP)	43.09	13.26
Antique	Cadiao, Rhodora	NUP	56.74	Javier, Exequiel (LP)	43.25	13.49
Davao Oriental	Dayanghirang, Nelson	LP	57.49	Almario, Thelma (NPC)	42.50	14.99
Misamis Oriental	Emano, Bambi	PADAYN	58.11	Uy, Julio (NUP)	41.88	16.23
Nueva Vizcaya	Padilla, Carlos	NP	56.22	Gambito, Jose (UNA)	39.90	16.32
Sorsogon	Rodrigueza, Bobet	LP	44.92	Anonuevo, Rolando (IND)	27.32	17.60
Pangasinan	Espino, Amado III	Aksyon	58.59	Cojuangco, Mark (NPC)	40.86	17.73
Zamboanga Sibugay	Palma, Wilter	LP	58.63	Jalosjos, Jan-jan (NP)	40.33	18.30
Samar	Tan, Ann	NPC	57.27	Zosa, Emil (LP)	38.95	18.32
Zamboanga del Norte	Uy, Berto	LP	58.97	Yebes, Gob. Lando (NPC)	39.78	19.19
Bohol	Chatto, Edgar	LP	58.41	Imboy, May (PDPLBN)	39.18	19.23
Surigao del Sur	Pimentel, BB	LP	59.77	Garay, Enciong (NPC)	39.48	20.29
Southern Leyte	Mercado, Mian	LP	60.28	Tan, Sheffered (UNA)	39.71	20.57
Negros Oriental	Degamo, Roel	NUP	60.00	Arnaiz, George (NPC)	38.73	21.27
Marinduque	Reyes, Nanay	LP	54.74	Lim, Vicky (IND)	33.00	21.74
Maguindanao	Mangugagatu, Esmael	LP	60.72	Midtimbang, Ali (UNA)	38.60	22.12
Lanao del Sur	Adiong, Soraya	LP	56.62	Salic, Fahad Panarigan (UNA)	34.25	22.37
Laguna	Hernandez, Ramil	NP	51.17	Ejercito, Jorge Antonio (IND)	28.41	22.76
Kalinga	Baac, Jocel	LP	48.87	Dieza, Conrado (UNA)	25.74	23.13

Table 2.2 *(cont'd)*

Province	Winner	Party	Vote share, winner (%)	Second-placer	Vote share, second-placer (%)	Difference (%)
Nueva Ecija	Umali, Cherry	LP	61.83	Antonino, Rody (UNA)	38.16	23.67
Bulacan	Sy-Alvarado, Wilhemino	LP	56.39	Dela Cruz, Josie (NPC)	32.35	24.04
Tarlac	Yap, Susan	NPC	63.25	Manalang, Ace (PMP)	38.16	25.09
Eastern Samar	Nicart, Aklan	LP	62.72	Libanan, Nonoy (NUP)	37.27	25.45
Sultan Kudarat	Mangudadatu, Datu Pax	PTM	64.24	Pallasigue, Diosdada (LP)	35.33	28.91
Camarines Sur	Villafuerte, Migz	NP	60.00	Fuentebella, Arnie (UNA)	30.93	29.07
Occidental Mindoro	Mendiola, Mario Gene	LP	64.19	Villarosa, Girlie (Lakas)	34.66	29.53
Siquijor	Villa, Jecoy	LP	60.02	Fua, Orlando (UNA)	29.30	30.72
Palawan	Alvarez, Jca	LP	62.08	Ventura, Art (IND)	30.79	31.29
Lanao del Norte	Dimaporo, Angging	LP	65.84	Lantud, Eleanor (UNA)	30.87	34.97
Basilan	Salliman, Hataman Jim	LP	67.95	Maturan, Joel (UNA)	30.37	37.58
Romblon	Firmalo, Eduardo	LP	68.34	Montojo, Gard (IND)	30.76	37.58
Northern Samar	Ong, Jun	NUP	70.16	Cerbito, Walter (IND)	27.53	42.63
Davao del Norte	Del Rosario, Anthony	LP	72.04	Suaybaguio, Victorio Jr. (IND)	27.95	44.09
Oriental Mindoro	Umali, Pa	LP	72.83	Andaya, Sally (SNDUGO)	25.11	47.72
Isabela	Dy, Bodjie (NPC)	NPC	75.27	Padaca, Grace (IND)	23.79	51.48
Sulu	Tan, Abdusakur II	LP	71.17	Tulawie, Cocoy (LDP)	17.23	53.94
Bukidnon	Zubiri, Jose Maria	BPP	79.51	Tabios, Diosdado (IND)	18.76	60.75
Sarangani	Solon, Steve	PCM	76.58	Aquia, Mohamad (LP)	15.13	61.45

(cont'd overleaf)

Table 2.2 (*cont'd*)

Province	Winner	Party	Vote share, winner (%)	Second-placer	Vote share, second-placer (%)	Difference (%)
Cotabato	Talino-Mendoza, Emmylou	LP	75.51	Monreal, Lito (IND)	13.30	62.21
Zamboanga del Sur	Cerilles, Antonio	NPC	86.92	Poloyapoy, Tirsendo (Aksyon)	11.84	75.08
Rizal	Ynares, Nini	NPC	87.35	Salonga, Steve (IND)	09.55	77.80
Capiz	Del Rosario, Antonio	LP	93.19	Belonio, Boss Doming (IND)	05.75	87.44
Albay	Bichara, Al Francis	NP	91.60	Hernandez, Jim (IND)	03.60	88.00
Leyte	Petilla, Leopoldo	LP	94.49	Falcone, Bal (IND)	02.77	91.72
Cavite	Remulla, Boying	UNA	94.15	Borral, Obet (IND)	02.31	91.84
Iloilo	Defensor, Arthur Sr.	LP	96.03	Lebin, Gil (IND)	02.00	94.03
Misamis Occidental	Ramiro, Herminia	NUP	97.41	Dologuin, Alex (IND)	02.58	94.83
Quezon	Suarez, David	NUP	97.07	Gonzales, Teodorico (PMM)	00.97	96.10
Mountain Province	Mayaen, Leonard	IND	100.00			100.00
Pampanga	Pineda, Nanay Baby	KMBLN	100.00			100.00
Apayao	Bulut, Elias	LP	100.00			100.00
Quirino	Cua, Junie	LP	100.00			100.00
Biliran	Espina, Gerryboy	LP	100.00			100.00
Camiguin	Romualdo, Baby	LP	100.00			100.00
Ilocos Norte	Marcos, Imee	NP	100.00			100.00
Ilocos Sur	Singson, Ryan	NP	100.00			100.00
Aurora	Noveras, Gerardo	NPC	100.00			100.00

Table 2.2 *(cont'd)*

Province	Winner	Party	Vote share, winner (%)	Second-placer	Vote share, second-placer (%)	Difference (%)
Dinagat	Ecleo, Mommy Glen	UNA	100.00			100.00
Negros Occidental	Maranon, Alfredo	UNEGA	100.00			100.00
Davao Occidental	Bautista, Claude	NPC	100.00			100.00
Bataan	Garcia, Abet	NUP	100.00			100.00
Agusan del Sur	Plaza, Eddiebong	NUP	100.00			100.00

LUZON

chapter **3**

Rinconada, Camarines Sur: Incumbency and Patronage as Determinants of Electoral Success

Duke Thomas G. Dolorical

INTRODUCTION

The Rinconada District in the Province of Camarines Sur is a hotbed of patronage and clientelism, practised and perfected with savviness by incumbent officials running for re-election (whether for their current position or another), as an art form requiring both technique and creativity. Well-entrenched incumbent candidates belonging to Rinconada's leading political alliance have dominated electoral contests partly due to the structural advantages of incumbency and other strategies employing money politics and populism.

Various works point out that incumbency advantages include greater name recall among voters and almost exclusive access to state resources and formal networks (Querubin 2015; Carson et al. 2007). The same advantages have been observed in the Rinconada District despite the term limits that have been institutionalised for all elective government positions in an effort to ensure equal opportunities among those desiring to be elected public servants. However, such policies have been ineffective in Rinconada District in limiting the monopoly of well-established politicians since many of them, after their term limits, vie for higher or lower positions.

Obviously, incumbent candidates have the convenience and expediency of access to state resources and formal networks necessary for financing an electoral campaign and securing a well-organised and beholden mobilisation structure. The result of the 2016 election in the Rinconada area is a testament to the above fact given that the majority of the winners were either (i) incumbent officials who were holding the same position they ran for (for example, District Representative S. Fortuno), (ii) incumbent officials who sought a higher position (for example, Buhi mayoralty candidate Aguinillo), (iii) incumbent officials wishing to stay in politics and vying for a lower post (for example, Buhi vice-mayoralty candidate and incumbent mayor Lacoste), or (iv) individuals affiliated with an incumbent official (for example, Frank Bernaldez of Bato replacing his wife as mayor and Madel Alfelor of Iriga City replacing her brother as mayor).

In this chapter, I assert that the widespread use of incumbency advantages to defeat challenger candidates reflects an unhealthy democracy that leaves little room for fresh faces and novel ideas in politics. In addition, I argue that incumbent candidates further their margin of electoral success by piggybacking on projects and programmes implemented during their terms, regardless of whether the credit belongs to the national government. Furthermore, the employment of state resources and networks that are only accessible to incumbent candidates as duly elected officials, and their deployment for clientelism and patronage-based campaign strategies, have been the most telling advantages against challengers and non-incumbent candidates in the Rinconada District. I then argue that it is these advantages that Fortuno utilised to capture power repeatedly in the congressional contest of the Rinconada District and fortify a seemingly self-reinforcing clientelistic network that reciprocally supports both patron and clients. To combat this incumbency advantage, non-incumbent candidates have resorted to the same patronage and clientelist-based strategies of campaigning, including money politics and populist strategies.

BACKGROUND OF THE RINCONADA DISTRICT

The electoral jurisdiction covering the Rinconada District consists of one city and six municipalities spread out at the southern tip of Camarines

Sur Province in the main island of Luzon. The area is bound together by a common language (although with variants) and culture, which are distinct from those of the other towns in the province. Serving as the fifth congressional district, it has a total voting population of 240,559.

Although there are several educational institutions situated in Rinconada, the district does not have development infrastructure to aid trade, or other special sectors such as tourism. Its geographical features define the area's economic activities: lowlands surrounding Mt. Asog are cultivated for agriculture, and Buhi Lake, coastal plains and the Bicol River provide livelihoods for fishermen. Despite these natural resources, the average poverty incidence of the Rinconada area as of 2011 is 47.98 per cent (Gumba 2011). In this chapter I contend that the topographical, religious and socio-economic profile of the district exacerbates non-incumbent candidates' incentives to utilise clientelistic campaign strategies to offset the advantages of re-electionists.

For example, since the population is predominantly composed of Catholics, followed by Protestants, Iglesia ni Cristo (INC) and Muslims, the challengers reach out to their local religious leaders, given that endorsements are highly valued, and in certain cases, certain denominations impose "bloc voting" among their flocks for the favoured candidates. This is particularly true for the Iglesia ni Cristo and some Protestant sects, from whom candidates often seek their leaders' endorsement through concessions and contributions.

For decades, Rinconada District was largely oligarchic and clan-dominated, namely by Iriga City's Alfelors and Villanuevas, Nabua Municipality's Simbulans, Bula Municipality's Canets and Decenas, and Baao's Gaite. In the province of Camarines Sur, the Villafuertes have remained uninterrupted in their control of the provincial government. Miguel "Migz" Villafuerte,[1] his father L-Ray Villafuerte[2] and grandfather Luis Villafuerte[3] have taken turns controlling the province in past decades.

---

[1] Camarines Sur governor from 2013 until present.

[2] Camarines Sur governor from 2004 to 2013 and incumbent 2nd District representative.

[3] Patriarch of the Villafuerte clan and served as the Camarines Sur governor from 1986 to 1992 and 1995 to 2004. He also served as 2nd District representative from 2004 to 2010 and 3rd District representative from 2010 to 2013.

Recent times, however, have seen the rise of "new men" in the political landscape, including Fortuno, who became a patron of municipal and barangay-level elective officials and other politicians-turned-allies such as Bagasbas of Balatan Municipality, Lacoste and Aguinillo of Buhi Municipality and Bernaldez of Bato Municipality. A third-term congressional representative of the fifth district of Camarines Sur, Fortuno has worked his way to becoming a dominant patron of lower-level politicians among local government units (LGUs) in the Rinconada District. Fortuno's political career was launched by his popularity as a local radio announcer. In the House of Representatives he was recognised for his perfect attendance and gained prominence for his opposition to the passage of the Reproductive Health Law. He took inconvenient stances against well-established clans, being the sole representative in Camarines Sur who opposed the division of the province into two separate provinces. He is credited with the implementation of previously neglected infrastructural projects for the mostly rural local government units of Rinconada area. Prior to being elected as Rinconada's congressional representative (1998–2001, 2010–13, 2013–16 and 2016–19), Fortuno was elected as provincial board member (two terms, 1988–95) and vice-governor of the province of Camarines Sur (three terms, 1995–98, 2004–10) respectively. In the 2013 and 2016 elections, Fortuno ran under the ticket of the Liberal Party (LP).

However, as these prominent politicians and political dynasties have sought to increase their clout and demand allegiance, this has created electoral tension in the form of violence, vote buying, harassment and other irregularities. The result is an environment that is not conducive to challengers—none of the non-incumbent challengers emerged victorious against their well-entrenched incumbent opponents in 2016.

THE POWER OF PATRONAGE IN A RURAL VOTING POPULACE

Incumbent and non-incumbent candidates have similarly used clientelist and patronage-based strategies in the Rinconada District. The difference is that the former can rely heavily on their privileged positions as current government officials, through: (1) patronage utilising state resources actualised in the form of goods, assistance and cash-distribution; and (2) mobilisation of networks created through that patronage.

Hicken's (2011) work on clientelism frames the main assumptions of this chapter, including what he identified as key elements of clientelism: dyadic relationships, contingency, hierarchy and iteration. Mares and Young's (2016) work is utilised to explain the types of brokers and networks that mediate the relationships and interactions among candidates and voters in the Rinconada District.

Incumbent candidates relied on their formal and informal networks. The use of state resources for either intended or partisan purposes benefitted them by producing positive perceptions of their capacities and qualities as public servants. As a supplemental strategy they were also prone to piggyback on national government programmes and projects implemented during their term of office to claim credit. For those facing serious competition and at some risk of losing, vote buying was also a strategic choice, and often done to counter the vote buying attempts of non-incumbent candidates. Incumbent candidates such as Salvio B. Fortuno utilise these resources to reinforce their existing clientelistic networks and fund patronage-based campaign strategies to ensure not only their own individual electoral victory but also the victory of their subordinate politician clients.

While non-incumbent candidates do not have the structural advantages of incumbency and cannot rely by default on the same strategies employed by incumbent candidates, they try to offset the advantages of their opponents by relying on their own resources and their largely informal networks.

Their second-best alternative strategies are as follows: (1) providing their own services, goods and assistance to voters as well as paying more when buying votes from voters; (2) informal mobilisation of networks that broker patronage on their behalf; and (3) framing the incumbent candidate's patronage as corruption and citing ineffective delivery of basic services. The majority of non-incumbent candidates in all the LGUs of the Rinconada District have provided blood donations, medical services and medicines. Aside from goods, many candidates have also given financial assistance to voters. Most of the non-incumbent candidates interviewed claimed to have recruited members of their mobilisation structure from among individuals disgruntled with their political opponents, along with family members, relatives and trusted individuals. Finally, one common strategy for non-incumbents is to point out the governance failings of the incumbent. In Buhi, for example, a group of non-incumbent candidates publicly questioned the allocations of funds loaned in the name of the LGU by some of their incumbent opponents.

FOOD-FOR-VOTES: GOODS, CASH, AND EXPECTATIONS IMPLIED

Goods, assistance and cash distribution are the most effective strategies used by candidates to secure votes. Rural districts are particularly vulnerable because basic needs are not met, and there is a misconception that candidates giving cash have more personal resources to run the local government. The majority of the candidates interviewed agreed with the statements: "voters expect candidates to distribute goods and cash" and "voters have already been conditioned to this practice".[4] They further claimed that it is in their best interest as candidates to comply in order to project an image of approachability and accessibility. Of course, such practices also give the candidates name recall among voters during election day. Voters, especially the risk-averse poor (Hicken 2011), often perceive these behaviours as the ability to understand and therefore empathise with and care for the situation of poor constituents.

Patronage is cyclical and reciprocal. Indigent voters are more likely to vote for candidates who have rendered them assistance as their way of "remembering and taking care of those who took care of us". Promises of patronage before and during the election are carried out post-election. Incumbents do so to maintain their existing base of supporters and entice new ones, thus expanding the network of clients who are beholden to the patron. This is especially true since many Filipinos feel debts of gratitude towards those from whom they receive help.

Non-incumbent candidates, on the other hand, rely on their own resources, limited party support, private contributions and informal networks to fund their campaign and provide a limited form of patronage to voters. In certain cases, the patronage practices of well-financed non-incumbent candidates even exceed those of their incumbent opponents. For cash-strapped non-incumbent challengers, however, it is critical that they seek party membership to augment their financial resources and gain access to mobilisation networks.

While candidates feel the need to respond to requests from voters, they do take steps to avoid being taken advantage of. The distribution of goods is systematised through the established formal and informal campaign networks of the candidate at the grassroots level. This ensures that goods are delivered to targeted beneficiaries. For example, some candidates require each solicitor (that is, the voter asking for cash or

---

[4] Interviews with various candidates and campaign staff, Riconada area, 25, 26, 28 April and 3, 4 May 2016.

assistance) to produce authentic copies of certificates of indigency issued by their municipality of origin, and original letters of endorsement from their village leader to validate whether he/she is a registered voter in the district. Even photocopied letters and certificates are rejected. In the case of non-incumbent candidates, verification is done through their ground-level coordinators or allied barangay officials.

PIGGYBACKING: FROM HONEST TO EXAGGERATED DECLARATIONS OF ACHIEVEMENTS

Incumbent candidates declared that among the most important campaign strategies is to highlight their accomplishments in office. In the Rinconada District, Fortuno, for example, has made sure that *all* road construction and rehabilitation projects in the district's seven local government units include signage announcing that these were undertaken during his and the allied mayor's incumbency. It is unsurprising that, like Fortuno, the majority of politicians in Camarines Sur prefer infrastructural projects because of their tangibility and visibility, especially if public structures are labelled with the politicians' names. Clearly, these privileges of using "state resources" are exclusive only to incumbent candidates.

It is also common practice among incumbent candidates to take credit and claim as their "own project" nationally funded projects such as DSWD's *Pantawid Pamilyang Pilipino Program* (4Ps) and *Kapit-Bisig Laban sa Kahirapan–Comprehensive and Integrated Delivery of Social Services* (KALAHI–CIDSS).[5] Incumbents thus strive to convince voters that in order to ensure the continuity of such beneficial programmes and projects they must continue their support for their candidacy. Indigent beneficiaries may also feel the threat that they will be removed from these popular programmes if they do not vote for the incumbent candidates in their locality.

Of course, the use of patronage by incumbents can sometimes be a liability. Generally, non-incumbent candidates try to offset the advantages of incumbent piggybacking and patronage by turning it against the incumbents. Through the use of social media and political rallies, they try to nullify the policy and infrastructural achievements of incumbent candidates by attacking their reputation and emphasising allegations of

---

[5] These agencies dole out cash assistance and projects beneficial to indigent constituents.

corruption and inefficient delivery of services under the latter's term. They campaign for voters' support by presenting themselves and their platforms as viable alternatives to what they frame as the "corrupt and inept" leadership of their incumbent opponents. Interestingly, there are also non-incumbents who resort to cheap tactics. For example, a non-incumbent candidate in Buhi was identified as the source of rumours that spread through SMS messaging and social media regarding accusations of infidelity and immorality of a rival incumbent candidate.

VOTE BUYING: INTENSE BUT "BUSINESS-AS-USUAL"

A common strategy utilised by incumbent and challenger candidates in Rinconada District is vote buying. Widely acknowledged by voters, candidates and election observers, vote buying goes beyond giving food and assistance as it places a price on the people's right of suffrage. For some incumbent candidates, it is done to maintain their base of loyal supporters or as an incentive for undecided voters and supporters of opponent candidates. Usually, incumbent candidates pay less money to their loyal voters and spend more on undecided voters or opponents' supporters. The former are long-time beneficiaries of their incumbent patron and thus only require a minimal amount of money to continue support.

While vote buying may seem the best alternative option for non-incumbents if a good platform is not sufficient to sway voters, most of them do not have enough resources to compete with incumbents. Their narrative of "change" in governance and policies is often overshadowed by the limitations of financial input necessary in order to (i) communicate this narrative to the wider populace, including those living in districts that require traversing mountains in terrible road conditions, or crossing the seas in uncomfortable outrigger boats; but also to (ii) fund inducements, such as goods and cash, in exchange for people's votes.

On the other hand, wealthy challengers did readily resort to vote buying, arguing that it is the accepted practice of all candidates in elections and in order to win, candidates must be able to "play this game". For example, there were reports in Nabua that a well-resourced non-incumbent candidate offered PhP 500 to 700 per vote, PhP 200 to 400 higher than the offer made by an incumbent opponent. In Iriga City a challenger's attempt to exceed by PhP 200 the PhP 300 offer per vote of an incumbent opponent was rendered ineffective when the incumbent alerted the police to place checkpoints in strategic places to thwart the vote buying attempt of the challenger.

An important actor in this arena is the seasoned political operators who convince their candidates to engage in buying votes. Akin to Stokes' (2005) concept of *perverse accountability*, candidates designate "poll watchers" who will ensure that bought voters will vote for them. In Nabua, Parish Pastoral Council for Responsible Voting (PPCRV)[6] volunteers tasked with assisting the Boards of Election Inspectors (BEIs)[7] and voters in many voting precincts were predominantly people identified with an incumbent candidate. An interviewee pointed out that co-opting these volunteers allowed the candidate to augment the number of poll watchers the candidate could tap to closely monitor[8] whether paid voters voted for them.[9] These workers were then also in place to try to persuade illiterate or older voters requiring their assistance to switch their support if the voter supported the opponent candidate. While this elaborate scheme is not commonly practised, the majority of candidates in the Rinconada District did employ poll watchers. In some precincts in Iriga City, poll watchers for a candidate even manipulated voters' queues to ensure that bought voters were given prioritised entry to the polling place.[10]

Vote buying strategies have evolved over time as candidates find ways to innovate. Aside from the typical pattern of "last hour" vote buying (that is, distributing cash to pre-identified lists of registered voters individually, by family, or by clusters of neighbourhoods before election day), the following creative schemes were also employed to conceal or legitimise vote buying in Riconada:

(a) *Loans.* Potential voters are identified, particularly indigents, and are offered loans with low interest rates by future candidates. The debtors are enticed by loaners to vote for a particular candidate, and, in exchange, the loan incurred will be forgiven if the candidate

---

[6] PPCRV is a Catholic Church-affiliated electoral watchdog and citizens' arm of the Commission on Elections (COMELEC).

[7] A BEI is composed of public school teachers deputised by the COMELEC to facilitate and supervise the election at the precinct level.

[8] In some precincts, members of the BEI co-opted by candidates (specifically the personnel in charge of cutting voters' receipts) work in concert with the candidate's poll watchers to determine whether a paid voter voted for that candidate. The BEI member simply nods to the poll watcher to indicate whether the voter whose receipt he/she is cutting indeed voted or not for the candidate in question.

[9] Interview with campaign staff A, Naga City, 19 March 2016.

[10] Interview with Candidate A, Iriga City, 25 April 2016.

wins. However, if the candidate loses the debtor will pay the loan with significant interest. This scheme thus motivates the debtor to vote and campaign for the candidate for purely monetary concerns. It was reported that a veteran political patron and businessman regularly employed this strategy among vendors and pedicab drivers in Baao.[11]

(b)   *Poll watchers.* An independent and an incumbent candidate both confirmed that candidates conceal vote buying under the guise of employing poll watchers. The cash given to these individuals by the candidate is made to appear as legitimate compensation, and those receiving payment are even given legitimate poll-watcher IDs. "One will be surprised to discover that candidates have 200–300 poll watchers belonging to a particular precinct but are not assigned actual poll-watching duties during election day", said one interviewee. This scheme has been one of the enforcement mechanisms employed by a well-entrenched incumbent candidate in Nabua.[12]

MOBILISATION STRUCTURES OF INCUMBENT AND NON-INCUMBENT CANDIDATES IN RINCONADA DISTRICT

The primary motivation for why national parties field and support local candidates, albeit sometimes minimally, is to encourage them to directly and indirectly carry the candidacy of the party's national candidates at the ground level. In exchange, local candidates choose to be affiliated with a political party at least *temporarily* to have official endorsements, party funding and logistical support.

The majority of respondents claimed that they rely heavily on personal effort and input and very little on their party structure in order to win. Reliance on the party is viewed as unnecessary, according to interviewees, who concede that while party membership may afford indispensable organisational and financial support, it is still best to depend on one's own campaign machinery and mobilisation structure. Since parties have to support local candidacies of their party members that serve as the ground-level machinery for their national candidates, allocation of

---

[11] Interview with campaign worker B, Baao, 26 April 2016.
[12] Interview with Candidate A, Iriga City, April 2016.

resources should be strategic. Thus, parties usually give support when they notice that the risks experienced by a local candidate will also affect the performance of national candidates. If parties notice that their local candidate's chances of winning are good, then parties will extend support, but very minimally.[13]

Furthermore, national party leaders do not allocate as many resources and as much logistical support to local candidates during general national elections compared to mid-term local elections, trusting the presidential race to carry the rest of the national team. Respondents in Baao and Balatan argued that when national party leaders think that a local candidate's candidacy is strong in terms of chances of winning, the party does not give as much support.

Respondents admitted that there is really no ideological coherence between parties and their local candidates. This relationship is obviously governed by transactional rather than ideological considerations. In Bula, the NP-LP alliance only supported the NP block of the latter. Villafuerte and Fortuno supported the mayoralty candidate and vice-mayoralty tandem of Benjamin Decena and Janice Cariaga, respectively, both of whom are from NP. The LP block under the leadership of mayoralty candidate Megay Ibasco (LP) and vice-mayoralty candidate Moises Soreta (LP) did not enjoy the support of the alliance. Bula's LP block consequently separately negotiated with gubernatorial candidate Arnie Fuentebella (UNA) to have the former act as the ground-level machinery of the latter in exchange for the latter's financial and logistical support.

Interestingly, this arrangement was entered into while all stakeholders involved stayed within their respective parties. Clearly, party structure and ideology are overridden by transactional and mutual patron-client considerations and are "merely labels that candidates ran under" (Kerkvliet 1995). Incumbent candidates are more concerned with boosting the support and services of their personal formal and informal networks than with building a party network (see Figure 3.1).

FORMAL NETWORKS OF INCUMBENT CANDIDATES

Figure 3.1 illustrates the formal and informal mobilisation networks that incumbent provincial and congressional candidates employ. These candidates work to secure the cooperation and alliance of incumbent

---

[13] Interview with campaign staff B, Balatan, 4 May 2016.

Figure 3.1

Example of campaign team structure of incumbent provincial candidate

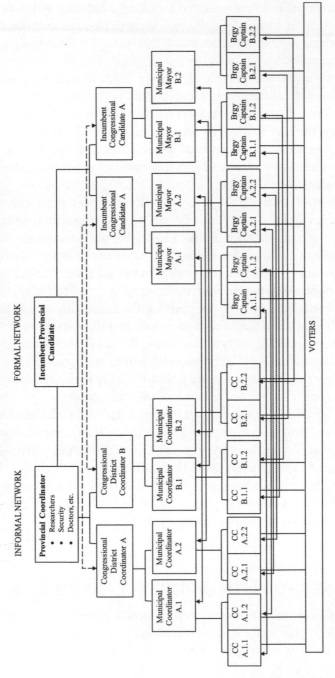

Note: * CC-Community Coordinators.

mayors, barangay officials and subordinate state employees who are positively motivated by existing or future administrative rewards or threats of obstructions or punishments (Mares and Young 2016).

The same machinery is also utilised to facilitate the delivery of goods and cash to voters or constituents. It is imperative that the congressional or provincial candidates are able to secure the alliance of incumbent mayoralty candidates or the endorsed candidates of incumbent mayors because the latter's office ensures the availability of human resources and funds for project implementation, wields authority over vital offices and individuals, and controls access to networks established through the specific mandates inherent to the mayoralty position.

A mayoralty candidate in Buhi argued that it is their people who act as advance parties that organise the locality, coordinate with community coordinators, secure the location, and gather people in case gubernatorial or congressional candidates wish to campaign in a specific locality under their jurisdiction. In exchange for these services, it is customary for the provincial or congressional candidate to give a substantial amount of funds to the mayoral incumbents.[14]

Accusations abound that Villafuerte and Fortuno each distributed PhP 5 million for each mayoralty candidate under their NP–LP alliance. Such is the importance of this structure that Villafuerte secured a 24-municipality machinery of incumbent mayors in Camarines Sur while Fortuno secured all of the incumbent mayors in Rinconada. On the part of mayors and their subordinate local officials, aside from monetary and administrative inducements (Mares and Young 2016), other factors that motivate them are clientelist in nature (Hicken 2011). The relationship between Villafuerte, Fortuno and their Rinconada municipal and city-level networks follows the typical clientelist pattern. The relationship is both hierarchical and personal, with each side having an expectation of *reciprocal* benefits and a future working relationship as patron and client. An interviewee adds that it is in the best interest of a high-ranking patron to ensure the electoral victory of a low-ranking political client, as doing so provides the patron added beholden machinery in future elections. If a provincial or congressional candidate is not allied with the incumbent mayor, then the natural disposition is to secure the support or alliance of the opposition or the political figures opposed to the incumbent mayor. This arrangement, however, is rare in the case of incumbents in the Rinconada District.

---

[14] Interview with Candidate B, Buhi, 3 May 2016.

NON-INCUMBENT CANDIDATES' CAMPAIGN AND MOBILISATION STRUCTURE

There are times when non-incumbent candidates do employ formal networks in the Rinconada District. This is, however, a rarity, and only happens when the individuals and personalities within the non-incumbent's formal networks hold minor offices or positions in the government. Non-incumbents instead rely heavily on their informal networks as well as approaching religious sects, extended families, professional associations, transport workers and other sectoral groups. I discuss each of these briefly below.

Religious groups

The voters in the district are predominantly Catholic but the candidates do not directly seek the endorsement of priests since the Church generally does not specify favoured candidates nor impose bloc voting upon its followers. In the case of Iglesia ni Cristo (INC), however, which openly requires its members to vote for certain candidates, the aspirants seek an audience with the INC local leadership and broker deals and concessions with its leaders in exchange for its endorsement among its bloc-voting followers.

Extended families

Candidates also muster the support of big families in their locality. This refers not only to big households, but also to the level of social influence family members have. Candidates seek the support of the patriarch or matriarch, assuming that the rest of the family will follow. In these meetings, concessions are made, such as offers of goods, according to a campaign team member of a congressional candidate in Rinconada. Concessions can also come in the form of scholarships for family members, employment for family members in the local government, easing or exemption from business permit processing, etc. Once agreements have been reached, the heads of the household may even be appointed as local coordinators of the campaign.

The candidate's own family network is also tapped, as in the case of a non-incumbent candidate in Nabua whose campaign team was composed of family members and whose financial resources came from his clan.

(Lacking a well-resourced family, another non-incumbent candidate requested an audience and meeting with the most influential families in Iriga City.) None of the political families in the Rinconada area have yet resorted to inter-marriage to secure the vote-base of Riconada area and the established mobilisation networks of other political families.

Professional associations

Among educated voters in Rinconada, clientelistic offers are subjected to meticulous scrutiny. Here Hicken's (2011) discussion of causal mechanisms behind clientelism and development applies. Most of the candidates confirmed that strategies of patronage and clientelism were ineffective among professionals. An interviewed candidate claimed that this sector is more interested in a candidate's track record, qualifications, accomplishments, educational and general background and proposed platform of governance.[15]

A candidate in Bula admitted that their campaign team is reluctant to offer cash or goods to this sector as this might be considered an affront to the sector's more discerning nature.[16] This is consistent with the assertion that as income rises, the marginal utility to a recipient of a given material benefit decreases (Hicken 2011). For example, when a public-school teacher who earns PhP 25,000 monthly was enticed with PhP 300, the natural tendency was to reject it since she based her candidate selection on qualification for the post.[17] It is to this group that non-incumbent candidates present themselves as the most preferable alternative compared to their incumbent rivals, especially if the incumbent is tainted with issues of irregularities, incompetence and corruption.

A mayoralty candidate in Buhi argued that their campaign does not focus on the educated sector. They instead focus where the highest proportion of voters is—among the masses who mostly have limited formal education— as they are easier to impress and convince.[18] However, two mayoralty candidates from Baao and one in Nabua argued that the endorsement of the middle class/educated sector is useful, especially in cases when the contest between candidates is tight. But even here incumbent candidates

---

[15] Interview with Candidate C, Nabua, April 2016.
[16] Interview with Candidate D, Bula, 5 May 2016.
[17] Interview with a public school teacher, Iriga City, 5 May 2016.
[18] Interview with Candidate B, Buhi, 3 May 2016.

are well-positioned to convince this sector since they have programmes implemented and general accomplishments to present.

Transport groups

Transport groups are among the most organised sectors in Philippine society and their electoral support is prioritised by candidates. Incumbents condone fare hikes and extend annual franchise registration of public transport vehicles to avoid being unpopular within this sector. Since public utility vehicle drivers interact with commuters and passengers daily, they have the ability to mainstream the campaign of the candidates that they are supporting. For example, candidates pay public utility *jeepney* drivers to play their campaign jingles, with passengers as captive audiences. Campaign posters and stickers are likewise conveniently placed conspicuously on the vehicle. In exchange, transport groups lobby for beneficial policy concessions with local government officials.

Having no policy or political capital to begin with, non-incumbent candidates promise more beneficial policy mechanisms and platforms for this sector. A non-incumbent candidate in Nabua, for example, committed to devote two months' worth of his salary to the establishment of terminals, vulcanising shops and cooperatives for transport groups. Another non-incumbent candidate in Buhi promised to build better roads. Still another non-incumbent candidate from Iriga City vowed to reduce the fees paid for the renewal of franchise registration for public transport, and extend registration from annually to every three years.

Other sectoral groups

Since Rinconada is an agricultural district, campaign strategies and speeches of candidates are often crafted in a manner that is enticing to farmers. Promises to farmers were declared everywhere. In Baao, a non-incumbent candidate guaranteed free seedlings and subsidies for important farming needs. In Buhi another non-incumbent candidate vowed to seek the help of the Japan International Cooperation Agency (JICA) to provide training on agricultural technologies, while in Iriga another candidate pledged economic and livelihood protection by designating a local farmers' produce section in the city centre.

THE EXERCISE OF PATRONAGE AND CLIENTELISM IN THE RINCONADA DISTRICT

Of the 240,559 total registered voters in Rinconada during the 2016 election, about 83.89 per cent or 201,814 individuals exercised their voting rights. In its congressional contest, Salvio Fortuno (LP) garnered 134,372 votes or 78.55 per cent of the vote, a very wide margin compared to his opponent Nancing Alfelor (UNA), who garnered a measly 21.44 per cent of the vote or 36,680 votes. In fact, *all* of the victors in the major contests of Rinconada were incumbent candidates allied to Fortuno, who has established a vast clientelistic network of incumbent candidates and secured the vote base of the area through patronage. With every victory also comes an opportunity for continued access to state resources, which deepen and fortify his patron-client network.

This vast network, together with Fortuno's various achievements,[19] explains his unchallenged reign as the three-term congressional representative of Rinconada District. His clients who initially captured power because of his patronage reciprocate by serving as his ground-level machinery during elections. They are incentivised by the fact that doing so allows continued rewards in the form of sustained support from their patron. Whatever project or programme that Fortuno implements is conveniently attributed to his clients as their shared accomplishment, which they can present to the people. The cycle thus represents a patron-client relationship.

In the case of non-incumbents, it is a question of what they can present as tangible signals of their ability as leaders and public servants. Since they do not have access to state resources, many resort to alternative privately funded patronage-based and limited clientelistic schemes in campaigning. For example, a qualified non-incumbent candidate in Nabua with an impeccable non-elective public service track record did not have the necessary amount of resources to win against an incumbent opponent whose unquestioned loyalty to Fortuno was reciprocated with generous patronage and access to the latter's clientelistic network. The non-incumbent attempted to offset such overwhelming odds by aggressively distributing goods, cash and assistance prior to the election. However these strategies were not enough to offset his lack of experience, resources and network.

---

[19] Congressman Fortuno is popular for his good-quality infrastructure projects in the various LGUs in the Rinconada area and for his perfect attendance in Congress. He is also very popular among indigent voters due to his accessibility to this sector.

While stressing the issues of incumbent incompetence and the lack of development of respective localities in Rinconada, non-incumbent candidates presented themselves as alternative candidates with general narratives of change, transparency and accountability. While this may have worked for the educated voting population, it was not convincing for the vote-rich impoverished sectors of Rinconada. Thus, non-incumbents who promised programmes and services for marginalised sectors under a platform of change still had to resort to aggressive vote buying in order to try to win.

CONCLUSION

This chapter finds that the patron-client relationships observed among public officials, candidates and the voting population continue to facilitate the ascension to power of incumbent political figures. In the Rinconada District, the patron-client relationships of incumbent candidates or incumbent-supported candidates have reciprocally assisted in the recapture of power of the patrons (Fortuno and Villafuerte) and clients (landslide victory of NP–LP alliance candidates in all Rinconada LGUs).

This reciprocal relationship spurs an almost self-reinforcing cycle within patron-client relationships. Moreover, non-incumbent candidates' lack of access to state resources and their consequent inability to employ strategies of patronage induce them to rely on vote buying strategies that often seek to exceed those of the incumbents. However, even those challengers who aggressively bought votes were unable to overcome a lack of established networks, resources, or name recognition, and the dominance of re-electionists.

This chapter therefore affirms that what determined success at the ballot-box for candidates was neither substantial qualification nor party affiliation but rather the combination of patronage, clientelism and money politics.

Table 3
Election results from Camarines Sur 5th District

Candidate	Party	Office	Per cent (%)
* Indicates Incumbent Candidate			
Fortuno, Sal*	LP	House of Representatives	78.56
Alfelor, Felix Jr.	UNA	House of Representatives	21.44
Villafuerte, Migz*	NP	Provincial Governor	60.00
Fuentebella, Arnie	UNA	Provincial Governor	39.04
Buenaflor, Roger	KBL	Provincial Governor	00.96
Peña, Fortunato*	LP	Provincial Vice-Governor	52.35
Alfelor, Peachy	UNA	Provincial Vice-Governor	47.65
Baao			
Gaite, Melquiades*	NP	Mayor	51.58
Bricenio, Gbb	NPC	Mayor	34.84
Sapugay, Cherry	UNA	Mayor	13.58
Besinio, Jeff	LP	Vice-Mayor	52.58
Bedural, Edwin	UNA	Vice-Mayor	30.99
Ballesteros, Boyet	NPC	Vice-Mayor	16.43
Balatan			
Bagasbas, Ernesto*	LP	Mayor	69.26
Borja, Nena	NP	Mayor	30.74
Villareal, Jimmy*	UNA	Vice-Mayor	53.50
Cuarto, Aurora	LP	Vice-Mayor	46.50
Bato			
Bernaldez, Frank	LP	Mayor	52.16
Sacueza, Alvin	UNA	Mayor	47.84
Ramos, Victorio	UNA	Vice-Mayor	50.31
Tino, Noel	NP	Vice-Mayor	49.69
Buhi			
Aguinillo, Margie	LP	Mayor	53.52
Balagot, Jofred	UNA	Mayor	46.48
Lacoste, Rey	NP	Vice-Mayor	55.44
Belza, Diones*	UNA	Vice-Mayor	44.56

(cont'd overleaf)

Table 3 *(cont'd)*

Candidate	Party	Office	Per cent (%)
Bula			
Ibasco, Megay	LP	Mayor	58.08
Decena, Benjamin	NP	Mayor	41.92
Soreta, Dok*	LP	Vice-Mayor	56.20
Cariaga, Janice	NP	Vice-Mayor	43.80
Iriga City			
Alfelor-Gazmen, Madel	LP	Mayor	65.45
Alfelor, Emmanuel Jr.	UNA	Mayor	33.87
Badong, Rodrigo	IND	Mayor	00.54
Botor, Rhoderick	IND	Mayor	00.15
Villanueva, Jose Jr.	LP	Vice-Mayor	48.57
Orolfo, Roseller	IND	Vice-Mayor	31.34
Alfelor, Avelino Jr.	UNA	Vice-Mayor	20.09
Nabua			
Simbulan, Delia*	LP	Mayor	62.71
Bearis, Ruben Jr.	UNA	Mayor	37.29
Velitario-Hao, Marissa	LP	Vice-Mayor	76.73
Cruz, Jaypee	UNA	Vice-Mayor	23.27

Second District of Camarines Norte: Are Patronage Politics a Socio-Political Condition or Cultural Syndrome?

Margie A. Nolasco

INTRODUCTION

Locals say politics in the province of Camarines Norte is like the pineapple: on the outside, it is very prickly and tough; on the inside, it is sweet or sour, depending on how it is cultivated and harvested. People in the province are known for their cordiality, friendliness and having a culture of showing a lot of warmth for one another. On the other hand, politicians are confronted with meeting people's expectations and being sensitive to the needs of the people. As a result, the effectiveness of politicians' campaigns can be determined through the impact on voters of the favours they provide, as well as politicians' attitudes in response to favours that voters solicit.

Camarines Norte politics is also interesting and entertaining. Its politicians, just like their cohorts in other parts of the Philippines, pursue their own agenda at any cost and seek to gain votes by any means. Most pursue strategies that place greater emphasis on image and personality-building than principles. Local traits or concepts such as *papogi* (appealing to), *makisama* (getting along with others well) and *damayan* (mutual aid) are important to most politicians to sustain their political careers. Politicians' desire to cultivate a good impression among and rapport with constituents in turn perpetuates political patronage. Political patronage, including various forms of allocation of favours and assistance to meet constituents' special needs, is the widely accepted means of mobilising voters.

It has been noted that the political system in Camarines Norte is a major contributing factor to why economic development has not happened as planned. The province has been economically overtaken by its neighbours. Moreover, efforts to pursue economic sustainability need to take into account the province's conservative cultural beliefs. Key political players in the province include barangay leaders, campaign managers, supporters and political candidates; this last group represent agents of "modern" patronage politics in the province. This chapter analyses how the patronage tactics and strategies of the political agents involved affect the traditional socio-political practices of constituents in Camarines Norte, as well as the possibility of political transformation.

BACKGROUND

The province's economy largely depends on agriculture, with grain crops, vegetables, coconuts, root crops and fruits as its main products. A university professor once described Camarines Norte as a "poor man sitting on a pot of gold" because of its widespread poverty amid a plenitude of mineral resources (Soltes 2011). Four of the 13 major manufacturing and processing industries in the province are mining (particularly gold and iron ore), jewellery craft, and the pineapple and coconut industries. The town of Paracale has large deposits of gold, which can be found throughout the town's riverbeds, flood plains, and even sink holes (Arumpac 2012). Still, the National Statistical Coordination Board (NSCB) disclosed in a 2012 survey of poverty incidence in the country that Camarines Norte's poor families comprise 21.7 per cent of the population. The lingering poverty is the result of the mismanagement of the province's natural resources by some public officials and a lack of innovative anti-poverty programmes by the national and local governments.

Moreover, the culture of the people in the province remains shaped by their socio-economic conditions, since local farmers develop camaraderie as they work the soil.

Linguistic pluralism also plays a vital role in shaping and influencing people's political attitudes and behaviour. Camarines Norte lies at the crossroads of the Tagalog and Bicolano cultures. The major dialects spoken in the province are Tagalog and Bicol, comprising about 63.1 per cent and 35.6 per cent, respectively. The greater number of Tagalog-speaking households can be attributed to Camarines Norte's being adjacent to the Southern Tagalog provinces, from whence the majority of migrants to the province come (Bicolanda 2010). To ensure equal representation of the two cultures, the Commission on Elections divided the province into two provincial board legislative districts in 2010 as per Republic Act 9725. The first district is Tagalog-speaking and the second district is Bicol-speaking. Presently, there are five municipalities under the first district— Capalonga, Jose Panganiban, Labo, Paracale and Santa Elena— and seven municipalities in the second district—Daet, Talisay, Basud, Vinzons, San Lorenzo, Mercedes and San Vicente. The town of Daet is the seat of government and the centre of education, commerce and trade in the province. Other growth centres are Labo, Jose Panganiban, Santa Elena and Mercedes. Each municipality is further divided into smaller barangays. Labo is the biggest municipality, occupying approximately 23 per cent of the total provincial area, while Talisay is the smallest.

The majority of elected positions are now held by members of political dynasties. These families include the Padillas, Vinzons, Chatos, Pimentels and Unicos. Some individuals, like Jesus Typoco, Egay Tallado and Elmer Panotes, are not part of a political dynasty, but are political powerhouses themselves (Bicol Initiative 2016).

During the 2016 election for local offices, 8 among the 15 incumbents in 2013 were re-elected. In the contest for the highest local positions, the incumbent governor and vice-governor won their races. Despite her being a political neophyte, Marisol Panotes, the wife of the late Congressman Elmer Panotes, successfully took over his post. Four of the seven mayors who won in the 2013 election were given another chance to serve their constituents. But only two out of seven vice-mayors retained their seats, while the rest of the winners were challengers and neophytes in politics.

CANDIDATE STRATEGIES AND PATRONAGE

Camarines Norte has a unique socio-political culture. What makes this province's political story unusual is that friendship is an important factor in the development of personal alliances in the province, and this is often associated with notions of family. It is normal for local residents who have known each other for a long time to address especially respected elders as *kuya* (brother) or *ate* (sister) and to consider them as extended family members. The province's strong value of *damayan*, or willingness to help one another, reflects this basis of friendship. Constituents give weight to politicians' attitudes and their personal relationships to them. This kind of personal alliance has a great influence on decisions in electing officials and is the reason why candidate-politicians are expected to pay attention to providing services based on personal needs and to show *pagdamay* (sympathy). One candidate-politician noted, "My performance was not the only factor that influences voters most but also on how I deal with my constituents, how I sympathised with them in times of their needs."[1]

Personal alliances are also linked to *utang na loob* (returning a favour to someone who helped in a time of crisis). Politicians use *utang na loob* to exploit constituents. Since political patrons provide help and indirectly buy the loyalty of constituents, the latter incur a debt, and feel obliged to "pay back" by supporting their political patrons during elections. This pattern is advantageous to politicians who have power and resources.

The campaign tactic of a typical political aspirant in the province is to be present during special occasions and gatherings, even if it is not an election time. If a candidate-politician rejects a constituent's invitation or personal request, that constituent might turn cold and withdraw his support for the candidate-politician's candidacy. A municipal leader states: "My candidate is expected to cater to voters' personal requests like giving financial aid to their birthday party, common items such as *pansit at sahog* [noodles and ingredients], and even *alak* [liquor]."[2] It is on special occasions like birthday parties and fiestas that residents can break from their everyday routine and take the time to meet friends and family. Residents prepare sumptuous food, then feel compensated if they have honoured personalities as their guests. (A special occasion without a politician present may seem a second-rate celebration to some constituents.) These events can be avenues through which politicians can market their candidacy to the voters present. That is why candidate-politicians find it hard to deny requests from constituents. One candidate explained that he learned how to "'dance to constituents' tune', always

---

[1] Interview with a politician, San Vicente, 5 May 2016.
[2] Interview with a barangay leader, Talisay, 21 April 2016.

cater to constituents' wishes whether I like them or not".[3] For him, this was the best strategy to attract votes.

Constituents are likewise fond of candidates who know how to get along well with the people. During the campaign period, voters preferred candidates who were extremely kind and flexible and who shared their time and resources, and even their talents, with their constituents. In the campaign sorties that I attended, I seldom witnessed politicians who did not sing or dance during campaign events. Finally, politicians in the province were driven by patronage transactions. A typical local candidate has to dispense political favours, such as donations for every possible project of the constituents, out of fear of losing valuable votes. A local leader involved with a 2016 campaign team confirmed, "… what makes [a] campaign very effective is when it is well-financed".[4] This pattern has made politics extremely expensive for candidates.

Part of the issue lies in a local political culture in which people are used to participating in extravagant campaign rallies. Supporters enjoy being entertained by the performances of volunteers, hired dancers and band members. In 2016, candidates even hired national celebrities for their grand rallies to keep their supporters entertained and to provide endorsements for the candidates. Packed foods and juice were also served to all supporters and attendees as a way to attract an audience, according to my informants. This is a burdensome and costly practice, particularly for poor but potentially effective candidates.

Candidates even engage in *pakulo* (gimmicks) during rallies and sorties to build name recall among those constituents who don't know them yet or who have forgotten their accomplishments or worth as political leaders. In one of the barangay sorties that I attended, participants were given numbered lottery tickets before the start of the meeting. Those who remained until the end exchanged their tickets for cash and gifts that were donated by the candidates.

Moreover, graft and corruption issues and controversies are common features of provincial politics. Elections offer the opportunity for a candidate to take action to weaken or destroy the opposition. As one of the mayoral candidates in 2016 admitted, "I am presently nervous on the implications made with my rebuttal to my powerful political opponent."[5] I witnessed a municipal rally in which the issues and shortcomings of the

---

[3] Interview with a candidate, San Lorenzo Ruiz, 5 May 2016.
[4] Interview with a candidate, Daet, 18 April 2016.
[5] Interview with a candidate, Vinzons, 3 April 2016.

other party's candidates were exposed and discussed in public by a rival. There were also some instances in 2015 in which the incumbents were accused of graft, corruption, and even immorality, only to bribe their supporters and use them to whitewash these issues and controversies. Some big-time politicians hired media personalities and paid huge amounts of money to clear their names or destroy the reputation of the opposition. Most of the municipal rallies I attended included visible media personalities who acted as campaign leaders. In 2015 a critic permitted a group to demonstrate at an event against an elected official's alleged immorality after a scandalous photo and video of that official surfaced and went viral on social media. Media personalities' opinions can help manipulate public perceptions and bolster a politician's candidacy.

That said, neither issues nor attacks seemed to decide many votes. Voters' decisions are still based on factors like a politician's accomplishments and campaign tactics. In fact, one politician em-broiled in controversies was re-elected and presently holds office. The evidence suggests that people still gave him their votes based on his accomplishments, like his giving out personal scholarships to students or jobs to constituents, and his strategic provision of a unique multi-services caravan. As this candidate's consultant explained to me:

> My candidate is personally supervising the mobile caravan which used to provide different government services to the different barangays all over the province. With the help of positive media reports of this caravan project, discreetly, they established rapport to his constituents.[6]

In addition, politicians adopted different patronage approaches for different social classes in light of their varied needs and expectations. Patronage generated more votes from voters of lower socio-economic status or in marginalised sectors than among other categories of voters. A 2016 candidate-politician explained that the strategies he uses in convincing people "vary".[7] Another political leader supported that claim, noting, "voters from the lower class mean business, *kung hindi makakuha ng pera, sa kabila* or if voters can't get cash or incentives for electoral support from one candidate-politician, they will vote for the opponent who can have [a] better offer".[8]

---

[6] Interview with a political consultant, Daet, 25 April 2016.
[7] Interview with a politician, Camarines Norte, 18 April 2016.
[8] Interview with a barangay leader, Talisay, 21 April 2016.

Politicians also have to find ways to win wealthier voters' support. The decisions of educated voters tend to relate to their own impressions of a candidate's performance, philosophy and management of provincial resources. Voters from these classes are generally less influenced by a political agenda. There were, of course, instances in which members of this class participated in patronage and vote buying by accepting money, gifts, donations and other services from candidates. According to one source, while it was against their moral values to accept such offers, they also realized that this was the only time when they could receive gifts, money, or services for "free". It is also widely expected that politicians will regain the money and resources they spent during the election once they assume office.

While the targeting of middle- and upper-classes relied on different tactics and was often candidate-politicians' last resort, it is important to note that at their core these exchanges relied on the same cultural norms and attitudes that underpin patronage among poorer voters. The support of some targeted voters is linked with the local norms of *utang na loob* and *pakikisama*. Voters, regardless of social class, often cast votes for those who have helped them in times of crisis.

In addition, vote buying dominates local races and has become part of local socio-political culture. Most candidates do not pay much attention to swing or undecided voters during the campaign period, although they do notice when these voters participate in opposing candidate-politicians' campaign events. Nonetheless, during "last hour" or "special operation" efforts—referring to vote buying transactions, three to five days before the election—some candidates take the risk to convince voters of low socio-economic status through use of financial resources or money. I witnessed such transactions two days before the election, while waiting for a candidate to emerge from his house for an interview. I saw a lot of people going into what I presumed was the house of a barangay leader allied with a local political aspirant. Two young men, having finished with their activity for the barangay leader, informed me that they had been given a "poll watcher's kit": an envelope with a poll watcher's identification card, sample ballot and money inside. There were also cases reported in the recent election period of undecided voters' trading their votes in exchange for money, as well as of *baliktadan* (back and forth) incidents, where voters, after accepting money offered by both political aspirants for the same position, voted for the politician who made the highest bid. The candidates in question were forced to *kung ano ang tugtog, yan ang sayaw* (go with the flow) because of their fear of losing the race.

MOBILISING STRUCTURE

The campaign period is the only time when some candidates make themselves visible all over the province, working to establish rapport with voters. In this campaign period, Camarines Norte appeared to be just like any other province in that candidates relied on supporters' work for the campaign. Aside from daily allowances, politicians gave these volunteers honoraria based on the resources available along with whatever the politicians had promised volunteers (cash, goods or employment) in exchange for their support and services. A political consultant explained, the "campaign period is [the] monitoring period".[9] One candidate-politician confirmed, "during campaign period, I constantly gather the barangay leaders for a 'loyalty check'".[10] For their part, barangay leaders hold regular meetings to update candidates on their vote tallies. It is also very common for candidates to assemble a team of their own trusted leaders, organised by municipality, barangay, and *sitio* (zone), who are responsible for identifying and monitoring supporters, undecided voters and potential last-minute/special operation targets. As a result, municipal, barangay and zone leaders played big parts in mobilising voters.

Some campaign managers were very open to talking about their budget allocations for candidates' activities and projects. A barangay leader declared, "When a constituent is embarrassed about asking for a favour from my candidate, my job is to assist him [to] transact with my candidate."[11] A candidate also said, "Patronage was done through the help of the organised supporters which comprised of different coordinators and leaders."[12]

Hence, each candidate had his own loyal community political leaders, most of whom did not belong to a political party.[13] Some politicians use influential persons or representatives of a large family in a particular community as political leaders. A candidate articulated that, "[the] size of the family and loyalty are important to me when I recruit volunteers to work on the campaign".[14] I gathered from informants that before the campaign period, these leaders had compiled *lista*, or tentative lists of

---

[9] Interview with a political consultant, Daet, 25 April 2016.
[10] Interview with a candidate, Mercedez, 20 April 2016.
[11] Interview with a political leader, San Lorenzo, 5 May 2016.
[12] Interview with a candidate, Talisay, 6 April 2016.
[13] Political parties can be an important source of resources for some candidates, but candidates primarily rely on their own efforts and resources.
[14] Interview with a candidate, Vinzons, 3 April 2016.

registered voters. These lists were the basis for identifying supporters and swing or undecided voters.

Money is the biggest contributing factor in winning a political race. It influences constituents to support a candidate and sustains activities throughout the campaign period. Local parties in the province have very stable and sustainable political machines that can mobilise large numbers of votes, but one cannot enter into politics without financial resources. Most candidates confirmed that the funds national parties allocate to a candidate will not cover the costs for the whole campaign period. However, candidates having a personal budget of millions of pesos were almost sure to win the race. Where do these campaign funds come from? One candidate explained that his budget for the campaign period came from his personal funds, as well as funds allocated by his party and help from family and friends.[15]

This study validates past research finding that incumbents have structural advantages over their challengers. Some incumbents use political privileges such as access to government resources to compete against their opponents.[16] As one candidate noted, "Sometimes it is disadvantageous to become a challenger because 'the incumbents' would normally brag [about] their accomplishments and their performances."[17]

Incumbents also have easier access to their party's campaign funds, especially if they become the national party's official representative in a locality and therefore need the support of the national party's machinery. Incumbents are also more likely to attract the backing of key financial supporters, and benefit from the enormous public exposure they enjoy while in office. They can also draw on public funds to finance services as well as "EPAL boards"—institutional ads that publish incumbents' accomplishments. These advantages have the direct effect of increasing votes, but might also be associated with patronage politics.

Other candidates do not rely on public funds directly, but on resources from either the party or financial supporters that can help them fulfil their political ambitions. As one campaign manager admitted, "budget allocation of the party supported my provincial candidate".[18] But most respondents declared personal money to be their main source of campaign funds. An independent candidate, for instance, complained that despite

---

[15] Interview with a candidate, Daet, 18 April 2016.
[16] According to key informants, some campaign funding in the province, including for campaign expenses, came from state resources.
[17] Interview with a candidate, Camarines Norte, 18 April 2016.
[18] Interview with a campaign manager, Basud, 4 April 2016.

his limited resources, "I spent too much money for campaign period."[19] But for him, an effective campaign requires sharing a little of something, whether time or money, among constituents. He believed that, as much as possible, candidates should not make promises, and instead hoped that being chosen by a large religious group like Iglesia ni Cristo (INC) for a bloc-voting endorsement would give him an advantage over his opponents.

To be able to secure valuable individual votes, local candidates start their campaign allied with organised political parties but end with more detached individual political races. Candidates and party activists worked as a group during events like rallies, meetings and some motorcades. But, in most cases, aside from the political activities of the party, the individual candidate conducted his own activities, such as house and follow-up visits, and other patronage transactions. Nonetheless, party members were encouraged to join the candidate and conduct similar individual activities.

Traditionally, politicians' initial electoral campaign plans were just to maintain their loyal core group and tap trusted leaders and their relatives as consultants. They believed that being surrounded by a trusted core group could make winning possible. According to one candidate, "a well-organised campaign structure and valuing core leaders are the ways to secure votes".[20] However, politicians' success depends on having comprehensive plans for the campaign. Aside from maintaining their loyal political core group, some politicians also spent large amounts of money to hire consultants and strategists who helped them with electoral decisions and managed campaign activities. Consultants monitored reports from the grassroots and provided strategic planning and technical support for campaigns. Indeed, in this election, the majority of politicians who hired consultants and strategists successfully won their races.

Thus, it cannot be denied that patronage is a useful strategy for a political candidate to win votes, especially since candidates win elections not through the strength of their party, but also through their personal capacity to attract voters. Though a campaign team may promote the full party slate, candidates still rely on personal networks rather than party machines to propel them into office.

---

[19] Interview with a candidate, Talisay, 4 April 2016.
[20] Interview with a candidate, Daet, 20 April 2016.

CASE STUDY

This case study traces the approaches of two candidates and how these affected their chances of winning. Since one candidate was an incumbent and the other a challenger, the comparison also sheds light on the value of incumbency. The two candidates were opponents for one of the highest local offices. They once belonged to the same major political party, but then the challenger was removed from that party because members accused him of "disloyalty". Thus the disappointed challenger moved to an opposing major political party and each candidate adopted contrasting philosophical approaches: pragmatism by the incumbent, and progressivism by the challenger.

The Pragmatist. This soft-spoken incumbent political aristocrat believed that day one of the campaign period is the day after official results are announced. Incumbency played an obvious part in his political career; it enabled him to provide services to his constituents during his term of office. However, his pragmatic approach was not the only factor that helped him gain votes. He is also the son of a former politician and belongs to a powerful, influential family that has served the province for many years. He has also enjoyed the backing of groups of trusted and loyal leaders.

It is his pragmatic approach that determines his political moves. Initially, he conducts an analysis of the needs and values of his constituents before he tries to convince them to vote for him. One of the best campaign strategies, per his pragmatic view, however, is being cautious in his actions and loyal to his party. He knows how to avoid getting entangled in major scandals or named in black propaganda by other politicians. His very simple, pragmatic policy is to deal with issues as they arise and offer detailed solutions that can work.

According to my sources, people are fond of his down-to-earth attitude and pragmatic approach. During his prior time in office, he empowered even lower-ranking unit heads to manage their units. Although he personally supervised activities of the office, if there were major decisions to be made, he consulted the grassroots before making them. Moreover, reflecting his own pragmatic approach and the role of incumbency advantage in gaining votes, the candidate used his managerial ability to provide government services to his constituents that would have real impact in their lives, then let his constituents decide the outcome of his candidacy.

According to him, as a long-time politician, he was already embedded in the political culture of the province and could assess constituents' relative loyalty. According to him, "vote buying is very rampant and that has been a campaign trait in the province". He explained that, despite the policies, gifts and ideas he provides, people would still take advantage of the campaign period by asking for and expecting additional handouts. He elaborated that in the many years he has been in politics, he had provided most of his marginalised constituents with individual favours, such as employment and other benefits. Nevertheless, during the campaign period, he offered incentives to the volunteers who worked for his campaign. Some supporters were also compensated with job opportunities after he won the race. That is why, like any other politician in the province, his office is packed with his political supporters.

The Progressive. The other candidate was a political progressive; he claimed he intended to be an *instrumento sa pagbabago* (instrument of change) and that positive economic developments happened when he was previously in office in one of Camarines Norte's municipalities. He expected his prior community to support his policies and campaign platform. He believed that his service to the people, credibility and previous achievements were his tools for winning the race. This challenger served one of the biggest municipalities in Camarines Norte for a decade and was an example of a dynamic leader who brought the municipality honour, while making a difference in the lives of his people. During his term of office, he played an important role in the success of both infrastructure development and institutional policies and programmes designed to extend welfare assistance to constituents. He had thus built a foundation for the future progress of his municipality; in his campaign, he emphasised this legacy and promised to replicate what he did over the entire province.

Despite a not-so-big budget, the challenger in this case was able to maintain grassroots support, as evidenced by volunteers who did not ask for any compensation, yet tirelessly campaigned for him. He was able to train campaign staff who engaged in strategic planning before the start of the campaign period to ensure higher voter turnout. As a challenger the candidate believed that being part of a major political party offered an edge. He benefitted from the resources of his party, such as advertisements, campaign materials and an effective working committee. However, even this candidate pointed out that during the campaign period, some voters expected politicians to help them with their personal needs. Most of the time, he entertained all kinds of solicitations through text-messaging.

Thus, both candidates had good points with which to convince voters. The cases presented reveal that factors aside from incumbency played important roles in the electoral race, since both candidates had held office previously. Other important factors, such as attitudes, patronage strategies and political party affiliation can help candidates' chances of winning.

CONCLUSION

Socio-political conditions are among the factors that may significantly affect the quality of elections and voting habits in a given province. Mutual benefits, sealed with personal relationships between constituents and politicians, are among the principal factors that shape socio-political culture in Camarines Norte. Parties are important in maintaining political machines and serve as vehicles for developing the campaign networks for candidates who lack a personal following.

Typical politicians will do anything to gain votes, including engaging in patronage transactions. One cannot enter the political arena without adapting to this political system, as patronage has been part of the socio-political culture since the birth of political powerhouses and "*trapo*" (traditional politicians) in the province. Politicians' self-sustaining patronage strategies affect the political system and economy of the province. This patronage system is driven in part by voter demands. During the campaign period constituents are able to challenge politicians to respond to their personal interests since they are aware that politicians will be able to recoup their campaign expenses when they assume office. This is true whether the candidate is an incumbent or challenger.

Most campaign activities in the province focus on strengthening personal relationships with constituents, through activities like house visits, heart-to-heart talks, attending to their immediate needs and other individual requests. The *papogi*, to constituents, are politicians' common campaign tactics, efforts which can be of great help in magnifying a candidate's name recall. Yet while candidates seek easy and effective ways to attract votes from all socio-economic classes, their efforts are not guaranteed to secure votes from constituents. In the election period, voters are still the ones who decide for whom to vote.

Furthermore, it is true that some incumbent politicians benefit from privileges like being able to utilise provincial resources to serve their constituents effectively or to advance their personal agenda. But political patronage is not only manifested in the practices of incumbent politicians. Challengers, even neophytes, have also adapted to the game of patronage politics before entering politics. Nevertheless, as the case studies demonstrate, politicians adopt different strategies and techniques that take advantage of the assets at their disposal and the disposition of the electorate.

Finally, in all elections, the outcome is often driven by elements and happenings beyond the control of the candidates and parties. Even strong candidates can lose the race by using inappropriate tactics among different social classes, since these classes have different needs and expectations. For example, some middle-class voters can react negatively to attempts to use traditional patronage politics to win their votes. My interviews suggest that local politicians despised the idea of the necessity of engaging in patronage politics within the province. The quality of constituents' voting in the province is being hampered by the temptation of costly political patronage transactions, to the benefit of a few powerful and rich politicians. Some poor political aspirants still opt to pursue political careers and challenge the notable political names in the province. However, most of these resource-poor aspirants fail, aware that the province's political system puts them at a disadvantage. But they are still hopeful for the province's positive transformation and that constituents will realise the ill effects of patronage on the political system.

Voters have become cynical about both government performance and the electoral process, and this leads to a self-reinforcing patronage-oriented system. Voters realise that governments consistently do a poor job of meeting their basic needs. Thus, despite massive ads on social media and comprehensive guidelines issued by the government on how to choose candidates, some people, especially those of low socio-economic status in this province, choose to trade their votes for temporary gain. After the election politicians seek to recoup campaign costs and acquire patronage resources, often at the expense of good governance. As a result, in this recent election, as in past elections, patronage proved a useful strategy for a political candidate to win votes. The prevalence of such tactics was an open secret to everyone.

Camarines Norte has a rich socio-political culture, which some politicians have taken advantage of to advance their own vested interests. The worst part is, politics has become a lucrative livelihood for some politicians. However, there are individuals and groups, including some non-governmental and religious organisations, that advocate for political reform, including rejection of the patronage-based political culture in the province. These attempts at socio-economic change could serve the common good of the people rather than the interests of traditional politicians. Nevertheless, for now, people remain trapped in a self-reinforcing system.

Table 4
Election results from Camarines Norte 2nd District

Candidate	Party	Office	Per cent (%)
* Indicates Incumbent Candidate			
Panotes, Toots	LP	House of Representatives	47.26
Chato, Liwayway	NPC	House of Representatives	39.45
Jerez, Senen	NP	House of Representatives	11.03
Asis, Donald	IND	House of Representatives	1.75
Napao, Napaoski	IND	House of Representatives	0.31
Balmeo, Bp Balmeo	IND	House of Representatives	0.20
Tallado, Edgardo*	NPC	Provincial Governor	47.26
Barcelona-Reyes, Cathy	LP	Provincial Governor	45.04
Typoco, Jesus Jr.	NP	Provincial Governor	5.84
Saniel, Clint	IND	Provincial Governor	1.52
Lukban, Antonio	IND	Provincial Governor	0.33
Pimentel, Jonah*	NPC	Provincial Vice-Governor	50.44
Sarion, Tito	LP	Provincial Vice-Governor	37.21
Pardo, Pamela	NP	Provincial Vice-Governor	11.77
Matubang, Zalvar	IND	Provincial Vice-Governor	0.58
Basud			
Davoco, Adrian	IND	Mayor	62.20
Mendiola, Helen	IND	Mayor	37.80
Quiñones, Jojo	IND	Vice-Mayor	52.61
Barrameda, Ramir*	NPC	Vice-Mayor	47.39
Daet (Capital)			
Ochoa, B2k	NPC	Mayor	44.44
Panotes, Concon	LP	Mayor	43.91
Ong, Ahlong	PMP	Mayor	11.15
Servaz, Sonny	IND	Mayor	0.50
Sarion, Connie	LP	Vice-Mayor	43.39
Tabernilla-De Luna, Joan	NPC	Vice-Mayor	37.38
Raymundo, Panday	NP	Vice-Mayor	19.23

(cont'd overleaf)

Table 4 *(cont'd)*

Candidate	Party	Office	Per cent (%)
Mercedes			
Pajarillo, Alexander*	NPC	Mayor	66.86
Tee, Maning	IND	Mayor	31.81
Santileses, Meo	IND	Mayor	1.32
Salalima, Brenda*	NPC	Vice-Mayor	41.41
Aguilar, Mandy	LP	Vice-Mayor	35.44
Abanto, Wenefredo Jr.	IND	Vice-Mayor	23.15
San Lorenzo Ruiz (Imelda)			
Delos Santos, Nelson	NPC	Mayor	52.71
Ramores, Edgar*	LP	Mayor	47.29
Villareal, Ma. Medina*	LP	Vice-Mayor	50.66
Factor, Oscar	NPC	Vice-Mayor	49.34
San Vicente			
Ong, Francis*	NPC	Mayor	72.15
Wisden, Emma	IND	Mayor	27.85
Villamor, Antonio*	NPC	Vice-Mayor	100.00
Talisay			
Magana, Ronnie*	NPC	Mayor	78.41
Abrio, Buboy	IND	Mayor	16.46
Cirera, Mark	IND	Mayor	5.13
Aguilar, Mahang	NPC	Vice-Mayor	49.17
Balauro, Eric	NP	Vice-Mayor	27.47
Ibis, Kuya Eming	LP	Vice-Mayor	23.35
Vinzons			
Segundo, Dra. Nory	NPC	Mayor	51.46
Ang, Agnes*	LP	Mayor	48.06
Chavez, Rodolfo	IND	Mayor	0.48
Herrera, Radam*	NPC	Vice-Mayor	54.79
Villafranca, Padi	LP	Vice-Mayor	45.21

chapter **5**

Fourth District of Laguna:
A Tale of Two Parties

Michelle Sta. Romana

INTRODUCTION

At first glance, Laguna's 4th District looks like a typical rural area where traditional political families and personalistic, patron-clientelist modes of campaigning persist. Most politicians battle for visibility by personally going down to small communities, practising *pakikisama* (a Filipino trait that encompasses heightened social efforts to maintain camaraderie within different groups) and engaging in everyday activities, like visiting a market or attending a celebration with constituents. This pattern then allows candidates to solicit votes easily and gives them a better chance to win in the next elections. Most politicians' supporters are their direct, personal beneficiaries. Giving cash and other necessities given during campaigns is therefore not necessarily perceived as a form of direct vote buying, but rather, as an extension of the candidates' willing service to their constituencies.

However, despite the similar traditional tactics that politicians use to win, there is evidence that candidates within a ruling political party/alliance have an advantage that extends beyond traditional family and patron-client ties. The Liberal Party (LP)–Nacionalista Party (NP) coalition that formed for the local Laguna races won by a significant margin over the formerly majority United Nationalist Alliance (UNA), smaller parties like National Unity Party (NUP), National People's Coalition (NPC) and the pre-existing networks of an old, established political family.

In this chapter I introduce the main groups and parties in the congressional race in the 4th District of Laguna and explore the common mobilisation tactics used by two congressional candidates and many local candidates. I discuss how, despite having similar narratives and methods to entice voters, the pre-election activities of an administration party, combined with their resource pool and their political network, sufficed to defeat two political dynasties within the 4th District of Laguna. Administration parties have wide-reaching networks, have government funding and programmes tied to their candidates and can engage in extensive collective action to destabilise frontrunners from opposing parties at the local level.

RECENT HISTORY OF THE 4TH DISTRICT'S ELECTORAL DYNAMICS

Despite the 4th district's remoteness, its 80.21 per cent (COMELEC 2016) voter turnout suggests that the district's citizens actively participated in the election cycle. As of 2016, Laguna had a total of 1,675,366 registered voters across the province, making it the fourth most vote-rich province (Lucero 2016). The 4th District is home to 328,032 registered voters, or merely 19 per cent of the province's voting population. National and provincial-level candidates tend to campaign in Laguna's more populous 1st and 2nd districts so as to be able to cover a huge voter reservoir in the shortest time (Cabyabyab 2016; Ilas 2016). Thus, the 4th district's heated election activity begins with the district-level race, from the congressional down to the municipal level. Although district-level races tend to be predominantly dominated by political families, political parties and alliances have increasingly played instrumental roles in securing electoral victories. Parties act as vehicles for mobilising resources for incumbents to implement their programmes, for which they then take credit throughout the candidates' terms.

In 2013, UNA was the most popular party. After the 2016 election, however, LP and NP were the most popular. Prior to the 2016 election, two major political events significantly changed the factional dynamics in Laguna. First, the LP and NP entered into an ad-hoc province-wide alliance which sent formal bets, party-mates and local slates into disarray as some candidates were cast aside in favour of others. Next, the

Commission on Elections (COMELEC) decided to allow disqualified ex-governor Emilio Ramon "ER" Ejercito to run again. Ejercito's subsequent attempts to secure his gubernatorial candidacy resulted in a temporary hiccup for UNA's stronghold in the 4th District.

In 2013, the UNA gubernatorial candidate, Ejercito, won against his LP opponent by more than 100,000 votes. UNA also secured mayoral posts in more municipalities than did any other party. However, the district profile has drastically changed since then. The 2016 election results, summarised in Figures 5.1 and 5.2, show the extent of LP–NP's increased influence as they defeated UNA in the gubernatorial race. No UNA candidate from the 4th District managed to claim a congressional post, while at the municipal level, UNA executive seats have also decreased.

Figures 5.1 and 5.2
Share of local mayoral and vice-mayoral seats, 2013 vs 2016, 4th District of Laguna, by party. Source: COMELEC 2013 and 2016.

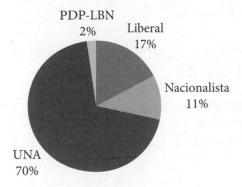

2013 Share of Mayoral and Vice-mayoral Seats Won, 4th District of Laguna (by Party)

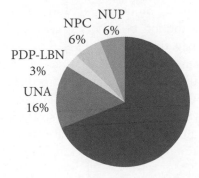

2016 Share of Mayoral and Vice-mayoral Seats Won, 4th District of Laguna (by Party)

In 2013, UNA controlled 14 of 32 mayoral and vice-mayoral seats, more than the LP (8), the NP (5) and PDP-LBN (1) seats combined. By 2016, however, LP topped UNA by securing 16 local executive posts, followed by NP with 6, effectively replacing the UNA majority with an LP–NP coalition (UNA's posts decreased to 5). A couple of NUP and NPC-affiliated candidates also won in Lumban and Majayjay. This was a new development, especially because there had been no strong local NUP or NPC candidates in these municipalities in 2013. The rise of these parties may be attributed to the added support of the San Luis family for NUP candidates and the popularity of the NPC-backed candidate, Grace Poe.

Despite the strong presence of LP-NP and UNA, two families still dominated the district: the celebrity clan of the Ejercitos (UNA) and the old political family of the San Luises (formerly LP, now NUP, with shifting alliances). Because of their losses, the Ejercitos faltered in 2016. However, they still maintained a stronghold in the municipality of Pagsanjan. Members of the San Luis family are also a presence on the provincial board and were significant drivers of the district's politics leading up to the 2016 election (Caronan 2016).

RAINING MANNA: COMMON TYPES OF CAMPAIGNING IN THE 4TH DISTRICT

> It's different [from the Three Gs]. The culture of Laguna is to entertain.
> Here, it's a battle of who has better character.
>
> – A campaign manager in an interview, 29 April 2016

Campaigns in the 4th District are spectacles, where politicians from traditionally political families and locally elected posts use personalistic, patron-clientelistic methods to secure votes. Most rely on flashy, loud entertainment campaigns, motorcades and positive inducements, such as the direct distribution of services, campaign goods, food and cash assistance, over negative inducements. Locals comment that the campaign period is generally "peaceful", "happy" and "fun". Violence among candidates is rare, although it has occurred in the past, especially in remote municipalities like Sta. Maria and Mabitac (Chua 2003).

Direct service plays a big role in campaign strategies by serving as the primary metric through which candidates are measured. If a political camp or candidate cannot provide pocket change for a beggar or PhP 100 when asked for gas money, it would reflect negatively on the candidate— the candidate may appear like a miser, "greedy" or *suplado/suplada* (snobbish). As a result, campaign teams are often given some pocket money—anywhere between PhP 1,000 and 3,000 in small-denomination bills—so that team members wearing campaign paraphernalia will not be accused of having these undesirable qualities. The amount is often fixed and excess funds are surrendered back to the campaign manager.[1]

During the campaign period, candidates go on house-to-house visits and participate in everyday activities. These activities are varied, and the candidate attempts to engage in *pakikisama*. Whether this effort involves a big and lively dinner, a baptism party, a birthday or wedding celebration, a funeral, a casual get-together, a drinking session, spending change in an informal small-town lottery,[2] or even showering in the house of a trusted constituent,[3] for as long as candidates are welcomed by willing constituents, they will partake in the activity. This is a way of building camaraderie with the community, securing their relationships and hoping that their good character will be seen and experienced, and word of it shared by their constituents. Candidates often conduct these events with their party members and family members. These strategies are so important that candidates will even pause a half-kilometre motorcade along a provincial side-road in order to pay their respects to a party in the community.[4]

Outside campaign periods, candidates actively participate in their constituents' celebrations through offering little gifts, entertainment or financial assistance—amounts range from PhP 300–500 for necessary document processing fees, or PhP 1,000–2,000 for take-home gifts as the godfather of a new baby, or sufficient funds to compensate for funeral and burial fees. If a candidate cannot attend a particular gathering, he or she might still lend portable tents or grant people access to personal venues in which to congregate or public spaces. These positive inducements are used regardless of whether the candidate is a newcomer or an incumbent official at any level of the government and allow the candidate to maintain visibility until the next election period.

Candidates host casual get-togethers over bottles of beer, whiskey, *lambanog* (low-cost coconut wine) and gin. A dinner becomes an opportunity to gather data or socialise with potential local links. Before

---

[1] Field notes, 29 April 2016.
[2] Field notes, Luisiana, 4th District of Laguna, 1 May 2016.
[3] Interview, 26 April 2016.
[4] Field notes, 1 May 2016.

leaving, a candidate may leave PhP 20–100 to "make up" for the drinks that he or she has consumed.[5] Candidates even sponsor liquor parties with alcohol bottles featuring pictures of themselves, increasing their own face and name recognition.[6] As two municipal councilor candidates admitted, it is difficult to reinforce voter loyalty without giving voters something in return, especially food and drinks. Such *salo-salos* (get-togethers over a meal) are practically "required" so that voters will be introduced to the candidate[7] and see how kind and generous he or she is.[8]

At their headquarters, candidates personally offer their open space as a venue for parties. They provide food, free medicines and financial assistance to the public. These resources, especially the immediate availability of money and medicine, represent necessary services or *tulong* (help) that needy constituents request from the candidate. When the candidate meets a constituent and delivers such a stipend, the candidate smiles, shakes hands and personally requests the beneficiary: "Please don't forget me/us this election".

MOBILISATION TACTICS

For the 4th District, last-minute negotiations may end up converting the voting preference of entire neighbourhoods. In the few days leading up to the election, candidates may meet and try to court certain political leaders in order to gain the support of the latter's local bailiwicks and the networks of voters who are loyal to the local leader. For example, during an afternoon break, a candidate received an urgent text.[9] The campaign team, in hushed voices, whispered that a municipal councilor they once thought loyal had been "taken in" by the opponent over a matter of *pera-pera* (money) to endorse an opposing candidate. The personal following of the incumbent councilor consisted of approximately 300 voters, enough to turn the tables in a tight, local race. The candidate and his team sprang into action, driving over to the councilor's house to woo back the councilor with drinks and cash.[10]

---

[5] Field notes, 1 May 2016.
[6] Field notes, 4 May 2016.
[7] Interview, 28 April 2016.
[8] Ibid.
[9] Name withheld to protect privacy of candidate.
[10] Field notes, 7 May 2016.

It is possible to infer how this system works by going down to the barangay level. To illustrate, a local councilor can permeate a populous *sitio* (a unit smaller than the local barangay) by talking with one of the *liders* (barangay/sitio leaders) there. These are often individuals who have huge social capital among a particular community. If the *lider* trusts the candidate, he or she will "take care" of them and follow up with a request for "a little extra", often *pang-merienda* (for afternoon snacks) for their efforts. The amount can be small, around PhP 300 to 500, divided among the *lider* and their community. After breaking the ice, the *lider* will accompany the candidate and talk up the candidate around the community, accompanying them and vouching for the candidate's good virtues and services.

A couple of nights prior to the election, when campaign-related activities are officially banned, the *gapang* ("the crawl") begins. *Gapang* involves discreet but straightforward vote buying tactics used by candidates, allied *liders* and campaign team members. *Liders* and campaign team members—rarely the candidate or any member of their slate—approach voters individually and give them money. These payments are accompanied by sample ballots that detail the candidates' allies and preferred slates. There is an implicit understanding that accepting this payment obligates the recipient to vote for the listed slate, although this commitment is not systematically enforceable. In turn, opponents stalk candidates and their vehicles, attempting to catch campaigners in the act in order to write up a report and disqualify the guilty candidate at the last minute.

Regardless of vigilantes and negative perceptions, vote buying remains a commonplace practice.[11] On the night before the election, one congressional candidate coursed through his local network to give PhP 500 with a sample ballot, while another was giving PhP 350. A mayoral candidate was giving PhP 1,000 for each vote. Others opted to give in kind rather than in cash. An example would be food for votes on election day, such as by inviting people to head to a local eatery for a plate of stir-fried noodles. Although the evidence is inconclusive, these efforts seem effective to some extent—some locals remarked that they were more likely to vote for the one who gave them more money, while others simply took home the goods without necessarily voting for that candidate.[12]

---

[11] Vigilantes are campaign members—often candidates' loyal right-hand men—who are tasked with tracking down and spying on rival candidates. This is done with the sole intent of catching the rival candidate buying votes.

[12] Field notes, 8 May 2016.

Having discussed the district profile, campaign tactics and mobilisation, we turn now to describing and analysing the campaigns of two major congressional candidates.

Former allies Congressman Benjamin "Benjie" Agarao Jr. (LP) and former Congressman Edgar San Luis (NUP) battled for the same congressional district post in the 2016 election. In some ways, the two congressional aspirants appear strikingly similar. They are both from political families that utilised similar techniques during their campaigns—nightly caucuses, *mitings de avance* (pep rallies), motorcades, poll watchers' gatherings and house-to-house campaigns packed their airtight schedules. Both are admired by their supporters as driven, approachable and benevolent providers of kindness, goods and services: they behave as expected by their constituency.

The primary differences between the two major congressional candidates can be traced to their immediate support bases and ways that their affiliations augment their campaign resources. I argue that, despite both candidates' usage of the same patron-clientelistic ties and positive inducements during elections, there is a marked difference in the mobilisation strategies of an incumbent party coalition versus those of the personal network of an old political family.

BEYOND PATRONAGE: HOW PARTY ALLIANCES NOW MATTER LOCALLY

One way that party alliances matter relates to the people within the parties, who can collectively act as catalysts of political change, to the benefit of the party. In the 2016 election, the LP–NP coalition battled UNA in the major Laguna races. UNA used to be an influential local force in Laguna, especially within the 4th District, where the Ejercitos were based. The events that led to this strengthening of the LP–NP coalition will be discussed in the next sections.

Pre-election blues and yellows: Party destabilisation tactics prior to the 2016 election

The 2016 election were not kind to the Ejercitos. This was in stark contrast to 2013, when ER Ejercito defeated former LP opponent Edgar "Egay" San Luis (then LP) by a comfortable margin. After the 2013 election, San Luis filed an overspending case against Ejercito. COMELEC's investigation determined that Ejercito had spent PhP 20 million on television ads on national broadcast station ABS-CBN (apart from spending on GMA-7)[13] for the 2013 election. This amount exceeded the allowable budget for a gubernatorial campaign. Ejercito was thus forced to abdicate his governorship because of his alleged overspending. Moreover, he was originally banned from running in the 2016 election, a decision that was only reversed late in the 2016 election campaign.

With Ejercito and UNA temporarily destabilised, two political actors rose to prominence under the new LP–NP Laguna coalition: gubernatorial candidate Ramil Hernandez (NP) and LP member Edgar "Egay" San Luis. The then vice-governor, Hernandez, became governor after Ejercito's disqualification from his post. For the 2016 election, Hernandez became the official LP–NP coalition candidate, effectively sidelining San Luis. San Luis stepped down as the LP Laguna Chair then transferred to the NUP, which also had an unofficial coalition with the LP. San Luis elected to run for Congress, instead of for governor, against former LP party-mate and incumbent, Congressman Benjamin "Benjie" Agarao, Jr.[14]

Hoping to keep the governorship in his family's hands, ER Ejercito entered his son Jorge Antonio (IND) into the gubernatorial race. But once the COMELEC ruled that ER could run, he withdrew his son's name, although the name Jorge Antonio Ejercito remained in the ballots. With two Ejercitos on the ballot, the plan backfired, as a huge chunk of the votes meant for ER went to his son, thus splitting the tally. Even so, the results show that the combined votes of ER and his son were not enough to overtake Hernandez.

ER criticised the initial COMELEC ruling and last-minute reversal as a deliberate plan to weaken the Ejercitos' and UNA's clout in local politics (Ponte and Cinco 2016). These factors confounding ER Ejercito's run for governor under UNA accordingly allowed the LP–NP to channel its solid machinery throughout the district.

---

[13] Ejercito vs. COMELEC and San Luis. Retrieved from http://www.lawphil.net/judjuris/juri2014/nov2014/gr_212398_2014.html (25 November 2014).
[14] UNTV Life, "Dating Laguna Rep. Egay San Luis, nagbitiw na bilang chairman ng Liberal Party". Posted 14 October 2015. https://www.youtube.com/watch?v=LI_hK1fKI14.

The LP–NP diaries: A symbiotic, institutionalised relationship

The LP–NP pre-election efforts to destabilise UNA combined with the coalition's doubled resources and capital for machinery enabled the alliance to take over the entire 4th District, advancing local LP–NP candidates over previous incumbents. While aiming for the victory of their national-level and provincial-level candidates, the high-visibility campaigns also provided an opportunity for multiple local candidates to take advantage of the machinery's structure and resources. This prospect encouraged local candidates to "turncoat", that is, switch from parties with less machinery to ones with more extensive resources and popularity.

Amidst the district's political dynamics, incumbent candidates running for re-election who were also members of the provincial administration party had the biggest advantage. They were given financial and material support, and had extensive political networks. If a candidate benefitted from government funding, institutionalised party support and other resources—for example, pork-barrel payouts to dispense, or quick approval and implementation of proposals—they were able to execute more programmes and leverage these as a measure of their own effectiveness as a political leader and government official.

Incumbents' campaign teams utilised this advantage by issuing campaign materials that doubled as government services. For example, polling precinct cards decked out in the candidate's colours listed voter-specific precinct information and featured the candidate's face and name. These were distributed *en masse* by the hundreds of thousands, and campaign teams expected a minimum 10 per cent vote return.[15] Another example was poll watchers' manuals with candidates' faces, names, numbers and slogans on them.[16] Other candidates tapped into human networks or used government programmes to promote their services throughout their term, maximising and maintaining their visibility.

Given these tendencies, the complications with ex-Governor Ejercito's (UNA) incumbency, due to the LP-backed COMELEC's case against him, represented a brilliant move to secure government resources for NP to deliver down to its lowest-level allies. By letting the NP vice-governor take over in time for the 2016 election, popular LP–NP incumbents were able to use coalition-financed resources, attract lower-level allies and turn this support into more party votes in the 2016 Laguna local elections.

---

[15] Field notes, 29 April 2016.
[16] Field notes, 26 April 2016.

The Agaraos remained the LP candidates for Congress and the provincial board for the 2016 election. The family served as an additional asset to the LP–NP coalition in securing votes within the 4th District of Laguna. The father, Congressman Benjie Jr., and the son, Board Member Benjo, both ran for re-election. The Agaraos utilised administration party funding and resources, channelled through different party-mates.

Upon entering the provincial capital in Sta. Cruz, one would have found it hard to ignore the Agaraos' posters. Against vibrant red and blue backgrounds, their faces appeared in numerous rows, above bolded lettering and their signature flame-shaped "A". Underneath were catchy slogans in Filipino: "For service that's steadfast, certain and keeps on going!" and "The true Congressman of the masses". Congressman Agarao's services to and activities for constituents had included programmes like rice distribution ("Agarice"), sports programmes, fundraising concerts ("Cong-zert"), scholarships, free medication and eye check-up facilities, all of which served as the basis of his campaign's branding him as an "action-oriented" congressman.

One of the keys to the Agaraos' high visibility lay in their extensive social capital. The camp rallied different sectors—including civil society assemblies and barangay captains in each municipality—to stage large campaign rallies, motorcades, *mitings de avance* and other events. Local candidates also enlisted the district's motorcycle drivers' associations and allied barangay captains to help win voters from their respective local communities. These influence-wielders endorsed the candidates to their barangay constituents. Often a campaign requested a particular number of voters per barangay—usually around 20–30. The number varied depending on the size of the barangay. These arrangements usually happened in barangays where the barangay captain was an ally to whom the candidate had previously given resources, such as funds for a barangay hall or health project.

To illustrate: Congressman Agarao's youth scholars assisted in campaign events as volunteers. They were provided with free transportation, food and drinks in exchange for their day-long efforts. They were also compensated approximately PhP 500–2,000 for additional transportation expenses,[17] depending on what day of the campaign period it was. Their activities included attending poll-watcher events, being in the front line of house-to-house campaigns and participating in rallies with other volunteers in each municipality on a daily basis. At the end of the day, these volunteers

---

[17] Field notes, 27 April 2016.

recorded their attendance, revealing an organised system and campaign structure. Some volunteers even perceived their daily efforts as a form of "giving back" to the congressman for supporting them through school with government scholarships.[18]

The explicit link between services and voter loyalty becomes more apparent at the municipal and barangay levels, where it becomes easier to track the flow of resources among smaller communities. In Sta. Cruz, an incumbent municipal councilor shared that since Hernandez (NP) became governor, the councilor's projects had been signed immediately.[19] He cited his government-backed feeding programmes, through which he provided around 2 kilograms of rice to needy families. A popular two-term incumbent, the councilor entertained numerous visitors to his house and office, most of whom were Sta. Cruz residents who knocked on his door. These visitors asked for resources or financial assistance—sometimes to process legal documents, to cover ceremonial fees, or a little for *merienda* (snacks). The candidate would hand them cash, ranging from PhP 50–500, depending on the amount requested.

Not one to forget his affiliations, the councilor and his wife would call out: "Vote Governor Hernandez! Don't forget! If it wasn't for Gov, this wouldn't be possible!" and "Vote Mar Roxas [LP's presidential candidate], too!" and wave goodbye at the voter.[20] The voter, cash in hand, would return a chipper: "*Syempre naman po! Boto namin yan!*" (Of course, we'll vote for them!)

While this was the norm in incumbent areas or locales with strong challengers, the campaign pattern looked very different in areas with a struggling candidate slate. This suggests that the LP–NP coalition used its resources mostly for precincts that were traditional bailiwicks (or areas with a huge voting population up for grabs). In the Pagsanjan municipality, where the Ejercitos (UNA) dominated with their slate of UNA incumbents, opposition LP–NP candidates found it difficult to expand their campaigns because donors channelled resources to LP's larger and more important races: heavily contested national, gubernatorial and congressional campaigns. According to Pagsanjan vice-mayor-elect Peter Trinidad (LP), "From calendars to tarpaulins, we got allowance enough to cover for the costs between each of us last election. But now, we were merely given a lump sum—a tiny one at that."[21] However minimal this

---

[18] Field notes, 27 April 2016.
[19] Name withheld by request.
[20] Field notes, 29 April 2016.
[21] Interview with Trinidad, 27 April 2016.

lump sum was, Trinidad conceded that without the coalition, his party-mates would have had no funding at all. In this sense, the LP–NP coalition helped ensure that such candidates had a chance to secure resources and continue their campaigns, encouraging them to remain in the coalition and expand the party's reach rather than opt for turncoatism.

The San Luises' loyal hold—how old families maintain linkages

> Always remember this—the glitter of gold is no replacement for the true love of a friend.
>
> – Edgar San Luis in a *miting de avance*, 30 April 2016

A core link common to events leading up to the 2016 election was former 4th District Laguna congressman, Edgar San Luis, a member of the political clan based in Sta. Cruz. The San Luises have held eight Laguna-based seats since 1960, including the forefather, who served as governor for 28 years. Their sustained local presence leaves them relatively free to field their own campaigns at any level, with the support of politicians who approach them. However, since the clan was able to snare only a provincial board seat in the 2013 election, the San Luises had had to rely extensively on these local networks to help maintain their visibility and service links.

Having left behind the resource pool and machinery of LP—which had carried Edgar in the 2010 election and won him about 450,000 votes for his gubernatorial post—the San Luises had no choice but to cope with a cutback in campaign resources this election season. Consequently, they ensured voters could see the juxtaposition of candidates through their relatively modest-looking campaign. Cheery pictures of their smiling faces were readily apparent in city centres and along roadsides, multiplying in number as one moved into the upland regions. Together, the duo reminded the district of their genuine desire to serve selflessly: "*Mahal namin kayo. God bless po!*" (We love you. God bless!)

The San Luises primarily relied on donations and endorsements from different personal connections and allied party-list sectors in this election (for example, the maritime- and legal-industry-based ANGKLA), because they could rely neither on LP–NP machinery nor on the vast network of allies in civil society that the Agaraos had. Many of these connections were from older ties, developed over the course of the San Luises' previous campaigns. In order to gain exposure and reinforce support among loyal voters, the San Luises campaigned with local politicians from different municipalities. Contrary to the concentrated efforts of the LP–NP coalition to campaign in populous bailiwicks, the San Luises specifically made an effort to target remote, neglected upland communities to reinforce or discover loyal voter groups. For instance, in the fifth-class upland municipality of Famy, the San Luises had historically been significantly more popular than the Agaraos, due to the fact that the San Luises delivered infrastructure projects to Famy during their clan-members' stints in Congress. Thus, the San Luises could often rely on these municipalities to deliver a number of votes during local elections.

Operating as independents, despite formally being part of NUP, the San Luises supported any candidate they pleased.[22] Since NUP did not have a full slate, NUP supported the San Luises and their networks, in return (Espina 2015). Though the San Luises' formal presidential endorsement was for Grace Poe (NPC), their names also appeared on sample ballots that supported Rodrigo Duterte (PDP-LBN) and Mar Roxas (LP) and their local allies, suggesting that the father-son duo was opportunistic in associating themselves with varied people and parties. The San Luises campaigned with each party's respective local candidates, including on LP–NP slates on which the Agaraos should have appeared, if proper protocol were followed (meaning slates should contain only members of the formal party alliance). This allowed the San Luises to garner votes and support from several different major parties. In effect, the family courts allies with its constant voter base—roughly one-third of the district's registered voters, or around 100,000 votes.

Thus, the San Luises have found value in their personalistic, multi-party approach. They even went so far in 2016 as to portray some political parties negatively. For example, congressional candidate Edgar would emphasise how LP "used" him, then cast him aside. Decrying what they called *pag-mumulitika* (politicking), the San Luises insisted that their members are not *balimbing* (starfruit: people who easily switch affiliations, named after the Filipino fruit with multiple flat sides); rather, when it comes to public service, the San Luises have simply never placed much importance on party affiliations. They merely wanted to continue serving their constituents to their own ability. During several *mitings de avance*, it was common for the San Luises to refer to their long friendships with various local mayoral candidates, stating that they went "way back" and noting how they were "always there for each other".[23] For instance:

---

[22] Interview, 29 April 2016.
[23] Field notes, 30 April 2016.

Let's do away with all these politics. It's possible that I hadn't been able to give him [former party mate] a contract right now, that's why he left me behind. But I have many friends that can give them the contract. Vice-Mayor Tape is with me![24]

These links were based on previous local candidates the family had helped before, back when the San Luises held a congressional seat and could move more resources to help local administrators execute projects. Now, these links helped the San Luises advance their services—for example, an allied, elected party-list party would consistently vouch for the San Luises in order to secure continued party funding for personal services. For example, the ANGKLA party-list party would vet constituents' requests for free medicine from a government hospital, because no incumbent San Luis had the direct power to do so.[25]

However, the family's relative inability to provide resources had consequences in the patron-clientelist political culture of rural Laguna, where success hinges on directly providing the greatest amount of help or services to the greatest number of voters. During the 2016 election period, their opponents portrayed the San Luises as candidates who had fallen on hard times and were unable to muster enough support for a big campaign. Thus, constituents doubted whether the San Luises could adequately provide for the needs of their constituents for the next three years. Voters mentioned that the San Luises had given less in monetary assistance ever since they had failed to win provincial-level posts— sometimes as little as PhP 20.[26] Although voters might still view this assistance as a nice gesture, Agarao supporters would highlight these rumours as evidence of their opponents' decreased influence, pointing out the San Luises' smaller motorcades, caucuses and caravans. Relative to the Agaraos' showy motorcades and celebratory torch rallies, the San Luises' events were indeed relatively modest in appearance.[27] The Agarao campaign team had elaborate motorcades consisting of jeeps and cargo trucks extending for nearly half a kilometre. The San Luises had similarly-sized motorcades, except with little pickup trucks and personal cars to carry all their campaign paraphernalia.

---

[24] Edgar San Luis in a *miting de avance*, 30 April 2016.
[25] Interview, 29 April 2016.
[26] Field notes, 27 April 2016.
[27] Field notes, 28 April 2016.

CONCLUSION

In summary, the LP–NP coalition played a significant role in re-shaping local district races, destabilising the previous UNA stronghold and unseating UNA incumbents in the 4th District of Laguna. Local officials rode along with the coalition and leveraged its resources to their advantage, often with the promise to garner support for other LP–NP candidates, as well.

In this election, an NP candidate won the gubernatorial seat in partnership with the national administration party, LP. When incumbent candidates that are part of the ruling party have government programmes and voter bases, it becomes easier to channel party funding to their campaigns and provide for their subordinates' and constituents' particularistic needs. Due to their accumulated experience and political capital, incumbents can tap into the social networks of their constituents and previous beneficiaries to expand their campaigns exponentially within a limited amount of time.

Although the 4th District experienced a massive win by LP–NP slates, the role of the traditional political family still holds some significance. Parties are still vulnerable in this regard. Old families hold power and loyal local networks—long-time partners and friends, political allies and entire cliques of barangay leaders that transcend party affiliation, premised on personal alliance as opposed to party alliances. Local allies, regardless of party, may call on family members to campaign with them, relying on the family's support, influence and endorsements in municipal-level campaigns. The combined power of their networks and resources spelled the difference during the last few days of the campaign, when many voters were most vulnerable to switching their preferred candidate based on additional inducements.

Despite the two candidates using similar tactics, their resource networks were different, with the results favouring the one with an incumbent national-level party. In the end, the LP–NP coalition won another term in congressional, executive and provincial board seats, offering evidence that aligning with a ruling party during the local elections may give candidates an advantage due to the party's extensive resource base. The San Luises won the same provincial board seat as previously, and they still maintained the support of one-third of the district. However, without leading-party support or an executive seat, the San Luises struggled to maintain power during the 2016 local election.

The dynamic described in this chapter may drastically change in the near future, now that the ascendant Partidong Demokratiko ng Pilipinas-

Lakas ng Bayan (PDP–Laban) has consolidated into a supermajority administration party and local party lines have become blurred again. In local elections, it may be that we see the same behaviour from administration and leading parties, suggesting that although a party structure and resource base matter, the actual party may not. The further study of Philippine local elections and party dynamics will thus be especially vital in the years leading to the 2022 election.

Table 5
Election results from Laguna 4th District

Candidate	Party	Office	Per cent (%)
* Indicates Incumbent Candidate			
Agarao, Benjie*	LP	House of Representatives	57.56
San Luis, Edgar	NUP	House of Representatives	41.69
Santos, Fidel	IND	House of Representatives	0.76
Hernandez, Ramil	NP	Provincial Governor	51.14
Ejercito, Jorge Antonio	IND	Provincial Governor	28.42
Ejercito, Emilio Ramon III	UNA	Provincial Governor	19.66
Alberto, Berlene	IND	Provincial Governor	0.51
Sucano, Nemesio	IND	Provincial Governor	0.26
Agapay, Karen	NP	Provincial Vice-Governor	45.61
Lajara, Christian Niño	UNA	Provincial Vice-Governor	32.12
Alarva, Angelica Jones	LP	Provincial Vice-Governor	19.75
San Sebastian, Bro Rico G.	IND	Provincial Vice-Governor	2.52
Cavinti			
Oliveros, Milbert*	LP	Mayor	51.44
Esguerra, Florcelie	PDPLBN	Mayor	29.07
Dela Torre, Bethoven	UNA	Mayor	19.49
Baeyens, Anita	LP	Vice-Mayor	64.67
Mesina, Jojo	UNA	Vice-Mayor	35.33
Famy			
Pangilinan, Edwin	LP	Mayor	37.86
Muramatsu, Renonia*	NP	Mayor	33.15
Acomular, Emmanuel	NPC	Mayor	28.99
Andaya, Ellen	LP	Vice-Mayor	39.96

(cont'd overleaf)

Table 5 *(cont'd)*

Candidate	Party	Office	Per cent (%)
Laminero, Melvin	NP	Vice-Mayor	33.62
Llamas, Vince Viii	PDPLBN	Vice-Mayor	26.42
Kalayaan			
Adao, Leni	NP	Mayor	32.02
Laganapan, Sandy	LP	Mayor	29.99
Ponce, Darwin	NPC	Mayor	29.25
Laganas, Russel	UNA	Mayor	7.52
De La Paz, Antonio	IND	Mayor	1.21
Lopez, Laarni	NUP	Vice-Mayor	38.34
Ragaza, Kenneth	IND	Vice-Mayor	37.72
Sasondoncillo, Marty	LP	Vice-Mayor	23.93
Luisiana			
Rondilla, Nestor*	UNA	Mayor	63.25
Rondilla, Manuel	NP	Mayor	36.34
Estrellado, Bobby	IND	Mayor	0.41
Jacob, Luibic	UNA	Vice-Mayor	66.19
Palad, Wilfredo	NP	Vice-Mayor	33.81
Lumban			
Ubatay, Rolan	NPC	Mayor	38.76
Añonuevo, Reynato*	LP	Mayor	35.04
Paraiso, Fredy	UNA	Mayor	26.20
Raga, Belen	NPC	Vice-Mayor	53.81
De Ramos, Pamela	LP	Vice-Mayor	26.60
Lagrosa, Mamerta	UNA	Vice-Mayor	19.59
Mabitac			
Sana, Ronald*	LP	Mayor	54.85
Fader, Gerardo	NPC	Mayor	45.15
Reyes, Alberto*	LP	Vice-Mayor	56.01
Olarte, Kian	NPC	Vice-Mayor	43.99
Magdalena			
Aventurado, David Jr.*	LP	Mayor	100.00

Table 5 *(cont'd)*

Candidate	Party	Office	Per cent (%)
Burbos, Tato*	LP	Vice-Mayor	100.00
Majayjay			
Clado, Jojo	NPC	Mayor	27.15
Mentilla, Larry	NP	Mayor	25.57
Estupigan, Godofredo	UNA	Mayor	14.12
Esmaquel, Allan	IND	Mayor	12.48
Rodillas, Victorino*	LP	Mayor	11.61
Gruezo, Froilan	PDPLBN	Mayor	5.40
Araza, Rolando	IND	Mayor	3.66
Amorado, Eulogio Wilson	LP	Vice-Mayor	40.13
Merestela, Avelino	UNA	Vice-Mayor	31.84
Vito, Manuel Danilo	NP	Vice-Mayor	14.87
Banawa, Rexford	NPC	Vice-Mayor	9.15
Barba, Jhoul	PDPLBN	Vice-Mayor	4.01
Paete			
Bagabaldo, Mutuk	UNA	Mayor	55.70
Cadayona, Arcel	NPC	Mayor	44.30
Bagayana, Gido	NP	Vice-Mayor	39.82
Paraiso, Aurelio*	UNA	Vice-Mayor	37.85
Calma, Elizabeth	NPC	Vice-Mayor	22.33
Pagsanjan			
Ejercito, Girlie*	UNA	Mayor	59.19
Gamit-Talabong, Terryl	NP	Mayor	40.81
Trinidad, Peter Casius	NP	Vice-Mayor	50.53
Madriaga, Melvin	UNA	Vice-Mayor	49.47
Pakil			
Soriano, Vince	NP	Mayor	55.37
Martinez, Totoy	NPC	Mayor	44.63
Familara, Melody Cabañero	LP	Vice-Mayor	37.01
Del Moro, Amy*	NPC	Vice-Mayor	28.72
Macuha, Rowen	IND	Vice-Mayor	21.55
Maray, Alfredo Jr.	UNA	Vice-Mayor	12.73

(cont'd overleaf)

Table 5 *(cont'd)*

Candidate	Party	Office	Per cent (%)
Pangil			
Rafanan, Ka Popoy	LP	Mayor	57.12
Reyes, Jovit*	UNA	Mayor	42.14
Acaylar, Freddie	IND	Mayor	0.74
Pajarillo, Al	UNA	Vice-Mayor	49.77
Astoveza, Jun*	LP	Vice-Mayor	45.20
Mendez, Nani	IND	Vice-Mayor	5.03
Pila			
Ramos, Edgardo	UNA	Mayor	54.91
Quiat, Boy*	LP	Mayor	39.68
Calubayan, Lorenzo	IND	Mayor	5.41
Alarva, Queen Marilyd	LP	Vice-Mayor	53.46
Relova, Querubin Jr.*	UNA	Vice-Mayor	46.54
Santa Cruz (Capital)			
Panganiban, Domingo*	LP	Mayor	69.07
Magcalas, Ariel	UNA	Mayor	30.93
De Leon, Louie*	LP	Vice-Mayor	55.99
Diaz, Efren	IND	Vice-Mayor	44.01
Santa Maria			
Carolino, Tony	NP	Mayor	100.00
Tuazon, Virginia*	NP	Vice-Mayor	100.00
Siniloan			
Tibay, Eddie*	NP	Mayor	51.63
Acero, Juanita	LP	Mayor	48.37
Acoba, Roberto*	NP	Vice-Mayor	62.50
Coladilla, Edgardo	LP	Vice-Mayor	37.50

chapter **6**

First District of Laguna: A Tale of Two Cities

Armida D. Miranda

INTRODUCTION

Campaigning and voting are comparable to sowing and reaping. The way politicians and candidates operate their campaign network is similar to the four laws of harvest: (1) they sow and usually reap in like kind; (2) they tend to reap in a different season than they sow; (3) at times, they reap more than they sow; (4) if they can do nothing about past harvests, they can plan and do something about future harvests.

It appears that most candidates, through their campaign arms or networks, start fertilising the "electoral soil" the moment they are elected. Those who did not win and were unable to reap the expected harvest usually continue their "civic activities" and try to sow seeds in strategic soils to produce new plants and roots that can later bear fruit. Whoever has the most resources can provide the most "seeds" and choose the most productive soil in which to scatter their seeds. This is how the electoral dynamics in the 1st Congressional District of Laguna, which is composed of the cities of Sta. Rosa and San Pedro, seem to operate.

San Pedro is the smallest town of the 1st District of Laguna and the third smallest in the entire province. It is the 37th most populous city and youngest city in the Philippines with the population of 325,809 (as of 2015), making it the town with the highest population density in the province of Laguna.[1]

As Laguna province's gateway to Manila, San Pedro has become a popular suburban residential community with its agricultural land converted to residential, industrial, and commercial subdivisions. Sta. Rosa City, on the other hand, is a First Class City in Laguna Province. It has also been known as "The Investment Capital of South Luzon" since 1994 and as the Detroit of the Philippines (due to the presence of car manufacturing plants). The city lies 38 kilometres south of Manila via the South Luzon Expressway, making it a suburban residential community of Metro Manila. It is also the densest city in the province, with more than 6,000 people per square kilometre. It is now the richest city in Southern Luzon in terms of annual income, which is PhP 2.3 billion.[2] That could be the reason why many politicians typically consider running for mayor.

It is partly because of these transformations that San Pedro and Sta. Rosa have become an interesting electoral arena and worth studying. In this chapter, I explore some of the ways candidates build networks of loyal supporters and the manner in which they conduct their campaigns in these two areas, drawing on the experiences of two coordinators and other campaigners.

BACKGROUND OF THE RESEARCH

There have been only two prominent names who have governed San Pedro since the early 1970s—the Cataquiz and Vierneza clans. One councilor candidate aptly summarised the history of these clans:

> Since 1971, the political climate in San Pedro has changed. During that time, whoever has the biggest clan was the sure winner. When the Viernezas entered the scene and knowing that they had to compete with a big clan, they started to use money. Since then, voters became used to that practice. When Calixto Cataquiz (husband of the incumbent) ran for mayor, he did the same. Vote buying in San Pedro

---

[1] http://www.wowlaguna.com/towns-and-cities/san-pedro-laguna-population-history-gov-officials-barangays-industries.

[2] http://www.wowlaguna.com/towns-and-cities/santa-rosa-laguna-about-laguna-population-barangays-gov-officials-industries/.

is now prominent. My grandfather has been through six presidential elections and has been used to being forced to contribute to whoever is campaigning because whoever will be elected tends to pressure big businesses. It has been a practice of my grandfather to set aside a certain amount for these politicians or else the operation of his business will be affected.[3]

In the 2016 local election, Lourdez Cataquiz (NP) and Iryne Vierneza won the mayoralty and vice-mayoralty race respectively, with Cataquiz garnering 52,348 votes (43.7 per cent) and Vierneza, 41,861 votes (36.7 per cent). This result was what many voters interviewed predicted. The elected mayor is a re-electionist and the vice-mayor is an incumbent councilor from the opposition. Out of 36 councilor candidates from various party groups, the elected councilors came from four party groups (LP, NPC, NP, PDP–Laban).[4]

In Sta. Rosa City, the huge amount of money needed to engineer an election campaign had narrowed down the field of candidates to three. The 2016 election worked in favour of the incumbent Liberal Party. Former 1st District Congressional Representative Dan Fernandez was elected mayor with 81,680 votes (59.8 per cent) and the brother of the outgoing mayor captured the vice-mayoralty race with 78,208 votes (59.8 per cent). Both were LP candidates. Sta. Rosa City has 181,664 registered voters but only 143,158 voted. Only 2 out of 30 councilor candidates from various other parties won and they came from the major opposition. The majority of the elected councilors came from LP.[5] In San Pedro, out of 165,073 registered electors, 124,294 voted. While in Sta. Rosa, out of a total of 181,664 registered voters, 38,506 failed to cast their ballot. Voters gave several reasons for not voting. Some did not turn up due to "abstention buying" wherein the voter was paid by the coordinator of a candidate (in this case, the mayoralty candidate for the incumbent or ruling party) to ensure that if the voter could not be convinced to vote for the particular candidate, the voter would not vote at all. Others blamed the difficulty of locating their names on the voters' list in their respective

---

[3] Interview with a councilor candidate, San Pedro, 2 May 2016.

[4] https://ph.rappler.com/elections/2016/results/philippines/Calabarzon/Laguna/San-Pedro-City/district/lonedistrict/position/6343/councilor?image=1&title=2016%20 and http://www.ivoteph.com/election-results/lag/winners-san-pedro-city-laguna-local-elections-2016-results/.

[5] http://www.ivoteph.com/election-results/lag/winners-santa-rosa-city-laguna-local-elections-2016-results/.

precincts, resulting in annoyance at the process and a loss of interest in casting their votes.

The campaign machineries of the candidates anticipated the second problem and helped voters find their precinct on the election day by placing booths at the entrance of the polling area complete with laptops and Wi-Fi connections. Names were searched from the Commission on Elections (COMELEC) website and afterwards voters were issued a card-like sheet with the face and name of a particular candidate with their cluster/precinct number indicated therein. In San Pedro, all parties set up their own individual booth to do this "public service", while in Sta. Rosa, only the ruling Liberal Party was observed setting up such a booth.[6]

CAMPAIGN STRATEGY AND THE ROLE OF PATRONAGE

The San Pedro and Sta. Rosa candidates used strategic mapping for their campaigning. They targeted specific groups for mobilisation, often with a house-to-house campaign, with or without the physical presence of the candidate. Among the groups most targeted were women, senior citizens, transport organisations, youth and church groups. Candidates also competed for the endorsement of the barangay captain as an additional effective means to saturate the grassroots level and expand the party's network. Recruitment of all these groups was on a per barangay basis and mainly through referrals. They were provided with identification cards which also served as their ticket to various social services. The incumbent mayor in San Pedro organised "*Lakas ng Kababaihan*" (Strength of Women) which served as their welcoming party in each barangay campaign. This group of women served as the advance party for each campaign stop, ensuring that events would have an impressive number of attendees. The wife of the outgoing San Pedro vice-mayor organised her own "*Gilas Kababaihan*" (Smart Women) which also served the same purpose. In Sta. Rosa, the outgoing mayor had her "*Angat Kababaihan*" (Rise Up Women), a purportedly non-government organisation that was, in fact, on the payroll, according to one re-electionist councilor.[7]

---

[6] In the case of the Sta. Rosa Liberal Party, sample ballots were used instead of the card.

[7] Interview with a councilor candidate, Sta. Rosa, 2 May 2016.

Senior citizens are also treated like royalty because of their influence on their families. Seniors were given special seats during campaign meetings and even provided with special uniforms. Candidates also fund youth projects, like summer sports fests and outings. Youth recruits are then usually connected to campaign coordinators and mobilised for the *Sangguniang Kabataan* (SK) or Youth Council elections.[8] Campaign coordinators are likewise recruited from within religious groups and tasked with influencing their churchmates and ensuring that candidates never miss an opportunity to be "prayed upon" by church leaders. Candidates also have their *suki* (regular transport providers) to bring people, *hakot*, to campaign meetings and *mitings de avance*. Finally, candidates sponsor projects among various transport organisations in order to cultivate the support of transport providers. The Sta. Rosa City Council, for example, enacted an ordinance that allowed tricycles to traverse the national road to shuttle passengers, leading to greatly increased traffic and a greater potential for accidents.

In addition to targeting key groups, most candidates direct resources to their constituents through a variety of channels. For example, provincial candidates sponsor summer basketball leagues, providing teams with uniforms and referee fees. Local candidates establish foundations or other organisations that sponsor medical missions, offer funding to local organisations, and distribute mementos like t-shirts and caps. National candidates also often support the repair and widening of roads and drainage, which is a way for candidates to claim credit for local public works.

Candidates, usually from the ruling party, sponsored private organisations' activities and responded to some personal requests. They were able to do so because they had considerable (government) funds to spend to strengthen their support base. Basic services were also provided, but interviews and casual conversations with many people show that those who were known supporters received benefits while those who were "outside the circle" needed an intermediary (barangay captain or campaign coordinator) in order to receive services they needed.

---

[8] An SK Council is elected in every barangay and oversees youth programmes in the barangay. The chairman of the SK Council also sits as an ex officio member of the Barangay Council. SK elections have traditionally been held every three years (with the last election in 2013), but new elections have been postponed as national legislators work to revamp the youth representation system.

Even the opposing party, which declared that it did not subscribe to the idea of patronage, donated benches and basketball boards, and even promised street lighting to get people's attention. Most opposition candidates engaged in the practice of "philanthropy" because they needed to build a good impression in order to win votes. An opposition mayoralty candidate, for example, used his own foundation to extend medical assistance. Another opposition candidate reported that disappointed voters tended to spread negative information if their request was declined, leaving candidates with no other choice but to respond to voters' requests:

> ... during [the] campaign period, the politicians are the victims of all kinds of abuse by many people. If you don't give they will ruin your reputation, they will make noise. ...[9]

In Sta. Rosa, the elected mayor appeared to have invested much in preparation for his candidacy as he was on his last term as congressman. He worked hard through his foundation to provide for the medical and hospitalisation needs of the constituency using pork-barrel funds. Although his original residence was in a different municipality within the same province, he worked early on to establish himself as a resident of Sta. Rosa. As both the congressman and the incumbent mayor were on their last term, it appeared that they devised a plan to maintain their hold over Sta. Rosa. The outgoing congressman authored House Bill No. 3917 to make Biñan (which is between San Pedro and Sta. Rosa) a new lone district which was easily enacted as Republic Act No. 10658 on July 2014.[10] As a result of the change, both the mayors of Sta. Rosa and Biñan ran for Congress unopposed, while the former congressman became the mayor of Sta. Rosa. All are Liberal Party members.

It is notable that, perhaps in anticipation of his run for mayor, the congressman concentrated most of his projects in Sta. Rosa, and mostly inside private subdivisions.[11] His major projects included bridges, footbridges, stadium/courts, and construction of and improvements to private subdivisions' structures, such as homeowners' association offices. His foothold in Sta. Rosa was strengthened by the "Movement", formed through his campaign director. Members of the "Movement" were issued a

---

[9] Interview with a councilor candidate, Sta. Rosa, 2 May 2016.

[10] http://www.gov.ph/2015/03/27/republic-act-no-10658/.

[11] Private subdivisions are attractive to many candidates because of the degree of organisation that usually exists within such communities, from homeowners' associations, to transport groups, to brotherhood organisations. Private subdivisions are well-defined markets that candidates seek to capture.

card which served as their ticket for access to various benefits that included scholarship grants (parents of students eventually become campaign coordinators) and medical assistance to indigents. The congressman also supported many barangay captains during the last barangay election, and as a result, all of the barangay captains of Sta. Rosa except one openly campaigned for him.

The outgoing mayor of Sta. Rosa likewise worked to build "relationships" with coordinators and barangay *liders* throughout the years of her term. One proof of such relationships was the flagrant display of the mayor's tarpaulin at the entrance to a particular barangay, with a declaration of support by that barangay. There were also tarpaulins seen in various places from other groups, such as a homeowners' association, pledging public support to the outgoing mayor and her vice-mayoralty candidate brother.

As the previous discussion suggests, candidates plant the seeds for election year-round by cultivating ties with local leaders and key groups, and responding to requests for assistance. As the election season begins, candidates cast their seeds more widely in an attempt to increase the harvest. Campaign meetings become a staple event, and at these gatherings (and other campaign events) voters can expect some sort of handout from the candidate. At one campaign meeting, I observed, for example, boxes of canned sardines and alcoholic drinks inside the open room adjacent to the campaign meeting area of one mayoralty candidate.

Candidates also distribute money directly to voters days before the election. During a casual conversation three days before the election, a tricycle driver from San Pedro told me that the opposition mayoralty candidate had already distributed money to supporters. The tricycle driver's neighbour and *cumadre* (godmother of his child) was a coordinator for that candidate and often invited him to join their group for added income. He related that coordinators had already received PhP 1,000 to work for the campaign while "members" (voters) received PhP 300 each. I observed a similar pattern in Sta. Rosa where incumbents or members of the ruling party typically distributed cash late in the afternoon or the evening before the election. Opposition candidates typically distributed their funds a few days before the election. Members/voters received PhP 200 each. In cases where campaign workers found household voters difficult to convince, those households would be asked to keep the money but stay in their houses on election day. Watchers would then be assigned to be sure that those voters did not go to the polls.

Observations at the headquarters of one campaign team revealed the kind of preparation campaigns undertake prior to election day. Lists of voters were noted inside open boxes, organised by cluster. Equally visible was a list of names from campaign headquarters, of newly recruited voters. Allowances (called transportation fare or money for cell phone loads) were provided to members of the campaign teams, depending on their position in the campaign organisation. Meals were regularly provided to visitors and campaign staff. All of these provisions were considered a motivation to "work harder" for the campaign.

Candidates differed in how much they coordinated with other campaigns. Meetings were usually held in plazas and open courts, where members of a party campaigned together. In San Pedro, they also typically went on house-to-house campaigns as one team. In Sta. Rosa, the ruling party and the opposition each campaigned in teams for some purposes (for example, house-to-house and at campaign meetings) but also pursued their own individual campaign strategy. In local elections, candidates appeared to be more open to adopting candidates from other parties. In the course of campaigning, whether house-to-house, in meetings, or in *mitings de avance*, it was common to see a mixture of candidates from various parties. This mixing strategy occurred in both locations but was more common among opposition campaigns that were not fielding a full complement of candidates. A local NPC team, for example, campaigned for the PDP–Laban presidential candidate, UNA gubernatorial candidates, and other board member independent candidates. Even some staff of Liberal Party councilor candidates openly wore the baller (customised wrist band) of Duterte. Endorsement of senatorial candidates was also mixed across parties.

Finally, another common strategy was distributing sample ballots to voters on election day. It was easy to detect who paid for the sample ballots as the name of the candidate who paid for the ballot is usually printed in bigger type than the other local candidates. In one case, a Provincial Board candidate altered the sample ballots he received from his party by pasting his name on top of the names of the other candidates for Provincial Board—a blatant message meaning "vote for me only".

How did candidates fund their campaigns? While the opponents' funds came from members of their families, supporters, and their own pockets, the campaign monies for candidates from the ruling party also came from government funds. For example, vehicles with government official plates were used during campaigns, with fuel expenses taken from municipal allocations. Likewise, incumbent campaigns were usually more generous in the distribution of campaign paraphernalia in both areas, often paid for with public funds. All this placed incumbents at a considerable advantage.

MOBILISATION STRUCTURE

The figure below shows the structure of the typical campaign network in San Pedro and Sta. Rosa:

Figure 6
The hierarchy of the campaign network

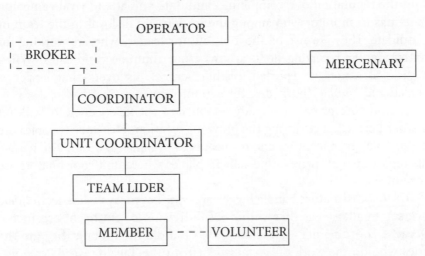

An **operator** is an individual who has such an expanded and established network that even provincial candidates hire his services. He is the chief strategist for the campaign. His "job" is often not confined to a single candidate or even a single team. In San Pedro, for example, operators help coordinate the campaign of candidates across the same team. By contrast, in Sta. Rosa operators tended to fill the role of campaign director/strategist/ manager for a single campaign. Operators in both areas conducted their own surveys to ascertain the "pulse" of the voters so that they could then act on the perceived "deficiencies" of their candidates. They also employed their own "spies" to monitor the behaviour of the other camp/s. As the election drew nearer, the operator kept watch on the overall race, including the campaigns of opposing teams. As election day approaches, a team normally drops "weak" (that is, less likely to win) members of their team or "*bando*" (band/group) in order to accommodate "strong"

candidates from other parties and thus boost the team's winnability. The operator's job is to merge the members of the opposing teams (*bando*) into one ticket. This strategy tends to work because when voters know that a *bando* also supports their chosen candidate, they reciprocate by extending similar support to the leader of the *bando*. In short, an operator supervises the overall "climate" of the campaign strategy of his client and advises the team on what they should do if he observes that the race is not favourable to his client.

There are also other "personalities" associated with the campaign. An older barangay employee revealed that **mercenaries** exist in many campaigns, and work under the operator. Their main assignment is to ruin the reputation of a competing candidate and attend rival campaign meetings to monitor who among the leaders are disloyal to the team or candidate. They are also on the look-out for leaders who are working for both sides or receiving honorariums from multiple candidates. When a disloyal leader is reported, his/her "career" is over—that leader is considered "*sunog*" (burned or thrown into the fire).

A **coordinator** has an already established clientele, generally built on his/her performance during the previous election. His "*tao*" (people) are based on a given territory and his task is to organise and mobilise people during campaign sorties, especially in places where unit coordinators are absent.

Unit coordinators handle bigger areas or barangays while team *liders* oversee smaller areas (like within a subdivision or cluster of precincts). Because coordinators are the ones who handle the money, they are the ones who do the work of "*gapangan*" (from the Tagalog word "*gapang*", which means crawl), that is, infiltrating the enemy's camp, usually on the eve of the election. Prior to the *gapangan*, coordinators identify the "weak" barangays in terms of sure votes. The campaign concentrates on those areas and targets influential intermediaries in the area who can help convince the voters to change their mind. Unit coordinators and/ or their intermediaries knock on the doors of each identified household to instruct them not to vote if they cannot be convinced to vote for their candidate. Unit coordinators receive regular pay as well as a "cut" from the amount they give to team members under their supervision. There are also some who just pocket the total amount for themselves rather than a percentage cut. These coordinators justify their "job" as a better way to earn money compared to just being idle or engaging in illegal acts.

Team *liders* each recruit 10–20 members, who, in turn, must enlist another 10–20 members within their area. In this way, a team works to saturate each area to secure "command votes". These members start as **volunteers**, and begin by wearing campaign shirts/caps and distributing propaganda sheets. In exchange for their efforts they receive food and free transportation to designated campaign areas. Those who prove good recruiters and help the network grow are rewarded with promotion to team *lider* with the equivalent increase in "income" (team *liders* are paid more than members). Members who show no interest in recruiting other members are just being "paid" to vote.

Finally, alongside the formal, official campaign structure is a network of **brokers** (dashed box). These are influential individuals with ties to the candidates and who mobilise votes on behalf of the candidate. *Liders* also serve as brokers but brokers can also include individuals who are not officially part of the formal campaign structure. Barangay captains are a prime example. In the Philippines, barangay captains are supposed to be non-partisan, but the rule is openly violated. A campaign manager declared without hesitation that the barangay captains have been part of their campaign machinery.[12] Barangay captains serve as **brokers**, with their *kagawads* (barangay councilors and barangay health workers) serving as coordinators.

Two women I talked to attending a campaign meeting disclosed that the Mayor of San Pedro gave each barangay captain a new car to ensure their support:

> *Bago mag-umpisa and kampanya, namigay si mayor ng bagong kotse sa mga barangay kapitan. Yung Kapitan namin di na binigyan. Kasi mayaman na s'ya tsaka makakalaban sa eleksyon* (Before the campaign started, the mayor gave each barangay captain a new car. Our barangay captain was never included among those who received it because he is already rich and he will be one of the opponents in the coming election.)[13]

A TALE OF COORDINATORS

Anybody's curiosity could be aroused upon seeing tarpaulins with the pictures of the officers of different organisations taken together with the

---

[12] Interview with a campaign manager, Sta. Rosa, 6 May 2016.
[13] Interview, San Pedro, 21 April 2016. A new car at one barangay hall at San Pedro was seen side by side with a new ambulance during an interview conducted on 4 May 2016.

incumbent mayor. Two messages were very prominent: (1) "We Support (*Name of the Candidate*)" and (2) "This Barangay is supported by (*Name of the Candidate*)". From the information I gathered, I learned that the barangay captain was a supporter of the outgoing mayor, who has been sponsoring their barangay neighbourhood association for a considerable length of time. The place used to have a single coordinator (Coordinator #1), but eventually one "down liner" (and local *lider*) formed a group of her own (Coordinator #2, who is also a barangay health worker), though she still supports the same candidate and party. Coordinator #1 assumed that Coordinator #2 formed her own group in order to enjoy the power and all the perks attached to being a coordinator.[14]

The barangay in question lies along a river and its residents are composed of informal settlers who have been living in the area for more than two decades. These coordinators have been in close contact with all levels of the local government—from barangay captain to the mayor. Coordinator #2 was thankful to the former congressional representative (who was elected mayor in 2016), because the latter provided funds to repair the bridge at the back of her house, thereby lessening the flooding in their area during typhoons.[15] When her husband suffered a stroke, the "Movement" founded by this candidate gave her family all the assistance they needed, including payment for all medical procedures and maintenance medicines. She also fully supported the barangay captain because, in her role as a barangay health worker, she knew she could call him whenever needed. She remained loyal to the barangay captain, even as stronger opposition candidates campaigned in the barangay promising better governance. She insisted that she believed in those who have already done something. She was prudent to resist possible monetary offers because a thousand pesos, for example, would be gone in a minute. But if the incumbent's team wins, the benefits they have been receiving will continue. She related what she has been saying to others as she campaigns:

> *Kung manalo ang sinusuportahan natin, ilang taon din natin mapapakinabangan ang suporta nila? Sa ngayon may boses tayo* (If the candidate we are supporting wins, just imagine how many years we can benefit from their support? Right now, they are attentive to our requests.)[16]

---

[14] Interview with Coordinator #1, Sta. Rosa, 3 May 2016.
[15] Interview with Coordinator #2, Sta. Rosa, 3 May 2016.
[16] Ibid.

She even gladly related to me that the outgoing mayor and her brother (the current vice-mayor) never hesitated to have meals with them (*boodle fight*) despite difference in their social status.

Coordinator #1 related that she met the incumbent mayor for the first time when the latter invited her to the oath-taking of officers of their neighbourhood association. She asked for the mayor's phone number and was surprised when the mayor willingly gave it to her. The mayor further endeared herself to Coordinator #1 when she replied to her texts, assuring her that the mayor was just a text away whenever the neighbourhood needed help. The mayor wholly supported whatever project she initiated, like the feeding programme she organised to coincide with their high school reunion, or her (failed) bid for barangay council *kagawad* (councilor). When one of her relatives died the mayor took care of everything so that her family never spent a single centavo. Likewise the mayor helped sponsor her daughter's grand debut celebration, and sponsored and supported her children's free education up to the tertiary level—something she can never forget.

Given the continued support from the mayor, this coordinator told me, it is simply fair that she return all the favours she has been enjoying. "It is now the proper time to pay back the benefit I have been enjoying from the present administration." She challenged those who will not accept her offer, reminding them that in due time they will need help and she can provide assistance from office-holders ranging from councilors up to the mayor. All they have to do is vote for the candidate for whom she is campaigning.[17] Because coordinators have easy access to the office of the mayor, a network has been established and residents allow themselves to be listed as "members" of the campaign party. This is a sort of assurance that they will be given priority for whatever assistance they will need in the future if this coordinator's candidates win.

Coordinator #1 has a retail variety store and she uses her daily contact with people to convince them to join her team to support her candidate. She is also planning to run as a *Barangay Kagawad* in the next election and if her candidate wins she is assured of his support for her own campaign. According to her, one of the advantages of being a coordinator is to be of help to many people. She can always act as a liaison bringing anybody to the elected officials any time, even outside of election season.

---

[17] The same gratitude was expressed by a barangay staffer in San Pedro who directly influences indigents to vote for the incumbent, mainly because she herself benefitted from the incumbent mayor.

Her connection with the candidates and elected officials is on a day-to-day basis via telephone. She pointed out that it is a reality that many voters in Sta. Rosa expect money during elections. Most would-be voters usually say, "*May pagkakaperahan ba d'yan?*" (Is there money in there?). This is street slang which means, "Can I earn something from that?" or "What will I gain in exchange?". One new candidate related that the previous mayor who lost the race reported that, "before, the voters would be happy for 300 pesos. Now they would even cuss you [if that is all you offer]".[18]

Coordinator #1 also noted that the deliberate distribution of money (PhP 200 minimum) has become the new trend. Those who attend the *miting de avance* receive a PhP 200 allowance plus meals. (It was also common to see "registration tables" during *miting de avance* where the money would change hands.) In her eyes this was just fair compensation for people's time, which could have been used for other productive activities. Over the years Coordinator #1 has worked for campaigns in a variety of capacities. Starting out as a "volunteer", she just received a t-shirt and meals. Once she became a coordinator she began receiving PhP 300 for every meeting she attended (*liders* receive PhP 200). In December 2015 this amount was upped to PhP 500 and all of the coordinators received Christmas gift packs. Those who distributed flyers during the campaign (which includes children) received PhP 100. The night before the election, the members (voters) on her list each received PhP 200 in exchange for their vote.[19]

Coordinators and leaders act as liaisons between people in need and people in positions of power, which probably creates a certain level of elevated self-esteem as well as identification with the position of power or feeling of self-importance. Rewards are both intrinsic and extrinsic. As Coordinator #1 puts it, "One of the advantages of being a coordinator is being able to help many people. I can always bring anybody to the elected officials any time even not during election season."[20] Coordinator #2 concurs, stating that, "I can come to the office of the mayor without passing through anyone except that I have to inform the Kapitan that I will be going to the mayor's office and request him to inform the staff that I will be coming, and that's it."[21]

---

[18] Interview with a councilor candidate in Sta. Rosa, 28 April 2016.

[19] Election day presents additional opportunities for some voters to make extra money. For example, tricycle drivers are hired by the campaign to shuttle voters to the polling precinct then back to their own barangay.

[20] Interview with Coordinator #1, 3 May 2016.

[21] Interview with Coordinator #2, 3 May 2016.

For candidates, the presence of a coordinator or a campaign leader within the family circle is a way of establishing solid support in preparation for future campaigning. A daughter of one campaign coordinator for the incumbent in San Pedro has already inherited the trade from her late mother, who reminded her children before she died to maintain their loyalty to the political family she had supported.[22] Her siblings are also coordinators now.

In another area, a barangay staffer who is a member of a religious group that says men should occupy positions of leadership said that her group ironically supports re-election of the incumbent (a female) because of their first-hand experience with her. The staffer said that the services provided by the local government had been continuous and did not favour any person or affiliation. On one occasion the staffer joined the mayor's house-to-house campaign and observed that the mayor never distributed any cash.[23] She pointed out that the mayor did not even know whom she had been helping and that made her admire the incumbent more.[24]

What can we draw from these experiences about why voters and campaign workers support certain candidates? Two Filipino concepts are helpful here: *pakikisama* (getting along well with people) and *utang na loob* (debt of gratitude). These may not be explicitly referred to by candidates or their supporters but they have been embedded in most Filipinos' consciousness. In his study of Philippine slums, Jocano argues that *pakikisama* "suggests a number of related-tendencies, like 'giving-in' to another person's wish, demands, wants, or desires. It is a subtle form of coercion, ranging from simple politeness to deliberate yielding of one's own idea, position, or principle in favour of those of another for future concessions or immediate reward" (Jocano 2002: 196–7). The Filipino culture is relational. A candidate's *pakikisama* time is a crucial tool in influencing voters, especially among the marginalised sector.

The second undeniably effective trait is the building of *utang na loob* (debts of gratitude). T-shirts, caps, food items, cash or assistance create a feeling of gratitude that can translate into solid support for a candidate.[25]

---

[22] Interview with a campaign coordinator, San Pedro, 29 April 2016. The incumbent covered the cost of her mother's wake and funeral.

[23] Distribution of cash does not happen during very public house-to-house campaigns because a spy from the other camp might document the act and file a case with the Election Commission (COMELEC).

[24] Interview with a barangay staffer, San Pedro, 4 May 2016.

[25] There are coordinators who campaign solidly for the mayor and his team but also accommodate other candidates for councilor for personal (not monetary) reasons, like their being a cumpadre, cumadre, friend of a relative, classmate, churchmate, etc.

There are a few (like the two coordinators discussed above) who never expected a favour at first, but experiences like a mayor's directly answering a text from a lowly constituent or a continuous supply of medicine for a sick family member overwhelmed them and produced a degree of indebtedness that no amount of money coming from the opposing candidates could change.

CONCLUSION

Based on the details presented in this chapter, the techniques that build an effective campaign strategy can be categorised into three levels: (1) establishing the target group of voters, some of whom can also be part of the campaign machinery itself; (2) investing in social relationships; and (3) constantly building and strengthening a network of supporters. The data also show that while most candidates promised to provide for the basic needs of their constituents, they still had to distribute money during elections in order to ensure their win. The simple reason for this is that they cannot directly and personally help enough voters to secure a victory. Those candidates who help their supporters and target communities at the grassroots levels by promising them that development will come if they choose the right candidate could still lose if they don't sow more seeds with cash during elections. In addition, voters increasingly demand instant gratification of their requests, and many candidates invest by providing for those demands to ensure votes.

Votes, in other words, have become a commodity and many voters are very particular about how they will personally benefit from the transaction. The buying and selling of votes is now part of the electoral process, and the more benefits voters gain before and during elections, the firmer their loyalty to the incumbent.

While politicians are incentivised to respond to voter demands for assistance, the current state of affairs reflects weaknesses in the Philippines' democratic system. Making access to some social services contingent on ties to a politician has created dependency on these politicians. As the people seek help for their needs, politicians' display of their personal "concern" for voters, coupled with answered requests, is an act of planting seeds and creates an instrumental link with voters. But the benefits of these personal interactions remain necessarily limited to a subset of voters. This personalisation and commodification of politics and elections has become a defining feature of democracy in the Philippines, to the detriment of a fuller, more participatory democracy.

Table 6
Election results from Laguna 1st District

Candidate	Party	Office	Per cent (%)
* Indicates incumbent candidate			
Arcillas, Arlene	LP	House of Representatives	100.00
Hernandez, Ramil	NP	Provincial Governor	51.14
Ejercito, Jorge Antonio	IND	Provincial Governor	28.42
Ejercito, Emilio Ramon III	UNA	Provincial Governor	19.66
Alberto, Berlene	IND	Provincial Governor	00.51
Sucano, Nemesio	IND	Provincial Governor	00.26
Agapay, Karen	NP	Provincial Vice-Governor	45.61
Lajara, Christian Niño	UNA	Provincial Vice-Governor	32.12
Alarva, Angelica Jones	LP	Provincial Vice-Governor	19.75
San Sebastian, Bro Rico G.	IND	Provincial Vice-Governor	2.52
City of San Pedro			
Cataquiz, Lourdes*	NP	Mayor	43.72
Campos, Raffy	PDPLBN	Mayor	27.92
Ynion, Eugenio Jr.	NPC	Mayor	26.25
Casacop, Michael	PRP	Mayor	2.11
Vierneza, Iryne	PDPLBN	Vice-Mayor	36.72
Tayao, Diwa	NP	Vice-Mayor	34.09
Solidum, Norvic	NPC	Vice-Mayor	29.19
City of Santa Rosa			
Fernandez, Dan	LP	Mayor	59.84
Gomez, Arnel	NPC	Mayor	35.01
Lazaga, Alice	PDPLBN	Mayor	5.14
Arcillas, Arnold	LP	Vice-Mayor	59.82
Aala, Tess	NPC	Vice-Mayor	27.16
Laserna, Sonia	AKSYON	Vice-Mayor	13.02

chapter **7**

First District of Makati: Signs of an Electoral Backslide and Challenges to a Local Dynasty

Cleo Calimbahin

INTRODUCTION

Makati is one of the 16 cities that make up Metro Manila. It is the Philippines' foremost financial, commercial and business district, generating an annual revenue of PhP 11 billion (Vilas-Alavaren 2016). Makati is home to the Philippines' old rich creole and Chinese mestizo families who control the economy and live in the gated exclusive communities near the business district. Makati is also where one finds multinational firms and international organisations who have their main offices in Ayala Avenue. But Makati's modernity and affluence are just two facets of the city.

Makati has two districts. District 1, the focus of this study, is composed of 20 barangays and these include both the gated and expensive barangay Forbes Park as well as Olympia and Pio Del Pilar barangays where a number of urban informal settlers reside. While the latter barangays are much poorer, they are the vote-rich areas of the city. Every politician knows that it is the support of Makati's urban poor that is key to winning and keeping an electoral position, more so than the support of wealthy Makati residents. The Binay family knows this. The family has been the incumbent dynastic family of Makati for the last 30 years. Yet what was very telling in the 2016 election was the slim winning margin of Abby Binay against Kid Pena. While Abby Binay scraped into victory, she lost in District 1, her father's bailiwick. Overall, it was not dynasty candidate Abby Binay who captured the most votes, but ally and candidate for Vice-Mayor, Monique Lagdameo, who got the largest number of votes at 172,950 and won both in Districts 1 and 2 (see Appendix for a table summarising the election results).

This chapter describes the closely knit national-local election campaign in Makati in the 2016 election, with Team Binay overtly campaigning as a family brand rather than as a party. By cultivating the Binay brand, the family courted personal votes through patronage and dispensing public services as personal favours. The family hoped winning the presidency, mayoralty, and local slates would secure the Binay family's control of its power base, Makati. The 2016 election was a watershed moment that shows some slight signs that the political landscape of the city is likely to change in subsequent elections. I will also review the broad political history of Makati and identify trends that have led to the expansion and contraction of the Binay dynasty.

BACKGROUND ON THE REGION

It was not too long ago when Makati was all swamp and *talahib* (overgrown grass). In 1951 the Ayala Company developed their property and created exclusive enclaves such as Forbes Park, San Lorenzo, Bel Air, and Urdaneta (Alegre 1998). One observer describes the change that followed: "The city, which used to be a poor muncipio teeming with tall and wildly growing hay grass, suddenly began to bustle with prosperity because of bonanza incomes from the business and property taxes that were generated from these Ayala development projects" (Abesamis 2016). The Ayala family remains the primary developer and land owner of Makati even as they have expanded their property portfolio in other parts of Metro Manila.

Today Makati hosts the main offices of the country's largest banks, insurance companies, multinational firms, holding companies and large luxury hotels used for international conferences and summits. Yet behind the façade of modernity is a Makati that is plagued with underemployment, illegal settlements, poverty, and illicit drug trade and use. Makati only gained cityhood in 1994. Makati's government suffers from allegations of corruption, kickbacks, and dynastic politics similar to many far-flung provinces in the Philippines. Makati has a history of traditional and tough political leadership, with limited turnover. Maximo B. Estrella was mayor from 1956 to 1969. Nemencio Yabut was mayor from 1971 to 1986. He was succeeded by Jejomar Binay in 1986 after the EDSA Revolution. As a human rights lawyer active in the anti-Marcos struggle, Binay was a trusted ally and supporter of Corazon Aquino. He was appointed Officer-In-Charge (OIC) of Makati to unseat Yabut, who was identified with the deposed dictator Ferdinand Marcos. Binay served as OIC for two years and won as mayor in the 1988 election. Since then, Jejomar Binay, his wife Elenita and their son, Junjun Binay have held the position of mayor. In 2010, Jejomar Binay ran for and won the position of vice-president. By 2013, three of his children held public office simultaneously with him: Nancy Binay as senator, Abigail Binay as congresswoman of the 2nd District of Makati, and prior to the Office of the Ombudsman's dismissal of him for graft, Junjun Binay as mayor. These developments constituted a clear vertical dynastic expansion, while keeping the local power base secured. In total, the Binays have controlled the City of Makati for three decades, with patriarch, presidential candidate, and incumbent Vice-President Jejomar Binay at the family's head. Typical of the dynastic nature of politics in the Philippines, term limits only mean the position is passed on to other members of the family, ensuring continuity.

Makati mayors had very strong ties with their patrons at the national level and projected fierce and tough images. A former Makati Councilor, Robert Brillante, observed that in Makati, "people need to fear you" (Gloria 1995: 92). All three mayors of Makati came from simple and poor beginnings. Maximo Estrella was born in Quiapo, a busy and commercial part of Manila that is also home to low- and middle-income families. Estrella worked as a seaman. Both Yabut and Binay came from less well-known parts of Makati, not the Ayala-developed gated villages where only the wealthy can afford to live. In the course of their public service, Yabut and Binay (along with the latter's children) eventually moved into those exclusive enclaves, although entry into those gated villages does not mean social acceptance by their residents. Tensions between the economic elite of Makati and the *municipio* or political elite arose from a combination of the dynamics of power and the personalities involved that is unique to Makati. Yabut, for example, experienced a rejection and cold reception from the old rich mestizo families of the exclusive Forbes Park when residents of this gated village petitioned the homeowners' association that the mayor not be allowed to move in (Gloria 1995). Junjun Binay (son of Jejomar), while mayor of Makati, was refused access to one of the exit gates in another posh Makati Village. Security video footage showed him and his bodyguards in heated conversation with the armed guards of the village (Diola 2013).

Upper middle-class sensibilities are also offended by the corrupt practices in the *municipio*. But political participation remains occasional and minimal for this social class. A few members of the economic elite might be vocal critics, and they might field one of "their own" against the Binays, but they are not part of the grit and grime of Makati politics. The economic elite of Makati are seemingly oblivious to the many poor people who enter these gated villages on foot every morning to service the fine homes, tend to their large, manicured lawns, and work at the Polo Club of Makati. These are the poor in and at the periphery of Makati, who vote for the Estrellas, the Yabuts, and the Binays.

Jejomar Binay built his career and reputation in part by responding to the needs of the poor in Makati. (Neither his wife nor those among his children who have held public office have had the same following as the patriarch.) Even those who worked for the campaign of Makati opposition candidates admired the older Binay and were quick to say that, "*si Tandang Binay, mabait talaga, madaling lapitan at matulungin sa amin. Lalo na noong bago pa lang siya. Wala sa mga anak niya ang katulad niya*"[1] (the older Binay is really kind and helpful to us, easy to approach especially when he was just starting. None of his children are like him. No one can dispute that Binay has extended popular social services to the elderly and poor of Makati. Under Binay, Makati provided yellow cards granting free hospitalisation, allowances for senior citizens, and free uniforms and education extended to Makati children: these are tangible and highly visible projects that win votes and hearts in the poor districts of Makati.

Makati's local government is often tied to national politics because of patronage ties to the presidential palace, Malacañang. The city gained prominence at the national level right before and after the 1986 People Power revolution that ousted President Ferdinand Marcos. When yellow confetti paper started falling down the windows of the tall buildings on Ayala in tribute to slain opposition leader Ninoy Aquino, it was a signal of an awakening of the elite and middle class. No longer were the anti-Marcos rallies limited to university students, the religious, or labour and peasant groups affiliated with the Communist Party; the rallies were now gaining broader support from the middle class. The yellow confetti symbolised the

---

[1] Interview with TeamKidKarla community leaders in a large meeting in Barangay San Antonio.

coming home of an opposition leader and support for his widow against the dictatorship. Post-Marcos Makati was often ground zero in battles for control of government. For example, the leaders of one attempted coup d'état against Corazon Aquino holed up in Makati's Atrium building and subsequent mutinies were staged in the Peninsula Hotel and in Oakwood Residences against President Gloria Macapagal Arroyo.

THE LOCAL–NATIONAL NEXUS

The 2016 election was a significant election for Makati as Binay aimed for the presidency. Of District 1's 189,215 registered voters, more than a third (35 per cent) were aged 24–35 and had not known any mayor other than Jejomar Binay and the Binay family. To understand what happened in the 2016 local election necessarily means discussing national politics and the 2016 presidential race, in which Binay competed. Known for careful planning and strategising, as early as 2010 when he ran for vice-president, Binay had a poster in his campaign headquarters with the following words, "*Ang dapat maging Pangulo ng Pilipinas*" (the one who should be president of the Philippines). What he did not foresee was that he would be fighting to hold on to the family's bailiwick and clear the name of his son who had been dismissed as mayor for plunder in 2015. For the first time in 30 years of electoral experience, Binay did not have all three factors in his winning formula: masses, money, and *municipio* (Gloria 1995: 90). Due to Junjun's ouster for plunder, a non-Binay family member and non-Binay ally was mayor of Makati in the run up to the 2016 election.

The 2016 election was a tense and tight race between Team KidKarla of the Liberal Party (LP) and Team Binay of the United Nationalist Alliance (UNA). Abby Binay and Monique Lagdameo led Team Binay, while the LP's Team KidKarla had acting mayor Kid Pena and Karla Mercado, daughter of Makati whistle-blower and former Binay ally, Ernesto Mercado. Kid Pena had climbed Makati's political ladder like most of the councilors from both LP and UNA. Initially active in youth-related activities, he graduated into barangay leadership and then eventually occupied regular council seats. Pena ran as an independent and won several elections, a testament to his popularity in District 1. Many residents of Makati know Pena as an avid motor biker. From his days working as a pizza delivery rider to his regular presence in funeral convoys as a rider, Pena could be seen in and around Makati on his motor bike (Inquirer Archives 2016). He won as vice-mayor in 2013, an upset that took everyone by surprise. Running alongside Pena for the 2016 election was political neophyte

Karla Mercado. Even though she had no prior experience running for a local position, the LP were banking on the Mercado surname. She is the daughter of Ernesto Mercado, whistle-blower against the Binays and a former close ally of the family. Both Pena and the older Mercado are very familiar with the way Makati is run by the Binays.

In this election, the Liberal Party knew they were within striking distance of ending the Binays' hold in Makati. But UNA could not afford to lose the Binay family bailiwick. As the ranking of Jejomar Binay in the presidential surveys declined and eventually dropped from number one to the trailing rank of third, what was initially an easy walk to Malacañang became an uphill battle. Complicating matters was the dismissal of Binay's son Junjun as mayor, and his subsequent disqualification from holding public office for life. It became necessary for daughter Congresswoman Abby Binay to run for mayor of Makati. Abby Binay, however, was looking to retire from politics and become a stay-at-home mom, admitting that in the past year, her husband Luis Campos had been meeting with the constituents of District 2 because the plan was for him to run for Congress once her term expired in 2016 (Cepeda 2015).

Running in tandem with Abby Binay for vice-mayor was long-time Binay family ally and congresswoman from District 1, Monique Lagdameo. Observers of Makati politics say both Abby and Monique are very good at the grassroots level and worked hard to do house-to-house visits during the campaign, despite Abby being a reluctant candidate. The young women were a formidable team.

As a result of Abby Binay and Lagdameo moving down the slate to run for mayor and vice-mayor, UNA had to revamp their slate and fielded less well-known allies to run for the House of Representatives for Districts 1 and 2. The focus was to secure city hall with Abby Binay, Monique Lagdameo, and eight very loyal councilors such as Ferdie Eusebio and Ichi Yabut (the Yabuts, previously foes, have become allies of the Binays in order to return to Makati politics). The councilors, all loyal to the family, once elected would be united behind both the mayor and vice-mayor. The LP's Team KidKarla were caught by surprise by the sudden change in the line-up of Team Binay—which was now fielding their strongest possible tandem against Pena's LP team—and realised that it was going to be tougher to win city hall for a full three-year term.[2]

The Binays' strategy was to secure city hall in the event that the plan to get to Malacañang fell through. All eight councilors of the UNA party won in District 1. UNA likewise secured District 1's seat in the lower house, a

---

[2] Interview with Nico Garcia.

position previously held by Lagdameo. The Binays usually campaign for the full slate in order to have a council that will not oppose them. A former ally of the Binays who served in the local barangay council talks about why it is important to secure the entire council: "Corruption goes unchecked in the municipal hall because the body supposed to balance the power configuration there tolerates the short-cut methods of allocating funds for certain projects. It is ... a rubber stamp council" (Gloria 1995: 81).

VULNERABILITY WITH VERTICAL EXPANSION

When Pena won in 2013 as vice-mayor, no one anticipated that it was crucial to secure that position with a trusted Binay family ally. In 2013 the Binay family engaged in a vertical dynastic expansion. The mid-term election marked the first time the Binay family simultaneously campaigned for two national-level positions, a seat in Congress and a seat in the Senate, while at the same time securing the mayoralty. In order to do this, the Binays broke away from PDP–Laban and created their own political party. Running a national campaign for daughter Nancy Binay for a seat in the Senate, and forming a newly-hatched party, UNA, the Binays were not able to focus on the vice-mayoral race. Kid Pena won as vice-mayor with 120,893 votes while Junjun Binay's running mate, Marge De Veyra won only 113,815 votes. Cracks were starting to show in the Binay campaign. That Kid Pena was not a close ally of the Binays became evident when Vice-Mayor Pena was given a small room on another floor in city hall for his office, a clear signal that he would have nothing to do with Junjun Binay and his allied councilors. Abby Binay and Monique Lagdameo, both elected to the House of Representatives from the two districts of Makati, took over Pena's office. Two years later, the unpredictability of politics actually put Pena in the right place, at the right time. The unexpected dismissal of Junjun suddenly made Pena mayor of Makati, the first non-Binay family member to hold the post in 30 years.

CAMPAIGN STRATEGY AND MOBILISATION STRUCTURE

Both the LP and UNA ran gruelling campaigns that showed how important the local Makati election was. For every round of house-to-house visits, small or large meeting each party had, the other party set up a parallel one. Posters put up in the morning would be torn down by night by the opponent. Mini-cabs with large speakers continuously went around District 1 playing campaign jingles and songs along with brief messages from candidates. Supporters calling house-to-house gave out flyers and leaflets. Long-time residents of District 1 whispered allegations that large families received PhP 5,000 from both sides, while another rumour said Pena's team leaders received PhP 100,000 to disburse.[3]

In building a reputation for social caring, the Binays could make use of two foundations attached to the family. One is the JC Binay Foundation, which provides financial and material assistance during calamities, and a lesser known one is called Serbisyong Tunay Foundation. The 100,000 members of the Serbisyong Tunay receive social services and benefits over and above what the Makati government extends.[4] These are a sure 100,000 votes that do not rely on seasonal dispensing of patronage. Getting figures on campaign expenditure and patronage payouts from both sides was difficult. Historically, a former Binay ally suspected that Binay spent PhP 20 million on the 1988 election and double that amount during the 1992 election (Gloria 1995: 94). In 2016, between the costs of Binay's campaign for the presidency and those that went into the effort to keep control of the family's local bailiwick in Makati, it is hard to believe Binay's Statement of Campaign Expenditure (SOCE) and UNA's declaration of expenses, which together only amounted to PhP 463 million (Gutierez 2016).[5] According to AC Nielsen records, Binay's TV advertising alone cost PhP 1. 6 billion (Rodriguez 2016).

In order to secure Makati while Binay fought to get to Malacañang, the campaign in Makati was focused on the name Binay. The team was called Team Binay. Their campaign song repeated the refrain "only Binay", and highlighted the benefits of living in Makati under Binay, such as free medicines, schools, etc. which other local government units could and should be dispensing but do not. It was also a stroke of genius to keep their tag lines as simple as Team Binay and Only Binay. Posters, which were prominently displayed, showed the elder Binay with Abby Binay. There were hardly any posters of individual councilors. The campaign was efficient because it combined a focus on Makati, specifically daughter Abby, with Jejomar's bid for Malacañang.

In contrast, the Liberal Party's Team KidKarla focused on "*ang bagong Makati*" (a new Makati). Initially, posters with the team colours

---

[3] Interview with Mang Ruben, 2016.
[4] See website of JC Binay and Serbisyong Tunay.
[5] This is apart from PhP 1.6 billion pre-election spending from TV ads from AC Nielson (Cepeda 2016).

of Team KidKarla, which were green and yellow, showed different faces of Makatenos enjoying the benefits of living in Makati. The message was an attempt to counter the Binays' penchant for putting their own family names and faces on every shed, bench, and building in Makati. It was simple but effective messaging. Even those who were unimpressed by the LP slate in Makati considered voting straight for the party because the Binays had started to manifest an overbearing sense of ownership of Makati.

In her proclamation rally, Abby Binay told the crowds, "*kailangan ng Makati ang serbisyong Binay at kailangan namin ang supporta niyo*" (Makati needs the Binay brand of service and we need you). In the same rally, Abby Binay shed tears while addressing her father, Vice-President Jejomar Binay. She also sang a song and, along with her husband, her vice-mayoral candidate and the rest of the council, danced to please the crowd. The host of the opposing Liberal Party's Team KidKarla pointed out in one large meeting, "*kalian niyo silang huling nakitang umiyak, kumanta at sumayaw? Ngayon na lang dahil alam nila na gusto na natin ng pagbabago*" (when was the last time you saw them cry, dance, and sing in a campaign? It is only now because they know that the people want change).[6]

But even as the people clamoured for change, strong networks built over time do not disappear overnight. Most of the barangay captains remained loyal to the Binays. The system of patronage dispensing that they built was mobilised in a very effective manner, including food distribution (for the proclamation rally, there was a designated area where those who came from the barangays with their leaders took their meals), attendance at small and large meetings, and disbursement of allowances. The incumbent advantage included the ties of Jejomar Binay to many voters as *kumpare* (godfather) in their marriages and baptisms, his ability to make quick referrals to the city's social services office, and his distribution of patronage in the form of offering work, including hiring constituents as poll watchers as a way to disburse money to the voters.

The rhetoric of change from the Liberal Party was riding on the wave of new information, charges, and allegations that tainted and threatened the Binay brand. When Ernesto Mercado whistle-blew on Makati land deals with Roberto Ongpin, the rigged procurement process that favoured contractors, and the complicated financial schemes involving close Binay allies as fronts, suddenly there was more substance to what many already

---

[6] Host in Team KidKarla parallel proclamation in District 1.

knew and talked about. Yet the ratings of Binay did not immediately plunge. In fact, foreign journalists asked why the people remained indifferent to the massive corruption allegations (Moss 2014).

Yet the result of the 2016 election shows that corruption as an issue matters for voters. This election was a close one—closer than people expected, given that the alternative ticket did not have a track record that could erase doubts as to how they were going to run city hall. What was clear was that a political opportunity for the opposition materialised. The disqualification of the heir apparent in Makati, Junjun Binay, threw a monkey wrench into what would otherwise have been a clear succession process among family members. But it was this expected succession that brought about the threat. Political allies who were loyal realised that at no point would they be part of the succession plan, so while they could still benefit from the Binay resources, they had little hope of ascending the political ladder themselves.

Very early on 10 May, at the Barangay Hall in District 1's Barangay San Antonio, the barangay of the Binay patriarch, I asked the police stationed there if the results were out. A man in civilian clothes—but who struck me as someone who could be a local *siga* (thug)—sitting alongside the uniformed policemen bellowed out with indifference, "*diretso*". By that he meant that the full Team Binay slate had won. Team KidKarla had made a strong showing, considering that they did not have the same resources and that fewer supporters showed up for their proclamation and *miting de avance* that attended Team Binay sorties.

It is also interesting to note that the most votes were received by Monique Lagdameo. A veteran of elections, starting as a member of the Sangguniang Kabataan (SK) or the Youth Council from Barangay Forbes Park, Lagdameo scored high in both Districts 1 and 2, while Abby Binay lost in District 1, her father's original district. Lagdameo had the advantage of support from Team Binay and UNA, yet could distance herself from the Binays because her name had not been mentioned in any of their corruption scandals involving procurement and government contracts. She was a loyal Binay supporter, and was widely perceived to be part of the core group of the Binay family, and so she could get the votes of loyal Binay supporters. But she also had crossover appeal and the ability to win votes from those not in favour with the Binays. It will be interesting to watch her future role in Makati politics. If she is sufficiently popular, she will need less Binay support in the future. If she is forward thinking and genuinely concerned with Makati, she could continue the Binay brand but with a new type of leadership.

The ties that bind Lagdameo to the Binays run deep. Enrique Lagdameo, Monique's father who comes from a well-to-do family, is the treasurer of the Boy Scouts, which Binay has led for the last 20 years (Vitug 2015). The Boy Scouts had recently been in the news because of a land sale that allegedly provided Binay with a PhP 600 million commission (Calonzo 2016). Enrique Lagdameo was likewise listed as one of the biggest donors for Binay in the 2016 presidential election (Ballahara and Magsambol 2016). Monique Lagdameo is poised to be a contender for the mayoral position in the future. The larger question remains whether Lagdameo can do it alone without the Binays' support, given her strong vote in 2016. Lagdameo can bring a new kind of leadership to Makati, one that is not tarred with corruption allegations. At the moment, however, it does not look like she will break from the patronage ties that bind her and her father.

DYNASTIC EXPANSION AND CONTRACTION

As mentioned above, in the 2016 election the local politics of Makati was even more linked than usual to the national politics of the Philippines. As one of the stronger contenders for the presidency, Binay's political opponents took advantage of the allegations of corruption against him and his family to strengthen their image in an election year, at the expense of Binay. For more than eight months, starting in the second quarter of 2015, the Senate conducted 25 hearings on allegations of corruption against Jejomar Binay and his son, Junjun Binay. It was continuous, aired on national television, and covered by media on radio and in print. The public saw pictures of mansions and a mistress that was all too reminiscent of how a former president fell from grace.

Just three years before, in 2013, the Binay family had successfully occupied the executive branch, had gained seats in the two houses of the legislative branch, and had controlled Makati's local politics. The country was witnessing the successful horizontal and, eventually, vertical expansion of a well-planned dynasty. But the dynasty experienced a contraction in 2016, buffeted by corruption scandals and by the disqualification from public office for life of then Mayor Junjun Binay. As a dynasty expands vertically, challenges from below at the level of local politics can combine with separate challenges from above. In the case of Makati, a local whistle-blower found an ally with national-level elites who saw the Binay dynasty as a threat. Dynastic families can decline in response to such dual challenges. In the case of the Binays, the challenge from below took out Junjun Binay as mayor while the challenge from above focused on the patriarch.

What caused the sudden contraction of the Binay dynasty was a confluence of events and decisions by personalities both within the Binay camp and among state actors outside the reach of the Binays. Binay ran Makati on a tight leash, like he runs his campaigns. Over the years, many people had become close confidants of Jejomar Binay. Over the years, he had also had a history of falling out with those close to him. The challenge from below came from a well-known Makati politician and close ally of the Binays who became a witness against his former patron. Ernesto Mercado had served Binay loyally as vice-mayor, and he was supposed to take over the mayoral post vacated when the older Binay ran for higher office. But the Binays reneged on the deal and let son Junjun run instead. When he blew the whistle on an overpriced Makati parking building involving Junjun, this was Mercado's way of getting even with the Binays. While the people of Makati can generally speak only in hushed tones about rumours of kickbacks and rigged contracts in Makati City Hall, Mercado knew the details. It was harder for the Binays to deny allegations when the witness was from within their own ranks.

Mercado was both a credible and an entertaining witness. Without missing a beat, he narrated in Senate Hearings how things worked in city hall and how Binay had managed to keep control all these years by generously distributing favours, gifts, and allowances. With Malacañang in Binay's sights, it was clear from Mercado's testimony that resources had to be generated to create a war chest to dispense patronage not just within Makati but nationwide. The procurement process for large government contracts favoured certain companies close to the Binays. Project costs were bloated. Findings of the Commission on Audit and the Ombudsman revealed overpricing and conflicts of interest.

Ernesto Mercado's whistleblowing was timed to diminish the popularity of Binay for 2016. Unfortunately for Binay, the Commission on Audit and the office of the Ombudsman were led by independent women who had made names for themselves by not tolerating corruption. Their efforts eventually led to the dismissal of Junjun Binay as mayor of Makati and a ban on his holding any public position.

As discussed above, Jejomar Binay had deftly used state resources in order to win the votes of the poor. In fact, providing public goods and social services became a hallmark of the Binays. Among their many social services they provided while in control of Makati, one that received a lot of attention was the distribution of birthday cakes to senior citizens. Non-Makati residents hearing of this service, and of local senior citizens' free entrance to cinemas, were envious. Despite a lot of talk, and jokes that the supplier of the birthday cakes was one of the Binay children, among the information shared by former Makati Vice-Mayor Ernesto Mercado was the detail that the supplier of the birthday cakes was a company owned by a known Binay supporter (Carvajal 2015).

However, in the course of Mercado's revelations, the public got confirmation that the Binays had benefitted from commissions and kickbacks from procurement contracts, and by favouring companies of close friends and allies. Mercado testified in the Senate hearing that Binay usually received 13 per cent of all government contracts (Salaverria 2014). One of Binay's close friends, Gerry Limlingan, received $29 million in security and janitorial contracts from city hall in three years alone (Rufo 2014). Limlingan was a former campaign manager and finance officer of Jejomar Binay. He was a board member in many companies and foundations linked to the Binays (Pascual 2015). A slogan of the Binay family that famously bragged about the public and social services they extended to their constituents, "*ganito kami sa Makati*" (this is how we are in Makati), thus had a dual meaning for many even before Mercado's testimony. According to some, one meaning was, "this is how we are in Makati": we give (bribes); a second was, "this is how we do things in Makati": we take (bribes).

The brand of politics developed by the Binays transcends political parties. As Hutchcroft and Rocamora point out, writing about the Estrada presidency, "the poor would have been best served by the emergence of strong political parties able to give them a voice in a political environment long hostile to their interests; what they got instead, sadly, was a corrupt populist claiming to help the poor while he made himself rich" (Hutchcroft and Rocamora 2003: 281). Much the same can be said about Makati under the Binays.

Even so, continued economic expansion and the growing concentration of employment in urban areas such as Makati, raises questions about the sustainability of urban dynasties like that of the Binays in the long run. How long can Makati's long-ruling, tough-talking mayors be able to sustain their hold on power amidst social change? Many among the influx of younger voters who are merely temporarily in the city for work have no political memory of the Yabuts or Makati politics before Binay, nor do they retain residual loyalty to the family as a result of years of receiving social services from them. The rising number of affordable condominiums in Makati suggests future elections will be dominated by younger, mobile, and transient residents who are outside the ambit of community and barangay leaders.

The highly personalistic and hands-on nature of Binay has made him repeatedly successful in elections. In his own words, "to most politicians, life and death in politics depend on their ward leaders. I win because I perform and because I don't rely on my leaders alone. I go straight to the people" (Gloria 1995: 90). For example, it is well known in Makati that Jejomar Binay frequently took the time to visit wakes of constituents who had died; by his own calculation he had visited 60,000 wakes (Avendano 2016). Councilor Ferdie Eusebio explained that even if the vice-president came from a long trip abroad, if necessary he would go to a wake straight from the airport before going home.[7] Binay utilised this same personalistic approach in his campaign and those of his children, setting him apart from previous Makati mayors. As one analyst concludes, "where Yabut relied on his leaders for victory, Binay relied only on himself at crunch time" (Avendano 2016). This is not to say that there was no team in TeamBinay. Binay's campaigns were very professionally organised, and clearly drew on more resources than those of their competitors, but it was the candidate himself and his personal reputation with voters that was the chief campaign asset.

In the wake of the corruption allegations, winning the 2016 election for the Binays was as much about winning back the *municipio* of Makati as it was about capturing Malacañang. Securing local offices would give the family leverage and a power base to retreat to and rebuild from in case the Binay patriarch did not make it to Malacañang. The Binay mayoral seat needed to be re-captured. Having had 30 years of rule in Makati, the Binays still had incumbency advantage. Yet even with a well-oiled machine, Team Binay remained insecure about whether they could win their urban voters. As long-time Binay ally Ferdie Eusebio said, "*siyempre ngayon hindi naming hawak ang municipio*" (of course we feel the uncertainty, we do not have city hall)—which speaks volumes about the way personalism and patronage in the use of state resources are often seen as the keys to electoral victory.[8]

By disrupting the Binays' control in Makati, albeit for less than one year, Pena likewise had a degree of incumbency advantage that no Binay challenger had enjoyed in the preceding 30 years. He had the support

---

[7] Interview with Ferdie Eusebio, April 2016.
[8] Ibid.

of the administration, some physical control over city hall, and the rare opportunity to show that he was a viable alternative for Makati's leadership. Pena's strategy, judging from how his team operated, was similar to that of other traditional politicians. There was little that made Pena distinct or different from mainstream politicians. To be sure, he distanced himself from the Binays and promised things would be run differently. But he lacked the time, the strong leadership and an efficient group of people behind him to be able to show that Makati could have a better-run city hall and city under his helm.

CONCLUSION

The 2016 local election produced some dynastic contraction for the Binays. Though she won overall, Abby Binay lost in District 1, the district of her father Jejomar Binay, where one would expect the Binays to have a lot of social capital and where the people had long enjoyed the benefits of Jejomar Binay's patronage. With son Junjun disqualified for life, and the patriarch losing the presidency, the plan to move the dynasty vertically into national politics was derailed, and the focus shifted to holding on to Makati. At the same time, the small margin separating Abby Binay and Kid Pena shows that there might be some traction to the corruption charges against the Binays. The incumbent Binay and Binay allies who occupy national positions are perhaps not as poised to sustain their gains as they were in the past.

The expansion of the dynasty to the national level made the Binays vulnerable to challenges at both the local and national levels. When the Binays expanded upward, local allies saw a potential vacuum, and an opportunity to occupy positions otherwise reserved for family members. At the same time, by moving upward, a strong local dynasty became a threat to other national-level politicians. Because Makati has a strong local-national nexus compared to other cities and provinces, national elites were quick to identify the Binays as a threat. The crescendo of corruption cases presented through the media for public and official investigations led state institutions to file formal charges. This led to a Binay decline in 2016. Buffetted by these blows, the Binays contracted. Even a strong local machine would find it difficult to offset such a two-pronged attack.

Makati's political landscape is likely to change in the coming years. The two questions that Makati voters are concerned with are: who can dislodge the Binays and can that winning candidate change the way

Makati is run as a city? If Jejomar Binay follows the same career path of Erap Estrada, he might return to Makati as its mayor. As the master of ceremonies at the ceremony where Abby was sworn in as mayor proudly announced, "we have proven to the whole world that Makati City is, and will always be, a Binay Country" (Samonte 2016). For now, that might be true. There are some Binay allies who are genuinely concerned about Makati who might strike out on their own just as Pena did in 2010. But rejecting patronage ties with the Binays is not enough. Voters want to see a credible challenger to a dynasty. After all, the Binays have shown their constituents what "serbisyong Makati" means in terms of government social services. But as the city changes, there is hope that the city will evolve out of dynastic politics.

Still, the task of unseating the Binays is a daunting one. In the *miting de avance* of the local Liberal Party in Makati, Ernesto Mercado did not give his usual impassioned barrage of corruption allegations against the Binays. Instead, moved by the number of supporters that showed up, he started pensively by confiding that he felt he needed to apologise to his daughter Karla. Karla, according to Ernesto Mercado, never joined him in his campaigns for the many elections he was in. Sharing the stage for the first time with his daughter, Mercado spoke as a father. He felt sorry that he asked her to run as Makati's vice-mayor, "*ang kalaban po niya ay hindi lang isang candidato kung hindi isang pamilya*"[9] (she is running against not just another candidate but an entire family).

Table 7
Election results from City of Makati

Candidate	Party	Office	Per cent (%)
* Indicates Incumbent Candidate			
Del Rosario, Monsour	UNA	House of Representatives (1st)	60.27
Garcia, Norman Nicholas	LP	House of Representatives (1st)	30.14
Talag, Willy	NPC	House of Representatives (1st)	4.75
Carreon, Eugenia	IND	House of Representatives (1st)	2.81
Latimer, Lourdesiree	IND	House of Representatives (1st)	2.03
Campos, Luis	UNA	House of Representatives (2nd)	54.01
Cruzado, Boyet	LP	House of Representatives (2nd)	42.09

(cont'd overleaf)

---

[9] Audio recording of Team KidKarla in the *miting de avance*.

Table 7 *(cont'd)*

Candidate	Party	Office	Per cent (%)
Perez, Levi	IND	House of Representatives (2nd)	2.30
Sarza, Joel	IND	House of Representatives (2nd)	0.85
Porciuncula, Vin	IND	House of Representatives (2nd)	0.75
City of Makati			
Binay, Abby	UNA	Mayor	52.67
Peña, Kid	LP	Mayor	46.73
Jumawan, Jimmy	IND	Mayor	0.60
Lagdameo, Monique	UNA	Vice-Mayor	60.12
Mercado, Karla	LP	Vice-Mayor	37.37
Enciso, Glenn	IND	Vice-Mayor	1.83
Padrigon, Edgardo	IND	Vice-Mayor	0.68

chapter **8**

Muntinlupa City: The Use of Monikers as a Manifestation of Programmatic Politics

Jose Aims R. Rocina

INTRODUCTION

This chapter focuses on how candidates use monikers to attract voters, specifically in the city of Muntinlupa. Such monikers as "Mr. Nebulizer", "Mr. Nice Guy", and "Mr. Education" play a big role in boosting candidates' chances of winning in the city's local elections.

Muntinlupa City is located in the southernmost tip of Metro Manila, cradling the cities of Taguig, Paranaque, Las Piñas, and Bacoor. It is bounded by the province of Laguna, specifically, Laguna de Bay. It is a city of extremes. The mega-rich of the city live in opulence in the plush Ayala-Alabang subdivision; more than two-thirds of the population wallow in poverty in the depressed areas near the rail tracks and along the dirty shores of Laguna de Bay. Known as the "Emerald City" of the Philippines for its glittering financial district, it is a microcosm of the pitiful lives of the majority of Filipinos; in a country where there is a huge gap between the rich and the poor and a minute middle class, the city has made economic progress by leaps and bounds, improving its local government classification from a fourth-class municipality in the 1980s to a thriving urban district in 1995, when it finally became a city.

The city was formerly known for housing the National Penitentiary (Bilibid Prison) which holds the country's hardened criminals. It has, however, already shed this dubious name tag and is better called nowadays the "Gateway to the CALABARZON" (an acronym for Cavite, Laguna, Batangas, Rizal, and Quezon) as it is the nearest city to this bustling economic zone in the south.

Its new-found financial clout, however, has also made it a haven of aspiring politicians who move heaven and earth to become part of its local government. In this regard, money politics has become the norm rather than the exception in local elections in Muntinlupa. Candidates do not hesitate to distribute anything that appeals to constituents, from money for votes, to the provision of education, health services, and even such an important commodity as water.

In this regard, one thing is clear in the city: he (or she) who does a better job of imprinting his legacy among the fickle-minded voting population wins. Incumbent Mayor Jaime F. Fresnedi of the Liberal Party relied on his long-standing education programme to entice Muntinlupa's inhabitants to vote for him, while his opponent, former Mayor Aldrin San Pedro of UNA (United Nationalist Alliance), promoted his free water programme among water-starved constituents living in low-class residential areas as the flagship of the services he provides. Consistent top councilor and vice-mayoral candidate, Atty. Raul Corro, talked with pride about the one thing that catapulted him to power: free notarisation of official documents. Finally, the Liberal Party's top bet in the congressional race, Congressman Ruffy Biazon, attracted thousands of followers with his travelling programme of free medical services and missions.

These distinctive services gave birth to a moniker for each aspiring candidate that became their hallmarks in voters' minds. Mayor Fresnedi was dubbed "Mr. Educator", Aldrin San Pedro became known as "Mr. Free Water", Atty. Raul Corro was called "Mr. Free Notary Public", while Cong. Ruffy Biazon became famous as "Mr. Health". These monikers stuck and helped their owners in a variety of ways. They helped voters to recall politicians' names, and boosted their popularity by acting as a reminder of their accomplishments. Indeed, in Muntinlupa the monikers became the backbone of the candidates' campaigns.

These monikers were not developed overnight; they were the product of services that were regularly delivered, usually free of charge, to the constituents across years or even decades. These monikers were designed by their creators to muster mass-based support. In promoting them, the candidates and their teams were trying to create in the minds of voters a belief that the candidate was the one responsible for a particular service, such that, in return, the voters need to consistently support the candidate at the polls. This courtship could last a long time, although this varied according to the capacity of the candidate and the type of service. If successful, voters attach these monikers to politicians known for delivering these services. They are trademarks that highlight each candidate's particular brand of programmatic politics.

Thus, it is safe to say that while the local elections in Muntinlupa were widely seen as a battle between the yellow army of the Liberal Party and the green mass of the UNA party, with all the usual use of money and patronage, they were also a conflict between rival monikers.

BACKGROUND

During the American period, Muntinlupa was part of the province of Rizal, together with Taguig and Pateros. However, in 1986, after the EDSA Revolution, when the late President Corazon Aquino rose to power, Muntinlupa and Las Piñas were combined into one legislative district. It was during the term of President Fidel V. Ramos that Muntinlupa was finally declared a highly urbanised city and, after a couple of years, received its own city charter. Since then, incumbent Mayor Jaime R. Fresnedi has held the reins of government, with his power only briefly interrupted between 2007 and 2013 when his now fierce rival Aldrin San Pedro was able to occupy the seat of power. Fresnedi made giant strides in the development of Muntinlupa's economy through his pet education programme and by establishing investment havens in its financial centre. On the legislative front, meanwhile, Muntinlupa's law-making politics has been dominated by the Biazon family, with both the father and son tandem of Rodolfo and Ruffy Biazon alternating as Muntinlupa's lone representative in Congress since it became a city. Rep. Ignacio R. Bunye was, however, the inaugural congressman in 1998.

Muntinlupa is divided into two districts with nine barangays. The northern first district consists of four barangays: Bayanan, Poblacion, Putatan, and Tunasan. The southern second district consists of the remaining five barangays: Alabang, Ayala-Alabang, Buli, Cupang, and Sucat. It has one district representative in Congress and 16 councilors, eight for each district. The biggest concentration of voters is found around Poblacion and Putatan. Thus, candidates usually exert more efforts to secure votes in these areas. Ayala-Alabang and Buli have the fewest voters because of their elite population and small area, respectively. Table 8 shows the winning candidates in Muntinlupa City in 2016. The table shows the dominance of the Liberal Party, which can be attributed to the fact that it was the incumbent party and therefore had more resources and influence than its main competitor. In the 2016 election, local candidates were either allied with the Liberal Party (associated with the colour yellow) of then President Benigno S. Aquino, Jr., or with the green-hued UNA of then Vice-President Jejomar Binay.

In terms of its geography, what stands out in Muntinlupa is its proximity to Laguna Lake, which makes it prone to flooding during the rainy season. Railway lines also traverse its inner territory and the super highway South Luzon Expressway (SLEX) cuts across its western shoulder. Its proximity to Cavite and Laguna provinces has boosted its economy, facilitating an inflow of workers, resources, and investments. Some of the candidates in Muntinlupa's elections were formerly residents of Cavite and Laguna, like Councilor Mark Lester Baes, whose family formerly resided in Indang, Cavite.

Top Philippine schools like De la Salle-Zobel and San Beda-Alabang, malls like Festival Mall and Star Mall, companies like Convergys, and giant industries like the North Park and other multinational corporations have established themselves in the city, boosting the coffers of the local government. But these investments have also produced a sharp economic divide between Muntinlupa's robust western part and its eastern section, resulting in the widening of inequality between the haves and the have-nots.

Candidates need to be innovative when designing their campaign strategies, as no strategy appeals to all constituents. In the affluent subdivisions, candidates must prove to the residents that they have been accountable for the funds entrusted to them. In such places, candidates can demonstrate good performance through the projects that have been built, such as schools and hospitals, or the services that have been rendered to the community.[1] For voters living below the poverty line, candidates must be more attentive to their basic needs, for example for water, food, and shelter. Poor residents are more likely to expect candidates to give them dole-outs in the form of cash or goods; the thing they most aspire to is jobs.[2]

---

[1] Interview with Mark Lester Baes, Muntinlupa, 22 April 2016.
[2] Interview with Neil Varias, Muntinlupa, 27 April 2016.

Most of the incumbents get re-elected in Muntinlupa. A reason for this success is the so-called Muntinlupeno mentality, where politicians must first prove themselves as worthy candidates before voters would support them. Once they get elected, they have to demonstrate that worthiness by doing a lot for the people, and, if they get re-elected, they are expected to do even more. Many incumbents use public funds to solidify their relations with their clienteles by patronage politics, making it very difficult for new candidates to win in local races, because incumbents tend to be proven suppliers of needed goods and services (Friedman and Whittman 1995). Indeed, with 28 councilor candidates vying for eight positions in 2016, it was very difficult for first-time candidates to enter the elite circle; it takes something special for a "newbie" to be elected. An example was Councilor Mark Lester Baes of the Liberal Party, who won despite running for the first time. Some of the reasons for his success were obvious: he is the son of popular councilor Robert Baes, and he is director of JCI Philippines (Philippine Jaycees, Inc), a leading development-oriented NGO which is mainly supported by elite families in the country. He also, he claimed, demonstrated his genuine sincerity and willingness to help people in need.[3]

The most challenging aspect of Philippine elections is the Filipino perception that the politician, whether incumbent or candidate, is the solution to all problems. People ask for virtually everything from their politician, even for trivial things such as money for fares, vehicle fuel for an outing, money for snacks, or for a movie, and so on. Sometimes people just approach a candidate and ask for money outright; if the candidate asks, "What for?" the person might smile and say, "*Wala lang!*" (nothing really) as an answer.[4] The pernicious aspect of this practice is that it can be hard for the politician to draw a line between giving and not giving. They can do little to determine who is really in need of help, and who is just pretending.

WINNING STRATEGY AND THE ROLE OF PATRONAGE

In Muntinlupa, monikers played a vital role in determining candidates' success or failure. But they were never enough on their own; candidates had to supplement their moniker-based appeals with other means of

---

[3] Interview with Mark Lester Baes, Muntinlupa, 22 April 2016.
[4] Interview with Neil Varias, Muntinlupa, 27 April 2016.

attracting votes. This can be attributed to the fact that a voter has many needs; as a rule, the candidate who can satisfy most of them wins. One of those needs is entertainment and relaxation.

In the weeks before the election, the following scene was typical of the strategy used by the Liberal Party of Cong. Biazon. It was a "Karaoke Night", which he typically hosted in the early evening, lasting till early dawn, with the aim of entertaining and giving comic relief to prospective voters. Selected constituents among the audience would sing their hearts out to the applause of neighbours, while being also the butt of jokes handed out by hired comedians. Laughter resonated in the entire venue as goods such as t-shirts and cupcakes were passed around the crowd. Late in the evening, politicians would also sing, and explain their causes and platforms in between songs, making the entire programme truly an affair to remember. Similarly, in the vice-mayoralty race, Vice-Mayor Dioko allegedly brought supporters and constituents almost daily to his private resort in Sucat, feeding them *lechon* (roasted pig), and letting them enjoy the amenities of the establishment.[5]

But providing entertainment was just one of the strategies candidates employed to win voters to their cause. Other strategies were also common. For example, for candidates to win, they also had to satisfy their constituents' basic needs, like food and shelter. Many campaigns handed out two-kilogram bags of rice to constituents during campaign sorties. This strategy was confirmed by the camps of Cong. Biazon and councilor candidate Neil Varias.[6] Residents of depressed areas, and informal settlers, especially appreciated such gestures. The provision of shelter was likewise an important tool to attract votes. Winning Councilor Mark Lester Baes personally delivered lumber, corrugated iron, plywood, nails, and other building material to a homeless family in Sucat,[7] while Cong. Biazon in previous terms had, with the assistance of Anak Pawis, a party-list group, and the Philippine Urban Solidarity organisation, provided decent housing to thousands of residents living near the rail tracks.[8] Such actions endeared politicians to voters, making them strong contenders.

Another key factor in the local race was the promise of jobs and livelihood programmes. Using this strategy was a way to build clientelist

---

[5] Interview with Raul Corro, Muntinlupa, 27 April 2016.

[6] Interview with Magdalena Maximo, Muntinlupa, 23 April 2016; interview with a Varias staff member, 27 April 2016.

[7] Interview with Mark Lester Baes, Muntinlupa, 22 April 2016.

[8] Interview with Ruffy Biazon, Muntinlupa, 21 April 2016; interview with Marie Grace Quizon, Muntinlupa, 23 April 2016.

relationships, as people need jobs to survive. If an electoral outcome determines whether a person works or is re-hired, such a person will do anything to support the candidate who is the key to employment success. In particular, a change of mayors means a change of employees, especially a change of those who are merely in contractual positions and serve at the pleasure of the executive. A staff member of former mayor San Pedro lamented that when Fresnedi replaced San Pedro in 2013, all of the former mayor's appointees were dismissed and replaced by the new mayor's loyalists.[9] Constituents also compete to be recipients of livelihood programmes, knowing the person in power will tend to give priority in such programmes to their own followers.[10]

Overall, of course, succeeding in the election required money. The production of paraphernalia alone required a lot of resources.[11] Candidates gave different answers as to what was the most expensive part of the election, with some saying it was the mobilisation of voters (as pointed out by a UNA councilor candidate, Pastor Varias),[12] while others listed the daily supply of food to supporters as the most costly item (as offered by party-mate, Alfredo Don Bunye IV).[13] However, one thing was clear: patronage politics and clientelism were dominant political modes in Muntinlupa City, and that made the election an expensive business.

While the primary clientelistic strategy was still cash distribution (Mayor Candidate Artemio Simundac, for example, always had bundles of 20 and 50 peso notes in his pocket to hand out to daily well-wishers), most agreed that this was no longer very effective at corralling the votes of service-starved constituents.[14] Similarly, constituents now took for granted such common gestures as sponsorships and donations for weddings, baptisms, birthdays, and other special occasions.[15] Even candidates who provided constituents who experienced a death in the family with free coffins, free memorial lots, funeral services with a stash of cash and complimentary tents, chairs, tables and vehicles for the burial parade, were no longer guaranteed victory.[16] Likewise, distributing cakes and serenades to celebrate the birthdays of constituents had lost its

---

[9] Interview with Lenny Esguerra, Muntinlupa, 28 April 2016.
[10] Interviews with Eleonor Panen and Magdalena Maximo, 23 April 2016.
[11] Interview with Baes and Bunye, April 2016.
[12] Interview with a staff member from Varias campaign, 27 April 2016.
[13] Interview with a staff member from Bunye campaign, 27 April 2016.
[14] Interview with a staff member, Muntinlupa, 6 May 2016.
[15] Interview with Eddie Babilonia, 27 April 2016.
[16] Interview with Lenny Esguerra, Muntinlupa, 28 April 2016.

lustre.[17] Make no mistake—candidates still had to engage in these types of patronage activities. However, such largesse was no longer sufficient to propel a candidate to victory. Increasingly, what made a candidate a winner was instead the lasting service legacy that he or she had provided to the people. Candidates who stood out for providing a high level of benefits over years of public service had a considerable advantage.[18]

One example was Alexander Diaz of UNA, who was running for his third term as city councilor. He was associated with the "FAITH" service programme. In the FAITH programme (in which FAITH stands for Food Always in the Home), Diaz provided seedlings (supposedly bought with his personal funds) of vegetables and fruit plants to his constituents, along with tools, fertiliser, other material, and training on how to cultivate the plants.[19] Recipients could not only consume the produce they grew, they could also earn extra income by selling their excess produce to the market, helping them to pay their bills, buy fares and medicine, and even send their children to school. The FAITH programme turned the backyards of residents in the city into gardens, aiming to divert youth away from drugs and other vices, and towards the mini-gardens. According to Diaz, the main goal of the programme was to give people hope that they would someday have better, more secure, and happier lives.

A new way of winning local elections involved buying not (only) votes, but also buying non-voters.[20] This meant paying supporters of a rival party not to vote during the election. The risk that voters will not keep their promise is much lower with this kind of transaction than with normal vote buying, because citizens must dip their fingers in indelible ink when they vote, meaning that it is easy to know whether they reneged on the deal. Amounts paid to non-voters can be much greater than in normal vote buying transactions, reaching into the thousands of pesos. This is in part because this strategy typically targets entire families rather than individuals. Families are usually paid in the range of PhP 2,000 to PhP 5,000, as compared to the usual PhP 500 and below given to ordinary individual voters. Accordingly, one dark side of the election was the hiring of motorcycle-riding henchmen who carried out the dirty jobs of paying off potential supporters of rivals during the campaign period. On the green side, I observed a motorcycle man who arrived at UNA headquarters and boasted that he had paid families who were Liberal

---

[17] Interview with Losino Gonzales, Muntinlupa, 27 April 2016.
[18] Interview with Raul Corro, Muntinlupa, 27 April 2016.
[19] Interview with Alexander Diaz, Muntinlupa, 8 May 2016.
[20] Interview with Lenny Esguerra, Muntinlupa, 28 April 2016.

Party supporters not to vote, thereby increasing the probability of a UNA win. On the other hand, an UNA poll watcher also told me that the night before the election, there were yellow men (that is, supporters of the Liberal Party) in their neighbourhood who were riding motorcycles and wearing masks to hide their identities. These riders allegedly distributed cash (ranging from PhP 200 to PhP 500), advising UNA supporters to vote for the yellow candidates.[21]

The usual campaign tactics also included harassing opponents. For example, police officers working for the incumbent arrested and detained many supporters of UNA for distributing flyers, which the police alleged was a cover for vote buying.[22] Most local politicians consider this sort of harassment to be part of the dirty game called politics.

Finally, some candidates made special efforts to court the votes of particular groups, organisations, or associations. Mayor Fresnedi, for example, was supported by the powerful religious bloc, Iglesia ni Cristo,[23] while winning councilor, Alexander Diaz, got the endorsement of the Couples for Christ, a Catholic lay organisation.[24] Tricycle groups and other transportation associations were also important: Neil Varias, a UNA candidate for councilor, engaged in boodle fights (that is, collective meals in which people eat with their hands) with tricycle drivers to establish rapport and camaraderie with them.[25]

MOBILISATION STRUCTURES

Most candidates in Muntinlupa reported that they relied more on their local team or machine than on the national party organisation, for both campaign and financial support. This was particularly true for the opposition candidates, who were provided with no support from their mother parties. Incumbents did report receiving more political sustenance from their main parties, but it was largely the politicians themselves who organised and funded their own electoral machines.

The main structure of a candidate's team usually consisted of coordinators, each responsible for a particular area, and, under them, leaders, followed by poll watchers and other personnel. It was the duty

---

21 Interview with Caress Lastrillas, Muntinlupa, 9 May 2016.
22 Interview with Paolo Calalang, Muntinlupa, 8 May 2016.
23 Interview with Caress Lastrillas, Muntinlupa, 9 May 2016.
24 Interview with Alexander Diaz, Muntinlupa, 8 May 2016.
25 Interview with campaign staff member, 27 April 2016.

of the campaign manager, who was connected most directly to the candidate, to put the coordinators in the right places. The manager would be the candidate's main person on the ground, the one who updated the candidate on whatever was transpiring in his or her assigned jurisdiction. The manager was the vital link in any successful electoral enterprise, the critical person for harnessing votes for the candidate. The manager was also the person who chose the coordinators based on his personal assessment of what it takes to muster support for the candidate. Thus, campaign managers were usually personally chosen by the politician, and were typically people the politician knew well, and could trust. By the same token, coordinators were generally known leaders, who had reputations for being reliable, and with good track records. Along with area leaders, they were the eyes and ears of the candidate on the ground, organising meetings, attracting recruits, convincing opposition supporters to switch, and searching for reliable watchers for election day.

These local machineries were tied to the candidate and not to the party. This was because parties, especially on the side of the opposition, did not provide financial assistance to their candidates, but instead only adopted them as supporters of the party. The incumbent party, the Liberal Party, however, did give some assistance, although it was not substantial. Despite the lack of institutional support, running-mates from the same party could save a lot of money by campaigning together. For example, all Liberal Party candidates, from the presidential candidate down to senators, congressmen, and local executives like councilors, attended a "Grand Rally" of the party in Muntinlupa on 20 April 2016.

The Liberal Party's congressional candidate, Ruffy Biazon, stated that his greatest advantage was his trusted political machinery, which he inherited from his father, the Marine General, senator and former congressman of Muntinlupa, Rudolfo Biazon.[26] This powerful political machine was primarily loyal to the Biazons, and it penetrated down to the lowest levels of society, making it an effective tool for the mobilisation of voters. Led by his main hatchet man, political manager Edgar Legaspi, Biazon's coordinators and area leaders were the primary reason he secured a seat in the House of Representatives. In turn, Biazon, an amiable and innovative politician, had mastered the art of taking care of his people. The members of his machine in fact expected little in the way of monetary compensation for their efforts; most of them were volunteers who rendered service virtually for free, receiving only a meagre allowance for transportation and food, as well as occasional

---

[26] Interview with Ruffy Biazon, Muntinlupa, 21 April 2016.

goods. What kept them together, and loyal to Biazon, was the belief that they would be the primary beneficiaries of government programmes, in the form of scholarships, medical benefits, and the like, after the election.[27] Many also felt the way the candidate treated them was of primary importance. The Biazons treated coordinators and leaders as part of their family. For example, they usually invited them for special occasions, such as celebrations of Biazon's birthday and Christmas, when they would visit the congressman's house for a succulent dinner and many raffle prizes as gifts.[28] Biazon claimed that his project funds came from the Priority Development Assistance Fund (PDAF), while his campaign funds came from his family, friends, and donors. The Liberal Party, according to him, only provided a small amount of money.[29]

Most electoral machines also contained core group members who played specialised roles. For example, Mr. Paolo Calalang was the main youth campaign manager for the UNA mayoral candidate, Aldrin San Pedro. Although young in age, Mr. Calalang was actually a veteran youth campaigner who had already had stints with previous politicians like former President Joseph Estrada and a candidate-actor Aga Muhlach. His duty was basically to mobilise the youth to be part of the green alliance, either as poll personnel, poll watchers, supporters, or even just voters. His job was made difficult by the fact that the UNA did not give any financial assistance to their local candidates.[30]

A candidate's campaign staff also included people hired to respond to requests for assistance. For example, Congressman Biazon had personnel in his office whose job was to cater to the medical needs of citizens. First, was a staff member who asked people what help they needed, checked whether they had the necessary paperwork (such as proof of residence, voter ID, doctor's prescriptions, and so on) and determined whether or not they could be processed immediately. This person would then connect the patient to the relevant service providers, for example, contacting the hospital about medical bills that needed to be paid or contacting drugstores to inquire about the price of medicines. A second staff member worked as an encoder who kept tab of all the transactions. Biazon's office could thus help constituents with varied medical needs, ranging from unpaid bills to securing anti-rabies shots and even dialysis sessions.

---

[27] Interview with Eleonor Panen, Muntinlupa, 23 April 2016.
[28] Interview with Maximo Magdalena, Muntinlupa, 23 April 2016.
[29] Interview with campaign staff member, 21 April 2016.
[30] Interview with Paolo Calalang, Muntinlupa, 8 May 2016.

Former Mayor San Pedro also employed two persons to help him run his free water delivery programme. They were a driver in charge of the water truck and his assistant. Every day they would deliver water to households. Every day, they passed by the UNA headquarters to make a tally of their deliveries before going to their assignments.

Education Mayor Jaime Fresnedi employed many people to distribute yellow "beneficiary" cards to deserving students, who had to show proof not only that the income of their parents was insufficient to meet their educational needs, but also that they (or their parents) were bona fide supporters of the yellow (Liberal) party. Yellow-card holders were then given priority in benefits such as scholarships, most of which were given to party members, supporters, and their friends during the election. Most of the students who received the cards were accepted and enrolled at the Pamantasan ng Lungsod ng Muntinlupa (University of Muntinlupa City).[31] Yellow-card holders also received priority treatment at the Ospital ng Muntinlupa (Muntinlupa Hospital).

Vice-mayoral candidate Atty. Corro also had personnel who helped him run his free notary service. First, was the processor, who determined the needs of individuals who came to him, categorised their problems, and determined whether they were actionable.[32] The processor also would check that the person was sincere, as sometimes people claiming to be in-need citizens were actually pranksters. A second worker would then schedule a meeting with Atty. Corro in order to work out how to address the person's needs, legal or otherwise.[33]

Usually, people who acted as the personnel of candidates were not well-compensated during the election campaign itself. They generally stay with the politician with the hope that they will be hired as additional manpower when the candidate wins, or that they will be given priority in the politician's programmes and services.

MONIKER POLITICS

The use of monikers greatly helped the cause of local candidates in Muntinlupa City. Monikers assisted candidates in gaining an edge in terms of media mileage, a result-oriented profile, and, consequently,

---

[31] Interview with Shiela Marie Alim, Muntinlupa, 8 May 2016.
[32] Interview with Losino Gonzales, Muntinlupa, 27 April 2016.
[33] Interview with Eddie Babilonia, Muntinlupa, 27 April 2016.

popularity. The monikers appeared everywhere: in newspapers, in the talk of voters, the speeches of candidates, and in election paraphernalia. Some candidates introduced themselves by their monikers, campaigned using them, and won as a result. The only limitation was that it was ordinarily only incumbents, or those who had previously served in the local government of the city, who could use a moniker.

Candidates generally did not choose their moniker from the outset. Instead, the monikers tended to emerge gradually, after a candidate first responded to constituents' needs and then later saw an opportunity to be known for the delivery of a particular service. Over time, such candidates realised that they could actually be synonymous with the service, and the moniker was born. While I focus on four candidates, the use of monikers was not limited to them. In the grand UNA rally on 1 May 2016, for example, one councilor candidate was introduced as Mr. Nebulizer.

I have already pointed out that service-starved Muntinlupa residents, especially those living in depressed areas, see elections as way of satisfying their needs. As a result, elections here become deeply integrated with service delivery. From the veranda of Mr. San Pedro's headquarters, I watched water trucks pass with the face of San Pedro pasted on their tanks. A Fresnedi staff member told me that: "Mr. San Pedro became known for his water programme while Mr. Fresnedi is widely appreciated because of his education policies."[34] In Biazon's headquarters, large numbers of people lined up daily for medical assistance.[35] In the house of Mr. Raul Corro, his campaign coordinator emphasised that Corro was a legend in Muntinlupa because of his free notarial service.[36]

It is important to note that some of these services, like health and education, were actually rendered by the government as part of its basic duties and functions. In other words, moniker politicians tend to take credit for services that would be provided by the government anyway. Their role is generally simply to facilitate citizens' access to the service.

Notably, two Liberal Party candidates (Biazon and Fresnedi) capitalised on two services which are very close to the hearts of Filipinos, but which are also basic government functions: health and education. Mayor Jaime Fresnedi, who took over from two-termer Aldrin San Pedro, gave education a major boost. He increased the previous administration's

---

[34] Interview with Ronaldo Catanyag, Muntinlupa, 22 April 2016.
[35] Interview with Ruffy Biazon, Muntinlupa, 21 April 2016.
[36] Interview with Eddie Babilonia, Muntinlupa, 27 April 2016.

meagre budget of PhP 5.5 million for education to an astounding PhP 163 million in 2016, in the process increasing the total number of scholars (students on scholarships) to 30,000. This high number of scholars was due to the fact that Fresnedi abolished the high-grade ceiling that had previously been a requirement for receiving a scholarship.[37] He also gave additional bonuses to students who graduated at the top of their class, or who were able to crack the entrance examinations of elite universities. This programme was of course, funded by city coffers. Given that education is so highly prized by Filipino voters, especially poor ones who see education as the only means of improving their standard of living, the moniker of Mr. Education worked wonders for incumbent Mayor Jaime R. Fresnedi. It also connected to his personal story, seeing he had worked very hard in his youth to make ends meet, and succeeded in life due to education.

At the congressional level, Congressman Ruffy Biazon became famous for his 6-K Programme: Karunungan, Kaunlaran, Kalusugan, Kabuhayan, Kapayapaan at Kalikasan (Education, Development, Health, Livelihood, Peace and Environment).[38] His flagship programme, however, was health. His office would issue Guarantee Letters to sick constituents for them to avail themselves of health subsidies in public hospitals such as the Philippine General Hospital (PGH) and the Ospital ng Muntinlupa. His programme was known as the Medical Referral System. Biazon also conducted dental and medical missions (from pork barrel allocations), and distributed Philhealth Insurance cards to thousands of his supporters. He was a strong advocate against cervical cancer, running an awareness campaign and providing medical assistance. This approach made Biazon a darling of women's groups, senior citizens, persons with disabilities, and other persons who could not afford to pay their medical bills or buy prescribed medicine. He admitted that he used pork barrel funds to finance his medical services.[39] Like education, health is a service Filipinos value highly. Given the very strong cultural tradition of "*utang-na-loob*" (which refers to a sense of gratitude and expectation of reciprocity), even a tablet or capsule can go a long way towards capturing the vote of the recipient of that medicine. The queues of people lining up daily in Biazon's headquarters for medical help were thus a sign of his strong electoral appeal.

---

[37] Interview with Ronaldo Catanyag, Muntinlupa, 22 April 2016.
[38] Interview with Ruffy Biazon, Muntinlupa, 21 April 2016.
[39] Interview with Edgar Legaspi, Muntinlupa, 21 April 2016.

Among the opposition, two UNA candidates had also delivered key programmes to Muntinlupenos. From 1990, vice-mayoral candidate Atty. Raul Corro, a top councilor, had rendered a particular service which became synonymous with his moniker: Mr. Free Notary. For a document to be notarised in the Philippines, people typically have to pay a fee of around PhP 300 to a private law firm; this is a large sum for those on low incomes. Notarised documents are usually affidavits and deed instruments, which are usually required in private and public transactions. As a lawyer, part of Raul Corro's obligation is to notarise documents. He decided to do this for free.

While few people would consider free notarisation to be a necessity like health or education, many voters gave it considerable weight due to their attitude of *utang-na-loob*. A steady demand for notary services is generated by the need for notarised documents for events like marriages and adoptions, and by the propensity of Filipinos to go to court to redress their grievances rather than reaching amicable settlements out of court. Atty. Corro believed that providing this service made him a legend in Muntinlupa politics. He claimed that he was the only politician in the Philippines to provide such a free service.[40]

Former mayor Aldrin San Pedro, meanwhile, gained much popularity with his free water service. Water trucks regularly roved around Muntinlupa City during the election period to deliver clean and potable water in areas where there was a dearth of the commodity. Water is a daily problem for many residents in Muntinlupa City, especially those who live in illegal settlements and are candidates for relocation. Water in the nearby Laguna Lake is highly polluted and undrinkable. For many residents, their only ways of securing water are from dole-outs or from illegal connections (which are cut by water company personnel when they are discovered). Accordingly, San Pedro saw this need as an opportunity to boost his votes. As a wealthy businessman, San Pedro decided to finance his water programme, which runs only during the election period.[41]

While these local politicians used monikers, and the associated services and programmes, as a primary tool to entice voters, they also engaged in other modes of money politics, for example vote buying and goods distribution. Delivering services, and earning credit as a result, became integrated into established modes of politics, it did not displace them.

---

[40] Interview with Raul Corro, Muntinlupa, 27 April 2016.
[41] Interview with Ellen Deang, Muntinlupa, 1 May 2016.

CONCLUSION

The 2016 election proved to be very competitive. In Muntinlupa City, and possibly in other parts of the Philippines, some local candidates were elected because of the services they provided. While there were other ways to attract votes, providing proven and tested services was one way for politicians to gain an edge, especially against new opponents who had not yet proven themselves to the people as worthy public servants.

Such services, as we have seen, earned the politicians providing them endearing titles from their constituents that made it even more difficult for challengers to defeat them. These titles were in the form of monikers which provided advantageous cues for voters. Monikers such as Mr. Free Notary for Atty. Raul Corro, Mr. Free Water for former Mayor Aldrin San Pedro, Mr. Educator for Mayor Jaime Fresnedi, and Mr. Health for Cong. Ruffy Biazon, helped make these candidates literally household names in the city.

One may argue, however, as to which of these monikers was more effective and enduring. It is safe to say that the most effective monikers were those that appealed to all sectors of society, to both the rich and the poor. Effective monikers also point to services that last longer, and are more important than services offered by rival parties or candidates. The most powerful monikers were thus arguably those highlighting education and health; while free water and notary services appeal primarily only to the poorest residents, health and education appeal to all types of voters. Well-off voters have water supplies in their homes and are able to pay notary fees but may still need financial assistance to pursue further studies or to pay medical bills. The results seem to bear this out. In the 2016 election, Jaime Fresnedi (Education) and Ruffy Biazon (Health), running for mayor and congressman respectively, won. Aldrin San Pedro (Water), also running for mayor, and Atty. Raul Corro (Notary), aspiring to become vice-mayor, both lost.

Table 8
2016 election results in the City of Muntinlupa

Candidate	Party	Office	Per cent (%)
* Indicates Incumbent Candidate			
Biazon, Ruffy	LP	House of Representatives	66.10
Ricketts, Ronnie	UNA	House of Representatives	33.90

Table 8 *(cont'd)*

Candidate	Party	Office	Per cent (%)
City of Muntinlupa			
Fresnedi, Jaime*	LP	Mayor	58.27
San Pedro, Aldrin	UNA	Mayor	31.78
Simundac, Temy	NPC	Mayor	9.55
Abas, Reynaldo Jr	IND	Mayor	0.26
Marmeto, Oscar	IND	Mayor	0.15
Dioko, Celso	LP	Vice-Mayor	50.37
Corro, Raul	UNA	Vice-Mayor	46.89
Nava, Baby Aguilar	NPC	Vice-Mayor	2.73

chapter **9**

Third District of Pangasinan: Weaning Away from Traditional Patronage

Gerardo V. Eusebio[1]

INTRODUCTION

Pangasinan has long been a politically strategic and significant province in the Philippines. It used to be the province with the highest number of votes and continues to be one of the top vote-rich provinces. Candidates for national positions risk losing if they ignore such a vote reservoir. It has also produced at least five senators and a president, Fidel Ramos, as well as a host of prominent national and local political leaders. The Third Legislative District of Pangasinan is in the centre of it all, with a political history characterised by dynasties, patronage, and violence. These are, of course, features of elections in some other parts of the Philippines as well. What makes Pangasinan interesting is the shift away from such traditional strategies and mechanisms that has been happening since 2007. Specifically, we see emerging in Pangasinan the beginnings of a new model of political organisation, which I label the "developmental machine".

---

[1] Eusebio, besides his academic profession, was a campaign strategist for a number of politicians, including former Representative of the 3rd District of Pangasinan Rachel Arenas in 2007. He was involved in the 2007 Arenas campaign from pre-campaign planning to the actual campaign in the district.

The main argument of this chapter is that while the longstanding political machineries of the Liberal Party (LP) and of other traditional parties have continued to operate and employ standard tactics in the district, these machineries have also begun to practise a new style of political engagement and mobilisation. Some machines have been trying to connect to the grassroots and build reputations as providers of public goods and services such as infrastructure, education, and health. Although traditional patronage continues to exist, with goods and services dispensed in exchange for votes and loyalty, this novel developmental mode has begun to transform politics in the district. Genuine participation of all stakeholders, especially the grassroots, has increased, as has the level of public goods provision. This combination of empowerment and performance, ultimately, has boosted the legitimacy of incumbent politicians.

BACKGROUND OF THE DISTRICT

Pangasinan is a province of the Philippines in central Luzon with a total land area of 5,451 square kilometres. According to the 2010 census, it has a population of nearly 2.8 million. Almost half of the people are Pangasinenses and the rest are descendants of Bolinao, Ilocano, and Tagalog groups who settled in the eastern and western parts of the province. The official number of registered voters in Pangasinan is just over 1.65 million.

The 3rd District of Pangasinan consists of one city and five municipalities: San Carlos City, Bayambang, Calasiao, Malasique, Santa Barbara, and Mapandan. Table 9.1 presents some basic information regarding the localities, last updated in 2007.

Pangasinan has been described as a gateway to northern Luzon and as the heartland of the Philippines. Pangasinan also occupies a strategic geopolitical position in the central plain of Luzon—known as the rice granary of the Philippines. Rice is the primary crop of the province, with 342,281 hectares of land dedicated to its production, and an annual yield of around 940,700 metric tons. Other crops include mangoes, corn, and sugar cane. Fisheries also contribute greatly to the provincial economy, yielding 121,765 metric tons of fish annually.

Like many provinces and districts in the country, electoral politics in Pangasinan has been characterised by a history of dynastic rule, the extensive use of money politics, and the occasional eruption of violence.

Dynasties are particularly prevalent, with a leading clan entrenched in each locality, notably the Rosuellos of San Carlos City, the Macanlalays of Calasiao, the Camachos of Bayambang, the Domantays of Malasiqui, the Calimlims of Mapandan, and the Zaplans of Santa Barbara. Heading the whole province is the Espino clan, led by three-term governor and Fifth District congressional representative Amado Espino Jr., and his son and incumbent governor, Amado III.

Table 9.1

Basic profile of the local government units of the 3rd District of Pangasinan

Locality	LGU Income Classification	Land Area (sq. km.)	No. of Barangays	Population
San Carlos City	Third Class City	78.67	86	164,061
Bayambang	First Class Municipality	183.05	77	96,609
Calasiao	First Class Municipality	42.42	24	85,528
Malasique	First Class Municipality	123.78	73	124,211
Santa Barbara	First Class Municipality	171.14	29	75,569
Mapandan	Third Class Municipality	19.44	15	33,210

Source: Government of Pangasinan, 2016.

In the 2016 election all the major national parties as well as regional parties, competed in the area. The ruling LP, Nationalist People's Coalition (NPC), Aksyon, Biskeg (a regional party), Kilusang Bagong Lipunan (KBL), and Lakas competed in races for representatives, governor, and vice-governor. The table at the end of this chapter lists the incumbent officials and their respective party affiliations.

While candidates from a number of parties were successful, the LP remained the top party in the province in the election. This is largely due to the LP's leadership in the complex inter-party and inter-candidate alliances that are normal fare in the province. The LP in general, and Rep. Arenas in particular, were allied with NPC and Aksyon, and with powerful dynasties such as the Espino, Rosuello, and Domantay families. Contenders to the leadership positions in the six local government units of the congressional district formed complex alliances and coalitions. These alliances mostly kept competition to a minimum, directing competition only against candidates from outside their particular alliances and coalitions.

CANDIDATE STRATEGY AND THE ROLE OF PATRONAGE

Generally speaking, the traditional patterns of Filipino electoral competition usually apply in Pangasinan. The traditional strategy of using the 3Gs (guns, goons, and gold) remains quite pervasive in the district, with most candidates employing this reliable and simple formula. In the past, they have used violence either to scare away potential and actual rivals, or to physically eliminate them.

On the surface, the 2016 election was largely peaceful, though with the usual noise coming from rallies and sorties. The last major instance of political violence in Pangasinan was the assassination of Mayor Julian Resuello of San Carlos City way back in 2007.[2] But elections in Pangasinan remain notoriously violent, to the point that the Philippine National Police included almost the entire province in its election watch-list in 2016 (CNN Philippines 2016). Within the district, all but Santa Barbara and Mapandan were included in the watch-list (Northbound Philippines 2016). And the watch-list is not unjustified: Councilor Mienrado Ynzon Sr. of San Carlos City was found dead in suspicious circumstances in December 2015 (Cardinoza 2015), while two separate cases of physical assault were recorded in the province by 29 April 2016 (Northbound Philippines 2016).

Meanwhile, most campaigns in this district continued to use goons, field operatives whose primary responsibilities were to collect intelligence and persuade the voters, using sometimes dark and violent means. They intimidated voters into either voting for their candidates, or not voting at all. They also attempted to intimidate campaigners and even opponent candidates into backing out from the election. Sometimes intimidation became instances of actual violence. There were also reports of alleged destruction of campaign paraphernalia (Northbound Philippines 2016).

As is the norm in much of the Philippines, the last of the 3Gs—the use of money—is pervasive in elections in Pangasinan. Not only do candidates rely on large amounts of cash to operate their overt campaigns, they also use it to fund their covert campaigns, which include the dispensation of most traditional forms of patronage. For example, in almost all the campaigns in the district, vote buying was and still is the norm. Some reports indicate that PhP 200 is the minimum amount negotiated for a vote in barangay elections, and that within a week before the 2016 election

---

[2] Interview with the mayor, 6 May 2016.

the amount could reach as high as PhP 2,000 per vote in congressional and gubernatorial races.[3]

The media, particularly AM radio stations, are another major recipient of patronage as they are key instruments in courting voters in bulk. Candidates usually dispense patronage to them in the form of "wining and dining" the journalists, as well as by providing other favours like jobs or cash payments. In return, the media are expected to take care of most of the communication needs of the candidates, especially by helping them disseminate the candidates' images, their platforms, and reports of their advocacy work. The media, especially the AM radio stations, are an important vehicle for electoral success because they have the ability to reach impoverished and remote constituencies—such as fisher folk—that candidates otherwise may have a hard time penetrating.

In my own observations of the election, I witnessed one congressional candidate hosting a dinner with select media representatives to discuss plans and strategies for improving the candidate's image, pointing out particular aspects that should be considered. After dinner, each media representative received PhP 20,000 in an envelope. The media outlets whose representatives attended seemed to oblige with the plans and strategies, subsequently touting the supposedly good reputation of the candidate while downplaying or even burying problematic issues associated with the same candidate.

In addition to money politics, dynastic politics play an important part in elections in Pangasinan. Political dynasties are not new in the province; dynasties have been the norm ever since elections were introduced during the Commonwealth era. Arguably, nowhere has the dynastic arts of "sliding down" (for example, running for vice-mayor from a position as mayor), "moving up" (for example, running for governor from a position as vice-governor), or moving horizontally (running for a congressional seat from a mayoral post) been as perfected as in Pangasinan. To the present, the elections in the province can be described as regular competitions amongst dynasties, instead of contests of individual candidates.

Regardless of whether or not they are part of political dynasties, elections are expensive affairs for candidates. While a few have resources of their own, most remain more or less dependent on resources (such as patronage) provided by political machines. Teehankee defines political machines as "specialized organizations set up for the purpose of

---

[3] Shadow Report by Gerardo V. Eusebio, 2 May 2016. Observation of political campaign in Pangasinan, Philippines.

mobilizing and influencing voter outcome through the dispensation of social, economic, or material benefits" (Teehankee 2002: 168). Political machines are the lifeblood of politics in Pangasinan. Machines serve as the major support system for candidates, and are key to their success.

Local political machines generally supplement their own resources by aligning with a political party at the national level that can provide them with additional funds. Emblematic of this is the Liberal Party's machine in the 3rd District. From the 2010 election, the Arenases allied themselves with the LP and with its then-presidential candidate, Benigno Aquino III. The Arenas team consisted of the mother, Rosemarie aka Baby, a local socialite rumoured to be a former president's mistress, and her daughter, Rachel. Baby attempted unsuccessfully to turn the scandal concerning her personal affairs into a stepping stone for a congressional seat in 1995 and 1998, while Rachel managed to gain the House of Representatives seat in 2007 and 2013. Being the national ruling party, the LP became the lead party in the district in the 2016 election, winning 6 out of the 17 major local contests, with the remaining 11 split almost evenly among NPC, KBL, and Aksyon (see Table 9.2). Furthermore, the alliances made by the Arenases and LP, as discussed earlier, ensured that LP has an effective control over the majority of the posts. It must be noted, however, that while the party's national machinery does provide additional financial and political resources for local candidates that boost their campaigns, their choice to access such resources in 2010 by aligning with the LP primarily hinged upon the expectation that Aquino would win, which he did.

Nevertheless, the LP machine was effective at distributing and delivering precious resources to the campaigns of the party's local candidates, especially during the period of its incumbency as the national administration from 2010 to 2016. LP incumbency made it possible to provide infrastructure and development projects, and other patronage resources across the board, not only to partymates, but also to power-holders from other parties in hopes of attracting them to the fold. These resources, especially the projects, would obviously follow the formal government organisation, that is, flowing down from the president and the Congress, to the local officials.

It is not surprising, then, that many of the campaigns in 2016 were particularistic and patronage-driven, targeted towards various captive constituencies. More programmatic promises never went beyond vague motherhood statements. For example, a vice-mayoral candidate revealed his dream of transforming his locality, Bayambang, into a business centre for Northern Philippines, but his plans were hazy.[4] Nonetheless, while the usual types of money politics were pervasive in the 3rd District, over the last couple of elections we have witnessed what may be the beginnings of a new type of political machine in Pangasinan—what I call a developmental machine.

This new kind of machine mixes traditional strategies with greater grassroots involvement and pays more attention than in the past to the provision of public goods and services. This new model has been the cutting edge of political stratagem in the district, and has been effective in winning elections. I discuss this new type of machine below.

MOBILISATION STRUCTURE

The traditional method of mobilising votes involves delivering patronage in the lowest politico-administrative level of the country: the barangay. Accordingly, in 2016, candidates and their teams mobilised barangay officials as ground-level distributors of patronage, local recruiters of supporters, and field intelligence operatives. These officials did much of the campaign legwork, together with the campaign headquarters, volunteers, and workers from the parties. They served as middlemen in the distribution of traditional patronage, especially money and employment, linking the supplying parties and candidates on one hand, and the demanding constituencies on the other.

An issue in this system, however, is that much of the allocated patronage was commonly understood by the major parties and candidates to have been pocketed by the barangay officials. These officials saw themselves as deserving ample compensation and favours for the work they provided for candidates and parties. In fact, campaign leaders commonly believed that constituents would be lucky to receive 50 per cent of the budget allocated for them by the campaign leadership. The campaign leaders have been unable to do away with these barangay brokers, however, since they rely almost exclusively on them for ground-level campaigning.

Meanwhile, funding for the campaigns usually came from donations by friends and supporters of the candidates, as well as from their respective national parties. There were local political and socio-economic elites who were willing to finance particular local campaigns. Funding from the national party level, meanwhile, was sourced mainly from the donations

---

[4] Interview with Vice-Mayoral Candidate A, 3 May 2016.

given by the national supporters of the parties. As with other districts nationwide, however, most of the funding for most local campaigns, at least 80 per cent of it, in the 3rd District had to be shouldered by local sources, as the focus of national funding is on national races, especially for the presidency.

But some changes in the mobilisation structures have occurred over the recent decade. Candidates began in varying degrees to bypass the barangay officials and attempt instead to connect directly to the people at the grassroots level, such as the urban poor, the farmers, the fisher folk, and workers in the transport sector. In other words, candidates have begun to shift away from relying on unreliable barangay officials for electoral campaigning in favour of using their own campaign staff to directly mobilise civil society. This is in part because they view their campaign staff, especially their volunteers, as more loyal and reliable than barangay officials. They prefer these staffs since their loyalty is based more on principles and long-term developmental vision, unlike the officials, whose loyalty rests on receiving immediate personal financial and political gains from campaigning.

Besides their frustration over the barangay officials' siphoning of the campaign funds, some candidates saw direct interaction and "sincerity" to be effective in recruiting civil society into their fold, especially when accompanied and reinforced by the indirect or collective targeting of social, economic, and material benefits that are needed and even demanded by community groups. Examples of these types of benefits include training, micro financing and livelihood programmes, and infrastructure projects. Providing such benefits could be a means to create links between voters and the candidate independent of barangay officials and their influence.

Meanwhile, hired poll watchers were the most prized campaign workers. Some of them started working in the early stages as campaign volunteers, but all were active come election day. They served not only as supposed guards of the electoral process on election day itself, but also as monitors looking into unusual activities during the electoral process, such as unexpected movements of candidates and voters, and delays and inconsistencies in the process.

What we observed in electoral mobilisation was increasing use of more direct and personal communications between candidates and supporters across campaigns in the district. It is not surprising, then, that direct recruitment of civil society members, both as campaign staff and key supporters, was on the rise, and that candidates relied more heavily on volunteers (who, though not expecting actual remuneration, were compensated with free meals, transportation allowances, and even small amounts of pocket money per working day) than in past elections. Communications and monitoring came in both traditional forms during meetings and sorties, and via more modern forms such as texts and emails.[5] Campaign coordinators were then present to strategise and organise all levels of the campaign, especially at grassroots and barangay levels, and, as much as possible, across the campaigns of their respective parties and alliances.[6] Their tasks included the coordinated manufacture and distribution of sample ballots for which the local parties paid.[7]

THE ARENAS DEVELOPMENTAL MACHINERY

As discussed above, over the past decade we have seen changes beginning to emerge in the methods of patronage distribution and machinery used in the 3rd District. For years, the success of a candidacy was determined largely by proficiency in the deployment of political machinery in support of traditional campaign strategies. Simply put, the better the candidate was at distributing patronage and in projecting himself or herself to the locale, the better his or her chance of being elected. However, this has begun to change.

These changes in the use of patronage in the 3rd District originated from a slight breakthrough in 2007, when Rachel Arenas ran for a House seat for the first time and won against three veteran politicians: former representative Generoso Tulagan Sr., former Customs deputy commissioner Gallant Soriano, and former representative Eric Galo Acuña. The Arenas family were relative newcomers to the Pangasinan political scene. Rachel is the daughter of Rosemarie "Baby" Arenas, Manila-based socialite and philanthropist who made headlines for being an alleged mistress of former President Fidel Ramos. Rosemarie failed in her initial bid to turn her celebrity into a Senate seat (1995) and House seat (1998). Calculating that they would have a better chance at winning a congressional seat from Rosemarie Arenas' home town of Malasiqui in the Pangasinan 3rd District, the family re-entered the political arena in 2007, with daughter Rachel as the standard-bearer. Rachel succeeded, and then successfully ran for re-election in 2010. In 2013 she stepped

---

[5] Interview with Youth Campaign Officer A, 5 May 2016.
[6] Interview with Campaign Coordinator A, 4 May 2016.
[7] Ibid.

down and her mother, Baby, replaced her and ran unopposed. In 2016, Baby won re-election against the two former representatives who had run against her daughter in 2007: Tulagan and Acuña.

Beginning in the 2007 election, and throughout their four successive successful campaigns, the Arenases employed developmental patronage machinery against the traditional campaigns of the more experienced politicians. In part, this was a strategic necessity, since at the time they lacked the well-developed patronage machinery of their competitors. What does this developmental machinery look like, and how is it distinct from traditional machinery? First, developmental machinery works by developing direct connections and networking links between the candidates and individuals and groups of voters at the grassroots level. This includes soliciting active participation from these individuals and groups.

To be clear, the developmental machine still makes use of patronage. The difference is that it attempts to establish direct links with voters, bypassing the barangay officials who have traditionally served as intermediaries in electoral networks, while taking their cut along the way. Shifting away from intermediaries has two beneficial effects from the perspective of the machine: (a) it strengthens the loyalty of voters toward the candidate; and (b) it means more resources actually go to voters, rather than being syphoned off by barangay officials.

This leads us to the second way in which the developmental machine is distinct from traditional party machines. Developmental machines work to cultivate a reputation for good governance—for being effective providers of local public goods and services to all voters, not just their own supporters. So, building on Teehankee's definition of political machines, the developmental machine could be defined as an approach which combines the provision of public goods and services with the direct delivery of patronage to participating individuals and groups at the grassroots level.

What do this participation and engagement look like in practice? Beginning in 2007 the Arenas machine began to directly partner with the local beneficiaries of patronage—for example, farmers, the LGBT community, local health workers, and similar groups—to help support the candidate, her campaign, and her advocacy work. In the past, political machines in the 3rd District rarely reached out directly to such groups, but relied on barangay officials to distribute patronage and mobilise voters.

Beginning in 2007 the campaign began to interact with these grassroots groups directly—assessing their needs, receiving their input, and providing patronage resources to these groups directly. This was a more progressive way to use and distribute patronage, involving the beneficiary groups directly, and resulting in their empowerment. It deviates from traditional patronage in that there is sustained engagement, coordination, and cooperation with, and commitment to, the constituencies. Traditional machinery treats constituencies as nothing more than a supply for their demand for political support and power, paid exclusively through patronage, while this new approach looks at constituencies as societal sectors with particular needs and aspirations that cannot be met by traditional patronage alone.

A good example of this progressive approach was work with health workers in the district. Since 2007, Arenas and her staff had been meeting with them, looking to assess their needs. The health workers related not only the usual needs of the public health services, but also proposed other programmes such as medical missions. This interaction resulted in the "Health is Wealth" programme that provided medical missions and supplies.[8] By demonstrating sincerity in assessing the needs of both the health workers and the larger public, Arenas was thus able to mobilise them to support her campaign. As this example demonstrates, the nature of the goods or service being provided is not necessarily different than what is offered by other campaigns—other campaigns conduct medical missions. The key difference is that the developmental patronage approach builds links with local constituency groups directly, rather than relying on local intermediaries, as done by traditional campaigns.

As a result, this relatively new approach has a natural indifference to the mainstream barangay political system. The Arenases purposely avoided the barangay system due to the fickle nature of its officials' loyalties and their perceived lack of integrity when distributing the entrusted patronage (and, it should be acknowledged, because the Arenases initially lacked good access to that barangay system). The campaign reasoned direct interaction with the constituents would be much more efficient and effective, despite the potential losses from shifting away from barangay officials. In particular, they waived the potential gains typically attained from the influence the barangay officials have in swaying constituents in favour of the candidates they support, and in distributing patronage resources.

This switch to a developmental strategy was made easier given that the Arenases were already renowned not only as local socialites, but also as philanthropists. They were known for their advocacy of social goods and services, such as infrastructure, education and health—areas which

---

[8] Interview with Volunteer Nurse A, 25 April 2016.

aligned perfectly with the needs of their constituents. Incorporating these kinds of policy appeals into their political machinery helped turn this reputation into a political asset that could be used in the acquisition of legislative power.

The two Arenas women made a good team. With Rachel looking out for the interests of the district in Congress, Baby worked to build the Arenas machinery back home. When Baby took her daughter's place in Manila after the 2013 election, Rachel accepted the position of governor of the Philippine Red Cross (PRC).[9] Upon closer inspection, it could be argued that her decision to accept this post was a conscious move aimed at maximising the advantages of developmental machinery. Another benefit from this decision was that she suddenly had the time to help her mother in managing the 2016 campaign, including running important errands for her, and appeared at many campaign functions.

By 2016, the Arenas campaign team had developed and perfected what I am calling here "developmental machinery" through their successive campaigns since 2007. They honed and tweaked their strategies over the years from their headquarters at the Arenas farm in Malasiqui, Pangasinan. One prime example of this strategy has been the mobilisation of health workers as election campaigners. This is not a standard practice. But since Rachel's first term to the present, it has been a distinctive feature of every Arenas campaign. Aware of the wavering loyalties of the barangay officials, the Arenases, from the start, relied instead on barangay health workers and other developmental groups. In return, the Arenases would create programmes and policies that would empower health workers and take care of the health needs of the whole district, such as the "Health is Wealth" policy mentioned earlier. In business parlance, the approach they adopted resembled taking the middleman out of a transaction.

This strategy was successful. Employing barangay health workers as campaigners newly politicised and, perhaps, empowered this group. In the end, the Arenas campaign found them to be more reliable than local politicians. Since 2007, they have used similar strategies to activate and engage other constituencies, including LGBT groups, religious workers, farmers, fisher folk, and the urban poor in San Carlos City.[10]

---

[9] Interestingly, Rachel was supposed to run as senator in 2013. However, the manner in which she distributed her pork barrel, which included exchanging projects with other members of Congress outside her district, caused some controversy within and without LP that necessitated some damage control.

[10] Interview with incumbent Representative, 3 May 2016.

A consequence of activating these groups was that the party machine now had regular, direct, and intimate consultations with numerous constituencies. As a result, the relationship with these groups did not merely involve efforts to use them for campaigning. In addition, the Arenas machine learned of community needs from these groups and partnered with them to develop together governance projects in the district. These projects, mostly in livelihood and social services, were implemented and sustained as the result of demands by these groups and with their full participation, with the representative playing the role of resource provider and overseer.

The creation of this developmental machinery not only legitimised the Arenases' tenure in office, but also involved visible attempts to improve the lives of these constituents. This became a virtuous cycle where, by partnering with these groups, the candidates developed reputations for delivering goods and services to their constituents, further empowering them to advocate for their needs.

Of course, the Arenases took full advantage of the development programmes implemented by the national government, working to indirectly link themselves with those programmes through appearances at the special events and activities organised by the programmes. The most remarkable of these linkages was forged in the administration of the Pantawid Pamilyang Pilipino Program (4Ps), the government's conditional cash transfer programme established in 2009. From the beginning of the programme, the Arenases, as district representatives, were always invited to attend transfer ceremonies throughout the district. Their appearances in these ceremonies helped link the Arenas to the national programme in the minds of many voters, despite the fact that the programme was administered by the government with little influence from local elected officials. Voters, rightly or wrongly, believed that the Arenases went to great lengths to ensure that the programme directed funds to the intended beneficiaries.

While the new developmental machine is a potential agent of change, it is worth noting that this effort at change has not occurred in isolation or unilaterally. We must bear in mind that the Arenases already had an advantage by running under the banner of a party that had the most effective national political machine during its heyday—the Liberal Party.

In 2016, with the party's standard bearer, Mar Roxas, fighting a daunting political battle against three popular and formidable opponents (then-Vice President Jejomar Binay, Senator Grace Poe, and then-Mayor of Davao City Rodrigo Duterte), the national party provided substantial patronage to vote-rich Pangasinan to ensure that the local machine operated well. Baby Arenas, in particular, belonged to the higher echelons of the party, which gave her province special entitlement when it came to the distribution of resources and patronage.

The political machinery of LP was a valuable asset in the 3rd District when it came to mobilising campaign and patronage resources. While the machine lost the race for president, the LP enjoyed a tight hold in almost all municipalities of the district prior to the election, with operations going down to the grassroots level. The LP National Headquarters partially funded the campaign activities of the collective army of local campaigners from the candidates in the six localities. These included the volunteers and campaign staffs who did the hardest work, including house-to-house campaigning in the remotest of barangays.

From an organisational standpoint, the Arenas machinery was an affiliate and client of the much wider LP machinery. But it must be noted that the LP machinery complemented the Arenas developmental machinery by undergoing similar shifts in its use of patronage.

Former Budget Secretary and LP stalwart, the controversial Florencio "Butch" Abad, explained that the nature of the party machinery changed under the Aquino administration. It was no longer a machine built out of pure patronage but one that empowered local officials, and one that increasingly emphasised programmatic performance. He claimed that not one province, district, or city could complain that it was neglected under the Aquino administration in the delivery of programmes like universal health care, conditional cash transfer, rural electrification, and infrastructure.

According to Abad, "the big change is whatever their party affiliations, the local officials provided basic programmes. They did not have to beg for it and they did not need to change parties. They genuinely appreciate this and want it to continue" (Rappler 2016). Certainly, LP gained the loyalty of local officials, such as the Arenases, at least temporarily, even if this local loyalty did not translate into the election of its national standard-bearer. Nonetheless, affiliation with the LP brought some advantages and extra resources to the party's local allies like the Arenases. However, once the LP lost the presidency in 2016, Baby Arenas, along with many other LP "loyalists", were quick to switch to the party of the newly-elected President Duterte.

Even more important than the affiliation with the national LP were the alliances the Arenases and the LP forged with other candidates and parties within the district, as noted earlier. These inter-party and inter-candidate alliances resulted in an extensive network of support and a sprawling clientele that the Arenases could, and did, tap. Their control of the congressional seat enabled them to spread patronage throughout the district without much opposition, which further solidified their emerging developmental machinery.

How did other candidates and machines respond? We do see evidence that some candidates tried, to some extent, to replicate the Arenas strategy. Former representative Tulagan had not been active in Pangasinan politics, particularly in the 3rd District, for nine years. So when he chose to run in 2016, he needed to "pull out a rabbit from his hat" in order to reintroduce himself to the population and present himself as a better candidate than the Arenas.[11] He tried to present his past service as congressman in a developmental light, while criticising the Arenas' over funding of projects outside the district.[12] However, his efforts to reinvent himself to the public were in vain, as evidenced by his defeat. His alliance with vice-presidential candidate Ferdinand "Bongbong" Marcos, a popular politician in the province, did not help; primarily because the senator was known to be tight-fisted, and he did not provide resources to help Tulagan's campaign.

The third candidate for the House, Eric Acuña, fared even worse than Tulagan. Former representative Acuña had not been seen in the district for more than 18 years since he lost to Tulagan in 1998. Thus, his campaign faced far greater challenges than Tulagan's. Acuña allied himself with then Mayor Duterte, boasting in social media and in public that he was the one who convinced Duterte to run for president. The association did not do much to boost his fortunes—Duterte visited the district only twice and was thought to have left very little money for the Acuña campaign.

Without support from a national party, Acuña worked hard to replicate the Arenas model to bolster his developmental credentials. At first, people were intrigued by his campaign theme and flagship product, both called *Ako'y Magsasakang Organiko* (AMO), a bottled fertiliser solution which his campaign distributed to the voters mostly in the agricultural sector. His campaign slogan was also *amo*, which means leader in Pangasinense. The campaign marketed AMO as the panacea to cure all agricultural ills, supposedly preventing drought while preserving the optimum quality of crops.[13] However, voters were ultimately unswayed by the hype and by the somewhat confusing nature of Acuña's campaign. AMO was an attempt

---

[11] Interview with former Representative A, 1 May 2016.
[12] Interview with Campaign Coordinator, 4 May 2016.
[13] Interview with former Representative B, 3 May 2016.

to appear developmental by connecting with the agricultural sector, but it simply didn't fly.

From the beginning, both Acuña and Tulagan were fighting an uphill battle. Despite making significant changes to their campaign tactics and structures, the Arenas developmental machine seemed invincible. By fulfilling their promises to deliver goods and services, the Arenases generated an army of loyal campaign workers. Despite their flirtation with developmental policies, the two opposing candidates, perhaps because they lacked resources, failed to directly and clearly engage the constituencies in the district. While they promised good policies, there was no attempt by either campaign to discuss and consult with these constituencies. By contrast, the Arenases had engaged in sustained dialogue with various community groups, resulting not in top-down, on-off patronage projects, but rather in projects and services that local constituents maintained themselves; these were projects that truly mattered to them, and which they had had a hand in designing. Thus, unsurprisingly, voters remained loyal to Arenas.

Of course, there are other factors that explain the staying power of the Arenases in the district. Their opponents' long absences from power, and their long political inactivity, also contributed to their defeat; they had not been able to distribute sufficient patronage to be remembered during those lengthy periods. Also, as discussed above, the Arenases had the advantage of being linked to the national governing party and its machinery. However, at the end of the day, it is unquestionably their developmental approach that ensured their political staying power.

CONCLUSION

Electoral politics in Pangasinan mirrors most of the general characteristics of political dynamics found in rural and semi-urban Philippines. The five municipalities and sole city face many of the same challenges that stymie development throughout the country, including the prevalence of long-lasting political dynasties, patronage politics, and electoral violence.

The recent elections, however, have indicated the beginnings of behavioural change among some local actors. The district has experienced an expansion of basic development infrastructure under the Arenases. By promoting development, the Arenases have created a new developmental machine, bringing together (a) the direct provision of goods and services to local constituencies in consultation with local stakeholders and (b) the mobilisation of those stakeholders during election campaigns. In addition, rather than running exclusive programmes meant only to reward loyal local politicians as in the past, this time, the Arenases included all local government units and provided them with basic programmes, regardless of party affiliation. This approach has contributed to the recent resilience of the Arenases.

Could the developmental machine be a model for other politicians? The Arenas strategy may seem similar to that of the late Naga City Mayor and Interior Secretary Jesse Robredo. Both Robredo and the Arenases were sincerely committed to good governance and delivered goods and services that truly improved the lives of their respective constituencies (see Chapter 10) (Kawanaka 1998). However, compared to the Arenases, Robredo did not rely as much on his party's machinery or on the available sources of patronage.

If the Arenases' strategy is replicated or adapted by other politicians, we may start seeing a shift away from the traditional machine politics and the old strategy of guns, goons, and gold, and towards the delivery of the functions and services mandated to them by law and demanded from them by their constituents. In other words, politicians might start being viewed as truly serving and empowering their constituents. Such changes might also lead to the transformation of political parties at all levels from weak and particularistic, to strong and programmatic. To be sure, such changes could also represent merely sly and pragmatic investments by traditional politicians trying to perpetuate their hold on power. It will be interesting to watch how this strategy continues to be used and evolves.

Table 9.2

Election results from Pangasinan 3rd District

Candidate	Party	Office	Per cent (%)
* Indicates incumbent candidate			
Arenas, Baby*	LP	House of Representatives	71.67
Tulagan, Generoso Sr.	KBL	House of Representatives	20.02
Acuña, Eric	PDPLBN	House of Representatives	8.31
Espino, Amado III*	AKSYON	Provincial Governor	58.57
Cojuangco, Mark	NPC	Provincial Governor	40.89
Salvador, Zaldy	IND	Provincial Governor	0.54
Calimlim, Ferdie*	AKSYON	Provincial Vice-Governor	49.32

Table 9 *(cont'd)*

Candidate	Party	Office	Per cent (%)
Macanlalay, Mark Roy	NPC	Provincial Vice-Governor	49.07
Torralba, Myrna	IND	Provincial Vice-Governor	1.61
Bayambang			
Quiambao, Cezar	IND	Mayor	60.00
Camacho, Zenaida	AKSYON	Mayor	36.51
Junio, Chato	LP	Mayor	1.72
De Vera, Leo	UNA	Mayor	1.70
Manalang, Adrian	NUP	Mayor	0.07
Sabangan, Nato	NPC	Vice-Mayor	52.25
Camacho, Ricardo	AKSYON	Vice-Mayor	46.16
Casingal, Feliciano Iii	LP	Vice-Mayor	1.11
Gosilatar, Freddie	UNA	Vice-Mayor	0.39
Lacap, Angelo	NUP	Vice-Mayor	0.08
Calasiao			
Bauzon, Joseph Arman	LP	Mayor	52.61
Macanlalay, Roy	NPC	Mayor	44.97
Gabat, Florante	IND	Mayor	2.42
Galang, Ferdinand	LP	Vice-Mayor	41.05
Chuson, Narciso Jr.	NPC	Vice-Mayor	37.32
Manipud, Virgilio	IND	Vice-Mayor	21.63
Malasiqui			
Geslani, Noel Anthony	NPC	Mayor	41.38
Pinlac, Renato	AKSYON	Mayor	29.52
De Guzman, Jebong	PDPLBN	Mayor	29.10
Domantay, Armando Sr.	NPC	Vice-Mayor	52.16
Soriano, Fe	LP	Vice-Mayor	43.36
Padilla, Domingo	PDPLBN	Vice-Mayor	4.48
Mapandan			
Tambaoan, Gerald Glenn	KBL	Mayor	46.21
Calimlim, Maximo Jr.*	NPC	Mayor	41.68
Morales, Jessie	LP	Mayor	12.12
Calimlim, Asuncion	KBL	Vice-Mayor	52.20

(cont'd overleaf)

Table 9 *(cont'd)*

Candidate	Party	Office	Per cent (%)
Mariano, Alice	NPC	Vice-Mayor	47.80
San Carlos City			
Resuello, Joseres	NPC	Mayor	59.87
Soriano, Wilhelm	KBL	Mayor	34.16
Cayabyab, Amelia	LAKAS	Mayor	5.97
Resuello, Julier	NPC	Vice-Mayor	70.45
Baniqued, Samuel	KBL	Vice-Mayor	22.70
Dela Cruz, Elma	LAKAS	Vice-Mayor	6.85
Santa Barbara			
Zaplan, Carlito*	LP	Mayor	53.74
Cabangon, Juan Emmanuel	NPC	Mayor	46.26
Delos Santos, Joel	LP	Vice-Mayor	37.45
Navarro, Roger	KBL	Vice-Mayor	37.12
Dalope, Norman	IND	Vice-Mayor	18.18
Jose, Ruben	NPC	Vice-Mayor	7.25

chapter **10**

Naga City, Camarines Sur: An Alternative Mode of Politics under Strain

Mary Joyce Borromeo-Bulao

Naga City is the only independent component city in Camarines Sur, in the Bicol Region,[1] and is the educational, religious, and commercial centre of the region. Naga City is also known for a unique governance system that was introduced by its former mayor, the late Jesse Robredo, who was first elected in 1988. This system, known as the Naga City Governance Model [hereafter Naga City Model], encourages popular participation and transparency, allowing ordinary people to take part in the governance of the city, and challenging the normal pattern of top-down control and clientelist practices common in Philippine local politics. The Naga City Model appears to provide an alternative form of politics in a country where political families dominate. As a result of this, the city government and Robredo himself have received much praise and numerous local, national, and international awards.

Naga City deviates from the usual political set-up in the province. Each of the legislative districts in Camarines Sur has been dominated by well entrenched political families—the Villafuertes, the Andayas, the Fuentebellas, and the Alfelors. In contrast, Team Naga, the local coalition established by Robredo and affiliated with the Liberal Party, has controlled Naga City politics for more than two decades. With the

---

[1] Independent component cities are self-governing and considered independent from the province in which they sit.

battle cry, "Ubos kun Ubos, Gabos kun Gabos" (vote for one, vote for all), the party has achieved victories for its entire slate of candidates in local elections there since 1992. Kawanaka (1998) attributed this success to two factors: first, Robredo's style of political mobilisation, which relied upon the incorporation of institutionalised popular organisations into public governance and, second, the government's performance and approachability. Kawanaka noted that Robredo initiated numerous innovations and projects that were well received by city residents across the socio-economic divide. Despite some variation across different social levels, residents generally perceived Robredo as having performed well.

As a result, the Naga City experience has been put forward as a model for reformers in other parts of the country, demonstrating that a strong local party with a broad mass base can programmatically and effectively deliver services to the people. The model has also avoided the usual clientelistic practices, instead institutionalising and establishing clear processes for delivery of services and public goods, rather than making them dependent on personal relationships between the governing and the governed.

After Robredo died in a plane crash in 2012, however, questions have been raised as to the continuity and institutionalisation of the Naga City Model. Can this new mode of politics be sustained after the death of its charismatic founder? The 2016 election shows that while there may have been challenges, Team Naga still wields considerable influence in Naga City. Building on Kawanaka's works, this chapter argues that the 2016 election success showed the extent to which the Robredo-style of politics has become institutionalised (Kawanaka 1998, 2002). However, it also exposed the vulnerability of this political experiment. Though the "Ubos kun Ubos" slogan—and the style of politics it points toward—remains influential, challengers are likely to try to unseat Team Naga through the use of money politics. While Team Naga was victorious in 2016, its response to such challenges in future elections will determine whether Robredo's political style further institutionalises or meets its demise.

THE POLITICS OF NAGA CITY

Naga City is an island of programmatic, reformist politics in a province dominated by political clans. Each of the legislative districts in the province has been dominated by a political family for decades. The first district has been dominated by the Andayas since 1984, when Rolando

Andaya Sr. was elected as congressman, while the creation of a new district in 2009 gave a new player, Diosdado Ignacio "Dato" Arroyo, the son of the former president Gloria Macapagal-Arroyo, his own turf.[2] Dato Arroyo's third term as representative ended in 2016, making the second district an open field contest. L-Ray Villafuerte ran for this post in 2016 and won against a former municipal mayor. The third district covers an area that was dominated by the Villafuerte clan for 15 years until Leni Robredo, the widow of Mayor Jesse Robredo, won the seat in 2013. The fourth district has been under the control of the Fuentebellas since 1909, with the political rule of this family beginning with the appointment of Mariano Fuentebella as *gobernadorcillo* in 1907. Finally, the Alfelor family dominates the fifth district. Ciriaco "Boboy" Alfelor was first to secure the congressional post in 1984. His father, Felix O. Alfelor Sr., started the family's political career when he became mayor of Iriga City in 1938. In short, were it not for Naga City, Camarines Sur would look like any other province in the country, with competing clans each lording over their respective fiefdoms.

Naga City was the domain of several political families before Jesse Robredo became mayor in 1988. Three prominent politicians—Ramon Felipe, Vicente Sibulo, and Luis R. Villafuerte, all of whom were from wealthy families—held sway over the city (Kawanaka 2002). Felipe and Sibulo started out as political opponents but eventually teamed up as mayor and vice-mayor of the city in 1963. When Felipe successfully ran for a congressional seat in 1965, Sibulo became Naga City's mayor. However, after President Ferdinand Marcos declared martial law in 1972, these politicians were displaced by Luis Villafuerte who rose to power because of his family's close ties with Marcos. In the 1980 election, running under Marcos' Kilusang Bagong Lipunan (New Society Movement) party, Villafuerte defeated Felipe and Sibulo who allied with Bicol Saro, a local opposition party. This marked the end of the Felipe-Sibulo reign in the city and the beginning of control by the Villafuertes. Villafuerte later left the KBL and joined the opposition, the United Nationalist Democratic Organization (UNIDO), in the waning years of the Marcos period. As a former part of the opposition, he was able to secure a key government position when Corazon Aquino became president. In 1986 Aquino

---

[2] Republic Act No. 9716, otherwise known as "An Act Reapportioning The Composition Of The First (1st) And Second (2nd) Legislative Districts In The Province Of Camarines Sur And Thereby Creating A New Legislative District From Such Reapportionment", was enacted on October 2009. The apportionment of legislative districts moved most towns in the former second district into the new third district.

appointed him governor of Camarines Sur, enabling him to maintain his considerable influence over Naga City politics.

In 1988 Villafuerte invited his nephew, Jesse Robredo, to run for mayor of Naga City, and with Villafuerte's support Robredo won narrowly. Robredo thus entered politics through his ties with an established political figure and relative, but subsequently abandoned the usual practices of family-based clientelism by severing ties with his patron. The rift between Villafuerte and Robredo started when Villafuerte tried to interfere in the city's affairs and disrupt Robredo's plans and goals for the city. Robredo tried to rid the city of illegal gambling revolving around a numbers game (*jueteng*), and was said to have been dismayed when he found out that his uncle, his political patron, was a beneficiary of these illegal activities (Scharff 2011). Villafuerte tried to unseat Robredo in the 1992 election by supporting Robredo's challenger, but Robredo easily defeated his rival and would go on to serve six terms as mayor. Villafuerte, then governor of the province, continued to field candidates against him, and against Robredo's party-mates after the latter's death in 2012, in the attempt to regain power in the city. However, these efforts have not paid off. In 2016, Villafuerte again fielded seven candidates in the Sangguniang Panlungsod (City Council), but lost once again.

JESSE ROBREDO AND HIS GOVERNANCE STYLE

Jesse Robredo could be considered one of the brand of "new men" referred to by Machado: a new set of politicians who lack the usual land-owning and dynastic backgrounds but instead rely on a political machine to get elected (Machado 1974). Robredo's family were not land owners nor did he come from a family of politicians; he was born to an ethnic Chinese family which owned a small wholesale and retail business in the city (Kawanaka 2002: 44). Lacking the personal or family wealth usually needed to sustain a political machine, Robredo institutionalised what he called the Naga City Model, which became the base for his political machine (Kawanaka 1998, 2002). It was an organisation unlike the classical sort of political machine portrayed by Scott (1969), as it did not rely on personal clientelistic relationships. Instead, it encouraged popular participation in governance, transparency, and accountability.

Robredo set up participatory mechanisms to enable citizens to take part in the government of their city, starting with the People Empowerment Program (PEP) in 1989. The PEP was an experimental response to the

Aquino administration's call for people's empowerment after the 1986 People Power Revolution. The PEP allowed the city government to engage in consultation with constituents about every significant decision it made through the various non-government and people's organisations in the city. The People Empowerment Ordinance in 1989 paved the way for the creation of Naga's Urban Poor Affairs Office (UPAO) in the same year, which in turn led to the birth of the Kaantabay sa Kauswagan (Partners in Development) Program. The Kaantabay sa Kauswagan Program was a land development programme especially targeting informal settlers in the city. It was supported by several additional initiatives in the subsequent years, including the Kaantabay Ordinance of 1997, which provided an opportunity for partnership between local government units and non-government organisations. This culminated in the creation of the NGO-PO Council in 1995 which eventually evolved into the Naga City People's Council (NCPC) in 1996.

The NCPC accredits non-government organisations and people's organisations from 14 sectors, namely, the urban poor, youth and children, business, labour, senior citizens, women, persons with disabilities, peasants, transport, Barangay People's Councils, education, civic, professionals and enthusiasts, and NGOs. Membership in these organisations ranges from a few hundreds to five thousand. Among the first of the organisations to be accredited was the Lakas ng Kababaihan ng Naga Federation (Power of Women in Naga Federation), which was formed to empower women in the city through different training programmes aimed at livelihood support for women at the barangay (village) level. This was initiated by the city government in 1989 and formalised in 1992, with Leni Robredo, Jesse's wife, as the head of the organisation. Each barangay has its own leader whose responsibility is to recruit members to the organisation.

Another pioneer organisation is the Barangay People's Organization, which is essentially composed of the Barangay People's Councils, consisting of officials and other figures who wield influence in the barangays. Other active NCPC member-organisations are the Senior Citizens League, the Naga City Padyak (Pedicab) Operators and Drivers Association (NACIPODRIF), the Trimobile Operators and Drivers Association, Naga Market Stallholders Federation (NAMASFED), Metro Naga Venders Federation, the Metro Naga Chamber of Commerce and Industry (MNCCI), different employer unions, cooperatives, and various non-government organisations advocating causes ranging from environmental protection and education to community development.

Most of these organisations had already been created prior to the creation of NCPC, but it was only after the NCPC was established that they were given a formal voice in the city's decision-making processes.

Under the Naga City Model, these organisations act as people's representatives in the city council (Sanggunian), and are invited to participate in deliberations on issues concerning their sector.[3] The NCPC has seats in the committees formed by the Sanggunian, which allows these organisations to represent the views of their constituents when relevant issues are discussed. Involving the NCPC in this way, as a non-partisan and non-profit association of NGOs and POs, has introduced an element of direct democracy to city governance alongside representative democracy. Constituents, through their involvement with NCPC, get to participate in committee deliberations on policy-making. The members of the organisations are able to work with elected officials in order to help them make more informed decisions on issues and problems in the city. They can air their concerns at the committee level so that officials can then echo these concerns during deliberation in the Sanggunian. NCPC can also put forward motions, suggestions, and objections during committee meetings and deliberations. Thus, while the ultimate decision-making authority still lies with the elected officials, this arrangement gives NCPC members the opportunity to share their views and be listened to, especially on issues concerning the member-organisations.

This model has been strengthened by other mechanisms designed to promote participatory democracy. For example, by providing NGOs and POs with formal accreditation, they have greater authority and more opportunities to lobby to promote the interests of their members. For example, NCPC-accredited tricycle drivers and operators' associations are able to lobby for fare hikes should they feel the need when gasoline prices go up. They are likewise able to offer their insights on traffic management policies based on their day-to-day experience in the streets. At the end of the day, therefore, the Naga City Model benefits both the members of these organisations and decision-makers in the city government.

---

[3] Interview, Dada Alarkon, head of the NCPC, 3 May 2016.

THE "UBOS KUN UBOS" PHENOMENON AND A STRONG LOCAL COALITION

At the centre of these democratic practices was Robredo, who people regarded as a leader who did not put himself above his constituents but acted as their social equal. Still today, people recall him as a hands-on mayor, recalling instances like after a typhoon when Robredo would be the first to grab cleaning equipment and start the clearing operations even before people had left their homes to clean their own backyards. He lived a simple lifestyle that people sometimes referred to as "tsinelas leadership" (leadership by flip-flops) because he was often seen going around the city and its far-flung barangays in slippers, asking people how they were faring. This populist personal style was a strong complement to the participatory governance model he initiated.

His distinctive style of leadership was also manifest in his election strategies. In 1992, when he ran for re-election, Robredo introduced the slogan, "Ubos kun Ubos, Gabos kun Gabos" (roughly translated, "Vote for One, Vote for All"). This was an appeal to voters to vote for the entire slate of candidates from Robredo's team, from mayor down to the councilors. During campaigns, Robredo emphasised the need to vote for his entire slate in order to push for city reforms. This approach signalled to voters his intention to distribute his power and influence among his team, making them a strong, solid group in the eyes of the constituents. Voters obliged, and from 1992 all the members of Robredo's team have won in every local election. This continued to be an effective strategy even after Robredo's third term ended in 1998, and he was constitutionally barred from standing for re-election. In his stead Robredo endorsed the candidacy of Sulpicio Roco Jr., helping to propel his whole team to victory in 1998. However, dissatisfied with Roco's leadership and management of the city, Robredo ran again for mayor and won in 2001. He subsequently held three more consecutive terms between 2001 and 2010.

Robredo's electoral success was not just due to his distinctive consultative, inclusive, and participatory governance style, but also because he built a strong political machine (Kawanaka 1998, 2002). The machine's base was the barangay-based organisations affiliated with the NCPC, which "gave him unitary and effective control of resources, effective control of grassroots leaders, smooth election campaigning, and a strong bargaining position vis-à-vis national figures" (Kawanaka 2002: 73). While most local politicians entertain people asking for help on a daily basis and respond to their requests in a very personal and clientelistic manner, Robredo institutionalised the distribution of aid to the city's needy citizens using both the resources of the government and the network of organisations he helped establish. If he received a personal request for help, he forwarded that request to either the relevant government agency or an organisation to which the person seeking help belonged. For example, if a woman came to him, complaining about ill health and lacking money for doctor's fees or hospitalisation, instead of just giving the woman some money to get herself treated (which would be the typical patronage style of a traditional politician), he would instead endorse the woman to the City Health Office, which would then provide her with assistance such as free consultation and medicine.

In this way, Robredo was able to remove clientelistic practices and put in place a systematised distribution of benefits. He was able to create patterns of goods distribution that lessened his personal discretion over who got what and how. For example, Robredo created programmes that would systematically identify poor families, individuals with medical needs, or children who deserved to be given scholarships. In an interview, incumbent Mayor Bongat explained that these programmes were designed in such a way as to minimise the discretion of the mayor or his staff.[4] This included creating the City Social Welfare and Development (CSWD) office, which operated apart from the mayor's office and decided on whether and how to extend help to needy residents. The mayor's sole role was referring people to the office.[5] Mayor Bongat described a number of programmes that operated in a similar way:

> The CSWD has programmes for people in crisis, for people in need. For example, when one gets sick, we have funds for that. Every year, regardless of whether there is an election or none, those programmes are funded. Aside from that, we also have the QUEEN [Quality Universal Education Empowerment in Naga] programme, which provides scholarships for public elementary and high school students. The city pays for their tuition fees, and for their mandatory fees. Then we also have the QUEEN rice distribution programme to motivate parents to continue supporting their children. We also have the Sanggawadan programme ["Helping One Another"—a conditional cash transfer programme in which recipients (indigent families) are provided rice subsidies, school supplies, health benefits, housing and livelihood loan assistance, so long as their children do not repeat a year level in school].[6]

---

[4] Interview with Mayor Bongat, 16 May 2016.
[5] Ibid.
[6] Ibid.

Having this network of organisations involved in the distribution of welfare placed Robredo in a strong position when it came to his election campaigns. Through this network he could coordinate and collaborate with barangay leaders who could help with his campaign, doing everything from organising house-to-house visits and planning rallies to mobilise enough voters in order to ensure victory of the entire slate. The strength of Robredo's vote bank in turn provided him and his supporters with bargaining power in dealing with candidates for higher, national posts. Robredo could offer votes in Naga City in exchange for promises of funds from national and provincial government programmes.

In 2010, facing again the constitutionally mandated term limit, Robredo endorsed John Bongat to replace him as city mayor. Bongat, a practising lawyer, inherited not only the position but also the established political machine that Robredo had built up over preceding decades. Bongat ran for office against Sulpicio Roco Jr. (the former mayor with whom Robredo had fallen out) with Robredo's blessing. Bongat was thus able to utilise the existing machine and all the benefits that came with it, propelling Bongat and the entire ticket to victory. Robredo also bequeathed to Bongat the Naga City Development Plan which he and his close allies had drafted to ensure that Robredo's vision of how Naga City should be developed would be achieved even without him as city mayor.[7] Robredo's choice of a successor who was not a family member showed that he was determined to bequeath to his city a political system far different to the dynastic politics and clientelism typical of most parts of the Philippines.

In the lead-up to the 2013 election, there were rumours that Robredo would withhold endorsement from Bongat because he disagreed with some of Bongat's decisions and priorities. However, Robredo died in a plane crash in 2012. Bongat ran for re-election in 2013, and he and his entire slate won again. Bongat and his team adopted the term "Team Naga" to show that they would remain a cohesive group even without Jesse Robredo endorsing them. It is worth noting that the name of the group did not refer to a person, but instead reflected an attempt to sell themselves as a local programmatic party, bigger than any one individual. While Robredo's team had previously relied heavily on the late mayor's personal appeal and his endorsement, Team Naga now tried to establish itself as a group of new-style political elites, or "new men", established for the specific purpose of molding political leaders of the city, very close to Machado's description of a modern political machine (Machado 1974).

---

[7] Interview with Frank Mendoza, 17 Jan. 2017.

THE 2016 ELECTION AND LOCAL PARTY INSTITUTIONALISATION

The 2016 election was significant because it provided clues as to the extent to which Robredo-style politics had been institutionalised in Naga City. John Bongat was running for his final term as mayor, with Nelson Legacion, a lawyer and native of Buhi, Camarines Sur, as his vice-mayor. The ticket was again called "Team Naga" and was affiliated nationally with the Liberal Party. What made this election interesting was the composition of the opponents of the Team—Fortunato "Tato" Mendoza, a very close friend of Jesse Robredo, ran for mayor against Robredo's endorsed group, while Nathan Sergio, a former Team Naga member and incumbent councilor, decided to jump ship and run for vice-mayor under Mendoza. Mendoza was a businessman who was well-known to be one of Jesse Robredo's closest friends. He had managed the central bus terminal under Robredo; however, this was stripped from him during Bongat's second term when the latter transferred the management of the bus terminal to the city government. At the same time, former governor Luis Villafuerte, Robredo's early sponsor, fielded seven councilor candidates, while another five independent candidates ran for the same posts. Finally, Leni Robredo, Robredo's widow, ran as the vice-presidential candidate of the Liberal Party—and won.

The opposition: Campaign themes and money

During the campaign, the Mendoza-Sergio tandem focused on certain critical issues which they believed had been neglected by the incumbent city government. These issues included the cost of electricity, which they argued was too high, the city's garbage disposal system, which they claimed was poorly run, and property and business taxes, which they said were also too high. Mendoza maintained social media accounts and a blog to promote his candidacy and to criticise the current administration on such issues.

In order to introduce the candidate to the voters and in an effort to secure votes, Mendoza's supporters attempted to build a campaign team that reached down through barangay-level networks, with the purpose of identifying "secured" voters who would support the team. One of Mendoza's election campaign team assistants said, however, that it was difficult for them to identify and recruit barangay "*liders*", or vote brokers.[8]

---

[8] Interview with Mendoza's key campaign personnel, 17 May 2016.

Although Mendoza had been close to Jesse and Leni Robredo, his team could not openly tap the powerful network of Robredo supporters because Bongat was the incumbent mayor and had been endorsed by Robredo's coalition.

This campaign assistant's task was to validate the names on the voter lists that were compiled by the *liders* in the barangay to check, "If they are really with me", he said, mimicking his boss. However, because of the difficulties they had constructing a grassroots network, these lists got to the campaign coordinators only towards the end of March (about six weeks before the election). This meant they did not have enough time to validate each name on the list. Thus, they ended up accommodating people who volunteered to support Mendoza despite also being affiliated with the other powerful people in the city like Sulpicio Roco Jr. and Luis Villafuerte. As a result, the assistant said, Mendoza was accused by some of compromising his principles by being connected with Villafuerte and the councilors he fielded in the 2016 election. Being aligned with Villafuerte had negative connotations for many people because Villafuerte had lost power in the city.

At age 67, Mendoza was no longer capable of undergoing the physical stress of a house-to-house campaign. Although he visited certain barangays during the first two weeks of his campaign, Mendoza's main approach was simply to invite constituents to his house, which has a vast garden where a stage was erected. This was where Mendoza presented his platform for government and where he held campaign events. The campaign assistant explained the organisation of these events: "The invitation comes from our office and goes to the barangay coordinators. We asked them to invite people in the list to come over on this specific date, but we asked them not to promise anything to them. We fed them and gave them PhP 100 for their fare. That was what we did one month before 9 May. But we did not promise them that they would get anything."[9] At the start of the campaign, according to the campaign assistant, the number of invitees was 100 per set, with two sets per day. However, as the election drew nearer, the number grew. There were around 20,000 names on their list but a total of only about 8,000 persons were actually invited and attended.

The assistant was firm that they did not pay those who were invited but only gave them free food and some transportation allowance. However, he did admit that people had begun flocking to Mendoza's residence with pleas for help starting in November 2015 when Mendoza announced his candidacy. Most people came to seek monetary support for health-related

---

[9] Interview with Mendoza's key campaign personnel, 17 May 2016.

concerns, while others simply wanted cash. Mendoza had projected an image of being the one candidate who was willing to provide help to anyone who needed it. Accordingly, members of his team were instructed to distribute money to those seeking help. Mendoza's instruction was to never let anyone who asked for help to leave without getting something, even if the payment was just a small amount. Campaign staff were tasked with considering requests from people who asked for help between November and December 2015, with a total budget for distribution of PhP 5,000 per day. In addition, the group attempted to get the support of the beneficiaries of the Pantawid Pamilyang Pilipino Program (4Ps) conditional cash transfer programme by giving them PhP 300 each.[10]

At the same time, because Mendoza had been a close friend of the Robredos, rumours circulated in the city that he was being supported by Leni Robredo; however, I was never able to verify this claim. Had Leni's support of Mendoza been confirmed and come into the open, it would have stirred people's interest in Mendoza but may have compromised Leni's relationship with Team Naga and her political party.

Given all these accounts, the strategy of the opposition was clear: it relied on propaganda and money. The Mendoza-Sergio tandem picked issues that could hurt the administration and were valid concerns of the people of Naga (especially because there had been growing complaints about an open-pit dump site used by the city), though the tandem provided little evidence to back up their accusations. On the use of money, some voters explained that they were given PhP 500 because they were on the opposition's "list" as election-day pollwatchers, though in fact they were never asked to render service during the election. They were only asked to vote for the candidate. While a campaign assistant denied that people on their list were given money, the free lunch or snacks and PhP 100 travel allowance given to persons who visited Mendoza's house would still have been a considerable inducement to those to whom PhP 100 meant being able to afford food on the table for a day or two. Moreover, as noted above, team members gave money to "help" anyone who came to ask for it. A PhP 5,000 daily budget from November 2015 could have amounted to a disbursement of up to PhP 900,000 by the time election day arrived.

---

[10] Interview with Mendoza's key campaign personnel, 17 May 2016.

Team Naga: Machine mobilisation and recruitment

In contrast to the more traditional methods employed by the opposition, Team Naga relied on its network, fashioned into a local party machine. The NCPC member organisations, especially the barangay-based ones, played a major role in the campaign. These member organisations have been supported through the years with projects which the city funded or helped to fund. Moreover, when the city government directs benefits—such as scholarships, rice subsidies, loans access—to residents, it directs them through the various organisations. Thus, election time is a time for these organisations to pay back the city government for its past support and a time to ensure access to further benefits. As a result, these organisations were easily mobilised by Team Naga to support its campaign. Though the Team Naga approach is not based on the individualised exchange of benefits that is so common in Philippine elections, there is nevertheless an important element of reciprocity in its approach, even if it is one built on organisations rather than personal networks.

In explaining how the campaign team was built, the incumbent vice-mayor Nelson Legacion emphasised the role of people at the barangay level, including supposedly non-partisan members of the barangay councils, the *tanod* (barangay police officers), members of the *lupong tagapamayapa* (judicial commissions—the barangay-level justice institutions), barangay health workers, barangay treasurers, members of the Lakas ng Kababaihan (a broad-based women's organisation), as well as others in the barangay who exercise social influence because of their businesses or other sources of authority. Team Naga's approach was based on mobilising figures drawn from these community-level organisations and the apparatus of local government.

The barangay organisations were deeply involved in the campaign at every stage. Members of these barangay organisations were the ones who went with Team Naga candidates during house-to-house visits in their own barangays, so that, for example, if Team Naga members conducted house-to-house campaigning in Barangay Santa Cruz, the members and officers of that barangay's organisations would accompany them. Legacion explained that this gave Team Naga a big advantage because people in the barangay knew and trusted the people who campaigned for it at the grassroots. In contrast, other candidates relied on a core group of supporters who campaigned across different barangays, with the result that the people they visited often did not even know, let alone trust them. When team members held campaign sorties (small-scale public campaign events) in every zone of every barangay, the same members and officers of barangay-based organisations were in the audience alongside residents. The barangay organisation members would also be in charge of setting up the venues for the campaign sorties, preparing the sound systems, stages, chairs, and food for the audience.[11]

Other non-barangay-based organisations affiliated with NCPC also played a role during the election period. These included the various drivers and vendors associations and even different businesses which were part of the Chamber of Commerce. Daryl, one of the campaign heads of Team Naga, explained that "What is good about these organisations is that they call for a separate meeting for all their members and invite the candidates of Team Naga to campaign."[12] Legacion and Bongat confirmed this approach and even revealed that they could hardly accommodate all the invitations they received from NCPC member organisations, as well as from business owners who expressed support for the team. They stressed, however, that these organisations did not formally provide support through NCPC but instead supported their campaign "independently".[13]

Another distinctive feature of Team Naga's electoral approach was the unique recruitment system it had in place to select candidates for elected office. This process ensured that only electable candidates who were committed to the Naga City Model were selected. Despite being based on a network of mass organisations and barangay-level bodies, at its apex the team sometimes resembles an elite membership group. Membership is usually closed, unless there is a vacant post, which occurs if a team member happens to have reached their term limit, run for a higher post, or left the group to pursue a different career. When such a vacancy occurs, the leaders of the different organisations registered at the NCPC, the city hall department heads, and members of Team Naga itself can make nominations for a replacement. Bongat explained, "[The] screening process is very consultative. We start with a long list of more than 30 names which were suggestions from the different organisations. Then, the team decides who may be included in the survey."[14] This process, Bongat said, was the same as that employed by Jesse Robredo during his time as mayor. However, in the present administration, there were rumours that people who wanted to be considered by the team had to pay a "membership fee" amounting to millions of pesos. However, no interviewee confirmed this allegation.

---

[11] Interview with city hall employee, 18 May 2016.
[12] Interview, 21 April 2016.
[13] Interview with Bongat, 16 May 2016; Interview with Legacion, 5 May 2016.
[14] Interview with Bongat, 16 May 2016.

After the preliminary list of candidates is prepared, informal surveys are conducted. One survey is conducted among the *punong barangays* (village chiefs), barangay councilors, leaders of the different organisations in the NCPC, and other organisations in the barangays. A commissioned survey is also conducted in the barangays among residents. This process ensures that the group chooses candidates who can win. According to one key informant, the commissioned surveys are conducted by the Lingkod Barangay Office, one of the offices created by the city administration in 1992, during the second term of Jesse Robredo as city mayor. This implies that resources of the city are used for the campaign of the team. However, no interviewee wanted to confirm the budget and source of finance for this survey. Sometimes, these surveys are repeated, usually when elections are nearing, in order to ensure that only popular candidates are nominated. Those who top these surveys are then considered to run for the post. The members of the team who currently hold office finalise the list of candidates.

This recruitment system is similar to those operating elsewhere in the Philippines as described by Teehankee (2012b) and Kasuya (2009), in that winnability is a critical factor. What makes Team Naga's approach distinctive is that this local machine possesses a broad and stable mass base, giving selected candidates a large chance of victory. Another distinctive feature is that Team Naga's internal control and selection mechanism ensures that candidates who are selected are committed to continuing the programmes and projects of the city government. The process also ensures representation of important sectors in the society: thus, the team of city councilors elected in 2016 included a senior citizen, a former college faculty member, a former Sangguniang Kabataan (Youth Council) Federation chairperson, a doctor, a lawyer, and many others.

As during Robredo's time, in 2016 Team Naga used the slogan "Ubos kun Ubos, Gabos kun Gabos" and campaigned as a team rather than individually. The mayor acted as the head of the campaign, planning the different activities and controlling the common fund which came from contributions from various sources. Bongat and Legacion emphasised that they tried to avoid distribution of goods and money during the campaign. When approached with requests for assistance from constituents, instead of giving their personal money, they would direct the person asking for help to the city hall. As Legacion explained:

> The city has programmes to help people in need, for example, medical assistance. But for those problems which are very personal, they should settle it on their own. At the start of the campaign, we try to

accommodate every request. We stretched what funds we had as long as we were able to help. For example, when someone needed PhP 1,000, we would give him PhP 100. That was until about two weeks ago, when we exhausted the budget. When someone comes to me, I tell him the truth that my office doesn't have any more budget for that and that maybe I can help him in another way or at another time.[15]

However, the Mendoza camp challenged the claim that Team Naga did not distribute money, alleging that three days before the election it distributed cash to voters. Specifically, one campaign worker claimed that Team Naga gave beneficiaries of the 4Ps cash transfer programme PhP 1,000 each, after the Mendoza team had distributed PhP 300 each to them, explaining Mendoza's loss of support in the group.[16] One pedicab driver explained that he received a box of groceries from the city government a few days before the election during a meeting of the Padyak Drivers Association Federation. It appears likely that such instances of distribution of money and goods were a response to the massive vote buying of the challenger's camp. One informant from the Team Naga campaign confirmed that the team was forced to distribute money and goods because some organisations pressured them to do so after receiving gifts from the other camp. However, it is not clear how widespread such practices were.

CONCLUSION

For three decades, Naga City has provided an alternative model of local politics in the Philippines, one in which organised linkages with people's organisations take the place of the personalised and clientelistic relationships that are typical of the country. However, the Naga City Model now shows signs of strain following the 2012 death of Jesse Robredo, the visionary who established the model and was so closely associated with it for decades. While the straight-ticket win Team Naga achieved in 2016 indicates that the local coalition that Robredo established remains strong, certain events in the 2016 election show that the system that Robredo founded is vulnerable. The unique recruitment pattern used by the team has assured continuity in the linkages between its leaders and its mass membership. However, the rumoured membership fee puts money in the

---

[15] Interview with Legacion, 5 May 2016.
[16] Interview with Mendoza's key campaign personnel, 17 May 2016.

equation for the first time, and may undermine the quality of leadership and the sectoral representation upon which the model is based. The mobilisation of mass organisations during the campaign likewise shows institutionalisation of the local party machine, despite the absence of the founder. However, the indications that Team Naga began to engage in the distribution of money and goods points to change and adaption to the dominant model of clientelisic politics. In general, therefore, while the weight of evidence in the 2016 election suggests that Robredo-style politics remains institutionalised, there are certainly signs that it is under challenge. How Team Naga responds to these challenges will determine whether the distinctive brand of non-clientelist politics pursued in the city survives.

Table 10
Election results from City of Naga

Candidate	Party	Office	Per cent (%)
* Indicates incumbent candidate			
Bordado, Gabriel Jr	LP	House of Representatives	55.26
Villafuerte, Luis	NPC	House of Representatives	44.74
Naga City			
Bongat, John*	LP	Mayor	66.75
Mendoza, Tato	IND	Mayor	32.01
Ortega, Luis	IND	Mayor	1.23
Legacion, Nelson*	LP	Vice-Mayor	63.98
Sergio, David Casper Nathan	IND	Vice-Mayor	33.93
Calleja, Bebot	IND	Vice-Mayor	2.09

THE VISAYAS

chapter **11**

Leyte: Where Only the Wealthy and Powerful Survive

Ladylyn Lim Mangada[1]

Politics in Leyte province, the northern part of Leyte island, are dynastic, and controlled by two wealthy and powerful elite families, the Romualdezes and the Petillas. Political parties are largely irrelevant since they do not have the mechanisms or structures to choose and field candidates. Instead, the two powerful clans align with political parties or groups opportunistically, and use their informal power to appoint their chosen representatives as candidates. This pattern was illustrated in the 2016 polls, when all candidates for the local races in the province's first legislative district were supported by one of the two dominant political families. Alliances between candidates and elite families serve a dual purpose: they strengthen candidates' chances of winning and help perpetuate a clan's reputation for public service. For many years, elections in Leyte have demonstrated that local voters primarily support officials with familiar and prominent family names. Electoral politics has thus facilitated the entrenchment of the province's political dynasties.

This chapter looks at the campaign methods and resources utilised by candidates in the local election in Leyte and provides a case study that illustrates how powerful families organise, manage, and sustain

[1] The author would like to thank Butch Corpin, Leon Rojas, and Sambo Yaokasin for their assistance with data collection. This research was partly supported by 2017 Roberto S. Benedicto Professorial Chair in Political Science.

their control over their bailiwick provinces. It examines the roles of money, political machines, and image-branding in election campaigns in Leyte, and shows how vote buying and patron-client relations structure the nature of political competition. All these make it difficult for programmatic politicians, or politicians lacking connections with the province's dominant political clans, to advance. Our particular case study centres on one mayoral race. I show how an outsider challenger became ensnared in this system, ultimately failing in his efforts to win his seat. The chapter concludes with a discussion of how dynastic politics of this sort weaken the democratic process and prevent the electorate from installing a government that can truly respond to the people's needs.

BACKGROUND

This chapter focuses on the first legislative district of Leyte, which comprises the highly urbanised city of Tacloban and seven municipalities. Most of these local government units are low-income municipalities based on the Department of Finance's income classification system. Two (Santa Fe and Tolosa) are fifth-class municipalities (the second-poorest classification possible); another two (Babatngon and San Miguel) are fourth-class municipalities, one (Palo) falls into the third income class category, and the last two (Alang-alang and Tanauan) are second-class municipalities. Poverty is a pervasive problem. Based on the 2015 Family Income and Expenditure Survey, the current poverty threshold stands at 47.3 per cent. Even before the devastation caused by super-typhoon Haiyan (locally known as Yolanda) in 2013, a majority of the district's population already suffered from poverty, unemployment, and hunger. Their dire condition was aggravated by unsatisfactory infrastructure and an inadequate system for responding to and recovering from acute emergencies. These problems became even worse after Haiyan, as recovery from the devastation was slow, and more typhoons inflicted further damage.

Leyte province—particularly the first district—is the bailiwick of the Romualdez-Marcos clan. Former First Lady Imelda Marcos, wife of the late authoritarian President Ferdinand Marcos, is from a politically connected family in the town of Tolosa. Her father (Vicente) was a lawyer who served as provincial sheriff of Leyte, an uncle (Daniel) became a speaker of the House, and another uncle (Norberto) became a delegate to the constitutional convention that drafted the 1935 Constitution. During the 20-year rule of the Marcoses, Imelda and her siblings controlled the province. The ouster of the Marcoses from national office in 1986 weakened their power, but they were still able to ensure that their loyal allies in Leyte remained unchallenged in the province. The provincial capital of Tacloban has never had a non-Romualdez protégé for mayor.

The other powerful family dominating Leyte politics is the Loreto-Petilla clan. This family emerged to prominence with the decline of Romualdez-Marcos rule in the late 1980s. In the beginning, the Petillas served and defended the Romualdezes during their halcyon days in the 1960s and 1970s. The founder of the dynasty, Leopoldo Petilla (Leyte governor, 1992–95), was Marcos' legal counsel, and his wife, Matin Loreto Petilla (governor, 1995–2004, congresswoman, 2004–07, and mayor of Palo, Leyte, 2010–present) served as the secretary to former governor and ambassador Benjamin Romualdez (Imelda's brother) during the Marcos years.

These two highly influential clans fielded candidates in different towns in the first district of Leyte. Though the Petillas can trace the origins of their power to the support they received from the Romualdez-Marcoses, the elections are now a competition between these two elite families. However, to maintain "peace" and their perpetual hold in the province and first legislative district, these two families seem to have negotiated and agreed on a division of the elected posts, for the most part avoiding competing directly with each other.[2] In Leyte in 2016, the Romualdez-Marcos dynasty fielded family members to run for positions in both the House of Representatives and the local government. Cristina Romualdez, wife of the outgoing mayor of Tacloban City, Alfred Romualdez, who is Imelda's nephew, took the post of her husband. Representative Ferdinand Martin Romualdez, another nephew of Imelda, has been replaced by his wife, Yedda Marie. Meanwhile, the Petillas have control of the provincial government of Leyte with Dominic Petilla as governor, a position he has occupied since 2013.

CAMPAIGN METHODS AND RESOURCES

As in most local elections in the Philippines, candidates in the first legislative district of Leyte rely on a combination of three kinds of resources: money, political machinery, and image-branding (Anderson 1998;

---

[2] The pact was initially negotiated during a prior election by national political leaders who hoped to secure the support of both clans.

Quimpo 2005; Landé 1965; Franco 2001; Hutchcroft 1998; Sidel 1997). Vatikiotis (1996) notes that democracy in the Philippines is dominated and manipulated by the rich and powerful—a phenomenon that many political scientists attribute to enduring patron-client politics. Kawanaka (1998) observed that this relationship framework is very personal and comprehensive, its power illustrated by the common practices of house-to-house visits and village-level caucuses. Campaign events, especially those held in the evenings, become entertainment events, complete with cultural presentations, snacks, prizes, and giveaways—small material gifts that are used to buy votes (Schaffer 2007).

In Leyte, patron-client strategies and electoral tricks, such as vote buying and the recruitment of community leaders to rally popular support for candidates, were observed in the 2016 election. The following sections outline the key campaign strategies.

MONEY, VOTE BUYING, AND PATRONAGE JOBS

The use of money is essential in any electoral competition. In the Philippines, it is a common practice for candidates to spend veritable fortunes on their candidacies. As such, elections are said to be the domain solely of the wealthy. There is a perception that money shapes electoral outcomes because sizeable funds are necessary to pay for the activities, services, and gifts that can secure victory. Election expenditures include salaries for key campaign personnel; allowances for barangay officials, leaders, and board of elections inspectors; bonuses for precinct leaders who deliver winning votes; free meals and snacks for staff and attendees of barangay meetings; payment for hired poll watchers; and, for some candidates, illicit activities like vote buying. (It is notable that the distribution of money was expected, even though in most races the two main families were not competing with each other.) A mayoralty candidate of the province's smallest town estimated that he needed PhP 10 to 14 million to win comfortably, with 60–70 per cent of those funds devoted to vote buying. In the charter city (highly urbanised city) of Tacloban, unofficial estimates provided by an insider in the campaign show the winning candidate spent around PhP 100 million during the campaign period.

Candidate-informants also noted a rise of solicitations and requests for donations during the election year. While some citizens may regard elections as a way to participate in and affect the conduct of government, most take an instrumental approach, seeing elections as an opportunity to extract money, personal favours, or other immediate returns for themselves and their families in exchange for their votes. The informants confided that among their expenses, the biggest allocation went to vote buying.

As can be seen in Table 11.1, most candidates engaged in vote buying. Of the candidates for which data were collected, only two did not hand out cash, and neither of these candidates won their seats. The table also reveals that the amounts of cash dispensed varied considerably, though the typical pattern was that the mayoral candidates made the largest individual payments, reflecting the considerable authority accrued to these positions in the Philippines' system of decentralised governance.

Table 11.1
2016 Election vote buying in Leyte

Winning Candidates	Amount (in PhP)
Maya (Congressman)	500
Tanzan (Mayor, One)	500, 1,500
Tiny (Mayor, Low City)	200–500
Dalagan (Mayor, Baga)	500
City Councilors	20, 40, 50, 100
Maria (Mayor, Earth)	1,000–1,265
Sicky (Mayor, Susmaryosep)	1,500 (selected barangays)
Losing Candidates	
Boxing (Mayor, Low)	100 (selected barangays)
Nanay (Mayor, One)	500
Yomar (Mayor, Ilang-ilang)	600
Cutie (Mayor, Susmaryosep)	1,000–1,450
Dump (Mayor, Baga)	800
Dockie	X
Furdoy (Congressman)	100
Board Members	X
Municipal Councilors	50, 60, 100

Note: The names of people and places have been changed to protect the author's sources.

Determining the amount to pay, however, can be a complicated business. As a rule, the benchmark figure is determined by whoever releases the money first, and teams go to some trouble to avoid leaking in advance how much they will be distributing. According to one informant, campaign teams often prepared several envelopes filled with cash of different denominations. They did this to make it difficult for observers to accurately say how much was being given to each voter; candidates sometimes spy on each other to determine the amounts enclosed in the envelopes.

Cash was mostly distributed in the few days leading to the poll. The timing of this practice was crucial—some candidates allegedly provided an additional amount to constituents once their opponent had finished distributing their incentives. This ensured candidates a "last touch" advantage over their rivals. According to candidates, past electoral observations showed that money was a factor that determines ordinary voters' voting choices. Candidates thus believe that vote buying remains the most effective way to influence the electoral choices of eligible voters. As one candidate put it: "*Kwarta la it lanat hit tawo sanglit dapat preparado ka hit last hour*" (Voters are only after the money so candidates have to be ready, especially at the last hour).[3] Another confirmed that, "The practice is the most expensive, but effective", while a voter explained that, "we will wait for the *badil* [election money]. We expect it to be a sizeable amount this time."[4]

For candidates, the utility of vote buying is to counter or neutralise the opponent. An informant stated, "All things being equal, *ada la ha kwarta magkakairiba. Gusto mo man dumaog so mapalit ka gud hin botos. Di gad ini maupay pero asya man it nadara ha tawo*" (All things being equal, we only differ in monetary resources. If you want to win, buy votes. This is not good but this is the way to sway voters).[5] All informants thus agreed that vote buying is significantly effective as a political strategy. They noted that they had not experienced an election when the practice was not employed.

Interestingly, the shrewder the politician, the more likely the amount dispensed to voters will vary. In one town, the multi-awarded mayor seeking re-election did not utilise a system of universal rates for his vote buying efforts. For barangays perceived to be on the candidate's side, he gave PhP 500. However, in "unfriendly or hostile barangays" he tripled the election money, hoping that the larger amounts would win over unsympathetic voters.[6] The strategy paid off: he won by a large margin.

---

[3] Interview with voter in Tacloban, April 2016.
[4] Ibid.
[5] Interview with campaign worker for candidate in Tacloban, April 2016.
[6] Interview with candidate in Tanauan, Leyte, April 2016.

The ubiquity of vote buying can partly be explained by the poor socio-economic condition of the voters in the first legislative district, and by the inability of democratic institutions to deliver public goods (Hutchcroft and Rocamora 2008). As a result of reluctance on the part of electoral authorities to prosecute and jail candidates who engage in the practice, and by the very fact that this practice is so entrenched, contestants and voters alike expect it to occur. But though vote buying is a pervasive phenomenon—an open secret in the local elections—most informants said they wanted the practice to stop, as they dislike spending so much money with uncertain returns. However, given the established nature of the practice, few candidates feel they can take the risk of abandoning it. Instead, candidates feel they must be ready to spend more than what was spent in the previous election, with costs rising inexorably. As most politicians say "it is better to be broke, yet a winner rather than being broke and a loser at the same time".[7]

Vote buying is not the only form of patronage politics. One enduring form of material assistance extended by politicians is hiring loyal supporters or community leaders to "Job Order" (JO) positions, that is, as temporary employees in their governments. Victorious politicians such as mayors, governors, and congressmen often assign their campaigners to be traffic enforcers, day care workers, or administrative staff. One such JO employee is Mr. Hero, whose house was destroyed when Super-typhoon Haiyan hit Leyte in 2013. He had no work, so he became an active leader in articulating Haiyan victims' concerns. Because of his influence within the community, he was hired by the mayor as a temporary worker for his village's local government in September 2015. Together with over a dozen other leaders, he reported to the housing office for work only once a week, on Mondays. As a JO employee, he received PhP 260 a day. The nature of his work was simple: to "monitor the political preferences and loyalties of the people", he said.[8] He did the monitoring on behalf of the outgoing mayor and his wife, who was standing for her husband's seat; it consisted of interacting with and listening to voters, while also keeping an eye on who else was visiting households in the area.

Another example is a former barangay captain. After his term ended, he joined one of the universities in the first legislative district as a member of the faculty. He was forced to leave a few years later because he failed to earn his graduate degree. The mayor then asked him to run in the local

---

[7] Interview with candidate in Tacloban, April 2016.
[8] Interview with informant in Tacloban, April 2016.

council, but he lost, in spite of the millions of pesos the mayor gave him as assistance. Despite the election law that prohibits losing candidates from working in government service for at least one year, he was still able to work in the local government unit as the "right hand man" of the mayor, troubleshooting on various political and administrative tasks as one of the executive assistants of the mayor. He claimed he was being paid using the mayor's personal funds. Today, he serves as a department head, once again appointed by the mayor.

Such examples illustrate Gutierrez's (1992) observation that voters and political actors usually align or identify themselves with political leaders who are mostly able to dispense patronage. In return these beneficiaries of political rewards become campaign workers who convince family members and friends to favour their patron, or they become the "eyes and ears" of the candidate/patron in the community.

MOBILISATION STRUCTURES

The organisation of election campaigns in Leyte, as in most parts of the Philippines, is based around personal organisations and networks of ward leaders built by individual candidates. This pattern has remained durable over time. Back in the 1970s, Machado (1974) noted that this machinery was composed of a leader and his or her followers and was built for political purposes, specifically, for the purpose of mobilising and influencing voting outcomes through the dispensation of social, economic, or material benefits. These benefits are essentially patronage in the form of jobs, services, favours, and money distributed to voters and supporters (Teehankee 2012a).

Though these organisations are informal and personalised, they can also be very long-lasting. In 2016 in Leyte, all of the incumbent local officials I encountered who were aspiring for the same or higher positions utilised their old political organisations. The oldest of these organisations dated back to the 1995 election. Political leaders insisted that the machinery should not be dismantled after the polls. To keep their people loyal, the patrons visit them or attend to their needs and problems whenever help is sought. In contrast, challengers who were running for the first time for single seats tended to share the electoral machines of their parties. This reflects the need for a larger machine and a more comprehensive investment in the constituency for single seat races. The number of votes needed to win a seat as mayor or vice-mayor is much larger than what is required for a councilor position.

As with the previous elections, informants affirmed that their organisations provided briefings and one-on-one coaching to new recruits, new campaign workers, and voters. Politicians have observed that campaign workers perform their best, especially in concocting strategies and techniques, when they are given material incentives. They believe that the best option is to provide tangible benefits such as allowances, food support or scholarships for children (Landé 1965).

Kasuya (2009) discovered that during an election campaign, machinery leaders operate as communication brokers between the patron-politician and the voters. They do house-to-house visits to distribute campaign materials and sample ballots, help prepare political caucuses, and engage in vote buying. This pattern was observable in 2016 in Leyte. One village leader said, "We list and monitor voters in the barangay. We also bring people to the venue whenever there is a scheduled campaign."[9]

Another informant recounted, "I go to every household to introduce my candidate and make assurances. Three months before elections, I go around to find out who among the constituents are for my candidate. I befriend the organisations and treat the people well so it won't be difficult to convince them to favour my candidate."[10] Such close interactions with, and monitoring of, voters continues to election day itself. As an informant in a place I will refer to as Low City explained: "We accompany voters who are not familiar with computers [such as those used as part of the voting process]. These are voters who do not know much of automation. It's not only persons with disability (PWDs) that we accompany. We try to convince voters to go by pair so they help each other and to ensure that they voted for our candidate. This gives us evidence that they truly voted for us."[11]

The informants maintained that the mobilisation structure depends on the position the candidate is aiming for and the size of the territory in which he or she must compete for votes. For example, the sitting congressman created a structure that was composed, at the bottom, of the organisation of precinct leaders; above them were liaison officers and then the municipal coordinator. The liaison officers monitored the precinct leaders, while the municipal coordinator and a leader of the barangay

---

[9] Interview with informant, April 2016.
[10] Ibid.
[11] Interview with informant in Low City, April 2016.

distributed the election money in the village. All election workers (precinct leaders, liaison officers, and municipal coordinators) were provided a monthly honorarium. Campaign staff revealed that months before the election, the congressman had created a private livelihood facility using both government and private funds. This facility trained underemployed women in some barangay in his constituency in preparing banana chips, managing rice dealerships, and raising hogs. All the beneficiaries of this programme became "volunteers" in the campaign structure when the congressman's wife began her campaign to take over her husband's seat.

In the race for the mayoralty post in Low City, an informant disclosed that her barangay had community leaders who possessed "tested loyalty and smartness". She, being the barangay chair and contact person of the barangay, reported directly to the mayor. All solicitations from her constituents for material assistance before, during, and after the election were coursed through her. In Low City, most of the barangay chairs were tapped to head the campaign at the village level. A barangay chair communicates directly to the anointed candidate of the mayor. The barangay chair submits to the candidate mayor the list of his/her team in the barangay. My informant explained that all she needed to do was spread the word that the mayor had been very helpful in barangay projects, and if his anointed successor won the election, more infrastructure projects would be poured into their barangay.

In choosing their campaign staff, candidates look not only for people who are dependent upon them. They also assess them based on their performance in previous elections, specifically their capability to promote candidates and undermine opponents. Social influence is also a key factor: most informants explained that the key figures in their political machinery were individuals who exercise power and authority in their communities (Mangada 2015). Many were barangay captains or officials, who were especially sought as campaign coordinators for two major reasons: first, barangay officials have usually earned the trust of the people because of the work they perform in managing community affairs and solving people's problems and, secondly, they are familiar with the voters in their barangays, and know how to convince people to vote for their candidate.

But there is more to winning an election than distributing money and building a campaign organisation. Candidates also need to be able to build a personal image that voters will find attractive.

For example, one incumbent councilor running for mayor portrayed herself as "God-fearing and morally righteous" to highlight her status as a born-again Christian. Whenever she visited barangays, she reminded the people she addressed not to backbite or utter bad words against her political foe. Instead, she would perform a song, to the delight of the audience. These attempts to endear herself to her constituents were apparently at least in part strategies to hide her lack of comprehensive knowledge on issues affecting the community. She never accepted any invitation to a public forum, or even bothered to explain her campaign tag, "*Diri la bangon-better*" ("Self made better"). This strategy seemed to help in that her opponent endlessly talked about the poor performance of her husband, and thus sounded too critical and negative. This councilor was elected.

Every candidate tried to build a distinctive image of some sort and to present themselves as approachable and good natured. But image building of this sort was also connected to patronage politics. All incumbents interviewed maintained that being able to respond to the requests of voters before the election was an advantage—for example, with medicines, employment, and funeral assistance. Politicians expect recipients to repay their helpful acts with votes in the next election. They show concern, kindness, and sincerity to constituents—including by demonstrating a personalised touch by visiting the sick or dying, or by participating in celebrations—in order for the beneficiaries to remain on their side.

Moreover, such acts of supposed charity do not only curry favour with a single person, but the recipient of the assistance will usually advertise the good deed to his or her family and friends. He or she then becomes a potential leader in the community, as anybody who publicly and courageously endorses a patron/candidate is tapped to head either a committee or a particular sector. Willem Wolters (1984: 198–9) described the granting of assistance as one of the many characteristics of patron-client relationships which bind higher-level politicians to lower-level ones, or local politicians to a handful of immediate supporters. Such interactions can give rise to long-lasting ties: if one has extended or received assistance more than once, both parties end up treating each other as "family" and the recipient is duty-bound to support the patron.

DYNASTIC AND MONEY POLITICS: A CASE STUDY

This section examines the campaign of a young candidate in the 2016 election in Leyte to demonstrate the interplay of the three types of campaign resources (money, political machinery, and image-branding) and the complicated result of their interaction.

Cutie Enchong (names of people, places, and political parties in this account have been changed to protect the author's sources) is a young entrepreneur in Tacloban City. He married a medical professional from Eastern Samar, whose dermatology and diagnostic clinic is also based in Tacloban City. In 2013, he ran as municipal councilor in his hometown of Susmaryosep, Leyte, under the ticket of Family A. He obtained the highest number of votes, thus ranking him first among the ten winning councilors. Using his family resources, he was able to give PhP 100 to each voter without relying on his party's political machinery.

In the 2013 election, it was only in Susmaryosep, Leyte, where Family A had a winning mayor. The other localities were controlled by Family B. In the local council of Susmaryosep, only the vice-mayor and Councilor Cutie were allied with Family A (the mayor is not part of the council). The majority of seats belonged to Family B. Being a "newbie" in politics, Councilor Cutie witnessed that Family B councilors were active, informed, and productive in their sessions. The Family B councilors were only too eager to mentor him in the law-making process, and he began to develop good working relations with them. Six months before the 2016 election, Family B councilors started sounding him out on whether he wanted to run for mayor. Meanwhile, Family A Mayor Sicky wooed him to become his vice-mayor, dumping the sitting vice-mayor, who was another Family A protégé.

Cutie decided to run as an independent candidate instead. He knew that the money of these two political families shaped electoral outcomes in his municipality, and the entire province, but he was uncomfortable with that reality. Being a native of Susmaryosep, he knew that no one in the municipality would spend beyond what one earns in public office, as there was no certainty in being able to recover the money spent. Recalling the 2013 election, Cutie also knew that the two families would financially support mayoralty candidates in 2016. Congressman Pirdi Rom (from Family A) gave PhP 7 million to Mayor Sicky in 2013, but Cutie did not know how much was released by Family B (headed by Jepe) to their endorsed candidate. Cutie's friends who were close to the Family B clan, however, claimed that Family B had given their candidate an amount that was similar to what the Roms had given Mayor Sicky, but that the money was embezzled. Talk of such large amounts of cash frightened Cutie.

Weeks before filing his certificate of candidacy, Cutie tried contacting then-Congressman Pirdi Rom to present his plan of running against the incumbent, who was a Rom ally, and to persuade him and the family to remain neutral in the mayoral race and help neither of them. But Cutie was not allowed by the cordon sanitaire to see Rom. He went ahead and filed his certificate of candidacy for mayor as an independent and continued to reach out to the congressman's office through other people close to Rom's cordon sanitaire. However, one of Rom's lawyers insisted that the family would still support Mayor Sicky. Meanwhile, Cutie's application to renew his business in Susmaryosep was rejected by the mayor. The mayor maintained that he was not a resident of the town. After several appeals, Cutie got a lawyer and filed a case with the Ombudsman.

A Family B-linked councilor soon offered to connect him to Jepe. In less than three days, he met Jepe somewhere in Leyte. Jepe offered to help him as long as he ceased being an independent candidate and aligned with Jepe's party. In Cutie's words: "I like dealing with Jepe, he advises and is accessible. He does not have layers of cordon sanitaire."[12] It took Cutie a week to decide to align with Jepe. Cutie was still hoping he could meet Pirdi Rom.

Cutie's initial electoral bid had two crucial weaknesses: lack of funds and absence of political machinery. He had barely enough to pay for tarpaulins (banners), meals, and fuel for volunteers. His campaign materials were signed by his wife, and they could not pay cash to print banners and posters. Campaign volunteers received PhP 150 per week just two weeks before the election, which is similar to what other candidates paid. To advance his political candidacy on the ground, a former mayor and incumbent councilor offered his political machinery. This person was aligned with Jepe. Cutie barely knew any of the people who came to help him, though his father and some key campaign volunteers handled the master list of voters that was given to his team by the barangay leaders who were tasked with identifying possible supporters. Most of these barangay leaders had been "donated" by the former mayor.

Cutie knew that he had no choice but to distribute cash to voters, but the process did not go smoothly. A few days before the election, these barangay leaders pressured Cutie to entrust the "*badil*" (election money) to their care, instead of to his relatives whom Cutie had put in charge of managing the distribution. A day before the election, some campaign workers threatened to stop working for him. Cutie also had trouble accumulating enough cash. Two days before election day, Cutie borrowed PhP 5 million from his in-laws who were businesspeople. Another senior

---

[12] Interview with candidate, April 2016.

politician closely related to Jepe released almost PhP 5 million as well. The funds came in two tranches: three million the day before voting day and the remaining amount on the morning of the voting day. This situation caused delay in packing and distributing the money. Cutie and his close relatives did not know how much to give: PhP 500, PhP 800, or PhP 1,000. Packing the money was done in Low City and only five people were involved. To win, Cutie decided to give PhP 1,000 per voter. Travel time from Low City to Susmaryosep was an hour, and only one service vehicle was being used to get the money from Low City.

In the second week of April, about a month before polling day, Cutie's rival had been rushed to hospital. Mayor Sicky stayed in the intensive care unit for a few days, and his wife campaigned in his stead. She also sought an audience with Cutie's lawyer, pleading with him to drop the case he had filed against her husband with the Ombudsman, considering Sicky's bad health. She also hinted that the money the couple had been planning to use for vote buying on election day would now be allocated to Mayor Sicky's treatment instead.

Cutie later suspected that this approach had been a trick to make him complacent. No one from Cutie's camp knew that Sicky was planning to continue to distribute money to buy votes in spite of his illness. He gave PhP 1,500 to each voter in three barangays where Sicky had houses and, therefore, close personal connections. The funds were released on the night before the election. Cutie had initially distributed PhP 1,000 per voter in these three barangays, but when he learned about the amount his rival was giving away, he tried to catch up by giving PhP 1,450 there.

In the end, Cutie lost the election by just over 300 votes, a narrow margin.

CONCLUSION

In this chapter I have argued that there are three critical components to electoral strategy in Leyte, as in other parts of the Philippines: money, machinery, and image-building. Of these tools in the election arsenal, the 2016 election showed that "big money" was the most important. The best-funded candidates—like Mayor Sicky—tended to prevail, winning in poor communities that had been burdened by a major natural catastrophe a few years earlier. Money played a direct role, in the form of vote buying, but it was also critical for funding the political machines and image promotion upon which successful candidates also relied. As a result, powerful and wealthy families called the shots in the local races. The province's two political families took advantage of their authoritative positions and connections to use patron-client strategies and personalistic ties to entrench their positions of dominance. In fact, almost all winning candidates in the last local election were identified with one of the two political families.

What do the results in the First District of Leyte suggest for broader questions about the nature of local democracy? To state the obvious, money can subvert competitive elections. This is particularly true when it is combined with dynastic politics. When its concentration in the hands of a few allows a narrow band of political elites to dominate the field, democracy is undermined. In such a context, citizen-voters have little opportunity or capacity to distil policy issues or to weigh carefully the outcomes of their voting decisions. The dominance of big money ultimately threatens the legitimacy of the electoral process and undermines the capacity of the resulting governments to respond to the demands and interests of the people.

Table 11.2

Election results from Leyte 1st District

Candidate	Party	Office	Per cent (%)
*Indicates Incumbent Candidate			
Romualdez, Yedda	LAKAS	House of Representatives	73.66
Clemencio, Fiel	IND	House of Representatives	25.75
Jacla, Ka-Poly	IND	House of Representatives	0.59
Petilla, Leopoldo Dominico*	LP	Provincial Governor	94.48
Falcone, Bal	IND	Provincial Governor	2.78
Nielo, Philip	IND	Provincial Governor	2.74
Loreto, Carlo*	LP	Provincial Vice-Governor	100.00
Alangalang			
Capon, Nalding	LAKAS	Mayor	53.15
Bague, Mario	LP	Mayor	46.85
Apurillo, Sarah	LAKAS	Vice-Mayor	54.04
Gayas, Marilou	LP	Vice-Mayor	45.96

(cont'd overleaf)

Table 11.2 (*cont'd*)

Candidate	Party	Office	Per cent (%)
Babatngon			
Galapon-Rondina, Maria Fe	UNA	Mayor	36.03
Chan, Joselito	LP	Mayor	32.47
Alde, Nico	PDPLBN	Mayor	29.90
Quintana, Ludy	IND	Mayor	1.60
Lugnasin, Leny	LP	Vice-Mayor	70.09
Elizaga, Jun	UNA	Vice-Mayor	27.59
Villanueva, Bimbo	IND	Vice-Mayor	1.52
Saballa, Boykia	IND	Vice-Mayor	0.80
Palo			
Petilla, Matin*	LP	Mayor	64.54
Sevilla, Teddy	IND	Mayor	35.46
Reposar, Bolingling*	LP	Vice-Mayor	100.00
San Miguel			
Esperas, Chekay*	LP	Mayor	56.54
Brazil, Pros	LAKAS	Mayor	43.46
Oballo, Atilano*	LP	Vice-Mayor	51.21
Agner, Ruben	LAKAS	Vice-Mayor	48.79
Santa Fe			
Monteza, Oca*	LAKAS	Mayor	47.53
Echague, Bong	IND	Mayor	44.54
Martinez, Joe	IND	Mayor	7.93
Lantajo, Ismael	LAKAS	Vice-Mayor	44.90
Parado, Froilan*	LP	Vice-Mayor	35.73
Jamora, Jovito	IND	Vice-Mayor	19.37
Tacloban City (Capital)			
Romualdez, Cristina	NP	Mayor	75.03
Glova, Neil	NPC	Mayor	24.58
Cabudoy, Golda Hilda	IND	Mayor	0.39
Yaokasin, Sambo*	IND	Vice-Mayor	91.58
Tolibas, Ramon Jr.	NUP	Vice-Mayor	8.42

Table 11.2 *(cont'd)*

Candidate	Party	Office	Per cent (%)
Tanauan			
Tecson, Pel*	LP	Mayor	45.56
Gimenez, Ina	LAKAS	Mayor	41.50
Pagayanan, Agapito Jr.	IND	Mayor	12.94
Flores, Doc Ronald*	LP	Vice-Mayor	100.00
Tolosa			
Ocaña, Erwin*	LP	Mayor	65.82
Junia, Ray	PMP	Mayor	20.15
Caadan, Hilario	LAKAS	Mayor	14.03
Legaspi, Rodolfo Jr.	LP	Vice-Mayor	57.23
Roa, Joyjoy	LAKAS	Vice-Mayor	26.94
Palaña, Virgie	IND	Vice-Mayor	15.83

chapter **12**

Second District of Leyte: Money, Machinery, and Issues in Fighting Local Dynasties in the 2016 Election

Donabel S. Tumandao

INTRODUCTION

The Second District of Leyte is an electoral district with 14 municipalities, the majority of which are poor. It has been ruled by dynastic clans for more than two decades. The recently concluded 2016 election displayed how politicians have converted their constituencies into their own family mass base, deftly expanding and extending their political powers by establishing and maintaining their own political dynasties. However, the 2016 election saw a significant change in the district's political landscape as some once-indomitable political clans met their demise. What did it take to challenge these political clans? How did the political challengers defeat the incumbency power of the dynastic candidates?

This chapter examines the clientelistic and patronage-based strategies employed by the political candidates in the Second District of Leyte.[1] It

---

[1] The information reported in the chapter is based on shadowing of and interviews with political candidates, campaign and operations handlers, strategists and workers, and observations of the various campaign and operations events during April and May 2016.

argues that the combination of ample amounts of money and well-oiled machinery, assets that dynastic candidates have had in abundance, in this case worked to the advantage of challengers and enabled them to secure victory. But in what way can new political players offset the advantages of dynastic candidates? This chapter presents a case study of political challengers who could match dynastic candidates in terms of money and machinery and thus posed a tough challenge to the incumbents. Moreover, these challengers' astute use of issues amplified their chances of defeating a once-resolute political clan in the legislative district.

BACKGROUND ON THE REGION

The Second Congressional District of Leyte is the largest district in the province in terms of land area, covering 147,672 hectares and encompassing 14 municipalities with a total of 501 barangays. The legislative district is located along coastline and is blessed with wide tracts of land; the majority of the constituents rely on agriculture for subsistence. The majority of the 14 municipalities belong to the lower income classes—seven (Julita, La Paz, MacArthur, Mayorga, Pastrana, Tabon-Tabon, and Tunga) are in the fifth class, two (Barugo and Capoocan) are fourth class municipalities and three (Dulag, Dagami, and Jaro) are third class municipalities. The two biggest municipalities in terms of population—Carigara and Burauen— are Second and First Class municipalities, respectively. In 2015, the province as a whole was ranked among the top 20 poorest provinces in the country, with an alarming poverty rate of 46.7 per cent (Philippine Statistics Authority 2017).

The political setting of the Second District of Leyte has been characterised by the resilience of dynastic clans. At the congressional level, the Second District has been politically controlled by the Apostols for the last 24 years. In the 2016 local election, this political family, which was affiliated with the Liberal Party, attempted to regain its bailiwick, Carigara, by putting forward Anlie Apostol, an incumbent board member and former mayor, to run against the first-term incumbent Mayor Eduardo "Boy" Ong. At the same, the Apostol matriarch, Trinidad "Ebbie" Apostol, a former Leyte Vice-Governor, former congresswoman, and former Carigara mayor, contested to replace Anlie in the provincial board, while incumbent Congressman Sergio Apostol sought to complete his third term. However, the veteran congressman, who held the position from 1992–2001 and from 2010–16—a total of 15 years—was challenged by Henry Ong, a political newcomer and brother of incumbent Carigara Mayor Boy Ong. This collision between the politically well-connected and moneyed Apostol clan and this equally affluent Ong brothers, was the highlight of the local elections in the Second District of Leyte, and resulted in the victory for the Ongs.

Aside from the electoral fray between the Apostols and the Ong brothers, six other municipalities whose incumbent mayors completed their third consecutive term in 2016 fielded their family members to replace them in their posts. These six incumbent mayors aspired to be replaced by their children (Capoocan, Dulag, and Jaro), wife (Barugo), husband (Burauen), or sister (Pastrana). The municipality of MacArthur, on the other hand, had a tandem of Leria siblings running for the mayoral and vice-mayoral posts.

In the 2016 election, the Apostols and all the incumbent municipal mayors in the legislative district, except for the mayor of Carigara, were affiliated with the Liberal Party. Even before 2010, such municipalities—particularly those ruled by political families—belonged to the same political party as the Apostols, which at that time was LAKAS KAMPI-CMD, the political party of then-President Gloria Macapagal Arroyo. The Apostol clan claimed to have the support of the 13 municipalities in the legislative district, anchored by the political family's long-established networks with local politicians.

CANDIDATE STRATEGY AND THE ROLE OF PATRONAGE

In the 2016 election, the strategies of the candidates were primarily clientelistic and patronage-based, including the use of vote buying, dispensation of goods, and promises of future employment opportunities for supporters. A common strategy among political challengers was to complement these strategies with a discourse of "change". They accused the administration of corruption, usually citing post-Typhoon Haiyan issues (see below) as examples of bad governance. In response, the incumbents delivered their accomplishment reports and campaigned on an "*ipadayon an serbisyo*" (continue the service) slogan. They particularly depended on pork barrel politics to woo voters in municipalities and in barangays.

The season of solicitations and contributions

The Philippine election period, which falls in summer, coincides with the festivities for different barangay fiestas and sports events (Perron 2009). April and May are the months of fiestas, when various barangays hold different activities and nightly talent and cultural shows. In order to sponsor various fiesta-related activities, organisers, such as barangay councils, youth ministries, and LGBT associations sought financial support from candidates. Aside from cash, the candidates were usually asked to donate trophies. Candidates were often willing to accept solicitations from these organisations as they expected that their names would be mentioned when the organisers publicly expressed their gratitude to their donors. Moreover, basketball players involved in inter-barangay and inter-town basketball tournaments asked the candidates to sponsor basketball uniforms. However, most of the candidates, be they incumbents or challengers, responded that basketball uniforms for an entire team were too costly, so instead they gave cash of between PhP 200 and PhP 500.

Another common experience among the candidates was dealing with voters seeking financial assistance for medical check-ups, medicine for sick family members, ultrasounds for pregnant women, and transportation to go to the hospital. The candidates and campaign workers argued that it was important to respond to such demands even if they believed that some of those who approach them were not really in need of help; not doing so would leave a bad impression, which they feared might have a negative impact on the election results.

Post-Haiyan issues hurled against the incumbents

The living conditions of constituents in the district were aggravated when Typhoon Haiyan (locally known as Super-typhoon Yolanda), the strongest and most destructive typhoon ever recorded in the country, ravaged the province of Leyte in 2013. Post-Haiyan issues mattered for the district's electoral contests, especially at the municipal level. Apart from the strategies mentioned above, political challengers took advantage of the grievances of typhoon victims by highlighting in their campaign sorties issues surrounding the distribution of post-Haiyan relief assistance. These political challengers accused the incumbents, especially the mayors, of using relief assistance funds to financially support their electoral bids. Moreover, some supporters of these political challengers claimed that during the distribution of relief goods and the Emergency Shelter Assistance fund, only the supporters of the incumbent mayors were listed as beneficiaries; non-supporters were left off the list. If these allegations are true, the distribution of post-Haiyan relief assistance was simply another form of patronage.

On the other hand, the incumbent candidates presented their accomplishments from 2013 to 2016. Central among these accomplishments was the reconstruction of buildings and projects destroyed by Typhoon Haiyan, such as markets, gymnasiums, schools, and drainage systems. Incumbents' campaign events were also venues for defending themselves against the issues thrown against them. They argued that such accusations were merely electoral tactics used by their political challengers in an attempt to tarnish their image before the voters.

The perks of being a dynastic candidate: Pork-barrelling and political branding

Owing to the agricultural landscape of the Second District of Leyte, there are various infrastructure projects in the barangays, most of which involve construction of farm-to-market roads. Kasuya declares that a "Filipino politician can translate pork barrel into a political advantage leading to re-election" (Kasuya 2009). One such translation tactic is credit-claiming, a direct advantage enjoyed by incumbent candidates and even by some non-incumbents who belong to political dynasties. On or besides these projects are posters flaunting the names of the elected officials who claim their efforts made the projects possible. Some of these posters not only bear the names of the elected officials but also include pictures of other family members who were running for office but, in fact, had nothing to do with the project. This is one of the notable perks of being a dynastic candidate: even a non-incumbent who is a member of a political dynasty can piggyback on his or her incumbent family members' achievements or credits.

In this vein, one congressional candidate promised to pour projects into barangays in return for the votes. To justify such electoral promises, he mentioned his family's previous projects in the barangays, which, according to him, indicated that his family has been true to its word. A candidate in one municipality confided that candidates directly negotiated with the barangay captains in their municipality:

Honestly, we have this strategy of "vote straight" (congressional level down to the councilors) and they will say a price . . . this barangay is let's say P3 million worth of projects or the barangay can identify the projects that they want.[2]

Still the most powerful weapon: Money for vote buying

Vote buying is still the most prominent type of money politics in Philippine elections (Hedman 2010). The previously mentioned strategies are all essential in building a candidate's "good" image and establishing name recall among the voters, but in terms of securing votes, most of the interviewed candidates and political strategists admitted that their major weapon is vote buying. Both incumbents and challengers argued that the act of giving cash, regardless of the amount, is a basic rule of the game. Some even remarked that the highest bidder has a better chance of winning. This most important strategy received the biggest budget among all campaign expenses; most candidates declared that vote buying comprised 80–90 per cent of their total budget.

Challengers who needed to offset the power of their opponent's incumbency, especially the dynastic challengers whose family names were already known to the people and who had established political networks, were enticed to match the amount given by the incumbent or to give an even larger amount. While more is better, regardless of the amount, in order to guarantee one's victory, a candidate had to dispense cash to as many voters as possible. Most of the candidates stated that they prioritised their own supporters and if it was a very tight competition, most were willing to penetrate the supporters of their opponents. This strategy depended heavily on the candidate's networks of *liders* in the barangays, which will be discussed in the next section.

MOBILISATION STRUCTURE

Most of the candidates admitted that party affiliation had only a nominal role during elections. Historically, the majority of the 13 incumbent mayors belonged to the same political party: that of the incumbent congressman who was aligned with the party of whomever was president. For example,

---

[2] Interview with a candidate for councilor, 3 May 2016.

their allegiance switched from LAKAS KAMPI-CMD during the time of President Gloria Macapagal-Arroyo to the Liberal Party of President Noynoy Aquino in 2010. These municipal candidates directed their loyalty not to the political party but to the congressman, who, after elections, could direct various projects to their municipalities. Party linkage, in this sense, was very tenuous. The candidates further acknowledged that party affiliation only matters during election periods and even then, the only benefit that they derive from it was the endorsement from their national candidates who campaigned in the district. Municipal candidates (for example mayor, vice-mayor, and councilors), regardless of party affiliation, referred to their local slates as their *partido*, which they relied on for their house-to-house campaigns, nightly barangay caucuses, and *mitings de avance*. But in terms of securing votes, they were on their own and did not even rely on their slate. The quest for victory, which mostly relied on vote buying, demanded a personalised machinery for each candidate, the maintenance of which has perpetuated clientelistic and patronage-based political organisations at the municipal and barangay levels.

Coming up with a political machinery that can be mobilised for the election period was a big challenge, particularly for non-incumbent and non-dynastic candidates who had to form their campaign teams and establish networks at the municipal, barangay and even *purok* (sub-barangay) levels without the resources and benefits of incumbency. In contrast, an already existing mobilisation structure added to the political advantage of incumbent candidates, who had built campaign teams and formed and utilised well-entrenched connections in the years that they had been in office. This was particularly true for dynastic incumbents, who could leverage broader and deeper networks. The political machinery of these candidates was composed of loyal supporters and *liders* at the barangay and *purok* levels. This machinery was usually divided into two groups: one was the central campaign team, devoted to various campaign activities, and the other was the mobilisation team composed of brokers and *liders*. This machinery was mobilised during the most intense days or hours before the election. A small core group of political strategists directed and coordinated the work of these two groups. The campaign teams for both political challengers and incumbent candidates were composed of relatives, friends, and loyal supporters.

During the campaign period, municipal candidates held house-to-house visits and various campaign sorties with their partido or local slate, accompanied by their own group of campaigners. The mayoral candidate of the slate usually provided the mini-cabs with large speakers that played the team's campaign jingle. Each candidate's group of campaigners posted streamers and distributed flyers to the voters. *Liders* extended assistance during the campaign by guiding the team and by introducing the candidates to voters in the barangays. They also played a key role in facilitating barangay caucuses, from arranging venues to drawing audiences to attend these campaign events.

When it came to finding brokers, political challengers established their networks of *liders* by choosing those regarded as influential figures in their constituencies, like former barangay officials, or others identified as being in opposition to the incumbent. Incumbent congressional candidates relied more on their allied mayors, while some incumbent mayoral candidates chose barangay captains as their *liders*. These incumbent candidates relied on their old political organisations on the ground; the dynastic candidates, in particular, counted on those *liders* who had proven effective in delivering votes in previous elections. Indeed, the fact that the clan could draw on the same network of *liders* for multiple races and across multiple elections represented another advantage for political clans (Coronel 2007).

The number of *liders* depended on the number of voters a barangay had. Barangays with the smallest voting population had one *lider* while bigger constituencies had a barangay coordinator as well as additional *purok* and family *liders*. These *liders* prepared a list of their loyal supporters and the names of swing voters. Such lists became the basis for the distribution of cash payments to voters. In addition, *liders* were also mobilised during the campaign for intelligence work, namely, monitoring and reporting on the movements of their opponents' *liders* and supporters. The candidates used this information to gauge their own strength in the barangays and make necessary adjustments. For example, if they found that they were weak in one barangay, in addition to securing their own loyal voters they would do more to try and make inroads among their opponents' voters. Incumbent and dynastic candidates again had an edge as they had a clearer knowledge of their strengths and weaknesses in particular areas from previous elections.

Candidates, their campaign supporters, and their brokers are bound by clientelistic linkages. The benefits that members of the political machine rake in are patronage-based, including money, services, jobs, and favours (see also Teehankee 2012a). All candidates shouldered the meals and transportation costs of their campaign supporters and workers; some also paid a daily salary to their supporters. Candidates were able to attract supporters to attend caucuses and *mitings de avance* through the provision of transportation, meals, t-shirts, and caps. A further manifestation of patronage the candidates' promises to prioritise their supporters in terms of employment opportunities and to provide future support to those *liders* who aspired to run for the upcoming barangay elections, were then scheduled for later in 2016.

IT'S NOT ALWAYS ALL ABOUT THE MONEY

Setting the political context in this municipality requires backtracking to the 2013 election. Both the mayoral contenders for that election were lacking political experience: one had served one term as a municipal councilor; the other was making her first attempt to run for an elected position, though she was a dynastic candidate and a scion of the most powerful clan in the municipality. According to informants, the dynastic candidate dispensed cash payments to more voters, and gave an amount three times higher than her competitor. As a result, when the more wealthy, dynastic candidate lost, some political pundits claimed that money was no longer the sole factor that determines electoral prospects in the municipality. However, the dynastic candidate's unpopularity was regarded as the biggest factor that contributed to her loss. According to informants, if the political clan's matriarch, then second-term incumbent mayor, had run instead, then the victory would had been theirs.

How had the political scene in this municipality changed by the 2016 election? That now-first-term mayor stood re-election and battled against another member of his previous opponent's political clan—this time, a candidate who was more popular and more politically experienced. The challenger was a former two-term mayor of the municipality and a two-term member of the Provincial Board. Money-wise, both candidates were equally affluent, enough to oil their respective machineries and to offer material and monetary inducements to voters. In terms of their political organisation at the barangay level, the dynastic mayoral candidate had more established connections and even claimed to have the support of more barangay captains than the incumbent mayor.

However it is interesting to note that the members of the incumbent mayor's slate, including the mayor himself and all of his allied municipal councilors, were all once affiliated with the dynastic clan. The political strategists and campaign handlers working for the incumbent mayor had also rendered their services to the political family in previous elections. Banking on the outcome of the 2013 election, in which money unexpectedly was not able to dictate the winner, the team of the incumbent mayor believed that the same pattern would hold for the 2016 election. But, just in case, they raised their own campaign war chest. Neither team discounted the importance of monetary inducements for voters during the electoral fray.

About a year before the election, the incumbent mayor, who wanted to factor in voter feedback in designing his electoral scheme, instructed one of his veteran political strategists to visit barangays and to ask the residents their views regarding his administration and that of the previous dynastic candidate. This was much earlier that the approach of most municipal candidates, who didn't conduct surveys intended to gauge or predict their odds of winning in the barangays until during the campaign itself.

The political strategist in question explained that, based on what had transpired in his barangay visits, it appeared that the residents were generally satisfied with the performance of the incumbent mayor. Moreover, voters, especially in the *poblacion* (the municipality proper) where the middle and upper classes reside (a group that comprised approximately one-quarter of the voting population) expressed repugnance toward the electoral bid of the dynastic candidate and claimed that they were fed up with corruption issues involving the political clan. The veteran political strategist explained that in interior barangays money could easily sway voters who weigh heavily the amounts candidates give. Voters in the *poblacion*, on the other hand, will always accept cash dole-outs, regardless of the amount, but then base their decisions on the candidates' track-records. These voters tended to be wary of political figures who had been linked to issues of corruption. He added that from the perspective of these voters, the ubiquity of cash payments during elections is viewed as common electoral practice. For them, corruption refers more to the exploitation of power by elected officials, including mismanagement of government funds, especially in the form of "ghost" and sub-standard projects.

Armed with this information, the incumbent mayor focused on ways to secure votes where money was less likely to ensure electoral victory. He instead, raised the profile of issues designed to capture the attention of voters. His team was so determined to convert a focus on issues into a winning strategy that, despite being the municipality in the district with the second highest number of barangays, they held nightly caucuses in all of these barangays. His team also conducted house-to-house campaigns, but they considered the nightly caucuses to be more important campaign venues. During these events most people were available and could be gathered in a single place to listen to both the candidates' platforms and to a full discussion of accusations hurled against their opponents. In these caucuses, not only was the dynastic candidate subjected to a salvo of negative attacks revolving around her alleged involvement in corruption and murder cases, but the rest of her family members were likewise implicated. To support these accusations, the team distributed copies of documents and evidence to the audience.

This strategy represented not only an attack on the image of the dynastic candidate, but it was packaged so as to demolish the family name of the political clan. In addition to raising corruption issues, the team of the incumbent mayor also came up with a strategy to counter a notable political advantage of political dynasties, that of credit-claiming, as mentioned earlier in this chapter. The incumbent mayor tried to offset this advantage by posting tarpaulins in the municipality's *poblacion* printed with the following statement:

> Ang pera ng bayan ay sa bayan, at hindi pag-aari ng kahit sino man o isang pamilya lamang. Kaya hindi mangyayari na ilagay ang pangalan ko bilang mayor sa ano mang proyekto ngayon at kailanman. (The government's money is the people's money and is not owned by anyone or by any family. That is why I cannot append my name as mayor to any project, now and forever.)

Furthermore, the team of the incumbent mayor explained that the corruption allegations against the political family actually triggered his breakaway from the clan. Political strategists and some supporters who had worked for the political family in previous elections now stood against their former political masters. The role of these political strategists proved indispensable throughout the electoral competition, given their knowledge of the political dynasty's *liders*, allies, and winning strategies.

Hours before the polling day, the two candidates both played the money politics game at almost the same level. However, looking at their larger campaign strategy and the election results, the strategy by the incumbent mayor's team to target voters in the *poblacion*—as voters who would not be swayed by money and whose decisions would take into account the candidates' track-records and issues—seems to have succeeded. The incumbent mayor won in all the barangays in the *poblacion*, where he garnered twice as many votes as the dynastic candidate. He was declared the ultimate victor in that electoral contest, thwarting the resurgence of the dynastic clan in the municipality.

LEVELLING THE ELECTORAL PLAYING FIELD: POLITICAL VETERAN VS POLITICAL NEOPHYTE

In order to win an election, a candidate must possess an ample amount of money and working machinery. A political veteran, who has been undefeated and who is part of a political family in power for more than two decades, can readily capitalise on these two essential attributes. How can a political challenger counter such an electoral advantage? One political neophyte, the very first opponent to seriously challenge the political veteran in question, entered the congressional electoral scene and embarked on an electoral bid with the aim of levelling the electoral game in terms of money and machinery.

In terms of money, the neophyte, who had been a businessman for 20 years, was as wealthy as the incumbent political veteran. However, unlike his opponent, who had a long-established political organisation, the neophyte had to build a mobilisation structure in the municipalities and barangays. It is worth pointing out, though, that one of his biggest assets was having key political strategists who had once worked for the political veteran and who had deep knowledge about the dynastic clan's previous strategies and network of brokers.

The political veteran relied on his key brokers: namely, incumbent mayors in the municipalities. He piggybacked on the local machinery of such municipal allies for his campaign and cash dole-outs. On the other hand, the operations team of the political neophyte had to look for its own brokers in the municipalities. They made a point of securing the support of at least one incumbent municipal councilor in the opposition in each municipality. At the barangay level, his team looked for local influential people who could be their *liders*. Most of those selected intended to run for barangay captain in the upcoming barangay elections. These chosen brokers in the barangays were all promised future support if the political neophyte were elected into office, indicating a relationship clearly built on clientelism and expectations of future patronage.

One of the biggest challenges that the neophyte had to deal with was his relative obscurity. To make himself known to the public, he put up numerous posters and streamers in the barangays, which far outnumbered his opponent's. His campaign team also worked to build his political image among potential voters. His strategists framed the electoral match as a battle between young and old, emphasising that the age of the political neophyte was half that of the veteran politician. Accentuating his relatively younger age, the neophyte's campaign team pursued a goal of visiting and campaigning in all the barangays in the legislative district. In such barangay visits, he talked to the residents—especially farmers, fishermen, senior citizens, and youth—asked about their problems, and offered ways to address such concerns if he were elected. The team used these visits to establish the image of an approachable candidate, arguing that the interests of constituents were better articulated when voters themselves could express them directly to the leader whose responsibility was to represent them in Congress. This challenger's ambitious goal to visit every barangay became the talk of the district, as local constituencies waited to see if he could indeed achieve such an ambitious target: no one—not even the political veteran—had ever visited every barangay before. In the end, the neophyte was able to visit and campaign in each of the 501 barangays in the congressional district, an achievement which also indicated how substantial his financial resources were.

After introducing himself to the public, the neophyte worked to convey to voters his anti-corruption campaign slogan, "*Waray itatago, waray korapsyon*" (Nothing to hide; no corruption). In his various campaign sorties, he adamantly attacked the incumbent official by asserting that the long years that this political veteran had held office, despite the fact that it was time for him to retire owing to old age, implied that he was greedy for power. He further pounced on the incumbent candidate's posters, placed beside infrastructure projects labelled with the words "*ipadayon an gugma han mga* [family name of the political clan]" (Continue the love of the [clan]). He argued that corruption is concealed in these various projects and that the political clan directs its *gugma*, or love, not at constituents, but at the contractors of such projects.

Apart from house-to-house campaigns, his team channelled their campaign slogans through social and broadcast media. For example, his team created a Facebook page in order to target those in the 18–40 age bracket, on which the candidate introduced himself and communicated his platform. The candidate also contributed some articles about his platform to an Eastern Visayas online news service. Moreover, his political ads were played on a local radio station, where he was also endorsed by two popular local radio commentators.

In contrast, the political veteran visited only few barangays, mostly just the poblacion in the municipalities. In his campaign sorties, he retaliated against his challenger by pointing out the neophyte's apparent lack of political experience. He was present for each of the *mitings de avance* of his allied municipal mayoral candidates, at which he also reminded the voters of his accomplishments. Days before the polls, through the mobilisation of the *liders* of his allied mayors, he also met with and distributed cash to senior citizens and youths. The barangay *liders* of the mayoral candidates gathered about ten senior citizens and ten youths in each barangay; the invitation was not made through the barangay senior citizen or youth organisations, but was purely based on the advice from local *liders*. The veteran appealed to these groups through his promises of continuing scholarship programmes for youths and other programmes for his fellow senior citizens.

In the most thrilling hours before the election, the political neophyte, armed with monetary inducements funded through his businesses, played the money politics game at the same level as the political veteran. However, the vote buying strategies they employed were different, with implications for the outcome of the election. According to informants in some municipalities, during the *ora de peligro* (dangerous hour), the veteran rode in with the local machinery of his allied mayoral candidates for the distribution of cash payments. The voters were instructed to proceed to the house of the barangay lider or coordinator, where the distribution of cash for the mayoral candidate and the political veteran took place. The neophyte's strategy, on the other hand, reflected the more common vote buying pattern in the district, in which *liders* go house-to-house to dispense cash. Informants in the barangays noted that the barangay *liders* just guided the neophyte's core operations people, who were actually the ones who gave the cash dole-outs to voters. Such a process guaranteed that the money was indeed received by the voters and did not stay in the pockets of the barangay *liders*. This strategy gave the neophyte a more direct way of monitoring his team's effort in the barangays than the veteran had; the latter largely depended on his allied mayoral candidates, who were concerned first with ensuring their own victory.

The equally wealthy neophyte, who had built his own machinery by oiling it with patronage, was the first-ever challenger who proved to be a match for the experienced veteran. The challenger lost by a wide margin in only one municipality, the hometown of his opponent. He was also defeated in four other municipalities, but only by a very slight difference in votes. Levelling the electoral game in terms of money and machinery, and offsetting the powers and advantages of his dynastic opponent's incumbency by a well-schemed campaign and astute use of issues, paved the way for the political neophyte's victory by a margin of about 12,000 votes.

CONCLUSION

The results of the 2016 election demonstrated that candidates and campaign strategists still regard money as the most important resource through which machinery is established, elections are won, and political positions are maintained. Success comes via patronage-based politics and clientelistic ties. The chapter affirms that dynastic candidates, who commonly possess money and machinery drawn from their long years of access to government funds and utilisation of well-established political networks, have capitalised on such political leverage to win previous elections. However, the chapter finds, too, that political challengers, deprived of the other advantages their dynastic opponents enjoy, but who could nevertheless match those dynastic candidates in terms of money and machinery, proved to be strong electoral competitors. Furthermore, while a lack of political experience may appear to be one of the biggest disadvantages that political neophytes face it is also an asset for political newcomers. The lack of political experience translates to no records, transactions, or issues of corruption for opponents to use in their propaganda against the neophytes. Conversely, the dynastic candidates' track-records and previous issues of corruption and ineptitude, accumulated over their long tenure in office and over the course of their clan's dominance, can prove to be a disadvantage. Where other aspects of electoral competition were equal (that is, money and machinery), focusing on corruption and reputational issues helped convince voters to choose political challengers over dynastic candidates in two contests within the district. This chapter thus argues that the astute deployment of political issues by political challengers to justify the need for dismantling a dynasty significantly can complement the combination of money and machinery.

Table 12
Election results from Leyte 2nd District

Candidate	Party	Office	Per cent (%)
*Indicates Incumbent Candidate			
Ong, Henry	NPC	House of Representatives	52.57
Apostol, Sergio Antonio	LP	House of Representatives	45.67
Hidalgo, Alberto	IND	House of Representatives	1.24
Ramos, Gary	PDPLBN	House of Representatives	0.52

Table 12 *(cont'd)*

Candidate	Party	Office	Per cent (%)
Petilla, Leopoldo Dominico*	LP	Provincial Governor	94.48
Falcone, Bal	IND	Provincial Governor	2.78
Nielo, Philip	IND	Provincial Governor	2.74
Loreto, Carlo*	LP	Provincial Vice-Governor	100.00
Barugo			
Avestruz, Ma. Rosario	LP	Mayor	70.02
Tiu, Toto	LAKAS	Mayor	20.83
Buñales, Dory	PMP	Mayor	9.15
Tiu, Josephine	LP	Vice-Mayor	84.24
Bugal, Danny	PMP	Vice-Mayor	15.76
Burauen			
Renomeron, Juanito	LP	Mayor	57.79
Serdoncillo, Roger	NUP	Mayor	40.01
Soro, Patrick	PDPLBN	Mayor	1.13
Gacgacao, Romulo	IND	Mayor	0.86
Balais, Erlinda	IND	Mayor	0.21
Alpino, Noel	LP	Vice-Mayor	57.50
Toreno, Antonio Jr.	NUP	Vice-Mayor	40.42
Sapdo, Tony	PDPLBN	Vice-Mayor	2.08
Capoocan			
Carolino, Fe Claire	LP	Mayor	51.50
Vallar, Lourdes	PMP	Mayor	48.50
Carolino, Federico Sr.	LP	Vice-Mayor	65.16
Oriel, Totoy	PMP	Vice-Mayor	34.84
Carigara			
Ong, Boy*	NPC	Mayor	55.29
Apostol, Anlie	LP	Mayor	44.71
Modesto, Mildred	LP	Vice-Mayor	39.80
Arpon, Ulpiano Jr.	IND	Vice-Mayor	31.67
Larraga, Joenlee	UNA	Vice-Mayor	28.53
Dagami			
Delusa, Deo*	LP	Mayor	63.06

(cont'd overleaf)

Table 12 *(cont'd)*

Candidate	Party	Office	Per cent (%)
Diaz, Antonio Jr.	UNA	Mayor	36.94
Bardillon, Bibi	LP	Vice-Mayor	53.44
Sudario, Lowi	UNA	Vice-Mayor	46.56
Dulag			
Que, Mildred Joy	LP	Mayor	56.44
Palabrica, Jeatte	IND	Mayor	43.56
Agullo, Jade	IND	Vice-Mayor	62.45
Labanta, Edwin*	LP	Vice-Mayor	30.50
Bautista, Dr. Boy	IND	Vice-Mayor	7.05
Jaro			
Celebre, Zharina	LP	Mayor	58.60
Elises, Getty	UNA	Mayor	41.40
Celebre, Rolando	LP	Vice-Mayor	60.75
Arbas, Rigo	UNA	Vice-Mayor	39.25
Julita			
Caña, Percival	LP	Mayor	37.30
Tinaya, Daniel	IND	Mayor	31.95
Daya, Geraldine	NPC	Mayor	30.75
Macaso, German	IND	Vice-Mayor	46.79
Tubi, Kim Berlin Marie	NPC	Vice-Mayor	28.58
Dy, Irvin	LP	Vice-Mayor	24.63
La Paz			
Lumen, Lesmes*	LP	Mayor	65.66
Yu, Asam	IND	Mayor	30.23
Andrade, Moises	IND	Mayor	4.12
Cinco, Joel*	LP	Vice-Mayor	85.94
Terado, Mario	IND	Vice-Mayor	14.06
Macarthur			
Leria, Rene*	LP	Mayor	60.93
Matoza, Roehl	LAKAS	Mayor	39.07
Leria, Alice	LP	Vice-Mayor	59.39

Table 12 *(cont'd)*

Candidate	Party	Office	Per cent (%)
Pantin, Xandrix	LAKAS	Vice-Mayor	40.61
Mayorga			
Adolfo, Valente	UNA	Mayor	49.96
De Paz, Alex*	LP	Mayor	49.63
Velasco, Raul	IND	Mayor	0.41
Beltran, Jairo*	LP	Vice-Mayor	46.21
Advincula, Jose	UNA	Vice-Mayor	44.64
Gabrieles, Arturo	IND	Vice-Mayor	9.16
Pastrana			
Opiniano, Alvin	IND	Mayor	59.31
Baclea-An, Evelyn	LP	Mayor	40.69
Empillo, Edgar Sr.	IND	Vice-Mayor	39.61
Ala, Jocelyn	LP	Vice-Mayor	33.33
Marcos, Maritess	IND	Vice-Mayor	27.05
Tabontabon			
Balderian, Rustico	UNA	Mayor	36.34
Gamez, Brendo*	LP	Mayor	35.18
Redoña, Efren	NUP	Mayor	28.48
Cinco, Edgar*	LP	Vice-Mayor	60.09
Bibar, Doyon	UNA	Vice-Mayor	39.91
Tunga			
Agda, Catalina*	LP	Mayor	39.28
Uribe, Jose Capoporo	NPC	Mayor	32.88
Valuis, Cardo	IND	Mayor	27.84
Costelo, Reinbert	NPC	Vice-Mayor	52.92
Costelo, Benjamin	LP	Vice-Mayor	47.08

chapter 13

First District of Bohol: Tradition, Innovation, and Women's Agency in Local Patronage Politics

Regina E. Macalandag

INTRODUCTION

The Province of Bohol has been ranked as the "Best Governed Province" in the Philippines (Inquirer.net 2016). Boholanos claim a collective "self-image" as politically conscious, borne out by a series of public opinion surveys conducted by the Holy Name University of Tagbilaran City since the late 1990s. Not surprisingly, they express a desire to make their needs and opinions known to their local leaders. They are also known to be pious and religious as a people. However, it remains a puzzle for election observers that during elections, it is not uncommon for people to succumb to cash offers in exchange for their votes, from "the same faces and familiar surnames in Bohol's election ring" (Udtohan 2015).

This chapter explores manifestations of patronage and clientelist politics in Bohol during the local 2016 election. It examines the discourse of *utang na loob*, loyalty, and the carrot-and-stick approach behind the patronage tradition to which candidates and campaign workers conform in order to be able to win votes in elections. It also discusses innovations in patronage politics as the local body-politic continues to

242

transition. Moreover, since the question of how patronage politics effects the gendered nature of election campaigns is under-analysed, the chapter also aims to add to the limited literature on patronage politics and gender through a case study of the specific ways in which female candidates rely on the politics of patronage and clientelism as winning strategies.

BACKGROUND ON THE REGION

Bohol is the tenth largest island in the Philippines. It comprises 47 municipalities and the capital, Tagbilaran City. Historically, the province made an imprint in the country's colonial past with the religious leader Tamblot, who resisted impositions of early Catholicism, and Dagohoy, who reputedly led the longest revolt against the Spanish in the Philippines.

Bohol is the foremost producer of major agricultural products in the region, though tourism also plays an increasing role in the island's economy, and investors continue to fund a robust infrastructure programme throughout the province. Though poverty remains high, poverty incidence has fallen from 50.2 per cent in 2000 to 30.6 per cent in 2012, according to National Statistical Coordination Board (NSCB) indicators.

There are three congressional districts in the Province of Bohol. This study particularly examines the political dynamics within the First District of Bohol to draw conclusions regarding money politics during the 2016 local election.[1] The First District comprises Tagbilaran City and 14 municipalities (Alburquerque, Antequera, Baclayon, Balilihan, Calape, Catigbian, Corella, Cortes, Dauis, Loon, Maribojoc, Panglao, Sikatuna, Tubigon). Based on the official list of the provincial Commission on Elections (COMELEC), District 1 had a total of 335 aspirants registered to run for local elective offices in the 2016 election. Of these 335 candidates, only 23.3 per cent, or one out of five, was female.

The majority of candidates in the First District were affiliated with the Liberal Party (LP). Independent candidates came in second, followed by those from the United Nationalist Alliance (UNA) and the Partido Demokratiko Pilipino–Lakas ng Bayan (PDP–Laban). An overwhelming majority of candidates—most of them incumbents—ran under the

---

[1] The total number of registered voters for Bohol as of 2015 was 798,768, as compared to 775,785 registered voters in October 2012. There are more female than male voters and the largest group of voters come from the 20–24 and 25–29 age brackets.

Liberal Party and were victorious in the 2016 election. Congressional- and provincial-level seats were virtually uncontested, as the well-established incumbents, Representative Rene Relampagos and Governor Edgar Chatto, were both running for their third and last term. Their opponents were political neophytes and thus stood little chance, even though several belonged to political families (for example, Joahna Cabalit-Initay and May Lim-Imboy). Most of the other incumbents at the mayoral and legislative council levels enjoyed a similar advantage.

In past elections, Bohol politicians tended to switch affiliation to whichever party was dominant nationally, as is usually the case in Philippine politics. This study suggests that in this election in Bohol, it was incumbency, with its concomitant access to both public and private resources (including monetary resources) and support from a massive and efficient mobilisation structure—rather than membership in a particular party—that gave a significant advantage in securing votes. This pattern is due to pervasive clientelistic patronage politics in the province, utilising the traditional network of strong familial connections.

CANDIDATE STRATEGY, MOBILISATION STRUCTURE, AND THE ROLE OF PATRONAGE

This section describes how patronage and money politics works in the context of Bohol, including in the winning strategies and mechanisms employed by local candidates in the 2016 election.

Utang na loob,[2] or debt of gratitude, provides the backdrop to the large-scale money politics characterising the 2016 election in this constituency. To cultivate *utang na loob*, candidates sow the seeds of patronage, starting long before the election period. A campaign worker of a mayoral candidate acknowledged that, "to win elections, a candidate has to do some sort of early campaigning, locally termed '*pamugas-pugas na daan*' (sowing seeds) to be able to build a momentum for a planned or continued candidacy".[3]

---

[2] The essence of *utang na loob* is an obligation to appropriately repay a person who has done one a favour. The favours that elicit the Filipino's sense of *utang na loob* are typically those whose value is impossible to quantify, or, if there is a quantifiable value involved, that involve a deeply personal internal dimension (Borja-Slark 2008).

[3] Interview with a campaign worker, Bohol, May 2016.

The patronage train rides from "womb to tomb" and has proved to be effective. Local politicians inundate constituents with sponsorships for various activities, year in and year out, ranging from birthday cash and in-kind gifts, to babies' christenings or dedications, to pledges as *ninong/ninang* (godparents), to mass weddings, to presents and other privileges offered to senior citizens, to financial aid for funerals (for example, a mayor giving a casket worth PhP 11,000 and rice). The "womb to tomb" approach is upgraded from a personal to a political level prior to, during, and immediately after elections, when government programmes are dangled before constituents in a "carrot-and-stick" way. This traditional and almost subtle way of ensuring loyalty ties is well-ingrained, not only among clients, but among patrons, as well. One mayoral candidate expressed it this way: "The way you do your work on the first day you assume office is already considered a campaign. You are already building your name. You build your reputation to the people."[4]

Pangulitaw (courtship) is the practice by which the campaign team (especially for incumbents) courts voters, starting long before the elections. The *pangulitaw* comes in the form of programmes and services that cannot be accessed by constituents unless they vote for the incumbent leadership. Gatekeepers take note of whether those seeking assistance have voted for the incumbent in past elections, as they appropriate government resources for the incumbent's patronage purposes. One campaign worker narrated,

> The whole year round, Mayor … does "allocative" programmes such as giving of college scholarships (PhP 5,000 per semester), employment opportunities for casuals (latest count of casuals at the city government is about 2,000+), burial and financial assistance (including rice), and other benefits. These programmes and services are declared to be intended for any constituent in need but gatekeeping power is exercised, for example, by the Burial and Financial Assistance staff (at the same time *purok* leader), hence such programmes may not be fully accessed by those not endorsed by the *purok* leader.[5]

Election Day becomes a day of reckoning, to collect on the loyalties and debts of gratitude that candidate-patrons have sown. It also serves as a barometer for the effectiveness of the clientelistic mechanisms that make

---

[4] Interview with a mayoral candidate, Bohol, May 2016.
[5] Interview with a campaign worker of a mayoral candidate, 22 May 2016.

up the political machine in which politicians have invested over the course of their incumbency and throughout the electoral cycle.[6]

Campaign efforts have evolved over time in terms of the distribution of patronage. They now employ technologies of management that include surveys, creative use of voter lists, and validation tables (identifying voters as supporters, non-supporters, or undecided). These tools are designed not only to keep track of mass support for a candidate, but also for gatekeeping purposes, especially in relation to the distribution of goods and other resources in exchange for votes.

For the 2016 election, the COMELEC designated an official campaign period commencing 90 days before the election, but the real campaign period started long before for certain mayoral candidates. As early as October 2015, an incumbent mayor had fielded his campaign team to conduct a survey to gauge support and update voter-turnout data from the 2013 election, particularly on who voted for which mayoral candidate, and to calculate the number of supporters for the mayor. The survey instrument barely mentioned the candidate's platform, nor did the interviewers attempt to sell their candidate. They just asked respondents upfront for whom their eligible household members would most likely vote. Although members of the campaign team were not required to mention the mayor's record in government, a regular spiel among them as they met constituents went, "*Si Mayor wala namulitika, motabang bisan kinsa* (The Mayor is not politicking; he helps anyone)".[7] The names of voters who failed to state categorically for whom they voted in the past election were labelled with question marks.

The survey results pointed the candidate's canvassers to where they should focus their campaign efforts. One campaign manager explained,

> Usually we come with a budget based on the number of voters. *Inangayan* (share) or *uwan uwan* (rain showers) is like a sharing of vote money from candidates with constituents. We try to appeal to them [ward leaders] that they are one of our keys towards winning. We tried to explain to them to ensure that nobody from our slate will be removed. They must vote straight for the full mayor/council ticket and no one must eliminate a candidate in favour of another party. If

---

[6] Explains a local scholar, "Political machines are specialized organizations set up for the purpose of mobilizing and influencing voter outcome through the dispensation of social, economic or material benefits" (Teehankee 2010).
[7] Interview with a campaign worker of a mayoral candidate, 22 May 2016.

they won't follow us, they [ward leaders] will be blacklisted by us in the next elections.[8]

The campaign manager holds tight reins on the ranks of campaign leaders and strictly monitors them. For instance, campaign leaders are prohibited from listening to caucuses of political opponents. For a leader to be seen doing this casts doubt on his or her loyalty. An instance of "disloyalty" earns "disciplining": the leader in question is asked to "open vote" on election day, which means to show his vote to a designated poll watcher who ensures a 12–0 vote cast in favour of the candidate's slate, and to verify that he or she has cast a vote for the candidate.[9]

As elections draw near, voters look forward to the *inangayan* and anticipate how much people will get from candidates. As one election observer noted,

> Residents of many barangays in the island province of Bohol usually greet each other with this question: "Is it raining over there? (*Wa ba'y uwan-uwan diha?*)". They are not talking about the much-prayed for rain to water the dried-up rice fields. They are referring to the cash and goodies that political candidates distribute to villagers to ensure victory in the polls (Resabal 2016).

While voters expect the *inangayan*, candidates, on the other hand, employ cost-efficient strategies to ensure that they draw a larger share of votes than their opponents. It is a common practice for candidates and their campaign teams to conduct a series of validations, including up to four stages, in order to streamline their campaign efforts and determine their actual supporters.

> *Ato* or Ours are the major supporters of the party. These people will undoubtedly vote for the party and they are considered priority in giving vote money. *Bali-bali* or the swing voters are those people who receive cash from both sides and don't tell [how they] vote. They remain neutral in order to benefit from both sides. Some of them will still be given cash anyways. The *palitunon* (to be bought) or the undecided ones are those people who will base their votes on the amount given by the candidates. In short, these are the people whose votes can be bought. Lastly, the *pusilunon* (to be shot) or *dili ato* (not with the party) are the people who are clearly with the other side. Nevertheless,

---

[8] Interview with a mayoralty campaign manager, 4 May 2016.
[9] Interview with a campaign worker of a mayoral candidate, 22 May 2016.

the people can be "shot" on the spot with money. They may have a change of mind once they receive the cash.[10]

The growing sophistication of technologies of management constitutes a significant innovation, and demonstrates ways in which machine-based campaigns override traditional networks like kinship or clan. Leaders compile lists of voters, recording the party or candidate affiliation of voters; categorising them as "supporters", "non-supporters", and "undecided"; and indicating the corresponding amounts of money the team has distributed. Surveys thus help campaign teams not just count and classify voters, but design interventions to manage electoral behaviour in a targeted way. They serve the purpose of "managing the social" by categorising constituents and designating appropriate interventions, in ways reminiscent of Foucault's concepts of surveillance and biopolitics. Armed with survey data, campaign teams also have the potential to be coercive. Professing support for another candidate would mark a voter as an adversary and angry canvassers which may subject such voters to violence, threat, or intimidation.[11]

Campaign managers of both the winning and defeated mayoral candidates underscored that the biggest challenge in this election was money. Putting in place a systematic mobilisation structure that reached down to the household level was costly and served as the focus of most campaigns, especially for incumbents.

A key point of contact in local campaigns is the barangay captain. Despite being officially non-partisan, barangay captains are the "go-to" brokers and municipal candidates rely on them during elections. It is common for incumbent mayoral candidates to leverage personal loyalty from barangay captains; their relationship is mutually beneficial. If the barangay captain does not offer campaign support to the candidate, his or her barangay will receive fewer projects after the incumbent's re-election.

This exchange is part of a continuous "carrot-and-stick" approach employed by candidates sitting as incumbents, who rely on these relationships as the strongest asset of their campaign. As one campaign manager related,

---

[10] Interview with a campaign manager for a mayoral candidate, 2 May 2016.
[11] Beyond using surveys to manage electoral behaviour, another mode of intervention during this electoral campaign involved manipulating the technology for automated voting, though this strategy was only available to well-resourced candidates. Rumours circulated that some campaigns were trying to use money to tamper with vote counting machines, but the claims were without evidence.

> How things operate here, the mayor has power especially in the
> allocation of funds … like if I win in this barangay, you will get
> projects from me. But if a barangay campaigns hard for the other
> group you will not get anything from me. That's just an example …
> We are campaigning from mayor to vice-mayor to councilors in the
> whole slate; we will give awards to them; for example, we tell them
> if the whole slate will win in their barangay, we give them 100,000 or
> 200,000 pesos (or more) worth of projects [roads, education, health,
> traffic, peace and order, among others].[12]

It is the character of this elaborate mobilisation structure—a web organised
from top to bottom, rewarded with political, social, and economic
(including monetary) favours, drawing on a bottom-up network of
loyalties from leaders and constituents alike, including bringing home
the vote during elections—that allows this patronage system to gain and
maintain currency.

Incumbent candidates have an edge against candidates not belonging
to the administration when it comes to creating and maintaining these
networks. This advantage is due, for the most part, to the human and other
resources accessible to and at the disposal of incumbents. Such resources
may include government programmes for which local politicians can take
credit and which they can appropriate as patronage resources for their
campaigns. This practice undermines the capacity of non-administration
candidates (except for those who have vast personal resources) to launch
campaigns comparable to those of incumbent candidates.

My research found that deviation from the norm that is patronage and
money politics is uncommon. The central moral challenge that candidates
face in every Philippine election is the difficulty or danger of deviating
from these "traditional modes" of securing local political positions,
including those described here for Bohol. These well-entrenched modes
have marred local and national electoral politics and had calcified any
reformist vision toward social transformation.

Having sketched broadly how clientelist patronage and money politics
play out in Bohol, I now turn to the experiences of women candidates. In
the next section I explore how women candidates navigate through the
masculine domain of elections and patronage politics, and thereby shape
the contours of the local electoral process.

---

[12] Interview with a campaign manager of a mayoral candidate, 4 May 2016.

CASE STUDY: WOMEN CANDIDATES CONFORMING TO OR SUBVERTING PATRONAGE?

The 2010–14 World Values Survey reports that more than half of the respondents in Malaysia (69.6 per cent), the Philippines (56.4 per cent), and Thailand (51.5 per cent) agreed with the statement "men make better political leaders than women do" (Tan 2016). It is not surprising, therefore, that the overall number of female politicians in Asia remains low, even given the success of elite women (for example, female presidents of South Korea, Thailand, Myanmar, Philippines) in recent years (Tan 2016). Boosting women's political presence continues to be contingent on factors that include political climate, electoral system, party affiliation, money, party system institutionalisation, political will, and sociocultural norms towards female leaders, among other issues. South Korea, for example, has fallen short of electing a significant number of female representatives because of a lack of political will and the inability to enforce gender quotas, attributed to its weakly institutionalised party system based on male-patronage networks (Tan 2016).

Understanding gender dynamics in patronage-laden electoral campaigns reveals how women navigate around and appropriate rather than undermine directly gendered expectations to secure representation and break the political glass ceiling.[13] Alternatively, this examination offers certain evidence of the potential of electoral campaigns as opportunities for the political empowerment of women, while moving the Philippines away from patronage politics in the long term.

I begin with the following question: Do women candidates conform to or subvert patronage-based strategies to win elections in the Philippines? Only 20 per cent of candidates in Bohol were women in 2016, an increase over past elections. This study examines selected cases of women candidates who ventured into local politics and tried their luck in the 2016 election. These women candidates, who come from varying backgrounds and had varying credentials, claimed to set out with similar idealistic notions of

---

[13] The glass ceiling is described as "those artificial barriers based on attitudinal or organizational bias that prevent qualified individuals from advancing upward in their organization into management level positions" (Martin 1991; Lorber 1994: 227 in Zamfirache 2010). Considered to be the reason why arenas of power have been dominated by men, the concept stresses the impossibility for women to advance in professions higher up the ladder than they already have, indicating that women do not lack ambition or strong will, but they are kept back by invisible obstacles (Lorber 1994 in Zamfirache 2010).

good governance and transformation to those of their male colleagues, yet the established ways of gaining entry into the political arena were still evident along their campaign trails.

One female candidate for mayor (Candidate A), for instance, explained how her approach changed between her first and second time running for office:

> To convince voters to vote for me the first time, I invited key stakeholders for a shared governance discussion and presented my platform of governance. It is easier this time in the 2016 election because people saw my achievements. But I cannot change tradition— that it's all about money.[14]

Candidate A began her first term in office with idealistic notions of shared governance in a town considered as a premier tourism destination. The town is also widely known in the province to have the highest amount of *sold* votes during elections. While admitting that elections in her area involved a lot of money and that she would rather spend money on her family, she nonetheless had to secure votes and go with the practice of giving out *inangayan* to constituents. For her, the overall clamour for change in political leadership and social transformation that had seemed to pervade at the national level, had not really translated to the local level as voters still expected money in exchange for their votes.

Another candidate for mayor (Candidate B) echoed Candidate A's hope that she could use her good track record as the basis for re-election. But she too acknowledged the daunting reality of money politics. She elaborated on her activities as a candidate:

> There are many avenues that I can avail to be near my people. I have a personal social media account. I use this to post the activities we have accomplished. This gets a positive response as people check on me and expect these activities to be posted. I also reach out to people by text messaging.... We have developed a slogan for our campaign, "For the sustainable growth of [our town]".... The biggest challenge as a candidate is to be able to make the programmes we promise to happen. It should have been better if campaigns are about competing in the best we could give rather than throwing attacks against each other.... Money politics cannot be avoided. It has been an accepted practice.... One has to give [money], no matter how small. I would like to see the day when election becomes a matter where people will really look into the things you are capable of doing and the things you offer.

---

14 Interview with Candidate A, 4 May 2016.

> Money should no longer be involved, much more violence. Clean and
> honest elections are very elusive.[15]

In fact, Candidate B distributed *inangayan* despite being against said practice. For her, a good track record was not sufficient to secure votes, even from her own supporters. She distributes money despite enjoying a large lead over her opponent, a benefit that her family name and marriage to a politician from a higher office in the province afforded her. Voters still expected money from her as a candidate during the election. While she expressed a desire for genuine service, accessibility and responsiveness to constituents, she nevertheless maintained an equivocal stance on clean and honest elections, as she vacillated between her (and her family's) experience of following the tradition of money politics and the desire to seek electoral reform.

Another candidate (Candidate C) who ran for legislative council, knew that money had already been widely circulated to ensure the administration candidates' victories. She managed to convince her non-administration teammates not to give money to voters in the election, and the result was a devastating loss. She admitted: "I believe that I and the rest of the team lost because of this. Money still played a large part in this election."[16]

Candidate C, a gender equity advocate, shared that she had been approached by a friend and former local candidate during the 2013 election, who advised her to distribute money in order to win. This friend and ex-candidate broached the idea to her of doing a parallel campaign aside from that done with her team/party-mates, which did not involve distributing payments. The friend (a gender equity advocate herself) explained that Candidate C could employ two women (Candidate C called them "political mercenaries") who are public school teachers and heads of women's associations in the area to run a parallel campaign for Candidate C in the 2016 election. They sought women's votes from their women's associations as well as among their extended networks. This was an unusual proposition to come from associations or social organisations in the area, especially since it was so upfront and transactional. The women leaders' asking price was a PhP 40,000 "allowance" for each mercenary. Candidate C revealed that she did not have that amount to pay these political mercenaries and even if she had, she said she would not use any, as this was against her principles and her own calls for change.

---

[15] Interview with Candidate B, 14 April 2016.
[16] Interview with Candidate C, 22 May 2016.

When asked whether her being a woman candidate helped her in any way during the election, Candidate C shared that she and her team tapped into "gender" messaging to win votes, especially from women. All but one member of Candidate C's slate of candidates were women and the team tried to sell the message that women make better leaders than men by touting their "housekeeping of the city", invoking "Mother Earth" for the protection of the city's environment, and stressing the nurturing qualities of a woman/mother. She reported that they were forced to be essentialist and to counter the more popular administration party. The party was headed by a male mayoral candidate, especially popular among young voters because of his celebrity looks and well-endowed coffers. They also aimed to increase the number of women city legislators. Her party even played up the class factor, talking about how one candidate began as a fishmonger and became a successful entrepreneur. But, at the end of the day, money still reigned supreme. At the close of the election, Candidate C herself shelled out a small amount as *suhol* (payoff) for youth volunteers hired to note any irregularities.

Candidate D was a neophyte in the political arena, but her maiden name was a familiar one to the voters, as she belonged to a political clan. She opted to highlight the family name in her campaign materials (with her married name taking a back seat) while espousing a "no to vote buying" position. She made good on her promise not to distribute cash during the election. Candidate E also benefitted from a political name, through her husband's family. She resorted to social media, inserting Bible quotes into her regular posts and projecting herself as a motherly and family-oriented candidate, in addition to the usual house-to-house campaigns and posting of campaign materials in strategic areas. While her party also avowed "no to vote buying" and participated in a "Clean Elections Pledge" or "No to Vote Buying" ceremony,[17] reports surfaced that her regular campaign sponsor had released and distributed cash to voters on her behalf. Both Candidates D and E lost in the election. Neither was a match for the extensive mobilisation network of the administration candidates, which included more than 3,000 campaign workers/ward leaders.

Their rhetoric notwithstanding, these women candidates still relied on their clientelist networks and played up their dynastic connections, when available. Attempts by women to break out from the mold and secure their own space in politics on their own merits were foiled by a more

---

[17] All parties but the administration party attended the ceremony.

deeply embedded patronage politics. Rather than subverting the system, they simply yielded to the power of patronage and money politics. They ended up offering equivocal pronouncements of good governance and clean and honest service, while taking on the benefits that accompany male-dominated patronage relations.

However, an alternative conceptualisation of agency is possible in which agency is not simply "a synonym for resistance to relations of domination, but a capacity for action that specific relations of subordination create and enable" (Mahmood 2001: 210). Seen through this lens, these female candidates may not be subverting the male-dominated patronage system, but working around it. But should the fact that they are playing the same game (giving out payments themselves, accepting their team's distributing money, and knowingly benefitting from those payments), as their male counterparts, stands out as an act of women's agency? Can this acquisition of political space via riding the patronage bandwagon be seen as women's tactical move to demonstrate their own brand of politics? Does this strategy then represent only the first innings in a longer-term, incremental game of instituting new norms for political effectiveness while shedding patronage politics in the process?

CONCLUSION

This chapter has explored the manifestations of patronage, clientelism, and money politics in the 2016 election in Bohol Province. It argues that while the local body-politics continues to transition, patronage and clientelistic relations linger. Conformity to the old rule of patronage remains more common than deviations from it. The practices of vote buying, sowing the seeds of patronage early on in the electoral cycle to allow candidates to exploit a sense of *utang na loob*, and investing in elaborate and efficient campaign networks remain as the principal components of the electoral strategies in the province. These tactics stymie the quest for electoral reforms and ensure the persistence of patronage distribution and clientelist politics. New developments, including the role of vote-counting machines, the rise of social media as an alternative political channel, and reformist calls for good governance, have caused cracks in this entrenched system, but these have had limited impact at the local level.

However, rethinking the concept of agency vis-à-vis the experiences of women candidates helps us to understand women's engagement with and challenges to patronage politics. Reforming the patronage-laden order may be a means to confront the challenges to women's meaningful participation and thus lead to longer-term reforms and more empowering forms of politics and democracy. However, as it stands, in running for local office, women may find a more expedient path in working around and through, rather than against, the system now in place.

Table 13
Election results from Bohol 1st District

Candidate	Party	Office	Per cent (%)
*Indicates Incumbent Candidate			
Relampagos, Rene*	LP	House of Representatives	79.53
Cabalit, Joahna	UNA	House of Representatives	15.30
Alturas, Chris Philipps	PDPLBN	House of Representatives	5.17
Chatto, Edgar*	LP	Provincial Governor	58.42
Imboy, May	PDPLBN	Provincial Governor	39.16
Garcia, Wenceslao	IND	Provincial Governor	1.74
Balagosa, Kary	IND	Provincial Governor	0.44
Gaudicos, Fer	KBL	Provincial Governor	0.23
Balite, Dioning	PDPLBN	Provincial Vice-Governor	51.94
Lim, Concepcion*	LP	Provincial Vice-Governor	48.06
Alburquerque			
Tungol, Epren*	LP	Mayor	59.46
Salibay, Egin	PDPLBN	Mayor	40.54
Doria, Cayetano Jr.*	LP	Vice-Mayor	100.00
Antequera			
Pahang, Jose Mario*	LP	Mayor	70.25
Rebosura, Amet	IND	Mayor	29.75
Jadulco, Leo*	LP	Vice-Mayor	53.05
Labado, Lani	PDPLBN	Vice-Mayor	46.95
Baclayon			
Uy, Benny	LP	Mayor	50.67
Cabahug, Jodel Theodore	NP	Mayor	49.33
Balangkig, Romy	NP	Vice-Mayor	50.12

(cont'd overleaf)

Table 13 *(cont'd)*

Candidate	Party	Office	Per cent (%)
Israel, Bebeh	LP	Vice-Mayor	49.88
Balilihan			
Chatto, Maria Puresa	LP	Mayor	87.63
Monton, Mark	IND	Mayor	12.37
Olalo, Adonis Roy	IND	Vice-Mayor	54.03
Asilo, Edgar	LP	Vice-Mayor	45.97
Calape			
Yu, Nelson	LP	Mayor	80.29
Dumalag, Delia	UNA	Mayor	14.01
Yu, Vicente	IND	Mayor	5.70
Yu, Sulpicio Jr	LP	Vice-Mayor	100.00
Catigbian			
Lurot, Virgilio*	LP	Mayor	54.31
Concon, Nato	IND	Mayor	45.69
Digaum, Necita	IND	Vice-Mayor	60.62
Lacea, Reynald*	LP	Vice-Mayor	39.38
Corella			
Tocmo, Jose Nicanor*	UNA	Mayor	46.95
Bandala, Danny	LP	Mayor	39.67
Ontong, Fabio Jr	PDPLBN	Mayor	11.04
Bolando, Epifanio	IND	Mayor	2.34
Daquio, Marizon*	UNA	Vice-Mayor	47.06
Rapal, Vito	IND	Vice-Mayor	36.56
Tocmo, Rex	LP	Vice-Mayor	12.11
Macarayan, Vanessa	PDPLBN	Vice-Mayor	2.64
Lumain, Nicanor	IND	Vice-Mayor	1.63
Cortes			
Lim, Lynn Iven	LP	Mayor	74.01
Tabanera, Bet*	IND	Mayor	25.99
Pabutoy, Leo	IND	Vice-Mayor	53.27
Labor, Tata	LP	Vice-Mayor	46.73

Table 13(cont'd)

Candidate	Party	Office	Per cent (%)
Dauis			
Sumaylo, Miriam*	LP	Mayor	62.43
Migriño, Victorio	PDPLBN	Mayor	37.57
Bongalos, Lulu*	LP	Vice-Mayor	68.00
Bomediano, Jobert	PDPLBN	Vice-Mayor	32.00
Loon			
Relampagos, Elvi	LP	Mayor	70.30
Go, Liezl	UNA	Mayor	29.70
Lopez, Lloyd Peter	LP	Vice-Mayor	72.99
Pasilbas, Damaso	IND	Vice-Mayor	16.29
Caresosa, Wilfredo	IND	Vice-Mayor	10.73
Maribojoc			
Arocha, Mer	LP	Mayor	53.10
Redulla, Tusoy	NP	Mayor	46.65
Cantoneros, Henry	IND	Mayor	0.25
Veloso, Jose	LP	Vice-Mayor	54.26
Pohl, Lalai	NP	Vice-Mayor	45.74
Panglao			
Montero, Nila*	LP	Mayor	51.14
Dumaluan, Doc Che	PDPLBN	Mayor	48.86
Fuertes, Pedro*	LP	Vice-Mayor	56.67
Alcala, Dodong	IND	Vice-Mayor	43.33
Sikatuna			
Ellorimo, Jose Jr*	LP	Mayor	100.00
Manigo, Jul*	LP	Vice-Mayor	53.37
Palgan, Billy	UNA	Vice-Mayor	46.63
Tagbilaran City (Capital)			
Yap, John Geesnell II*	LP	Mayor	83.21
Karaan, Arlene	IND	Mayor	15.80
Kapirig, Edgar	IND	Mayor	0.99
Veloso, Jose Antonio*	LP	Vice-Mayor	92.13

(cont'd overleaf)

Table 13 *(cont'd)*

Candidate	Party	Office	Per cent (%)
Hontanosas, Alfred	IND	Vice-Mayor	7.87
Tubigon			
Jao, William	LP	Mayor	51.03
Amila, Marlon*	UNA	Mayor	48.97
Fortich, Billy*	LP	Vice-Mayor	56.83
Flores, Ever	UNA	Vice-Mayor	43.17

chapter **14**

Antique Province: Old Money, Same Players, and the Politics of Patronage in the 2016 Election

Juhn Chris P. Espia

INTRODUCTION

The Lone District of the Province of Antique covers a constituency of 18 municipalities, which are among the poorest in the country. While the area still remains largely rural, many of its old, wealthy landowners have been on political hiatus for nearly three decades and have instead allowed professional politicians to hold the majority of the key provincial and municipal positions.

The 2016 election saw a few surprises. Among them was the first electoral setback of former congressman and governor, Exequiel Javier, who had not lost an election in 30 years. Drawing from interviews of several candidates and members of their campaign teams, this chapter concludes that while vote buying was still deemed as "indispensable", other forms of patronage, such as college scholarships and job offers, ties with religious and volunteer groups, and the extensive use of the local media, were also as important. Money alone did not guarantee victory; it needed to be complemented by an effective political machinery and an effective image-making tool. The chapter examines this formula in the context of electoral contests at the provincial level and uses it as a model to explain this major setback to the Javier dynasty. The chapter concludes that given the prohibitive costs of the prevalent and culturally accepted practice of vote buying in the province, only those who are wealthy or those who have wealthy patrons can effectively contest for seats.

In the 2016 election, there were 21 races for key positions,[1] 18 of which were for mayor and vice-mayor. In the mayoral races, 13 involved incumbents (Barbaza, Belison, Caluya, Culasi, Hamtic, Laua-an, Pandan, Patnongon, San Remigio, Sebaste, Sibalom, Tibiao, and Tobias Fornier) while five were open seats (Anini-y, Bugasong, Libertad, San Jose, and Valderrama). In the vice-mayoral races, there were also 13 which involved incumbents (Anini-y, Barbaza, Belison, Caluya, Culasi, Hamtic, Laua-an, Patnongon, San Remigio, Sebaste, Sibalom, Tibiao, and Tobias Fornier) and five that were open seats (Bugasong, Libertad, Pandan, San Jose, and Valderrama).[2]

A total of seven candidates were officially part of the race for the House of Representatives post. However, the real competition was between the incumbent Paolo Javier (son of the gubernatorial candidate, Exequiel Javier) (who captured 56.60 per cent of the vote in the 2013 election) and Roquero, a long-time family rival (who garnered 42.17 per cent of the vote in 2013). The rest were considered as either "splitter" or "nuisance" candidates. The race for governor was a one-on-one race between Rhodora Cadiao and the elder Javier, while the vice-gubernatorial race was a three-way contest. The table in the appendix provides a summary of the 2016 election results for the key positions of congressman, governor, vice-governor, mayor, and vice-mayor.

Figure 14 provides a comparison of seats won in the 2013 and 2016 elections based on party affiliation. In the 2013 election, the majority of the seats was won by the Liberal Party. In the 2016 election, while the Liberal Party lost two of the top three positions (governor and vice-governor), it won 19 out of the 39 available seats. Many of the candidates in the 2016 election remained loyal to their respective parties from the

---

[1] This does not include races for the Antique Provincial Board or the Sangguniang Panlalawigan. The members of this board are elected via plurality-at-large voting: the province is divided into two districts, each sending five members to the provincial board; the electorate votes for five members, with the five candidates with the highest number of votes being elected. The Vice-Governor is the ex-officio presiding officer, and only votes to break ties.

[2] The incumbent mayor of Culasi and the incumbent vice-mayor of Hamtic ran unopposed.

2013 election, except for many UNA-affiliated candidates who transferred to NUP.[3] Of the 39 available key positions in the 2016 election, 20 were won by incumbents, while 19 were occupied by challengers.

Figure 14
Comparison of seats won by party affiliation in the 2013 and 2016 elections

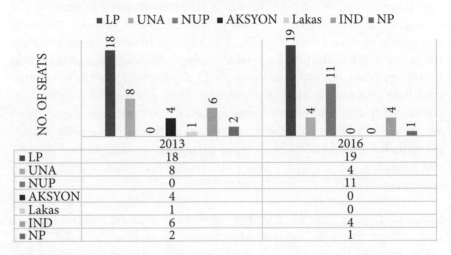

	2013	2016
LP	18	19
UNA	8	4
NUP	0	11
AKSYON	4	0
Lakas	1	0
IND	6	4
NP	2	1

BACKGROUND ON THE REGION

The province of Antique is one of the six provinces comprising Western Visayas (Region VI) and one of the four provinces located in Panay Island (the other three being Iloilo, Capiz, and Aklan). Antique is a lone congressional district and has 18 municipalities, 14 of which are found along the coast; three are inland and one is an island municipality (Caluya). Currently, the province has 590 barangays spread across 272,920 hectares (Province of Antique 2008).

Antique is an agricultural province that produces crops like *palay*, sugarcane, corn, legumes, vegetables, and other cash crops. Farming,

---

[3] UNA stands for the United Nationalist Alliance and NUP stands for the National Unity Party. While UNA candidates transferred their official affiliation to NUP, they remained allies with former UNA partymates. UNA and NUP formed the united opposition in the province. The increased presence of NUP in the province can be explained by the availability of better funding through the party compared to what was available under UNA.

fishing and small businesses are the primary sources of livelihood for the majority of the population. The province has a total coastline of 307.45 kilometres and traverses the Cuyo East Pass, a body of water which is considered a rich fishing ground, being one of the "tuna highways" of the Philippines (Philippines Statistics Authority 2017). In terms of population, the province ranks fourth in Region VI at 546,031; of these, 288,338 are registered voters. Population density is relatively low at 200 persons per square kilometre. Based on the data published by the National Statistical Coordinating Board (NSCB) in 2012, the rate of households on or below the poverty line in the province is decreasing—from 42.5 per cent in 2006 to 34.5 per cent in 2009, and down to 23.6 per cent in 2012. While this may look like a significant improvement, it is still relatively high when compared to the 2012 national average of 19.7 per cent and the regional figure of 22.8 per cent. Of the six provinces in the region, Antique is the poorest. In 2009, families in Antique earned an average annual income of PhP 124,667, significantly below the PhP 206,174 nationwide average annual income (Philippines Statistics Authority 2017).

The 1986 assassination of former governor, Evelio Javier (the elder brother of gubernatorial candidate Exequiel), a Liberal Party stalwart and known figure in the anti-Marcos circles during the martial law years, brought the province's politics into the national limelight. Since the assassination of Evelio, occasional violence has been a key concern during elections in Antique. This history led the COMELEC, the Antique Provincial Police Office (APPO), and the Philippine Army to initiate a "unity walk" and "peace covenant signing" on 13 March 2016 to ensure a secure and fair election. The event was attended by 297 candidates from all over the province (Checa 2016).

CANDIDATE STRATEGY AND THE ROLE OF PATRONAGE

The doling out of patronage remains the most effective strategy in winning votes in the province. Vote buying and the promises of college scholarships and jobs are frequently used by candidates and brokers to secure votes. Prior to the 2016 election, local analysts and media practitioners all agreed that vote buying was rampant in the province. In fact, the province was part of the National Citizen's Movement for Free Election's (NAMFREL) list of areas where vote buying happened in the 2013 election (Rappler 2013a). NAMFREL is the country's first and, arguably, most credible election watchdog, whose origins date back to the

1986 Snap Elections (Hedman 2006). Getting onto the list is an indication of the pervasiveness of vote buying in an area, enough to merit national attention.

The majority of the candidates and campaign staff interviewed for the project admitted that they or their candidates were engaged in vote buying in one form or the other. Most recalled many instances in the past when politicians won because of it; the 2010 election is particularly perceived as one of the worst in terms of vote buying incidence in the province. In the 2016 election, money was distributed through "special operations", which were usually done late at night or early in the morning. The majority of those who were targeted by vote buying were voters belonging to Classes C, D, and E. Amounts varied depending on the position that a candidate was vying for, ranging from PhP 50 for *Sangguniang Bayan* members, to as high as PhP 2,500 per voter per head for provincial candidates. The *listadores*, which were usually barangay-level brokers, created lists of the names of potential voters and released funds directly to them either in three tranches starting two weeks before the elections or on the day immediately before the polls. These partisan brokers possessed a good knowledge of voter preferences and partisan inclinations in the locale (Stokes et al. 2013).

In some places in the province, aside from brokers proactively filling their lists, certain intermediate brokers also practised proactive "vote selling", where they commit a certain number of votes to the highest bidder. Those who "sell" their votes belong to Classes D and E and see elections as a rare opportunity to earn some much-needed cash. Some voters have even refused to go to polling precincts if they have not received money. According to a mayoral candidate "People come here to the campaign headquarters and sell to us votes. If we buy don't them, they will definitely sell to my opponents."[4] The fact is that vote buying is culturally acceptable to the majority of the electorate—not a surprise in a province that is considered the poorest in the region.

Indeed, in many cases, voter expectations or beliefs mattered for distinguishing between positive and negative strategies and what form of inducements a candidate should adopt. Although this difference was quite subtle, it still impacted voter behaviour (Mares & Young 2016). In Antique Province, many candidates viewed vote buying as "indispensable", where any candidate who hopes to win a seat should be prepared to buy votes. A few viewed it as a "necessary evil"—candidates are forced to buy votes if

---

[4] Interview with a mayoral candidate, San Jose de Buenvista, 6 May 2016.

their opponents do so because no matter how little the amount is, people's decision-making will still be greatly affected by money and other tokens. While this forced them to increase the size of their campaign coffers, many of them were willing to shoulder the cost since they viewed vote buying as effective. In addition, candidates and parties typically adopted the same type of vote buying practices; the main difference being that the latter tended to pay more since voters were expected to vote for an entire slate.

COMELEC is fully aware of vote buying practices but was generally perceived by both candidates and operators as "weak and toothless". The provincial and municipal COMELEC are severely understaffed and have to wait for a formal complaint before they can act on an election law violation. The last two known actions by the poll body in the province were cases of overspending—in 2010, Congressional candidate Mallares was found to have spent 164 per cent over the allowable limit of PhP 865,014, while in 2013, Belison town incumbent Mayor de la Flor spent 104.72 per cent more than the total allowable amount (Rappler 2013b). This is typical in the Philippines, where many candidates find regulations for campaign and campaign finance hard to comply with, but it does not stop them from amassing and spending vast amounts of money and violating election laws (Teehankee 2009).

Patronage was also an important tool in campaigning. Candidates, particularly incumbents, also invested in providing services such as poverty alleviation, health and livelihood programmes, and seed and livestock distribution. These programmes had a strong appeal, particularly to poor and marginalised voters. In order for people to avail themselves of these government services, they often need to be aligned with winning candidates. Because challengers do not have access to these strategies, they frequently become the most virulent critics of these programmes and were more inclined to use vote buying and promises of employment and college scholarships (when they win) as strategies. As a result, promises of scholarships and jobs before elections have become the norm, especially for those running for provincial-level positions. College scholarships, which include tuition fees and a monthly stipend for those who wish to obtain a college degree in one of the province's public colleges, are usually given as political favours.

While direct vote buying was relatively more effective, more widely practised, and could cover a larger segment of the electorate, these alternative patronage strategies presented one important advantage: scholarships and employment prospects allow for more engagement between a candidate and a supporter. During the campaign period, past and future recipients or their relatives were almost always part of a candidate's machinery and campaign team. How these networks are formed and facilitate repeated and constant relationships of exchange between politicians and segments of the electorate will be discussed in greater detail in the succeeding sections.

But money and other forms of patronage do not always guarantee victory. To complement these strategies, candidates also utilised a number of approaches to help secure votes. First, both provincial- and municipal-level candidates made sure to maintain their often extensive kinship networks. Family ties not only give any candidate a good chance of winning by giving them a reliable voting bloc, but also give them the advantage of name-recall, especially when one comes from a family of former politicians. Second, the use of *Iglesia ni Cristo* (INC) endorsements was consistent throughout the constituency. Comprising around 10 per cent of the total voting population and with a guarantee of an 80 per cent compliance to the command votes, politicians regularly seek the endorsement of INC's Central Committee in order to mobilise those command votes (Teehankee 2012a). Endorsements come in the form of letters, vouching for a particular candidate, that are circulated among church members. The same role was played by local transport groups such as Tricycle Owners and Drivers Associations (TODA), which in large towns such as San Jose and Sibalom, could reach memberships of up to 4,000.

Third, the role of image-making in complementing patronage was important in Antique. Candidates and their campaigns often spent considerable resources and energy to shape the electorate's general perception of a candidate in order to capture "market votes" (Teehankee 2010). Candidate images are "cognitive representations" and may sometimes bear little resemblance to reality (Laylo & Dagdag-Laylo 1999). Candidates project an ideal image and articulate a stance on an issue in the hope of gaining popularity. In places where the media is strong, campaigns tended to be "hybridised", that is, media-centred campaign practices blended with traditional practices that utilised patronage networks (Teehankee 2010).

The role of the local mass media in image-making was key in Antique. In particular, local FM stations were deemed to be very effective in promoting politicians and running smear campaigns against their opponents. While the television has replaced the radio as the main source of information for the masses (see for instance, Teehankee 2010), community-based radio stations remain popular in rural areas. Listenership cuts across all segments of the electorate. In some towns, candidates dread the power of these stations, leading one candidate to say that "Radio stations should only broadcast the qualifications of a candidate and not run black propaganda against another. Black propaganda is as dirty as vote buying."[5] Aside from traditional media, social media was also becoming an important medium of political messaging, especially with the increase of internet access in far-flung areas. Many of the candidates interviewed for the study had social media accounts made specifically for the campaign that were aimed at the younger segments of the voting population.

OF BROKERS, VOLUNTEERS, AND PARTIES

Two weeks before the May 9 poll, many of the candidates and operators interviewed were set on the idea that they needed at least 50 per cent of the votes to win their constituencies and that at that point, very few of the voters were undecided. It is at this stage that candidates had to intensify campaigning and "troubleshooting operations". Many of the candidates also did "straw-voting" to help them determine their winning chances. Straw-voting involves calling a large meeting involving all of a candidate's campaign team where they identify on a list or a map which areas they would likely win or lose and by how much. This is done throughout the campaign period—at the start, in the middle and one week before the election. They conducted "troubleshooting" operations in areas where they were not comfortable with their margins. These either involved the distribution of more cash or further promises of future projects, jobs, or scholarship grants to local leaders and brokers.

To help them do all of these, candidates in Antique Province relied on their machinery and a dedicated campaign staff. As with many national and local machines in the Philippines, the composition and membership of these machines vary across elections and are a key feature of Philippine local politics (Teehankee 2012a). Typically, a local candidate's political machine was comprised of grassroots leaders who were mostly elected barangay officials and "people of consequence" in their communities. When current barangay officials belonged to their opponent's camps, candidates usually tapped former barangay officials to help them campaign on the ground. These barangay-level leaders were expected to communicate and commit a requisite number of votes to municipal leaders who were either

---

[5] Interview with a mayoral candidate, Belison, Antique, 1 May 2016.

local elected officials or those who were handpicked by the candidates. These political operatives were professionals, well-versed in politics and know their fellow villagers well (Finan & Schechter 2012). With the barangay elections fast approaching, many incumbent and prospective barangay officials picked municipal and provincial candidates that had the highest chances of winning, with the expectation that these candidates, when elected, would support them in upcoming barangay elections.

Second, all of the candidates and operators interviewed for the study reported having dedicated campaign staff to help them run the day-to-day campaign operations, with staff size ranging from 5 to 50 individuals. These campaign staff were either paid or were volunteers. Paid campaign staff were those that were either hired specifically to run the campaign and were compensated according to their qualifications, or they were local government employees who were hired due to their connection to the incumbents and were therefore compelled to render part of their time (paid by taxpayers) to help run the campaign. Volunteers, on the other hand, were either a candidate's relatives, people hoping for future job opportunities, or members of youth groups/movements directly affiliated with a candidate. Choosing to hire paid campaign staff or to rely mainly on volunteers varied by candidate. Many of the political operators involved in the campaign were also members of civil society organisations, making it easier for them to network with groups such as the INC and the business sector.

Candidates with large families enjoyed the benefits of having readily available campaign staff to help run the campaign, but volunteers who seek job opportunities by supporting were deemed to be more fervent campaigners, as their hiring or promotion to permanent post depended on the ability of their patrons to win a seat. In a province where job opportunities are limited, having a political patron in power spells the difference between having a job or not. According to one campaign staff member, "I am hoping to get a permanent post in the municipal hall after the elections as I am currently a contractual employee. If my boss wins, more likely I will get a permanent position. If he loses, I dread the idea of going to Manila to find a better job."[6]

In addition, youth groups also constituted an important volunteer network that was used in conjunction with candidates and party machinery. It useful to note that while a few are drawn to these groups because of their idealism, the majority join because of offerings of college

---

[6] Interview with Lian Atienza, San Jose, Antique, 5 May 2016.

scholarships and job opportunities. While volunteer youth groups were found in all campaigns throughout the province, two major youth groups participating in the 2016 election in the province are noteworthy: vice-gubernatorial candidate Denosta's Movement for Righteous Leadership (MRL) and the Antique Youth Association (AYA), which is affiliated with the Javiers. While most volunteer youth groups tend to be loose and informal, these two groups have well-defined organisational structures and have chapters in every municipality in the province. They performed similar functions to their parties' machineries and operated in parallel to these machines. In most cases, they performed the bulk of the manual labour needed to run a campaign—posting fliers and streamers, the preparation of rally and caucus venues, and the preparation and distribution of campaign paraphernalia. All volunteers were given free food and received transportation and communication allowances.

For all three types of campaign workers—local leaders, paid staff, and volunteers—the relationship between principals (candidates) and agents (brokers) was informal and relied largely on trust and presumed loyalties built over years of continued and repeated transactions. This holds true even in the case of paid staff, who were recruited based on these presumed loyalties. Constant communication and regular gatherings between elections was key to maintaining this loyalty. Whenever loyalty issues arise, candidates typically did loyalty checks. These checks could come in the form of last-minute, impromptu meetings; no-shows with no plausible excuses tended to raise suspicion and were subjected to monitoring by other campaign team members. Those found to be disloyal to the team were ostracised by the entire group. Loyalty issues tended to be a more salient concern in key provincial-level positions (congressman, governor, and vice-governor), where stakes are higher, the campaign organisations larger, and where the election was more tightly contested.

Party affiliation in Antique was important, whether one is talking about national or local parties. While candidates continued to change party leaders according to their convenience (Kerkvliet 1995; Teehankee 2012a), parties in the province helped provide the necessary machinery for mobilisation as well as additional funding support. In fact, in prior elections, while there were a number of candidates who registered as "independent", many of those who won had forged alliances with major political groups in the province. National party funds were coursed through the provincial party leadership; these leaders had the option of whether to distribute the funds equitably or to keep the funds for themselves. In fact, this became a significant issue which prompted a few candidates to switch from one party to the other. Affiliation with a local group allows for the pooling of monetary resources with other candidates and, for the local group, access to national party funds.

STAYING POWER: MONEY, MACHINE, AND IMAGE IN THE ANTIQUE PROVINCIAL ELECTION

The previous sections emphasised that while money is important, without political machinery and effective image-making, the doling out of patronage will not be effective. There is no better demonstration of formula than the result of the 2016 provincial election and the province's longest running and most powerful political dynasty.

Due to its status as a lone congressional district, Antique elects its representative to the Lower House through a province-wide vote, the same as the governor and the vice-governor. For this election, Exequiel Javier ran as governor alongside his vice-gubernatorial candidate Victor Condez and his son, Paolo Javier as congressional candidate. On the other side Rhodora Cadiao ran for governor allied with Edgar Denosta (vice-governor) and Ray Roquero (congressional candidate) to form the unified opposition against the Javier slate.

The Javier family's 30-year hold on power was secured after the outpouring of popular support in the light of the assassination of his elder brother, Evelio, a former governor and staunch anti-Marcos leader, by scions of a rival, pro-Marcos clan (allegedly, the Pacificadors) days before the EDSA 1986 People Power Uprising. Evelio subsequently became a symbol of the fight against an oppressive yet often negligent central government and his death continued to resonate across succeeding administrations, as many areas in the province remained out of touch with the national government. Exequiel Javier, the younger brother of Evelio, capitalised on this popular imagery to serve as representative of the province's lone congressional district for six terms—from 1987 to 1998 and from 2001 to 2010. He was also governor from 1998 to 2001 and 2010 to 2013. His son, Antique Rep. Paolo Everardo Javier, was standing for a third and final term to Congress in 2016 and was being groomed as heir to the 27-year-old dynasty.

Prior to the 2016 election, local analysts and members of political camps alike viewed the race for governor as a very close one. Exequiel Javier won the governorship in 2013 by garnering 52 per cent of the votes, but was eventually disqualified by the COMELEC for suspending the mayor of the municipality of Valderrama, who was the wife of his son's major rival in the 2013 and 2016 congressional race (Roquero). Cadiao, who won as vice-governor in 2013, was eventually installed as governor in the place of her rival, Javier. Cadiao's bailiwick included the vote-rich southern and northern towns while Javier's support came from the towns in the hinterlands and the mountainous barangays as well as the vote-rich central towns. The race was a repeat of the 2010 contest between the two, which Javier won by garnering 56.48 per cent of the votes to Cadiao's 41.50 per cent. To add to the drama, Javier was finally reinstalled as governor on 28 March 2016, just days prior to the election, after the Supreme Court overturned the COMELEC's decision. Cadiao returned to the vice-gubernatorial post. This was seen by some local analysts as a development that could potentially swing the momentum in favour of Javier. However, they were proven wrong as Cadiao won handily by getting 56.77 per cent of the votes to Javier's 43.22 per cent (see Table 14).

Exequiel Javier had never lost an election after his brother was assassinated 30 years ago. The 30-year dynasty rested on a foundation of patronage distribution and his brother's populist appeal as well as a vaunted political machine. In previous elections, the elder Javier had an overwhelming advantage over his opponents in terms of his ability to dole out patronage, from vote buying to jobs and scholarships. However, this election year his political opponents, particularly the Cadiaos, were willing to spend their money. As one campaign staff member said, "Our regret last time is that we did not spend enough. This time we will be willing to match how much their camp (the Javiers) will spend."[7]

Cadiao's campaign machinery was also much more extensive and effective in 2016. In the 2013 election, only two mayors openly declared their support for the opposition, but this number increased to nine in the 2016 election. Many of these switches can be attributed to the conflicts arising out of the unequal distribution of Liberal Party (which Javier heads) campaign funds. Many of these mayoral candidates found Cadiao to be "more fair" in terms of fund and patronage distribution, as per their experience during the campaign period and in her short stint as governor. For example, one mayoral candidate, a cousin to the Javiers and an ally in previous elections, noted that, "When I transferred to the Cadiao camp this year, the percentage of party funds in my campaign chest rose to around 40 per cent, from just around 20 per cent when I was with the Javiers."[8]

---

[7] Interview with Cadiao campaign staff, San Jose, Antique, 5 May 2016.
[8] Interview with Tobias Fornier, Antique, 6 May 2016.

Another interesting point of comparison between the Javier and Cadiao campaigns is how promises of college scholarships were used to attract voters. While the Javier camp promised to retain the status quo (2,000 provincial scholars per year at PhP 2,500 stipend per semester), Cadiao promised to increase the stipend to PhP 5,000 per semester and increase the number of scholars to 2,500—an increase in the annual budget for provincial college scholarships from PhP 20 million to PhP 50 million. Interviews with representatives from the Cadiao campaign indicated that "more incoming freshmen and their voting relatives flocked to the Cadiao camp than to the Javiers".[9]

Furthermore, over the years, the populist appeal that the Javiers had historically banked on began to wane. Proof of this erosion began to appear when then-Governor Sally Perez challenged (and lost by a slim margin to) Exequeil Javier in 2004. The image of a staunch defender of human rights, the poor, and the marginalised that Exequeil Javier had repeatedly invoked also proved to be a double-edged sword. A series of unpopular decisions, including withholding of provincial employees' salary increases under the Salary Standardization Law (SSL), combined with a number of graft and plunder cases, began to chip away at his popular appeal. The three years prior to the election had also seen previously unthinkable defiance by ordinary citizens, namely a solo protest by a disgruntled provincial employee in the capital town's central park named after Evelio Javier, and people turning their backs and spitting on the ground whenever Javier's campaign truck passed through and played his dead brother's theme song, "Impossible Dream". The campaign continued to believe in the strong appeal of the family name as well as in the inability of his political opponents to match his fiscal resources and patronage networks during elections—this proved a miscalculation.

Cadiao, on the other hand, had cast herself as a reformist ever since she first ran as governor against Javier in 2010. When she sat down as governor for a year in 2015–16, she further enhanced this image by instituting a People's Day, where people from all walks of life could visit the governor and request assistance. This proved to be a more effective means of distributing aid, with an added personal touch, and was in stark contrast to Javier's perceived image as stand-offish towards his constituents. Both candidates had at their command the biggest local radio stations in the province—Real BOSS Radio for Javier and DYKA and Spirit FM for Cadiao—who were paid to run ads and commentaries on their respective

---

[9] Interview with Cadiao campaign staff, San Jose, Antique, 30 April 2016.

candidates. Both candidates also had a dedicated team of campaign staff who controlled their social media accounts ("Cadiao Cares" for Cadiao and "Antique sa Guihapon" for Javier). Because of the logistical impossibility of having to do caucuses in all of the province's barangays, both traditional and social media emerged as the most efficient and cost-effective way of communicating with the public, a trend that has been consistent in the last few Philippine elections (Teehankee 2010). While Cadiao embarked on a media campaign promoting her policy agenda and her image as a reformist, the Javier camp focused on running a smear campaign against Cadiao. This negative campaign eventually backfired.

In contrast to his father's failed campaign, Paolo Javier was successful in his bid for Congress. Paolo banked on a strategy which ultimately won him the seat—the use of "splitter" candidates. While the real race was between Javier and Roquero (see Table 14), two other candidates for office, Delfin and Villaflor, were suspected of being paid to run by the Javiers in order to divide the votes of the opposition. This was widely reported in a number of local media outlets (except those that are controlled by the Javiers). Oft-cited proof of this was the fact that both of these candidates had run in previous elections (in 2010 and 2013) and garnered a significant chunk of the votes from opposition areas, such as the towns of Sibalom and Bugasong, without doing anything by way of campaigning. Three other candidates, namely Mallares, Pidoy, and Combong, also stood for Congress and were all deemed to be pure "nuisance" candidates.

In the 2013 election, the close race between the Paolo and his opponent, Ray Roquero, was seen as a sign of the erosion of popular support for the Javiers. Roquero, despite the fact that he was unable to campaign due to a short prison stint during the 2013 election campaign period, was able to keep the race close. In the 2016 election, Rocquero ran again and although he was able to campaign for the entire election period this time, he still lost the election to the younger Javier. Part of the reason was money politics—Paolo was much better resourced—but the younger Javier was also able to cultivate an image separate from that of his father—populist, pro-poor, and pro-youth. He insisted on going around without armed bodyguards (or at least liked to appear that he did) and did not hesitate to go on house-to-house visits while on the campaign trail—a stark contrast to his opponent Roquero, who was generally perceived as a *trapo* because of previous involvements in political scandals (as evidenced by his short prison stint).

The race for vice-governor was also seen as a close one, with all of the candidates either sitting as incumbent members of the *Sanggunniang*

Panlalawigan (SP) or having previously held the position. Condez, a former SP member, was supported by the northern towns, Denosta by the southern towns, and Fortaleza by the central towns. Fortaleza, a celebrated lawyer and a former Cadiao ally, ran as an independent candidate. Denosta was vice-governor in place of Cadiao when she was installed as governor. Denosta won by getting 47.71 per cent of the votes to Condez's 40.89 per cent and Fortaleza's 14.36 per cent. While Fortaleza was a relative newcomer with few resources and weak machinery, Condez ran with a lot of resources and banked on the same strategies as his allies, the Javiers: vote buying and the doling-out of patronage, the use of a powerful political machinery, and the extensive use of local traditional media as a campaign tool. However, as a long-time politician and a close associate of Exequiel Javier (he was perceived as Javier's main man in the *Sangguniang Panlalawigan*), Condez had trouble separating himself from Exequiel's eroding popularity, and struggled to shake his *trapo* image.

Denosta, on the other hand, was a classic example of a professional politician who invested heavily in a particular following and in building a reformist image. While his general strategy was not noticeably different from the other winning candidates, he took advantage of his youth network which worked in conjunction with his other networks. The group he founded, the Movement for Righteous Leadership (MRL), is made up of around 5,000 members, with student leaders comprising the bulk alongside representatives from government employees, farmers and fisherfolk, the transport sector, religious groups, business groups, and professionals. Each of the 18 towns in the province has an MRL chapter. Mr. Denosta's profession as an engineer and part-time university professor allowed him to access this particular age-group. In fact, all of the core members of MRL were volunteer student leaders from the University of Antique, where he taught part-time. He met with MRL leaders every other day as they acted as his machinery, working in parallel with the NUP machinery. However, not all MRL members carried the NUP ticket, as they were only focused on the candidacy of Mr. Denosta. While many of the candidates relied largely on traditional patronage networks, Mr. Denosta was able to sustain a core group of followers by catering to their idealism as well as their need for traditional patronage goods, and he used them to build an effective political machine and cultivate his image as a reformist.

CONCLUSION

Patronage-driven politics has always been at the centre of the conversation on electoral politics, more so in the case of poor, rural areas like Antique Province. However, instead of the expected long-term dyadic relationship between the rich landowners and poor peasants, the province's politicians are, in the words of Kit Machado, "professional politicians" (see Machado 1974; Kimura 1998) who have had fruitful political careers through the successful use of money politics and political machineries.

As this chapter demonstrates, while vote buying is deemed indispensable, it does not always guarantee electoral victory. Rather, it needs to be complemented by other forms of positive inducements such as scholarships and other forms of aid, political machinery, and both traditional and social media. While party membership still remains ephemeral, party machinery and funding is still seen by many politicians as important to winning, even by those who list themselves as "independent". The 2016 election in the province also marked a shift towards candidates who espouse a combination of reformist and populist appeals. The extent to which this might continue in future elections is an interesting subject for political inquiry.

While there has been a collective sigh of relief among many in the province after getting the "change" they wanted, many voters and candidates still lament the fact that the prevalence of vote buying is extensive and allows only those who are wealthy or who have wealthy patrons to effectively contest for seats. Because of the restrictions imposed by a lack of resources, in the end, change might have been simply surface-deep. Perhaps in Antique, one set of elites has simply replaced another. The *rigodon*[10] continues.

---

[10] The first and also the last number of formal Filipino dances. This Spanish-era legacy is reserved mostly for the members of the ruling class and revolves around the changing of dance partners.

Table 14
Election results from Lone District of Antique

Candidate	Party	Office	Per cent (%)
*Indicates Incumbent Candidate			
Javier, Paolo*	LP	House of Representatives	52.37
Roquero, Raymundo	UNA	House of Representatives	38.27
Delfin, Robert	NPC	House of Representatives	4.80
Combong, Junior	IND	House of Representatives	1.67
Mallares, Narzal	PMM	House of Representatives	1.66
Pidoy, Rodelo	IND	House of Representatives	0.74
Villaflor, Antero	KBL	House of Representatives	0.48
Cadiao, Rhodora	NUP	Provincial Governor	56.78
Javier, Exequiel*	LP	Provincial Governor	43.22
Denosta, Edgar	NUP	Provincial Vice-Governor	46.33
Condez, Victor	LP	Provincial Vice-Governor	39.72
Fortaleza, Eduardo	IND	Provincial Vice-Governor	13.95
Anini-Y			
Pollicar, Maxfil	NUP	Mayor	38.81
Pahilga, Opet	LP	Mayor	37.46
Sampior, Jorrey	UNA	Mayor	23.73
Hernaez, Glenn*	NUP	Vice-Mayor	58.94
Cazeñas, Inday Magda	LP	Vice-Mayor	41.06
Barbaza			
Necor, Gerry*	LP	Mayor	58.39
Francisco, Faith	NUP	Mayor	41.61
Necesario, Ramy	LP	Vice-Mayor	54.70
Untal, Artchebal*	NUP	Vice-Mayor	45.30
Belison			
Dela Flor, Darell*	LP	Mayor	52.46
Piccio, Christopher	NUP	Mayor	47.54
Otayde, Elfe	LP	Vice-Mayor	56.29
Jacaba, Acay	UNA	Vice-Mayor	43.71

(cont'd overleaf)

Table 14 *(cont'd)*

Candidate	Party	Office	Per cent (%)
Bugasong			
Pacete, John Lloyd	LP	Mayor	58.53
Pesayco, Joemarie	NUP	Mayor	41.47
Pesayco, Bernard	NUP	Vice-Mayor	48.39
Dava, Renante	LP	Vice-Mayor	46.77
Pacete, John	IND	Vice-Mayor	4.84
Caluya			
Reyes, Genevive*	LP	Mayor	70.00
Dingcong, Nonong	UNA	Mayor	30.00
Egina, Dads*	LP	Vice-Mayor	61.41
Frangue, Rey	UNA	Vice-Mayor	38.59
Culasi			
Lomugdang, Jose Jeffrey	LP	Mayor	100.00
Alagos, Ariel*	IND	Vice-Mayor	50.41
Herco, Bibiano	IND	Vice-Mayor	49.59
Hamtic			
Pacificador, Junjun*	NUP	Mayor	64.74
Javier, Jason	LP	Mayor	35.26
Pacificador, Julie*	NUP	Vice-Mayor	100.00
Laua-An			
Baladjay, Francisco Jr*	LP	Mayor	56.08
Samillano, Joean	NUP	Mayor	43.14
Necor, Marialyn	KBL	Mayor	0.77
Baladjay, Aser*	NP	Vice-Mayor	57.06
Espartero, Robert	NUP	Vice-Mayor	42.94
Libertad			
Te, Bebot	NUP	Mayor	43.45
Valenzuela, Toto Rapol	LP	Mayor	28.93
Raymundo, Daday	IND	Mayor	27.29
Tumbokon, Bert	IND	Mayor	0.34
Mangilaya, Jean Condez	LP	Vice-Mayor	48.10

Table 14 *(cont'd)*

Candidate	Party	Office	Per cent (%)
Raymundo, Berting	IND	Vice-Mayor	30.71
Desullan, Ygna	UNA	Vice-Mayor	19.86
Loriega, Boy	IND	Vice-Mayor	1.32
Pandan			
Tan, Jonathan*	LP	Mayor	50.50
Sanchez, Plaridel Vi	NUP	Mayor	49.50
Tugon, Doc	UNA	Vice-Mayor	55.66
Tan, Jeremy	LP	Vice-Mayor	44.34
Patnongon			
Bacongallo, Johnnyflores*	LP	Mayor	74.36
Abellon, Alex	NUP	Mayor	25.64
Solis, Benjamin	IND	Vice-Mayor	53.62
Magbanua, Eduardo*	LP	Vice-Mayor	46.38
San Jose (Capital)			
Untaran, Elmer	NUP	Mayor	42.91
Plameras, Toting	LP	Mayor	37.98
Salazar, Boyet	IND	Mayor	18.67
Arangote, Renato	IND	Mayor	0.44
Saldajeno, Felix	IND	Vice-Mayor	30.10
Encarnacion, Toto Edel	NPC	Vice-Mayor	29.97
Galindo, Pacifico Jr	NUP	Vice-Mayor	22.40
Delgado, Edwin	LP	Vice-Mayor	17.54
San Remigio			
Cabigunda, Glenn*	LP	Mayor	90.37
Panes, Sme	UNA	Mayor	9.63
Coloso, Elizabeth*	LP	Vice-Mayor	87.18
Petinglay, Rito Sr	NUP	Vice-Mayor	11.56
Loquinario, Junie	IND	Vice-Mayor	1.26
Sebaste			
Varona, Jose Christopher*	LP	Mayor	58.33
Bulos, Isabelo	NUP	Mayor	40.09

(cont'd overleaf)

Table 14 *(cont'd)*

Candidate	Party	Office	Per cent (%)
Rendon, Vicente	IND	Mayor	1.57
Recopuerto, Baby Gas	NUP	Vice-Mayor	53.46
Azucena, Noracil*	LP	Vice-Mayor	46.54
Sibalom			
Occeña, Joel*	LP	Mayor	60.07
Lotilla, Boy Erick	NUP	Mayor	39.93
Tubianosa, Doc Berns*	LP	Vice-Mayor	61.08
Ovivir, Norman	NUP	Vice-Mayor	38.92
Tibiao			
Bandoja, Bando*	UNA	Mayor	50.78
Buenafe, Randy	LP	Mayor	48.44
Quibete, Pelay	IND	Mayor	0.78
Lim, Xz	NUP	Vice-Mayor	65.02
Alvarez, Fe*	LP	Vice-Mayor	34.98
Tobias Fornier (Dao)			
Fornier, Jojo*	IND	Mayor	57.68
Lignig, John	IND	Mayor	42.32
Tajanlangit, Morit*	UNA	Vice-Mayor	75.54
Cazeñas, Nolet	LP	Vice-Mayor	24.46
Valderrama			
Posadas, Joy	LP	Mayor	52.60
Roquero, Kristoffer Ray	UNA	Mayor	47.40
Castillon, Josefino	UNA	Vice-Mayor	53.12
Lacson, Leo	LP	Vice-Mayor	46.88

MINDANAO

chapter 15

Compostela Valley Province:
Machine, Logistics, and Solicitations

Neil Pancho

INTRODUCTION

In the middle of an interview inside a rural hotel, a young boy with a companion his age sheepishly handed over a solicitation letter to a candidate for the town council. The candidate was running under the Liberal Party (LP), the administration party in the 2016 national and local election. The candidate said, "*Kinsa ang nagtudlo ninyo ani*? (Who taught you this?)". The boy replied, "*Si Coach* (Our coach in the basketball)". The candidate told the boy, "Ingna si Coach, '*dili formal ang letter*.' *Tan-awa pa gud ni* (read the letter). *Ingna si Coach nga mangayo og pormal nga letter. Unya ipadala sa balay, ha?*" (The letter is not formal. Look at this. Tell your coach to draft a formal letter and send it to my house)". The boy nodded. The candidate turned her attention to the interviewer and raised her voice, "*Dili in-ana kay mura tag nangayo og limos* (It should be like this because we look like we're giving alms to a beggar)". After the boy left the candidate then poured out all her misgivings about the solicitation letters delivered to her house as well as to others during the campaign period.

Her frustration was not without basis. Solicitations from constituents are business as usual during the election period. Candidates expect a flood of requests to come to their doorsteps as the campaign heats up in the mineral-rich province of Compostela Valley. Constituents' requests range from local fares to medical emergencies, and candidates must respond if they hope to win elections. Relationships between voters and candidates are cultivated year-round—ongoing clientelism shapes the local politics of the province—but around election time these solicitations increase exponentially.

This chapter explores electoral dynamics in Compostela Valley. As is clear from Table 15, Compostela was a stronghold of the Liberal Party (LP). The provincial LP swept the local positions of governor, vice-governor, and the entire slate of the provincial board in the first district. In the second district, LP got three of five positions. In this chapter, I draw on fieldwork to analyse the conduct of the 2016 election in Compostela Valley. I focus on two competing local machines within the province—the Uy-backed Uswag/LP machine, and the Amatong-backed Aksyon machine. This comparison helps shed light on how candidates build their support networks and the role patronage networks play in cultivating, maintaining, and mobilising the support networks. The case of Compostela Valley provides numerous examples of the advantages governing machines have over the opposition.

BACKGROUND ON THE REGION

Compostela Valley Province was organised in 1998 from the mother province of Davao del Norte. The province is composed of eleven municipalities in two legislative districts. The first district has five towns; the second district has six. The population stands at 4,468,563. The ethnic composition of the province consists of migrants from Central and Eastern Visayas (provinces like Bohol, Cebu, and Leyte) living together with the indigenous population (Mansaka, Mandaya, Dibabawon, Mangguangan, and Manobo). Economic and political control is in the hands of the migrant population.

The population relies on agriculture, with income derived from agricultural products such as rice, coconut, cacao, coffee, papaya, mango, durian, and banana. Banana exports constitute the main bulk of agricultural output. The province is also home to gold rush areas located in the towns of Monkayo, Pantukan, New Bataan, and Maragusan. The biggest gold rush area is Mt. Diwata in the town of Monkayo.

According to the National Economic Development Agency (NEDA) in 2012, poverty incidence in Compostela Valley stood at 25 per cent which makes it a typical province in the Philippines. Unemployment stood at 5 per cent in 2012. In the last election, 350,529 voted out of 408,539 which translates to 86 per cent turnout—on the high side for Philippine elections.

Davao del Norte politicians rose to power by controlling profitable enterprises like logging concessions and the commercial banana export, with the port of Davao City as the shipment hub for these products. Lorenzo Sarmiento, who owned a logging company (L.S. Sarmiento) entered politics and became Davao del Norte's representative to the House of Representatives (Hirsch and Warren 1998). When timber supplies dwindled, Sarmiento lost his clout to the new industry emerging in the 1980s—gold mining. The son, Rogelio Sarmiento, ran for governor in the newly-created Compostela Valley Province but lost to a human rights lawyer, Jose Caballero. After serving for three terms as governor Caballero was replaced by Arthur "Chungkee" Uy in 2007. Uy, a naturalised Filipino of Chinese descent, also completed three terms as governor. In 2016, facing term limits, he fielded his 30-year-old son as a candidate for governor. This ended speculation that he would field his son as a candidate for the first district congressional seat, challenging long-time ally, Maricar Zamora, the daughter of Manuel "*Way Kurat*" (no fear) Zamora. (The elder Zamora was the incumbent vice-governor of Uy.) Both Uy and Zamora won their provincial races.

Amatong-Uy Rivalry

One of the defining features of Compostela Valley (Comval) is the rivalry between two families—the Amatong and Uy clans. Rommel Amatong started his career in Congress in 2007, replacing his aging father and long-time provincial politician, Prospero Amatong. In the same year, Arturo Uy won the governorship of Comval. Both men ran under the Lakas Party and formed the political alliance, "*Uswag Comval*" (literally translated as "progress" for Comval) the following year, along with two other leaders, Representative Manuel Zamora from the first district and Vice-Governor Ramil Gentugaya. Uswag became the political machine of Uy, Zamora, Gentugaya, and Amatong, with each of these leaders commanding an overlapping loyalty of board members and mayors.

Since its founding in 2007 Uswag has allied itself with various national parties. It initially affiliated with Lakas, but a few weeks prior to the 2010 election, it switched to the Nacionalista Party (NP), throwing its support behind the NP presidential candidate, Manuel Villar. While the NP lost the national election, the Uy's local party, Uswag, won in the province, continuing its dominance. After Benigno Aquino III won in 2010 Uswag joined the new president's Liberal Party. The following year, Uswag, headed by Governor Uy, swore allegiance to LP in Balay National Headquarter in Quezon City, thereby formally shedding its NP coat to become an administration party once more.

The unity of the Uswag team lasted only as long as Governor Uy's time in office. As his term drew to an end, the members of Uswag tried to position themselves or one from their circle as the next governor. After much negotiation among the provincial leaders of Uswag, Governor Uy fielded his son Jayvee Tyron Uy as his replacement, with the support of Zamora and Gentugaya. The young Uy, 30 years old, was a graduate of Bachelor of Science in Medical Technology in Cebu City. Before entering politics, he used to work in the family food business, Tagum Barbest Cue Foods Corporation and Penong's Seafood and Grill Corporation. He was an incumbent provincial board member before filing the certificate of candidacy for governor in 2016.

The negotiation for the 2016 election affected the prospects of Manuel Zamora, a former congressman in the first district, and the sitting vice-governor. Zamora had planned to run for governor, but the mayors in Comval opposed his bid. They did not find him to be a serious chief executive for the province. Zamora casually walks around in a t-shirt, cargo pants, and slippers typical of a *tambay* (local thug). His folksy language endeared him to the masses but alienated local political leaders. He is known for his antics, including throwing a slipper to the laughing crowd and promising to pay a hundred pesos to whoever catches it. Dared by one politician to crawl before Poblacion's landmark, he did so, enlisting fellow Uswag leader Ramil Gentugaya as his accomplice, while their supporters looked on giggling and filming (a supporter later published the video on social media). With town mayors opposing him and Uy backing his son, Zamora opted to run for vice-governor for a second term. His daughter Maricar Zamora stood for re-election as representative of the first district.[1] Ramil Gentugaya,

---

[1] As mentioned previously, it had been rumoured that the younger Uy was planning to challenge for the seat, but the bargain gave the Uys the governorship and retained the congressional seat for the Zamoras.

a member of the provincial board and Uswag leader, decided to run for mayor in the town of Monkayo. Meanwhile, the incumbent governor, the older Uy, remained the leader of Uswag and elected to stay in politics and run as a board member in the second district of the province. In election rallies for the LP, local leaders continued to acknowledge his role in the province as though he were not ending his term.

The bargain made by these provincial leaders was just enough to keep most of the Uswag together. The leaders (Uy, Zamora, and Gentugaya) accepted their chosen elective positions, and the consensus was rebuilt. However, on the outside looking in was Representative Amatong, the three-term Congressman from the second district.

Shut out of the prime posts within Uswag, and left with no other option, Amatong left the Uswag/LP and allied himself with Aksyon Demokratiko (Aksyon), running for governor against Uy. Within the province, he assembled a slate of candidates to compete with the Uswag/LP provincial slate of the elder Uy. Both slates supported the Roxas-Robredo LP presidential ticket, and the administration's senatorial slate, but they competed bitterly for the posts of congressperson on down.

The Uy camp united against the defector, while Amatong drew on his base of support from the second district of the province, where he was completing his third term as Representative. The two camps vied for national LP support. Ultimately, the LP favoured the Uy camp, justifying its support by invoking the party policy of "equity to the incumbent". Also, the key to securing their support was the role of Representative Maricar Zamora. Zamora, the congressional incumbent from the first district, was a leading supporter of LP in the province in the 2016 election. "The silent operator running the budget process" in Congress, she co-chaired the House Committee on Appropriations and oversaw national public expenditures (Coronel et al. 1998: 68–9). She was a rising star within the LP and she reciprocated by eagerly working as a campaigner for the party in the province. She urged her party mates to rally behind Roxas against the tide of public opinion but in the end, her efforts were not enough to win the province for Roxas. The province voted for Rodrigo Duterte, the mayor of Davao City, as the new president of the Philippines.

With both the national LP party and the Uswag against him, Amatong's local party was at a serious disadvantage. Things might have turned out differently had Duterte not delayed filing his candidacy. Without Duterte in the race, Amatong had to pick from what was available nationally, and he chose to ally with Aksyon. Had Duterte filed earlier, one Amatong campaign worker believed Amatong would have run under the PDP of Duterte.[2]

CAMPAIGN STRUCTURE, LOGISTICS, AND IMAGE

The campaign in Compostela Valley Province evolved into a battle of local machinery consisting of a multitude of contacts with constituents animated by patronage. The administration party headed by local kingpin, Arturo Uy, had a great advantage. Uy had a solid control of the province, having won three elections as governor and having built political machinery from the province down to the barangay.

Uy built his campaign teams by tapping the campaign structures built by incumbent mayors. Almost all the mayors were loyal to him and with their help he was able to establish a structure in every municipality in pyramid fashion, with him on top, the mayors in the middle, and the barangays on the bottom. These municipal campaign structures delivered bodies during rallies, conducted informal surveys within the municipality, recruited poll watchers, and reported intrusions from other parties. Barangay leaders [from the barangay captains, to the *kagawads* (barangay councilors), to the *purok* leaders] were the backbone of this structure. Within the campaign, the barangay coordinator worked with these functionaries to coordinate campaign activities within each barangay. By contrast, Amatong appeared to have a hard time attracting leaders. This was not surprising—the administration machine usually has the upper hand in recruitment. Barangay leaders gravitated to the party with the most resources.

The symbiotic relationships between Uswag and barangay leaders was longstanding, and had been forged and maintained over three previous electoral cycles. Uy and his clique drew strength from the barangay and vice versa. The barangay leaders needed him for the community projects, and the governor needed them to support his administration and deliver votes during the election. Once this relationship is forged between elections, the campaign becomes a matter of affirming previous commitments and revisiting old acquaintances. Uy also had the practice of keeping tabs on former town officials who had completed their three terms. He would hire them as executive assistants before supporting them

---

[2] Interview with campaign worker, Montevista, Compostela Valley, 8 May 2016.

again as candidates to their towns.[3] Providing jobs to these local leaders was a way to keep them employed while waiting for the next election and was a way of maintaining their loyalty.

Campaigns go to great efforts to determine the partisan leanings of barangay captains. Most sided with the sitting governor—mediated through the mayor. Once the governor got the support from the mayor, he usually brought the barangay captains with him. Why would barangay captains be beholden to the mayor? The words of two barangay captains during a rally neatly explain their motivation: *"Gipadagan ko ni mayor"* (The mayor allowed me to run) and *"suportahan ko ni mayor"* (The mayor supported me).[4]

Campaigns were fought in the barangay with a mixture of big gatherings and *pulong-pulong* (small campaign meetings), organised on a daily basis. It was at this local level that Amatong was at the greatest disadvantage. Barangay captains already knew whom they would support even before the campaign started. Amatong did manage to get a few village leaders on his side but things proved especially difficult for him in the first district where he had no personal support base.[5] The first district was the bailiwick of former Representative "Way Kurat" (No fear) Zamora. Zamora, an ally of Uy, lorded over the first district for three terms. He then handed down the district to his daughter in the 2010 election. The elder Zamora, a *sabong* (cock-fighting) aficionado, built extensive ties with barangay leaders during his incumbency.[6] These were ties his daughter and successor worked hard to maintain. As a result, while Amatong's team included incumbent mayors in the second district, in the first district his team consisted entirely of individual opposition candidates for mayor.

Amatong was furthered hampered by his inability to raise a war chest to sustain his campaign. Uswag under Uy formed an alliance with other prominent and wealthy families like Zamora and Ramil Gentugaya from the vote and mineral-rich town of Monkayo. Uy himself has an interest in the food business and mining operations in the province, while Gentugaya's wealth comes from landholdings and investment in banana plantations. His family also runs the biggest rice mill in the town and

---

[3] Campaign event, Poblacion, New Bataan, 9 April 2016.

[4] Campaign rally, Compostela Valley, May 2016.

[5] It was in the second district where he worked as a district representative.

[6] One time he brought leaders to Bohol, an island in Central Visayas known for its tourist attractions, for an educational tour. He also ferried village chiefs in a Metro Shuttle bus—a company owned by the brother of the Governor Uy, Rey Uy, the incumbent mayor of the nearby Tagum City.

extended credits to farmers. Zamora operates cockpits and gold mines. Together, the resources available to Uswag were formidable. Amatong had only one rich financier on his side: Jose Brillantes, a former mayor of Monkayo whose family drew its wealth from mining. However, Brillantes' influence was limited to his hometown while Zamora and Gentugaya covered the entire province due to their positions as vice-governor and provincial board member respectively.[7]

Indigenous communities and women

Apart from barangay officials, two groups of voters received much attention from candidates in 2016: the indigenous population and women's groups. Leading politicians from both camps targeted tribal communities, usually through town mayors. In New Bataan, for example, LP Mayor Gerald Ford Balbin promised to set up the first village for tribal members in the centre of the town (Poblacion). This campaign promise went side by side with pledges to improve farm-to-market roads and to build a school building in the upland community. These promises were communicated by three brokers: the *datu* (tribal leader), a religious leader, and the barangay captain, each of whom claimed to speak for the community. The datu is the remnant of the old tribal system that existed for generations in many upland communities. Religious leaders are tribal members who adopted Protestantism courtesy of American religious missionary efforts in far-flung communities of Mindanao. Protestant churches are a common sight near indigenous populations. Finally, the barangay captain represents the administrative structure of the local government. In New Bataan and other towns, the local government institutionalised the participation of the indigenous population by creating a tribal council composed of datus from the different upland communities. They shared ideas related to mining, peace and order, and religious rituals with the government.

The young Uy was particularly active in seeking support from indigenous voters. He visited an upland indigenous community in Barangay Manurigao, travelling for five hours in *habal-habal* (modified motorbike for public transport), crossing hills and challenging roads a few months before the filing period. The visit was intended to get to know the needs of the community. During his visit, he promised to open a high school building, explore opportunities for tourism, and improve the road

---

[7] Gentugaya had also served as the vice-governor to Uy before Zamora.

network leading to the town centre. He then sent medical teams from the province to carry out medical missions for the indigenous community.

Targeting women was another common way of seeking a set of votes. Here the campaign was more subtle. Women were invited to participate in a summit where they were taught livelihood projects and how to take care of their health, with the assistance of rural health workers, who lent credibility to the activity. A candidate running for a local town council announced that the first 20 participants would receive free mobile phones, and afterward the participation in the summit increased greatly. After the summit, the same candidate took the names and mobile numbers of participants. A few days later, they received a personalised letter from the candidate who organised the activity and text messages thanking them for supporting the activity.

Logistics and image

The election provides the opportunity for candidates to meet the voters, where logistics and images come to play for local political contests. Here again, the administration party of Uy seemed to have a great advantage. Incumbent mayors mobilised resources derived from their position. For instance, temporary employees of the LGUs participated in a candidates' forum organised by a parish priest in the town of New Bataan. They all wore the colour of the administration party. The local opposition party affiliated with Amatong was much smaller. The Amatong-backed mayoral candidate, Nelson Cabuñas, an indigenous person from Mandaya and self-made businessman who earned his wealth from a gold mine, found himself in an awkward position after a barrage of questions were flung at him. Later, sources confided that the administration party in New Bataan had planted individuals from their side to embarrass Cabuñas with difficult questions.[8]

The presence of temporary employees or job orders (JOs) was also visible in many areas. In one *pulong-pulong* in the neighbouring town of Compostela, for example, temporary workers attended and worked on behalf of the mayor, who was running for another term. Employing contractual staff has been the practice of incumbents for a long time, leading to criticism that the practice saps the resources of the LGU in the long run by diverting funds from needed activities and programmes.

---

[8] Interview with campaign worker, New Bataan, May 2016.

Organising a province-wide campaign is a logistical challenge. The campaign structure must reach most corners of the province, and this gives a definite advantage to the administration party. The established machinery on the ground enables the administration party to hop from one *pulong-pulong* to another while drawing on their ability to ferry constituents from the hinterlands to the venue. In *mitings de avance* and Poblacion rallies in Compostela, candidates used trucks, buses, pickups, and motorcycles to carry constituents into the town. The local campaign committee coordinated with the governor's campaign team in preparing food for the crowds attending the rallies.

The glitz and glamour of entertainment are also an important part of most campaigns. Campaign rallies resemble popular noon-time shows on the television, with entertainment scattered in between candidate speeches. In the *miting de avance* for the LP in Compostela, bright lights beamed on the candidates on stage, while a TV camera focused on the speaker perched on an elevated platform. A projection screen magnified the image of the speaker for the benefit of those watching from the side of the stage or watching from afar. The audio was professionally amplified while young dancers gyrated to their dance numbers. Jingles that ripped off popular songs were played regularly at campaign sorties. The campaign, in short, was a fiesta for many, with colourful banners, tarpaulins, and t-shirts.

Uy's machine was conscious of projecting an image of unity and the ability to deliver service to its constituents. They made life-size billboards for all their respective slates. Each town had a billboard with the entire provincial slate, while Amatong had no billboards to match those of the administration party. At a disadvantage, the opposition party changed tactics. It began applying negative campaigning against Uswag and Uy. The opposition attempted to destroy the image of the administration party by raising the issue of corruption, particularly of the funds intended for victims of the typhoon in 2012. They even popularised it in a song. The lyrics go:

> *Nilabay si Pablo sa among baryo* (Pablo passed in our village)
>
> *Kadaut daghan kaayo* (he brought devastation)
>
> *Guba ang balay, Lupad ang yero* (he destroyed houses)
>
> *Ang Katawhan naguol og napuryesyo* (The people were sad and desperate)
>
> *Dugay hinabang nga ihatagay* (inaudible)

naay cash gihatag, dyes mil, dyes mil (Cash was intended for them)

asa na ang dyes mil, iuli ang dyes mil (10,000/10,000/where is the 10,000?)

kay amo ang dyes mil (It belonged to us).

The song was so popular that even children and ordinary people could mimic the lyrics. Amatong's actions placed Uswag in a defensive position. They went to great lengths to explain what happened to the PhP 10,000 emergency shelter assistance provided by the administration of President Benigno Aquino. In every rally, Uswag had to address the "*dyes mil*" issue. In a *miting de avance*, Uswag even employed a lawyer to explain the details of *dyes mil* coupled with an audio-visual presentation before the mobilised crowd.

THE ROLE OF PATRONAGE

Patronage animated the campaign structure, logistics war, and image-making. Candidates discretely admitted that they need to prepare a large war chest leading to the election. Funds had to be set aside in advance to cover the expenses of the 45-day campaign. This included cash for "*tag-tag*" (the local expression for vote buying, translated as "distribution") during "*oras de peligro*" (delicate time) when candidates start to "*kamang*" (crawl) to buy votes. Interviews with supporters and candidates from LP and Aksyon parties revealed similar preparation.

To facilitate *tag-tag*, the common practice in Compostela Valley Province during the election was to keep a list of the members of each household. *Purok* leaders prepared the list in coordination with barangay captains. They claimed to know if a family or an individual in a family had shifted allegiance. They did so by observing who people associated with or based on stories circulating in the community. Initially, the lists are quite expansive, including nearly everyone in the *purok* (sub-village). However, as the election drew nearer, the lists were whittled down to those who were strong supporters. An LGU employee who discreetly moonlit with the Aksyon of Amatong reported that initially, the LP list contained his name. Once the block leader, who worked with provincial LP, learned of his association, his name was removed from the list.[9]

---

[9] Interview with LGU employee, Compostela Valley, 17 April 2016.

Cash

Cash is king during election season. A candidate for local council admitted that they received allowances from an administration candidate in the province affiliated with LP, but most of their funds for all campaign activities came from personal contribution.[10] She lamented the lack of material support from the national headquarters of LP or Roxas himself. National party leadership rarely deals with councilors. Instead, they focus on governors and congressman.

The Amatong camp accused the administration party of distributing "yellow cards" to buy votes. Yellow cards recorded the weekly distribution of money to voters under the control of the *purok* leader. (In some areas, they use bloc leaders—a leader who manages ten households.) Allegedly, Uswag copied the practice from DSWD and the Red Cross, who used the card to designate victims of the typhoon in 2012. The card contained the date and donations of specific items from the government or international organisations. The purpose of the card was to ensure transparent donations and an even distribution among the population. During the election, Uswag issued a similar card for the purpose of monitoring the recipients' weekly cash allocation. Barangay coordinators moved around in coordination with the *purok* coordinator to dispense cash.

Vote buying comes in various modalities, with various intentions, sources, and waves. Each party prepared to buy votes, and each accused the other of buying votes. Both were aware that it is illegal to buy votes but acknowledged this as part of the game. The primary purpose of vote buying is to get voters to either vote for a straight ticket (province and towns) or to induce them to vote for one candidate. In a straight ticket, the money comes from whoever is running for governor or mayor respectively. In contrast, individual candidates may also independently buy votes in support of their candidacy, not content to rely on party affiliation to secure the victory. Seldom do two or more candidates pool their money together to buy votes. While vote buying is intended to reward core supporters, it can also be used to protect votes from slipping into the hands of the opponent.

The funds for vote buying come from those running for the top position of the province all the way down to the last town councilor. The capacity to buy hinges on the ability to accumulate a war chest leading up to the day of the election. Campaigns have to prepare an amount of money to cover official expenses for the 45 days and amass another amount for the *oras*

---

[10] Interview with LGU employee, Compostela Valley Province, 7 May 2016.

de peligro to buy votes. One respondent campaigning for a local council seat in a First Class municipality admitted that his family prepared PhP 800,000.00.[11] Kagawads who run without sufficient funds have to rely on a mayoral candidate to pay for their campaign expenses. Kagawads under Uswag in one town complained when they were asked to contribute to the campaign kitty because they expected the mayor, who was running for re-election, to cover them.[12] Similarly, board members also depend on the governor for the campaign.

A day before the election, the campaign officially stops. Ironically, this is the actual climax of the campaign. This is when vote buying comes to play. Vote buying comes in waves. One candidate for the provincial board was reported to be leading, but resigned himself to losing after learning that the administration party spent twice as much money as the opposition had spent on vote buying.[13] In one barangay, a voter received PhP 2,100 after three waves of buying.[14] Parties acknowledged that money is important in the last phase of the election. All parties participated— they only differed in magnitude. The party in power has more resources than the opposition to buy votes and, if needs be, can give cash on a weekly basis leading to the day of the election. A response from the opposition to counter one wave of vote buying with more buying would elicit yet another round of buying from the administration at a higher cost.

Not all voters received funds from candidates. Campaigns first prioritised their supporters, targeting marginal supporters only if needed. In general, leaders also avoided the middle class, professionals, and those who might not respond to offers of money, such as pastors and church leaders.

Vote buying is not without risk. To minimise the risk of voter defection, the parties emphasised straight voting. The parties also attempted to enforce the mandate from the provincial campaign team to encourage loyalty in the party and discouraged candidates from campaigning individually. However, a candidate affiliated with Uswag confided, "*Bisan sa Partido, laglaganay man gihapon*" (even inside the party, there is a practice of dropping candidates).[15]

---

[11] Interview with the candidate, Barangay Poblacion, Compostela, 18 April 2016.
[12] Interview with a candidate for local council, Kagawad, Compostela Valley Province, 16 April 2016.
[13] Interview with the candidate, Compostela Valley, May 2016.
[14] Personal correspondence with the candidate, Davao City, 14 May 2016.
[15] Interview with the candidate, Compostela, Compostela Valley Province, 16 April 2016.

In kind

Constituents seemed to believe that candidates are awash with cash during an election. Candidates were expected to be generous. However, buying votes does not always have to be in cash. All candidates also provided a variety of goods and services to voters. For example, an opposition candidate in one town said that her party provided in-kind donations to improve the access of the community to potable water.[16] Others allocated an amount for repair of basketball courts and the provision of the uniforms for the basketball players. Other gifts included a tent for the *habal-habal* terminal (motorbikes used as a public utility), improvements of barangay hall compound, signage for the village, and other community needs. Providing educational scholarships was another common tactic. Councilors kept a list of their scholarship students in primary school. During campaign sorties, they boasted of having scholars in many elementary schools located in their town. They would always tell their audience that if elected they would continue and expand the number of scholars.

Returning to the opening anecdote in this chapter, candidates do not have to look far to find people in need of assistance. During campaign season they are inundated with requests, big and small, for assistance. Amatong, for example, converted his garage into a receiving area for constituents who needed medicines and endorsements. Representative Zamora expected poor constituents to come to her for medical support after a visit to the local health unit located near the congressional office.[17] A chief of staff of one candidate running for the provincial council said that they had to prepare petty cash in anticipation of solicitation letters coming in. He feared that any voter turned away was a lost vote.[18] Thus, candidates had to assign staff to take care of the solicitations coming to their door the moment they chose to run for public office.

It is also important to note that assistance does not disappear after the election. As the saying goes, money is for the election, projects for regular days. Between elections, barangay officials solicited help from the governor, the congressman, and the mayor for small projects like the improvement of the drainage system, installation of street lights, and

[16] Interview with the candidate, New Bataan, Compostela Valley Province, 17 April 2016.
[17] Interview with Representative Zamora, Compostela, Compostela Valley Province, 2 May 2016.
[18] Interview with campaign staff, Wengie Villanueva, 8 May 2016.

building of basketball courts. The mayor and the barangay captain would claim credit for these projects before their constituents.

CONCLUSION

In the end, the 2016 election was a battle between two unequally matched machines. Uswag won that battle because its machine was better able to carry out the necessary activities of the campaign. In the battle of logistics, Uswag was more adept at ferrying its constituents to rallies, feeding them during the long hours of sorties, and projecting positive images of the party via billboards and streamers. The party could also tap its resources to provide better service in the form of the physical and visible projects voters expected them to deliver. At the end of the day, the opposition's attempt to discredit the administration was blunted by the ability of Uswag to activate its machine to mobilise voters and project a proper image.

The patronage system underpins these machines. Political machines are simply vote generators to ensure more or less solid support on the day of the election. The machines reach all corners of the province. The machine is the pipeline and patronage is the oil that flows from the top provincial campaign down to the last block in the community. Therefore, machine and patronage go together, and each depends on the other to exist.

Table 15
Election results from Compostela Valley 1st District

Candidate	Party	Office	Per cent (%)
*Indicates incumbent candidate			
Zamora, Maricar*	LP	House of Representatives	63.43
Brillantes, Joselito	AKSYON	House of Representatives	36.57
Uy, Jayvee Tyron	LP	Provincial Governor	50.92
Amatong, Bobong	AKSYON	Provincial Governor	48.64
Cañaveral, Josue	IND	Provincial Governor	0.44
Zamora, Way Kurat*	LP	Provincial Vice-Governor	59.52
Tito, Franco	AKSYON	Provincial Vice-Governor	40.48
Compostela			
Bolo, Lema*	LP	Mayor	53.45

(cont'd overleaf)

Table15 *(cont'd)*

Candidate	Party	Office	Per cent (%)
Ang, Dolfo	AKSYON	Mayor	46.55
Castillo, Rey*	LP	Vice-Mayor	100.00
Maragusan (San Mariano)			
Colina, Ate Maris	LP	Mayor	66.25
Colita, Emmie	AKSYON	Mayor	33.75
Colina, Cesar Sr.	LP	Vice-Mayor	75.57
Saballa, Rv	AKSYON	Vice-Mayor	24.43
Monkayo			
Gentugaya, Ramil	LP	Mayor	50.54
Brillantes, Junjun	AKSYON	Mayor	49.46
Brillantes, Janet	AKSYON	Vice-Mayor	53.06
Cabag, Nonoy	LP	Vice-Mayor	46.94
Montevista			
Jayectin, Topoy*	LP	Mayor	61.68
Basalo, Cirilo Jr.	AKSYON	Mayor	38.32
Juario, Jose	AKSYON	Vice-Mayor	55.70
Abucejo, Roel*	LP	Vice-Mayor	44.30
New Bataan			
Balbin, Gerald	LP	Mayor	53.76
Cabuñas, Nelson	AKSYON	Mayor	45.85
Namoco, Doming	IND	Mayor	0.39
Pagalan, Larie	AKSYON	Vice-Mayor	57.07
Corpuz, Boy*	LP	Vice-Mayor	42.93

chapter **16**

Tagum City, Davao del Norte: When a Local Boss Fails

Tetchie D. Aquino

The 2016 mayoral election in Tagum City were dramatic. The newly elected Speaker of the House of Representatives, Pantaleon Alvarez, described them as "Do or die elections wherein whoever loses will see the end of his political career."[1] The election pitted former allies, who were now bitter enemies, against one another. Allies-turned-enemies is the best way to describe the relationship between incumbent Mayor Allan L. Rellon and former Mayor Rey T. Uy, who were running against each other for the first time.

The Uy–Rellon tandem started in 2004 when they ran as Liberal Party (LP) candidates for mayor and vice-mayor respectively. The partnership was a success, and both won the same offices in three consecutive elections: 2004, 2007, and 2010. However, in 2013, because of the mandatory three consecutive term limit imposed on local elective positions, Uy and Rellon could not run for the same posts again. Usually, when a politician reaches the mandatory term limit, he or she either seeks higher office or takes a break for three years, stepping aside in favour of a relative or other trusted associate. In 2013, Uy decided to take a break from the elections. The residents of Tagum City expected that he would support the candidacy of Rellon, who was running as mayor.

---

[1] Interview with Pantaleon Alvarez, 30 April 2016.

But that did not happen. In order to keep his family name in the mix in Tagum, where name-recall is very crucial during elections, Mayor Uy asked his young son, De Carlo "Oyo" Uy, to run against his former ally instead. Oyo was supported by the Liberal Party since his father headed the local chapter. Rellon, on the other hand, had to transfer to the opposition Partido Demokratiko Pilipino–Lakas ng Bayan (PDP–Laban). PDP–Laban became the party of President Rodrigo Duterte in 2016 and is the current ruling party in the Philippines, but in 2013 the party was weak both nationally and locally. Nonetheless, Rellon won a landslide victory, garnering a total of 51,136 votes against Oyo's 30,303 votes. Oyo had the backing of a large political machinery and the incumbent mayor, but that was not enough for him to win the election.

In 2016, the Uy patriarch stepped in to regain his old position. He ran for mayor against his former ally, Rellon. The Tagum City electorate was split in between these two strong and experienced candidates. But, in the end, with a very small margin of 55,388 to 53,369 votes, Allan L. Rellon won again.

This chapter describes the 2016 mayoral election in Tagum City. It explains how the rival teams won votes through tried and tested campaign strategies, such as barangay-based campaigning, "handshaking" activities, political rallies, and the like, as well as by testing new strategies involving the use of social media. It discusses how one man, who campaigned by adopting a strong stance against criminality and who was backed by a strong political machinery, lost the election. It also describes how, despite allegedly having the guns, goons, and gold, the local boss failed. In the end, I argue that the rival machines were so evenly matched in terms of their mobilisation capacity that the election turned on the inability of Uy to win the support of blocks of voters outside his core group of supporters.

BACKGROUND

Tagum City, the capital city of the Province of Davao del Norte, is located in the southern part of the island of Mindanao. It has a total land area of 19,580 hectares, most of which is used for agriculture, with banana and coconut being the dominant crops. As of 2015, Tagum City's population of 259,444 persons was the largest in the province. Located 55 kilometres north of Davao City, travel from Davao takes an hour or two and the city is distinguished by its streets lined with palm trees (an initiative of Mayor Uy during his first term that was initially criticised by residents for being too expensive, but is now widely appreciated as a beautification project that sets the city apart from others).

Tagum City, once a sleepy municipality, is fast developing into a bustling urban centre, with numerous development projects underway, and business establishments such as shopping malls increasing. In a recent study conducted by the Asian Institute of Management (AIM), Tagum was ranked among the 20 most viable component cities for business in the Philippines (Tagum City 2016).[2] For people in the surrounding provinces of Davao del Norte, Compostela Valley, and Davao Oriental, Tagum is an important commercial hub. The city employs thousands of people from across the region and houses many students, drawn in part by a cost of living that is lower than in Davao.

In recent years, Tagum City has attracted many internal migrants from other parts of the Philippines. Economic opportunities, especially in mining, in Tagum and neighbouring municipalities have drawn people to the city. Originally, various indigenous peoples (called Lumad), including the Mansakas, Manguangans, Mandayas, and Kalagans, inhabited Tagum. Though there are some from these groups still residing in the city, most have resettled to nearby municipalities.

THE TAGUM CITY 2016 ELECTION

The 2016 mayoral election in Tagum was a competition between two traditional politicians, both of whom had long track records as public officials. Though each of the rivals was backed by a different party, party loyalty did not count for much during the election, since most residents based their votes more on the reputations of the candidates rather than on their parties' platforms. In this regard, the Tagum City election was typical of elections through much of the Philippines.

The incumbent, Mayor Rellon, was born and raised in Davao del Norte. Coming from a family of public servants and teachers, some of whom also served terms in political office (two mayors have served terms as mayor of Island Garden City in Samal), Rellon finished his Bachelor's degree in education, majoring in mathematics, at the University of Mindanao's

---

[2] On 23 June 1941, by virtue of Executive Order No. 452 issued by then President Manuel L. Quezon, Tagum was created as a municipality. On 7 March 1998, more than 50 years later, R.A. 8274 was ratified, creating Tagum as a Component City of Davao del Norte.

Tagum Campus, and also obtained a Masters in Public Administration from Ateneo de Davao University. A former college instructor, Rellon started his political career as a Municipal Administrator of Tagum in 1993 and served as city councilor from 1998 until 2004. In 2004, he was elected as vice-mayor, a post he held for nine years. In 2013, he won as mayor and finished his first term in 2016. Though Rellon won lots of awards for the city as its chief executive, his term as mayor also had its fair share of controversies. His opponents accused him of being responsible for various problems, including rising crime involving minors and overspending by the city government due to the overemployment of political appointees, including ghost employees.[3]

Former Mayor Rey Uy was also born and raised in Davao del Norte. However, he is of Chinese descent, with parents born in China. Despite being born in Tagum City, Philippine laws did not recognise him as a natural-born Filipino citizen; upon reaching the age prescribed by law, he was naturalised as a Filipino citizen. He finished his elementary and secondary education at the Ateneo de Davao University and graduated with a degree in Bachelor of Science in Agriculture at Xavier University, Cagayan de Oro City. He went on to develop a career in business, building on the success of his family, and became well known as co-owner of the Davao Metro Shuttle, a major bus company that operates in Davao del Norte and Compostela Valley. Upon the urging of his brother, who told him that Tagum needed a businessman in politics, Uy entered politics in 1988 at the age of 32, serving as a member of the Sangguniang Panlalawigan for Davao Province.

Uy was first elected as mayor of Tagum City in 1998 but lost in 2001 when he ran for re-election. One reason for this defeat was his plan to replace the tricycles in Tagum with jeepneys. Tricycles are the major form of public transportation in the city, and the tricycle drivers campaigned against him. In 2004, Uy ran for office again. He won and was able to win three consecutive terms (2004–07, 2007–10, and 2010–13). During his terms as mayor, Tagum City won a lot of awards for public administration and local governance. Reflecting the city's rising income Tagum was also reclassified as a First Class Component City.

Mayor Uy was a controversial figure, in part because his name has long been associated with vigilantism and violence in Tagum City. These allegations came into public view in May 2014, when Human Rights Watch released a study entitled "One Shot to the Head: Death Squad

---

[3] Interview with Mayor Rey T. Uy, 4 May 2016.

Killings in Tagum City, Philippines" (Human Rights Watch 2014). The study focused on killings carried out by a vigilante group called the Tagum Death Squad (TDS) which, it alleged, was linked to Mayor Uy. The report drew on extensive interview materials to detail alleged personal involvement in, and direction of, killings by Uy. According to the study, the TDS was deployed by Uy to reduce the presence of alleged criminals and other "weeds" (a term often used by Mayor Uy) in the city—drug dealers, petty criminals, and those who inhale solvents.

The study noted that though it is not clear when TDS was created, many of the extrajudicial killings carried out by the group were rooted in Uy's public anti-crime campaign. The killings, which happened between 2007 and 2013, served as warnings to those who intended to carry out crimes in the city. According to the study, it was Uy who directed the operations of TDS, including providing payments and equipment for the operations, and using the Civil Service Unit as cover to lawfully issue guns and motorcycles used in killings.

To this day, Mayor Uy denies his involvement in, and even the existence of, the Tagum Death Squad. In an interview he said that "the killings were done by different people for different reasons—business rivalries, drugs, love triangles, non-payment of debts, revenge, and so on".[4] He added that "killings happen anywhere, even in America".[5] These extra-judicial cases have yet to be resolved by law enforcement agencies.

Campaign strategies, patronage, and money politics

Despite the tension that was inherent in this competition between allies-turned-foes, the campaign period started peacefully. Candidates tried to promote name recognition by using jingles played through loudspeakers attached to vehicles that went around the city, running print, radio and television advertisements, sending teams out house to house to distribute handbills and pamphlets, and by putting up political posters—usually violating the rules set by the Commission on Elections (COMELEC) in the process. According to one Uy campaign worker, black propaganda was quite rampant, especially in social media where trolls from both sides were paid to spread rumours about their opponents.[6] Campaign workers and volunteers were tasked with responding to negative

---

[4] Interview with Mayor Uy, 4 May 2016.
[5] Ibid.
[6] Interview with Uy campaign worker, 6 May 2016.

commentary against their candidates and with writing posts highlighting their achievements. Even so, though social media played a large part in the national election, it did not play a big role locally, since most social media users were young voters who were either studying or working outside the city.

During the campaign period, the candidates' day started with "handshaking". Usually conducted in the mornings in public places such as parks, markets, and basketball courts, these activities were designed to allow the candidates to personally "meet and greet" the voters. The candidates could personally interact with ordinary citizens and listen to their needs and aspirations. Uy, in particular, believed that this activity was essential for demonstrating personal contact with constituents.[7]

Since the campaign period happened during the hot/summer season, the temperature compelled most people in Tagum City to stay indoors during the afternoons. The candidates use these time as an opportunity to rest and conduct meetings with their partymates and campaign teams. They would update each other on the overall status of the campaign—assessing whether the campaign strategies employed were successful or not, or whether they needed to develop new strategies to get more votes. They also used the time to prepare for the political rallies in the barangays, usually conducted in the evening.

These rallies were usually coordinated and hosted by the political parties, one of the few contributions of parties to the local contests. The rallies were the venues where the candidates could introduce themselves to the people and deliver promises that could either be programmatic—about what the candidates intended to do for the city as a whole—or highly targeted. For example, in one meeting, I heard a congressional candidate repeatedly instructing his political party mates to tell barangay officials that they would be given PhP 1 million for the barangay "development fund" if the residents there "voted straight"—that is, delivered victories for all of the candidates on the party's ticket.[8] Since political rallies are rather long, usually lasting for three or four hours, some candidates entertained the populace by singing and dancing. Sometimes they would ask celebrities to come to increase the crowd size.

In Tagum, barangays were usually notified ahead of time if political rallies were to be conducted. During the early months of the campaign, both the Uy and the Rellon camps announced the schedule of their

---

[7] Interview with Mayor Uy, 4 May 2016.
[8] Field Notes, 30 April 2016, Tagum City.

political rallies publicly and in advance. However, during the months nearing the election, the Rellon camp had to change track and conduct rallies unannounced. According to a Rellon campaign worker, they noticed that the Uy camp was sabotaging them by conducting political rallies wherever the Rellon camp was scheduled to appear. He said that if, for example, PDP–Laban scheduled a political rally in Visayan Village, Friday, at 8 pm, LP would go to the same place, on the same day but at an earlier time, such as 7 pm, effectively ruining whatever plans the PDP–Laban had for the night.[9]

Death threats were another reason why the Rellon camp had to schedule their rallies unannounced. According to Rellon's campaign manager, their campaign office received threatening calls and campaign workers also noticed suspicious unidentified men attending their political rallies. He said that for their candidates' safety they had to switch to conducting rallies unannounced.[10]

During field research, I personally experienced the difficulty of tracking the political rallies of PDP–Laban. Even people closely associated with the Rellon camp had to go through back channels before being able to learn where the rallies were being conducted. Usually, decisions on where to go were finalised an hour before the actual rally. The time and location of the rally was spread by word of mouth, from one neighbour to another. During data gathering, I found myself going from one barangay to another following leads, often ending up finding that either the rally was already over or that it had never happened. On one night, when I finally chanced on a Rellon political rally, it was possible to feel the nervous tension in the air. I had to make myself known to the people around me to avoid suspicion and I had to allow Rellon's official photographer to take pictures on my behalf rather than trying to take them myself.

In the same rally, I witnessed Rellon telling the audience about the death threats he had been receiving. He told the people that he was not afraid of these threats and urged those who were present not to be scared as well. He added that there was no need to be scared of a "fake Filipino"—an obvious allusion to Rey Uy's Chinese background—who only knew how to bully the people. For his part, Mayor Uy denied making these death threats and said that Rellon was just being paranoid.[11] He said

---

[9] Interview with a mayoral campaign worker, 30 April 2016, Tagum City.
[10] Ibid.
[11] Interview with Mayor Uy, 4 May 2016.

that Rellon's people should have a mechanism for distinguishing whether such a call was a serious threat or not.

Vote buying

As elsewhere in the Philippines, patronage politics was central to the campaign strategies of the majority of candidates. Vote buying was rampant. Candidates employed various tactics to buy votes. For example, they usually gave out small bills, ranging from PhP 20 to 100, to people who attended their political rallies or handshaking activities. Campaign workers also conducted house to house "surveys" to ask how many registered voters were residing in households and to check on their voting intentions. After a few days, they would be back to distribute a handbill or a sample ballot with an attached amount of cash, usually ranging from PhP 100 to 500 per registered voter. The amount varied depending on the time of distribution—it got higher as election day neared. According to some informants, some voters were being asked to take their electronic voting receipts out of the polling place to prove that they had cast their vote in favour of the candidates, though this was a clear violation of electoral rules. Likewise, there were some reports of abstention buying, where known supporters of a candidate were paid around PhP 2,500 or more by campaigners for an opponent, just for them not to vote during the election.[12] Though I cannot confirm how widespread these last two practices were, the more everyday forms of vote buying and cash distribution were highly visible and ubiquitous.

In an interview with Mayor Uy, he mentioned that the people of Tagum expected him to give them gifts. Though he did not mention the specific amount and purpose, he said that it was "normal" for people to ask him for fares. He added that even when he was not the mayor anymore, people would still visit his home to ask for medical assistance. Some requested to borrow a bus from his company to be used for personal reasons. He would help these people and now, he said, they were helping him during the campaign.[13]

---

[12] Interview with a mayoral campaign manager, 30 April 2016, Tagum City. Indelible ink was also used to ensure negative vote buying. In the Philippines, indelible ink is placed on the finger of the voters after they have cast their votes to prevent them from voting again in other precincts.
[13] Interview with Mayor Uy, 4 May 2016, Tagum City.

MOBILISATION STRUCTURES

The barangay is the most basic subdivision of local governments in the Philippines. Tagum is divided into 23 barangays. Both Mayor Uy and Mayor Rellon knew that in order to win, they needed to be able to mobilise support in these barangays.

Figure 16 shows how the Uy campaign team mobilised support in the barangays. The central campaign team was headed by a campaign manager, Oyo Uy (the candidate's son, and failed mayoral candidate in 2013), who had his office in the Uy residence that served as the campaign headquarters. Oyo oversaw each of the barangay coordinators, who in turn each created their own teams in each *purok*—a subdivision of a barangay, usually comprising approximately 20–30 households. Each *purok*-level team was composed of four campaigners headed by a Civilian Affiliation Officer (CAFO). These *purok*-level campaigners were the persons who conducted the bulk of the house-to-house campaigning, surveys, and distribution of election paraphernalia.[14] According to those I interviewed from the *purok*-level teams, most were volunteers and did not receive any salary for the campaign work that they did. They had a modest food allowance but otherwise they didn't receive any monetary support. They admitted, however, that they were promised that once Uy won as mayor, they would be given jobs in the city.[15]

Figure 16
How the Uy campaign team mobilised support in the barangays

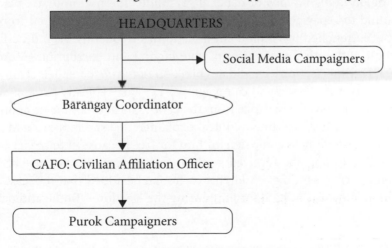

---

[14] Interview with an Uy campaign worker, 3 May 2016, Tagum City.
[15] Ibid.

As discussed previously, in addition to the legwork done by campaigners, the Uy campaign team also had two to three social media volunteers working directly under the supervision of the campaign manager. They were tasked with writing about Uy's achievements as a mayor and to respond to attacks aimed against him, which primarily focus on his alleged link to the Tagum Death Squad and his not being a "true Filipino". These social media volunteers were not given any "salary", but were given modest food allowances. They were also promised jobs in the city if Uy won the election.[16]

The Rellon campaign team also recognised the importance of campaigning in the *puroks* and built a similar campaign structure. Like Uy, they organised their campaign teams at the barangay level and then assigned workers in each *purok*. But, according to Giovanni Rellon, campaign manager and cousin of Mayor Rellon, they also created three additional teams: a team in charge of electoral education, a team whose job was to periodically conduct opinion surveys, and a team to canvass the votes. The main job of the electoral education team was to go to each barangay and educate the voters about the importance of the election and why they had to vote. Most importantly, the education team aimed to educate the voters about election procedures, especially stressing that it was illegal to take voting receipts out of the voting precincts. The canvassing team was created to monitor the counting of the votes in order to prevent any cheating during the counting of the votes.[17]

On both sides, the candidates constructed their campaign teams by relying on *utang na loob* or debts of gratitude. The notion that a person is bound to repay acts of kindness that he or she has benefitted from is deeply entrenched in Filipino culture and has frequently been described as contributing to the practices of vote buying and corruption (Montiel 2002). During elections, candidates bank on *utang na loob*; their strongest supporters, volunteers, and campaign workers are typically persons who previously received assistance from the candidate at one time or another. In Tagum, for instance, one volunteer explained that she supported Mayor Uy and was willing to campaign for him for free because of *utang na loob*. According to her, she received a job in the government because of Uy, enabling her to send her children to school. She added that the least she could do now was to fight for him during the election.[18] Both candidates,

---

[16] Interview with an Uy social media campaign worker, 4 May 2016, Tagum City.
[17] Interview with the campaign manager of Rellon, 30 April 2016.
[18] Interview with an Uy campaign worker, 6 May 2016, Tagum City.

having each served as mayor and thus having been in charge of the local government budget, civil service, and assistance programmes, had been able to build up considerable debts of gratitude among civilians throughout the city, and called these debts in when building their campaign teams.

CONCLUSION: WHY THE LOCAL BOSS FAILED

In 2016, though Uy ran under the Liberal Party banner, he did not support the LP presidential candidate Mar Roxas. Instead, like most politicians in Davao, Uy supported the candidacy of then Davao City Mayor Rodrigo Duterte. Presumably, he was partly motivated by Duterte's great popularity in Davao as a local son tilting at the nation's highest office. On his own account, he also admired Duterte's iron leadership and harsh policies toward illegal drugs and graft (Caduaya 2015).

Uy and Duterte were very similar in many ways. Both were from Mindanao and had served as local city administrators. Both had similar views on how to deal with criminality and they both considered gangs, criminals, and drug addicts as "weeds" that should be eliminated. Both were also allegedly linked to vigilante groups, Duterte to the Davao Death Squad (DDS) and Uy to the Tagum Death Squad (TDS).[19]

Why did Uy lose but Duterte win, given their great similarities? Of course, it should be noted that the Tagum City election was a close fight. Only 2,019 votes separated Rellon from Uy. In such a close election, with two equally resourced competitors, a myriad of factors could have tipped the balance. Uy's alleged links to extra-judicial killings and his ethnicity certainly reduced his popularity in the eyes of some voters. But Rellon struggles with scandals of his own. In the end, while the two political machines were fairly evenly matched and both able to mobilise their core supporters, Rellon's team seemed better able to win the support of blocks of voters outside their core group of supporters. As other chapters in this volume discuss, one of these blocks is Iglesia Ni Cristo (INC). INC voters tend to vote as a block, but in most contests, their numbers are not great enough to sway the outcome. However, in a close contest, the "Iglesia Vote" can prove crucial. In the Tagum case INC came out for Rellon as mayor of Tagum, giving the Rellon campaign the advantage.

---

[19] After he came to office as president, Duterte became a controversial figure worldwide for his endorsement of a campaign of extra-judicial killings throughout the Philippines.

In addition, Rellon's campaign strategy was very effective. He painted himself as an underdog who was no longer afraid of the threats of the rich bully Uy. Like in many Filipino movies and dramas, Filipinos have a soft heart for the underdog and wish for him to fight and win. Many sympathised with this beloved son of Tagum. At the end of the day, the underdog defeated the local boss.

Table 16
Election results from City of Tagum

Candidate	Party	Office	Per cent (%)
* Indicates Incumbent Candidate			
Alvarez, Pantaleon	PDPLBN	House of Representatives	40.63
Olaño, Arrel	NPC	House of Representatives	30.85
Suaybaguio, Nicandro Jr.	IND	House of Representatives	24.55
Mahipus, Saboy	IND	House of Representatives	2.56
Welborn, Richard Dexter	PMP	House of Representatives	1.41
Del Rosario, Anthony	LP	Provincial Governor	71.72
Suaybaguio, Victorio Jr.	IND	Provincial Governor	28.28
Dujali, Alan	IND	Provincial Vice-Governor	82.76
Estrada, Jessie	IND	Provincial Vice-Governor	17.24
City of Tagum (Capital)			
Rellon, Allan*	PDPLBN	Mayor	50.93
Uy, Rey	LP	Mayor	49.07
Gementiza, Geterito*	PDPLBN	Vice-Mayor	58.65
Bermudez, Oscar	LP	Vice-Mayor	30.39
Suaybaguio, Paulito	AKSYON	Vice-Mayor	10.96

chapter **17**

Lanao del Sur: Gold, Goons, Guns, and Genealogy

INTRODUCTION

The cornerstone of democracy is the freedom of the people to choose the leaders they believe will serve their interests best. Unfortunately, when that freedom is undermined during elections by such practices as vote buying, intimidation, violence, or the primacy of filial ties over democratic choice, then the entire democratic process can fail to produce leaders who will pursue the people's interests. This outcome, it shall be argued in this chapter, is exactly what happened during the 9 May 2016 General Election in the province of Lanao del Sur, located in the Autonomous Region in Muslim Mindanao (ARMM) Mindanao. This area is the poorest part of the Philippines.[1]

---

[1] ARMM was established by virtue of Republic Act No. 6734 as mandated by the 1987 Constitution as a solution to the secessionist movements and conflicts in Mindanao. The secessionist movements and resulting conflicts were based on the notion that the Bangsamoro has never been historically part of the Philippines and that the present political arrangement did not provide meaningful self-rule nor address the grievances of the Bangsamoro. These grievances range from economic dispossession, land-grabbing by settlers from other parts of the country, being treated as second-class

As in previous elections, in 2016 what determined which candidates won was the amount of gold, goons, guns, and genealogy they could mobilise. Put simply, the election in the province was not about competition over platforms of governance or which candidate was most competent. It was not about choosing the best local executives but was rather about which candidates could most effectively draw upon these Four Gs of power.

People aspiring for an elective position in the province need to put up an enormous amount of money to fund their campaign, gather together enough goons and political operators to run it, collect guns to arm those enforcers, and call upon relatives and in-laws for support. Miss any of these vital elements of power and a candidate's chances of winning diminish. One can have enormous wealth, but without goons to enforce and intimidate voters there is a high likelihood of being short-changed and deceived by voters. A candidate may possess goons, but without guns, he/she will rarely be able to intimidate voters or rivals, and will in fact often be brushed aside by those who possess the means to inflict violence. And of course, kinship plays a pivotal role; indeed, the number of relatives and in-laws a candidate can mobilise can make the critical difference when opposing candidates are otherwise equally matched.

BACKGROUND

This chapter focuses on electoral processes in the province of Lanao del Sur. In 2010, the province had a total population of 933,000 persons, 503,000 of whom were registered voters. The province has large number of local government units relative to its size and population. For example, the city of Iligan in neighbouring Lanao del Norte province has only 44 barangays for a population of around 342,000 while Marawi City (the capital of Lanao del Sur) has 96 barangays for just over 200,000 residents.

According to 2012 figures, Lanao del Sur was the poorest province in the whole country with poverty incidence of 68.9 per cent, an average life expectancy of 64 years, and per capita income of PhP 30,744 (in comparison, the per capita income of Metro Manila was then PhP 183,747 and around PhP 65,904 for the Philippines as a whole). Its Human Development Index (HDI) in 2009 was around 0.416—one of the lowest in the Philippines and comparable with African countries such as Mozambique and Sierra

---

citizens, marginalisation, and lack of genuine support from the national government, among others.

Leone (HDN 2013). Corruption, institutional mismanagement, perennial conflict, economic dispossession, marginalisation, and lack of genuine support from the national government, among other factors, are root causes of the massive poverty and underdevelopment in the province (Jubair 1985; Concepcion et al. 2003; Ferrer 2010).

Figure 17
Map of Lanao del Sur and the Autonomous Region in Muslim Mindanao

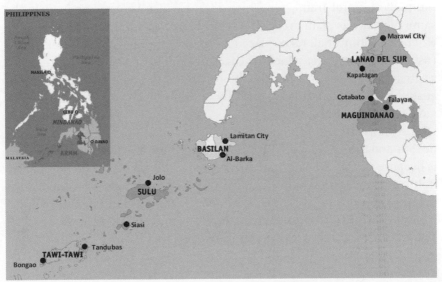

More than 90 per cent of the population of Lanao del Sur are Muslims and belong to the Meranaos tribe, which literally means "People of the Lake". As with the rest of the Bangsamoro region, Lanao del Sur is different from the rest of the country, in part a reflection of the fact that it was never colonised by Spain. The Meranaos managed to maintain their own culture and traditions, notably the importance of filial ties and clan membership. For example, traditional leadership structures based on sultanate and *datuism* (leadership of clan elders) are still robust in many areas. Such factors create a unique political environment and dynamics that are not comparable with the rest of the Philippines, while being broadly comparable with other parts of Muslim Mindanao. Moreover, the kind of democracy being practised in the region is quite different from the rest of the Philippines (Co et al. 2010).

Despite a history of conflict, elections in Lanao del Sur are typically highly anticipated and participatory events. The enthusiasm for election among Meranaos is due to their clannish nature, where candidate(s) belonging to a clan will call upon relatives and in-laws for support in order to help to prove that their clan is the best in the community. Thousands of Meranaos living elsewhere in the country, and even some residing abroad, return home to take part in the electoral process. The province exhibits one of the highest rates of voter turnout in the Philippines, ranging from 90 per cent to almost 100 per cent. Indeed, there were instances, prior to the introduction of automated elections in 2008, when voter turnout exceeded 100 per cent, reflecting both widespread enthusiasm, but also rampant electoral fraud, for which the province is also known.[2] At the same time, however, in every election in Lanao de Sur there are also places where no voting at all takes place due to violence or security breakdowns (usually in remote areas due to the lack or limited presence of government security forces). Unfortunately, the eagerness of some clan members to ensure that their candidate(s) win by hook or by crook often resulted in violent confrontation.

Elections are also frequent events. There are more elections in Lanao del Sur and the rest of the ARMM than anywhere else in the country. This is because, as the only autonomous region in the country, the region also holds special elections and regional elections. A typical voter in Lanao del Sur votes during barangay, local, national, presidential, and regional (that is, ARMM) elections. Over the last 25 years, there have been 17 elections held in the ARMM. All these elections require the investment of huge amounts of funds, time, and resources by candidates, especially by incumbent local executives who can use government resources to their advantage. As a result, residents of the province often see elections as a moment of wealth redistribution where the loot accumulated by local politicians is shared with their constituents in the form of vote buying and other dispensation of pecuniary benefits. As one voter from of the Municipality of Mulondo puts it: "the election is harvest time for us, so we take advantage of the blessings as much as we can".[3]

As usual, the 2016 election in Lanao del Sur was a contest for political supremacy among the various clans. The political hegemony of the Adiong-Alonto clan in the gubernatorial seat of the province was challenged by Fahad "Pre" Salic, City Mayor of Marawi, who allied with various clans

---

[2] The first automated election in the Philippines was conducted in the ARMM on 11 May 1998, however, due to technical issues the COMELEC reverted back to manual counting. The fully automated election was successfully carried out in the ARMM on 22 July 2008 during the regional election—two years before it was fully implemented in the entire Philippines during the 10 May 2010 General Election.

[3] Interview with Jalil Tago, Municipality of Mulondo, 31 March 2016.

(for example, the Dumarpa, Abinal, Macadato, etc.), families, and interest groups.[4] In the City of Marawi, the fight was between Salic's brother, former Mayor Omar Ali Solitario, standing against Atty. Majul Gandamra, who was backed by the Adiong-Alonto clan. Political competition in other areas of the province was also delineated along clans, family affiliation and blood ties. Basically, elections in Lanao del Sur are a clash of clans where a clan needs to prove that they are the best and, therefore, deserve the booty that elective positions bring.

THE BUSINESS OF ELECTIONS

Residents see elections as a moment for personal profit because of the role elections themselves play in processes of local elite formation. Put simply, local elites view elections in Lanao del Sur as more like a business venture than an instrument of change, development, and progress. Political dynasties and wealthy individuals consider elections as a moment when they can further their own interests by acquiring access to the riches, influence, and power that comes with local political office. Often, rich Meranao businessmen residing in Metro Manila or other urban parts of the country will be prodded by their relatives to return to the province to run as mayor, vice-mayor or other elective positions. While incumbent officials are running to further strengthen their hold on power and demonstrate their political dominance, others, like drug lords, regard winning in an election as a way to protect their illicit businesses, avoid prosecution, and obtained legal armed escorts (in the form of policemen under the influence of local executives).[5]

Winning in an election brings substantial benefits to the victorious candidate and also his or her clan and supporters. In a winner-takes-

---

[4] The Alonto clan has a long history of political power in the province of Lanao del Sur dating back to the late Senator Domocao Alonto in the 1950s. When Mamintal Adiong Sr., also from a strong political clan, married into the Alonto clan, it established one of the most powerful political families in Lanao del Sur. The late Mamintal Adiong Sr. was a three-times congressman of the 1st District of Lanao del Sur who subsequently become the governor of the province for three consecutive terms until his death. His son, Mamintal "Bombit" Adiong Jr., also served three consecutive terms as governor. Currently, the wife of the late Adiong Sr., Bae Soraya Alonto-Adiong, is the governor of the province of Lanao del Sur.

[5] McCoy (2009) shows how the political, economic, and illicit sectors are interlaced with each other.

all contest, the winners will treat government resources like personal property, freely distributing them to families and supporters. The benefits to the clan and supporters range from employment in local government offices to monthly allowances from elected officials, from barangays all the way to the governor. This is one of the reasons why electoral politics strengthens reciprocal relationships between local elites and their supporters. As Kerkvliet (1995: 401) notes, "Philippines politics revolves around interpersonal relationships—especially familial and patron-client ones—and factions composed of personal alliances." With office being such an important prize for candidates and their supporters, it is not surprising that they invest great resources and effort into winning it. Let us briefly review the main components of this investment.

Gold

It was widely believed by key informants that vote buying and bribery of government officials, especially employees of the Commission on Election (COMELEC), was very widespread in the May 2016 election in Lanao del Sur. Almost all candidates engaged in the practice. Since vote buying and bribery is an accepted norm, it created a rather efficient market for the prices of votes and the value of bribes. Owing to the ability of voters as well as government officials to pass information amongst themselves they could easily find out which candidates paid the most. And with the advent of mobile communication the sharing of information regarding the price of votes and value of bribes became even more effective.

Voters, officials, and other stakeholders in an election expect political operators from various candidates to entice them with the best offer for their votes and services. This has the tendency to raise the price of votes and bribes as individuals select the most beneficial choice among different options provided by political operators. Generally, voters support the candidate who pays the most and/or provides the best benefits after winning office. "The key to winning is money, money, money and more money," said Hadji Abdullah, a former mayor in the Second District of Lanao del Sur, "Without money, you might as well forget running during an election", he added.[6] He explained that everyone needs money to move or even vote. Everyone expects to be paid—from the officials of the COMELEC, members of the armed services, teachers who serve as Board

---

[6] Interview with Haji Abdullah, Marawi City, 2 April 2016.

of Election Inspectors, and even your own relatives. This is especially true of your voters and supporters, who assume they will be given a good price for their votes and efforts.

Vote buying during the 9 May 2016 general election in Lanao del Sur reached epidemic proportions, and was more openly practised than in previous elections, with many political operators openly advertising that they were seeking citizens who were ready to take money in exchange for vote. The atmosphere was akin to an open market for votes. Almost every candidate engaged in the practice—from the gubernatorial candidates all the way to town councilor candidates. According to Mike Saud, a poll watcher, the price of votes for governors ranged between PhP 1,000 and PhP 2,000 while those for vice-governor were between PhP 500 and PhP 1,500. The cheapest votes were those for municipal councilors at between PhP 100 and PhP 200, depending on the locality.[7]

Mayoral votes, meanwhile, were most expensive, ranging from PhP 3,000 up to PhP 15,000 per voter. In the Municipality of Lumbayanague, where family feuds existed, it was reported that the price of a vote for mayor reached PhP 25,000.[8] The high price of votes in Lumbayanague can be attributed to the tight contest (where tens of votes could decide the outcome of the election), the large internal revenue allotment for the municipality (the larger the resources of the local government the higher the payoffs to winning and, thus, the larger the investment), and the candidates being from wealthy families with millions of pesos to spare. Vote buying, however, is a complicated business. Candidates, together with their core team members, start by calculating how much money they will spend, the number of voters they need to buy from each barangay, the strategy they need to employ, as well as the number of political operators they need to employ to accomplish these tasks. They draw up these plans by using the official voter lists they obtained from the Election Commission.

Candidates also need to determine how to organise their vote buying efforts. Some candidates purchased votes in tandem with other candidates on a single ticket, sharing costs to buy votes for governor, vice-governor, congressman, and mayor running as a group. These efforts could come in many combinations such as the "three-in-one" ticket, in which a vote for a gubernatorial, vice gubernatorial, and congressional candidate as a single packet were priced at around PhP 3,500, or the "five-in-one"

---

[7] Interview with Mike Saud, Municipality of Tugaya, 30 April 2016.
[8] Interview with Malik Mamoalas, Marawi City, 15 April 2016.

approach when, say, these three candidates would combine with a couple of municipal council candidates. Many combinations were possible, especially given that some tickets also included national candidates running for posts like president, senators, and party list representatives. Some candidates, however, acted on their own and distributed cash payments without cooperating with others. Others literally purchased the ballot, wherein the vote buyer asked the voter to hand over his/her ballot so the buyer could fill it out before returning it to the voter to be inserted in the counting machine. This practice was quite common in remote municipalities or precincts inaccessible to media or election observers, or where candidates agreed not to interfere with each other.

To organise their vote buying efforts, candidates employed political operators. These political operators were usually recruited from close relatives of the candidate and served as agents in gathering information, recruiting supporters, and assisting in campaign efforts (among other things). A candidate tended to have at least two political operators in every barangay, depending on the population—the larger the population, the more political operators. These political operators compiled the lists of people willing to vote for the candidate in exchange for cash. Usually, political operators start with a copy of the Official Lists of Voters issued by the COMELEC (available upon request from the COMELEC office) and then check the names of residents they already consider as supporters of their candidate (that is, voters who accepted money). At times, different political operators working for competing candidates compared notes or discussed amongst themselves which residents were "open for discussion" or could still be "persuaded" to support their candidate. This practice of touching base with rival political operators was to avoid double payments to the same voters, which could lead to wasted vote buying expenditures.

A key informant involved deeply in the process, who declined to be identified, explained that political operators distributed down payments or "partials", as they are often called by residents, to voters to secure their support two to three weeks before the voting day. The down payment was typically 50 per cent of the total price of the vote. The remaining balance was paid on election day itself, or after the voter showed evidence that she/he voted for the candidate by presenting their voting receipt. Payments depended on the locality: in hotly contested areas the payment for a single vote for mayor was around PhP 10,000 per voter, while in the least contested area it was roughly PhP 3,000.

The 2016 election was the first time that voting machines issued voting receipts recording the candidates chosen by the voter—a fact candidates tried to use to their advantage.[9] Once a voter accepted the deposit from a candidate, he or she was barred from accepting money from rivals. The fact that the province is in the countryside, where everybody knows everyone else, means it was difficult for voters to engage in double-dealings with other candidates. In addition, the threat of violence from the candidate's goons also made it risky to do so. Because candidates were operating based on the voter lists and other intelligence submitted by their political operators in the barangays, some days before the election they could usually already predict whether they would win or not.

Where they could see that they had not bought enough votes, or that they were being outperformed by rivals, the candidate would try to outbid previous buyers by paying more than twice the amount already paid. In such cases, the voter would typically return the deposit to the previous buyer of the vote and keep what remained. In local parlance, residents call this practice of outbidding "vote-squatting". The term arises from "squatters", commonly defined by Filipinos as someone who illegally occupies someone else's property or land. It can be expensive, but it is also effective, especially in a close contest. In response, some candidates will increase the down payment to avoid vote-squatting. This can lead to an ever-increasing price for a vote as election day draws near, as candidates try to outbid each other.

An alternative to vote-squatting is intimidating a rival's supporters and inhibiting them from going to the precinct to vote. There are instances where candidates will use bomb threats or even throw grenades close to voting areas to scare people away. In the Municipality of Tamparan, for example, a rival candidate, fearing a landslide for his opponents, orchestrated a gunfight in the stronghold of his opponents to scare voters away or cause a failure of election. A "failure of election" occurs when COMELEC officials elect to postpone or suspend an election due to violence, terrorism, or other unforeseen circumstances. It is not surprising that since the electoral process was introduced in the province, there have always been failures of election. Surprisingly, some voters seem to welcome it—especially the voters in the area where the failure of election is declared since they will be reaping a higher price for their votes when elections resume as candidates try and outbid each other.

---

[9] An eleventh hour ruling by the Supreme Court required COMELEC to produce a printed receipt for each vote cast, which voters could inspect at the polls and which could be used as a paper back-up in the event of a recount. The rules required voters to deposit their receipt before leaving the polling station, but those rules were not always enforced.

On the other hand, not all voters were easily intimidated or merely passive recipients of cash payments. Some voters waited until election day to extract the best deal they could for their votes. According to Bong Mangondato, a resident of Marawi City, clan elders of large families delayed supporting candidates up to the eve of election day.[10] Their goal was to induce candidates to bid for the support of the clan. The bigger the clan the higher the bid, which often reached around PhP 100,000. Because elders sometimes have the capacity to decide whom the clan will support, they can be in a position of strength to bargain with candidates, especially in a close contest where the clan's support could decide the outcome of the election.

Goons

Money alone will not secure an election victory if a candidate does not have goons to back up the agreement reached with voters. Successful vote buying depends on the ability of the giver of the money to punish those who do not keep their end of the bargain. A candidate may be able to purchase all the votes in the list of voters; however, this will not translate to actual votes if voters know they can cheat and get away with it. This is where goons come in—they monitor and enforce agreement. For example, there were some wealthy individuals who ran as mayor and managed to buy more than 75 per cent of the vote, yet still lost the election because they could not protect their own supporters from intimidation and violence. In addition, when voters feel that they can renege on their deal without repercussion, they tend to do so.

Candidates typically recruited goons from among the toughest and most notorious members of their own clan. Some of them were offenders or persons known for having brushes with the law, while others were former rebels (for example, from the MNLF or the MILF) and former soldiers. One common denominator among the goons was their willingness to do the bidding of the boss without questions. Goons must be willing to intimidate, to physically harm or even kill opponents without hesitation. However, muscle and numbers of goons alone could only do so much to influence the behaviour of the people and intimidate rivals. Guns were needed to project power and the ability to inflict

---

[10] Interview, MSU Campus, 2 May 2016.

suffering.[11] According to the Philippine National Police roughly 90 per cent of known private armies in the country operate in the ARMM (Cudis 2016). In the Municipality of Butig, for example, candidates conducted campaign sorties escorted by at least 30 goons with high-calibre firearms to project power and as a deterrent from being ambushed by rivals. In nearby Magindanao province, during the heyday of the Ampatuan Clan, the size of their heavily-armed private armies exceeded 2,000 men. This was apart from military units that were loyal to the clan and assigned as official "security details" (HRW 2010).

Guns

Decades of secessionist conflicts, Martial Law and clan wars have created a local political culture in which guns are considered part of normal daily life. It is common belief that almost every home in the province possesses at least one handgun and one automatic rifle. The indispensability of guns in the local community makes it necessary for any person running for office in the province to amass numerous high-powered firearms to show that he or she can back up their words and cannot be trifled with. As one local executive interviewed for this report explained, "ownership of large cache of guns is not only a sign of wealth but projection of strength; whenever some relatives are in trouble they will come to you to borrow rifles and machine guns and this translate to more support and following".[12] In the province, the more guns you own, the more respect and fear you earn.

It is mostly mayors, congressmen, and governors in the ARMM who maintain private armies and possess large caches of firearms. A typical mayor in Lanao del Sur tends to have around 30 to 50 men to serve as private army with high-calibre firearms. The higher the office, the larger the private army. Local executives that have existing *rido* (clan conflict) generally maintain a larger private army, with members reaching up to a hundred. These local executives need to project power not only to

---

[11] A documentary video of the election in the Municipality of Tugaya, Lanao del Sur, filmed by foreign observers (KODAO Production) can provide a glimpse of the kind of election in the province and allow readers to appreciate the extent of the problem in local politics and the violence involved. Available at <http://www.kodao.org/video/foreign-observers-kodao-reporter-witness-gunfight-tugaya-lanaodel-sur> and <https://www.youtube.com/watch?v=yufgKrUwjas> [accessed 20 May 2016].

[12] Interview with Abdulkhalid Gamor, Marawi City, 16 May 2017.

establish control in their bailiwicks, but also to serve as deterrent against rivals. Their access to government resources and influence, meanwhile, allows them to sustain private armies and easily acquire firearms. Very often, the private army of a politician can also serve as protector and defender of the politician's clan when called upon. In case of *rido* (clan war) or other armed confrontation, for example, the private armies of the local executive can be sent as reinforcements to relatives in need.[13]

Although the Armed Forces of the Philippines and the Philippine National Police are aware of the existence of politicians' private armies there seems to be some unwritten rules about not interfering with local politics. As a result, there is minimal enforcement of gun control rules and few arrests of armed men at election times. In fact, during armed fighting between clans, the armed services typically serve as referees, seeking only to prevent rival clans from annihilating each other, rather than trying to eliminate *rido* altogether.

The proliferation of politically aligned armed groups, and the associated use of intimidation and coercion resulted in numerous cases of bodily harm and even death during the 2016 election. According to one informant, a volunteer from the election watchdog KASALIMBAGO, the estimated deaths directly related to the 9 May 2016 election in Lanao del Sur were more than 20, with many more suffering injuries.[14] Unfortunately, due to lack of official reporting the number of fatalities and collateral damage cannot be verified.

Indeed, violence could change electoral outcomes. In Marawi City, for example, many political observers predicted that Omar Ali Solitario would likely succeed his brother as mayor of the city. However, in an incident on the eve of his election, two relatives of his rival, Atty. Majul Gandamra, were killed, and this changed the outcome. Fearing retaliation, some political operators, supporters, poll watchers, and relatives of Mr.

---

[13] Clan war or *rido* in local language is a state of recurring hostilities between clans and kinship groups characterised by a series of retaliatory acts of violence carried out to avenge a perceived affront or injustice. *Rido* stemming from political rivalry is the most violent, deadly and long-lasting. See Torres III (2007) for detail on *rido* or local clan feuds in Mindanao.

[14] Interview with Amani Macapaar, Marantao, 13 May 2016. The national figure for election-related deaths was at least 30 (Sauler 2016). The KASALIMBAGO Movement is a network of government and civil society organisations committed to the strengthening of democratic ideals in the province through electoral reforms and other activities that would broaden people's participation and representation in realisation of peaceful, orderly, free, and credible elections in the province.

Solitario avoided polling places and mostly stayed home during the election day. Some relatives of the victims, who had previously supported Mr. Solitario's candidacy, switched sides in sympathy with their fallen relatives. This resulted in Atty. Gandamra winning the mayoralty seat in Marawi City by a margin of more than 200 votes, although many observers had predicted Mr. Solitario would win handily.

Genealogy

Politics in Lanao del Sur, as in other parts of the ARMM, is usually drawn along clan lines, rather than being based on platform, promises, or party lines. This system of clan-based politics is deeply rooted in the region's culture and history. Before the introduction of democracy, there was already a deeply embedded system of clientelistic relationships based on traditional clan-based forms of governance in the province. During the pre-colonial period, the government was based on the sultanate and the *datu* system.[15] In the colonial period, foreign powers such as Spain and the Americans dealt with the existing leadership in the region, such as the *datus* and the sultans, to further their policies and support those that were friendly to their cause. Even after the Americans granted full independence to the Philippines, the practice of dealing with and appointing local elites to political positions continued (Gutierrez et al. 1992). As late as the 1950s, the president of the Philippines still appointed mayors in Lanao del Sur from the ranks of influential families (Bentley 1993). Such practice further entrenched the influential families and enabled them to carve out their own political fiefdoms. For example, the Adiong-Alonto-Lucman Clan has dominated the politics of Lanao del Sur while the neighbouring province of Lanao del Norte has been dominated by the Dimpaoro Clan since the early 1960s.

Clan politics is certainly out in the open at election time. In the lead-up, it was very common for various family reunions, gatherings, weddings,

---

[15] The traditional system in Lanao del Sur divided society into the ruling class (*pagawidan*) and the common people (*pagawid*) or viewed another way into patrons and clients. Similar forms of governance also exist in the rest of the country, prior to the advent of Spanish colonial rule from 1521 to 1898, which was soon replaced by another clientelistic relationship based on land ownership where the landed elite became the patron and the peasant population, who are mostly farmers, the clients (Tan 2009). Nowadays in Lanao del Sur the clientelistic relationship is between the local executives and their supporters who are mostly relatives, in-laws, and close associates.

and social events to be held, with the aim of renewing kinship ties and consolidating the support of the clan around its candidates. Candidates either contributed to the expenses of the events or even bankrolled them completely, especially if they were given a free rein on how the event was organised. When advertising themselves, some candidates promoted their ancestral connections by listing the names of every clan they could possibly belong to, no matter how distantly. Accordingly, it was common to see banners or pamphlets in which candidates had paragraph-length lists of family names.

The 9 May 2016 general election, like previous elections, was a battle between influential clans and political dynasties. In the municipality of Maranatao, for example, the mayoralty contest was between Racma Abinal, wife of former Mayor Mohammad Abboh Abinal, against Samson Adiong and Jasmin Adtha-Magancong, both from powerful clans. In Marawi City, the mayoralty race was between the Gandamra clan, supported by the Adiong-Alonto, against the Salic family, with their allied clans. The patriarchs of the Adiong-Alonto and the Salic clans, meanwhile, were competing against each other in the gubernatorial race in Lanao del Sur. Former governor Mamintal "Bombit" Adiong had completed three consecutive terms as governor, the maximum allowed, and so was running as vice-governor alongside his mother, Soraya Alonto Adiong, as governor. They were competing against Sultan Fahad "Pre" Salic, who had completed three consecutive terms as the Marawi City mayor, running alongside deputy governor candidate and party mate, Mohammad Abinal, who was a three-term mayor of Maranatao.

An election was not only a contest between opposing parties but also a fight between clans over who would emerge as the best and strongest clan in the locality. Honour, pride and clan standing, therefore, were on the line. And in a place where sense of honour (*maratabat* in local parlance) is of paramount importance, it is not surprising that in every election, the situation is like a powder keg waiting to explode.[16]

Meanwhile, in areas where one clan had already established total control of the political landscape, the battle was sometimes between members of the same clan. Examples include the municipalities of Tamparan, where the mayoralty contest was between cousins (in the preceding election the rivalry had been between husband and wife) and Binidayan where it was between two brothers. Such rivalry between close kin happens whenever

---

[16] See Torres (2007) for clan wars (*rido*) precipitated by Maratabat, most still unresolved that date back to the 1930s.

the clan patriarch dies and the leadership is not formally transferred, or there are feuds within the family. In one instance, for example, a wife ran against her husband after the husband elected to marry a second wife.[17]

Even so, there were times when clan ties were trumped by money. As one candidate puts it "blood is thicker than water; but money, especially if it's a bundle of 1,000 pesos, is much thicker than blood".[18] The dire poverty in the province suggested that blood ties alone would not suffice to guarantee support from clan members for victory. These ties needed to be supplemented by pecuniary benefits to ensure clan members' endorsements and votes. There were times when voters would sacrifice blood ties in favour of a bigger payoff from other candidates outside of their clan. This was common among the poor and marginalised members of the clan. Thus, having a larger clan did not guarantee victory without the corresponding vote buying scheme.

Politicians were also able to draw upon other sorts of networks and brokers, like barangay chairmen, who were often the key to victory. They served both as political operators and dispensers of funds for candidates. The barangay chairman, generally the leader of the dominant clan in the village, wielded considerable influence and control during elections. Thus, incumbent local executives who had already cultivated years of clientelistic relationship with barangay chairmen, had greater chances of winning. Gamal Disoma, a political operator both for a mayoral and gubernatorial candidate, related that during the election barangay chairmen could collect as much as PhP 3 million in total from local and national candidates.[19] These funds were used as campaign money to distribute to voters in his barangay. As usual, the lion's share of the funds went to the chairman. The larger the number of registered voters in the barangay, the bigger the booty for the chairman.

Having briefly outlined how gold, goons, guns, and genealogy operate in elections in Lanao del Sur, we are now able to see how they operate in combination, and to analyse how this system has become so entrenched. At its worst, clan politics in the region generate large-scale localised political violence and local authoritarianism. When political families face off during election, violence often results, resulting in injuries and even death. Such clashes can give birth to *rido* that often last several generations,

---

[17] Presidential Decree 1083, otherwise known as Code of Muslim Personal Law of the Philippines, governs the civil relationship among Muslims in the country, which allows Muslim men to have up to four wives.

[18] Hanafi Datumulok, Ditsaan-Ramain, 26 April 2016.

[19] Interview, Buadipuso Buntong, 2 May 2016.

entangling clan members in cycles of vendetta and retaliation. Clan conflicts are easily rekindled every three years, along with the election cycle, as old scores are settled, injuries are repaid in kind, and competition between clans for political office is renewed.

In some instances a political family in certain areas gains the upper hand and totally obliterates their rivals, forcing them to migrate out of town. Those that remain either switch sides to support the winning family, or keep a low profile within the community.[20] In some places, the power of a political dynasty becomes so great that they can even change the name of the municipality to their clan name.[21]

Once a political dynasty establishes political hegemony in certain municipalities, elections there can become masquerades, superficially complying with existing laws, but in fact simply serving to cement the dominance of the ruling family. In such cases, the people have lost their freedom of choice and become subservient to the whims of the ruling political family. Accordingly, in the 2016 election, there were reports that in some locations voting took place inside the Municipal Hall or even in the house of an incumbent local executive.[22] In such places, voting was "tabled"—meaning rather than allowing citizens to come in and cast their votes, political operators of the ruling dynasty instead simply filled in the ballots on their behalf, conducting the entire electoral process according to the wishes of the local ruling family. In such cases, the poll watchers, election watchdog, and government officials tasked with safeguarding the sanctity of the ballot, were silent. They were either incorporated into the

---

[20] The Maguindanao Massacre that occurred on 23 November 2009 is perhaps the most well-known political violence in Muslim Mindanao. It resulted in the death of 58 people. The case is being heard in court and the families of the victims are still awaiting justice (see HRW 2010 for detailed accounts of the massacre). Killings and violence also occurs in the province of Lanao del Sur, but unfortunately, they are seldom mentioned or reported in mainstream media.

[21] For example, the Municipality of Bumburan was renamed Municipality of Amai Manabilang in honour of the patriarch of the ruling political family. In Maguindanao, the municipalities of Datu Unsay, Datu Saudi Ampatuan, and Datu Hofer Ampatuan were named after the sons of Andal Ampatuan Sr. (the patriarch of the Ampatuan Clan) while Shariff Aguak, Datu Paglas, Datu Abdullah Sangki, Datu Anggal Midtimbang, Datu Odin Sinsuat and many others were named after important persons or former patriarchs of the political clan that ruled the municipality. In Lanao del Norte, the Municipality of Sultan Naga Dimaporo is named after the brother of the late governor Sultan Ali Dimaporo.

[22] Interview with Macky Mamao, Marawi City, 2 May 2016.

ruling clique by way of genealogical ties, frightened by their goons and guns, or gold had sealed their eyes and ears.

As one election watcher observed, "cheating, intimidation and use of violence to influence the result of election regularly happens in the province but nobody complains or tell authorities or the national media about it; people are afraid that once authorities or the media left they will be at the mercy of the people behind the cheating, intimidation, and violence; so, nobody really want to take the risk".[23]

How and why has politics in Lanao del Sur reached this state? Obviously, the situation has emerged over many decades and is the product of many factors. Even so, it is possible to identify several driving forces. To begin with, the fight to win elective positions is primarily motivated by the need to control public funds. In a province where there is a scarcity of opportunities for social or economic improvement, steady sources of income from elected positions are worth fighting for, and in some instances, worth dying for. As Haji Abdullah, a former mayor, put it during an interview, "I know of no other business or sources of livelihood other than being mayor of my municipality and I am willing to sacrifice a lot and do anything to keep the position within my family."[24]

Ironically, the greater political autonomy and fiscal responsibility devolved to local government units (LGUs) under the 1991 Local Government Code has helped to entrench the politics of predation and violence in the ARMM. This law was based on the idea that local executives chosen by the people would better understand the needs of their constituents and should therefore be given greater freedom to manage development projects, financial assistance programmes, Internal Revenue Allotments (IRA), and other public resources. This approach also hinged on the theory that if the people choose a corrupt or ineffective local executive they could always replace him or her at the next election. However, in Lanao del Sur this accountability function of local elections has been undermined in some areas by entrenched local politicians able to mobilise financial resources, clan networks, and coercive power to capture the institutions of local governance. In other areas greater political autonomy and fiscal responsibility have raised the stakes of elections and thereby contributed to making them more violent.

One way of judging the effect of this dynamic is to look at politics at the barangay level. Previously, barangay elections in Lanao del Sur were

---

[23] Interview with Cosain Amerol, MSU Campus, Marawi City, 10 May 2016.
[24] Interview with Haji Abdullah, Marawi City, 2 April 2016.

peaceful and uncontroversial events. Elders or traditional leaders simply nominated barangay officials from among the most active members of the community, without even having an election. However, since the IRA were introduced at the barangay level in the early 1990s, these elections have become among the deadliest and most fiercely contested. Village residents, usually related by blood, are pitted against each other and the elections sometimes trigger deadly clan conflicts that last for years, tearing the social fabric that binds the community. As Hutchcroft (2012: 113) states, "for all the celebrated talk of promoting local autonomy and instituting fiscal decentralisation, the IRA is also very much a story about the enhanced access of local politicians to patronage resources".

But there are other reasons why the politics of gold, guns, goons, and genealogy continues to be so entrenched in Lanao del Sur, as in other parts of the ARMM. First, the national government often tolerates misdeeds in local government in the periphery in exchange for political support and votes. Mindanao is not only reputed to be a "dumping ground" for incompetent and under-performing government employees from other parts of the country (Diaz 2003), but, as Sidel (1990) observed, local executives there work to guarantee stability and deliver votes to national-level politicians in exchange for them not interfering in local politics. National politicians have little incentive to enforce anti-corruption laws against local politicians when they rely on those same politicians to deliver votes during elections (Hutchcroft 2007). For example, the notorious Ampatuan Clan in neighbouring Magindanao gave former president Gloria Arroyo more than a million vote margins against Fernando Poe, Jr. in 2004, and delivered a solid 12 senatorial seats to the government, dislodging opposition senatorial candidates from the ARMM in favour of pro-administration candidates in 2007.

Another factor entrenching predatory politics in the south is the "*Goberno a Saruang*" syndrome. This phrase literally means "foreign government" in Meranaw, and expresses the view held by many people from Bangsamoro that the current system of government is imposed from outside and is not their own. This lack of a sense of ownership means that people are disinclined to complain when local executives misuse government resources. It also creates a "winner-take-all" attitude among politicians and their families, who regard local government not as a public good, but as a family business that can be handed down to family members. As Gutierrez and Vitug (1996: 203) observed, the "concept of the state is not well-developed in these areas. That is why people find more security in their clan or in their *datus*. Thus, government becomes an alien structure imposed from Manila. Using public funds and equipment for public use may be seen not as criminal acts, but as the normal and logical exercise of the authority of the *datu* or politician in dealing with an alien authority."

Finally, the brutality of electoral competition in Lanao del Sur can also be partly attributed to the lack of economic growth and opportunities for employment and self-advancement in the region. Being the poorest province in the Philippines means local elites and ordinary people have few options for improving their lives through the private economy, but instead are dependent on state resources or the illicit economy. What is at stake in every election is therefore the fortune of the entire clan—whether it will live in abundance or suffer in scarcity. The clan's future prosperity, and thus its honour, is at stake, dramatically raising the stakes of electoral politics and making candidates willing to use intimidation, violence, and even killing to win. In this respect, the politics of intimidation, family ties, and vote buying are not dissimilar to other parts of the Philippines; they just find their most extreme forms here.

CONCLUSION

A mayoral candidate, who requested anonymity, summed up politics in Lanao del Sur as follows: "If you don't have money, relatives who are willing to die for you, guns and clan to back you up during election you might as well not join because you are simply wasting your time. A politician must be willing to kill to win and be prepared for any eventuality from such a clan war."[25] This bleak assessment matches the analysis I have presented in this chapter. The 2016 general election showed that what I have called the Four Gs of Power—gold, goons, guns, and genealogy—still decide who wins electoral competition in Lanao del Sur. Since elections replaced the traditional sultanate leadership in choosing local executives in the province I have not found one candidate, including in the 2016 election, who did not employ all the Four Gs of Power. This style of politics has become so entrenched in the province that politicians and voters alike find its logic difficult to escape. Politicians have learned that using the Four Gs of Power is the surest path to victory, and now the system has reached an equilibrium wherein anyone who plans to join politics must employ its logic or face likely defeat. Of course, a candidate can always present a strong policy

---

[25] Interview, Marawi City, 27 April 2016.

platform and reform agenda. But history shows that such candidates do not win elections in Lanao del Sur. Voters in the province do not see their vote as a medium of systemic change or as a tool for promoting development. Most see it as a commodity that can be sold to the highest bidder. In turn, since candidates win elections by buying votes and using other unlawful means, they do not feel bound to serve the people.

These dynamics create a vicious cycle wherein local executives plunder government coffers to amass wealth in preparation for future elections, and the electorate, witnessing that plunder, feel they should use elections to partake of the spoils. Alim Sadat, a religious leader, explained this logic: "politicians are only interested in keeping themselves in power by looting the government, they have little interest in development or building public works; that's the reason people take their money during election because that is the only way they can benefit from the government".[26] While we should not rule out future progress, for the time being, Lanao del Sur—like much of the ARMM—appears to be locked in a pattern of clan politics, political violence, and predatory behaviour that will be difficult to break.

Table 17

Election results from selected areas in Lanao Del Sur

Candidate	Party	Office	Per cent (%)
* Indicates Incumbent Candidate			
Adiong, Ansaruddin*	LP	House of Representatives (1st)	54.62
Dumarpa, Faysah	UNA	House of Representatives (1st)	44.91
Otara, Calawanan	IND	House of Representatives (1st)	0.31
Paiso, Mar	IND	House of Representatives (1st)	0.16
Papandayan, Jun	PDPLBN	House of Representatives (2nd)	50.64
Balindong, Yasser	LP	House of Representatives (2nd)	47.68
Marohom, Mohammad Hafez	NPC	House of Representatives (2nd)	0.94
Alonto, Rommel	IND	House of Representatives (2nd)	0.75
Adiong, Soraya	LP	Provincial Governor	54.96
Salic, Fahad Panarigan	UNA	Provincial Governor	34.54
Balindong, Pangalian	IND	Provincial Governor	8.26
Lucman, Jahl	IND	Provincial Governor	1.52
Abdulcarim, Ahmadjan	IND	Provincial Governor	0.04

---

[26] Interview, Tugaya, 20 May 2016.

Table 17 *(cont'd)*

Candidate	Party	Office	Per cent (%)
Sarip, Abdulfatah	IND	Provincial Governor	0.32
Adiong, Bombit	LP	Provincial Vice-Governor	77.20
Abinal, Mohammadali	UNA	Provincial Vice-Governor	19.45
Balindong, Caharoden	IND	Provincial Vice-Governor	2.23
Sarip, Abet	IND	Provincial Vice-Governor	1.11
Binidayan			
Datumulok, Abdullah*	LP	Mayor	61.35
Datumulok, Aman Misbac	UNA	Mayor	36.98
Raraco, Salac	NPC	Mayor	1.11
Dimaporo, Mohammad Hosni	IND	Mayor	0.38
Bassar, Samen	IND	Mayor	0.17
Datumulok, Akida*	LP	Vice-Mayor	51.94
Datumulok, Punudaranao	UNA	Vice-Mayor	42.65
Olama, Patah	IND	Vice-Mayor	5.17
Hadjimacmood, Ombra	IND	Vice-Mayor	0.24
Bumbaran			
Manabilang, Jamal*	IND	Mayor	100.00
Manabilang, Saidamen Leo	IND	Vice-Mayor	100.00
Butig			
Macadato, Ibrahim*	UNA	Mayor	50.90
Pansar, Dimnatang	LP	Mayor	48.50
Macadato, Nassif	IND	Mayor	0.20
Aboca, Zapata	IND	Mayor	0.11
Mama, Mamasao	IND	Mayor	0.10
Bao, Edris	AKSYON	Mayor	0.09
Amatonding, Faiza	IND	Mayor	0.05
Cosain, Abdulrahman	IND	Mayor	0.05
Adilao, Abunail	IND	Vice-Mayor	45.65
Kiram, Monabantog*	LP	Vice-Mayor	20.62
Mindalano, Amer Jr.	IND	Vice-Mayor	15.01
Macadato, Nasip	IND	Vice-Mayor	11.04
Ditual, Pauli	AKSYON	Vice-Mayor	7.05

(cont'd overleaf)

Table 17 *(cont'd)*

Candidate	Party	Office	Per cent (%)
Hakim, Muhaimen	IND	Vice-Mayor	0.38
Dimaporo, Gomander	IND	Vice-Mayor	0.09
Dimaro, Baser	IND	Vice-Mayor	0.04
Palawan, Jalilah	IND	Vice-Mayor	0.04
Serad, Abdulmalic	IND	Vice-Mayor	0.04
Rondato, Abdulmalik	IND	Vice-Mayor	0.03
Pangandag, Aslainie	IND	Vice-Mayor	0.01
Lumbayanague			
Gunting, Ansary	LP	Mayor	54.02
Asum, Salamona	UNA	Mayor	45.45
Gunting, Simpan	IND	Mayor	0.52
Salo, Alexander	IND	Mayor	0.00
Macre, Mangondaya	LP	Vice-Mayor	51.38
Asum, Arimao	UNA	Vice-Mayor	44.94
Gunting, Muamar	IND	Vice-Mayor	3.68
Marantao			
Abinal, Racma*	UNA	Mayor	55.27
Adiong, Samson	NPC	Mayor	30.18
Adtha-Magangcong, Jasmin	LP	Mayor	10.30
Tanggote, Mohammad	IND	Mayor	4.22
Tahir, Kiram	IND	Mayor	0.02
Maruhom, Alden	UNA	Vice-Mayor	48.37
Cornell, Ben	NPC	Vice-Mayor	41.95
Palao, Azis*	IND	Vice-Mayor*	09.18
Abdulkarim, Alya	IND	Vice-Mayor	0.20
Macalangcom, Anwar	IND	Vice-Mayor	0.19
Acab, Ali	IND	Vice-Mayor	0.12
Marawi City (Capital)			
Gandamra, Majul	LP	Mayor	52.23
Ali, Solitario	PDPLBN	Mayor	47.74
Tomawis, Ismael	LDP	Mayor	0.04
Salic, Arafat*	PDPLBN	Vice-Mayor	59.30
Abdul Rauf, Anouar	LP	Vice-Mayor	40.19

Table 17 *(cont'd)*

Candidate	Party	Office	Per cent (%)
Sultan, Sheikh	IND	Vice-Mayor	0.51
Tamparan			
Disomimba, Sittie Amina	LP	Mayor	64.35
Aliponto, Acmad Jr.	IND	Mayor	31.50
Ali, Zamzam	PDPLBN	Mayor	3.44
Dima, Jamael	IND	Mayor	0.51
Cabuntalan, Malik	IND	Mayor	0.20
Tomawis, Kapitan*	LP	Vice-Mayor	84.19
Batara, Johayr	IND	Vice-Mayor	8.09
Ali, Zainal Abidin	PDPLBN	Vice-Mayor	6.92
Pacasirang, Caironia	IND	Vice-Mayor	0.81
Tugaya			
Pacalna, Alfattah	LP	Mayor	55.01
Pukunum, Naip	UNA	Mayor	35.99
Pangcoga, Ayonan	IND	Mayor	5.73
Abangon, Suhaili	PDPLBN	Mayor	1.75
Pukunum, Jamilon	IND	Mayor	1.39
Decampong, Solaiman	IND	Mayor	0.08
Sarip, Hasan	IND	Mayor	0.05
Balindong, Alber	LP	Vice-Mayor	53.98
Maongco, Mohammad Azharre	UNA	Vice-Mayor	31.05
Disoma, Misug	IND	Vice-Mayor	14.41
Barangai, Moamar	PDPLBN	Vice-Mayor	0.55

Bibliography

Abesamis, Teresea S. "The Truth About Makati: Grassroots and Governance", *Businessworld*, 3 February 2016. Available at http://www.bworldonline.com/content.php?section=Opinion&title=the-truth-about-makati&id=122506 [accessed 30 May 2016].

Abinales, Patricio N. *Making Mindanao: Cotabato and Davao in the Formation of the Philippine Nation-state*. Quezon City: Ateneo de Manila University Press, 2000.

Abinales, Patricio N. and Donna J. Amoroso. *State and Society in the Philippines*. Lanham: Rowman and Littlefield, 2005.

Abocejo, Ferdinand. "The Veracity of Vote Buying: Perspective of the Philippine Electoral System", *International Journal on Graft and Corruption Research* 2, January 2015. Available at http://philair.ph/publication/index.php/ijgc/article/view/301 [accessed 17 August 2017].

Agpalo, Remgio. *The Political Elite and the People*. Manila: Regal Printing Corporation, 1972.

Ajana, Btihaj. "Surveillance and Body Politics", *Electronic Journal of Sociology*, 2005. Available at http://citeseerx.ist.psu.edu/viewdoc/download?doi=10.1.1. 606.6750&rep=rep1&type=pdf [accessed 13 October 2016].

Alegre, Edilberto. "Re-building a Nation", in *Up From the Ashes: The Story of the Filipino People*. Asia Publishing Limited, 1998, p. 274.

Ana-Liza Vilas-Alvaren. "Makati Posts 14B in Revenues", *Manila Bulletin*, 17 January 2016. Available at http://www.mb.com.ph/makati-posts-p14b-in-revenues-for-2015 [accessed 25 May 2016].

Anderson, Benedict. "Cacique Democracy in the Philippines: Origins and Dreams", *New Left Review* 169 (1998): 3–33.

Andreo Calonzo. "VP Binay Got Up to 651 Million from Boy Scouts Land Deal", GMA Network News, 18 February 2016. Available at http://www.gmanetwork. com/news/story/439735/news/nation/vp-binay-got-up-to-p651m-from-boy-scouts-land-deal-ex-ally-mercado-claims [accessed 12 May 2016].

Arumpac, Alyx. "Paracale's Real Treasures are not Gold", Public Affairs, *GMA News Online*, 3 July 2012. Available at http://www.gmanetwork.com/news/story/263976/publicaffairs/iwitness/paracale-s-real-treasures-are-not-gold.

Aspinall, Edward and Mada Sukmajati, eds. *Electoral Dynamics in Indonesia: Money Politics, Patronage and Clientelism at the Grassroots*. Singapore: NUS Press, 2016.

Aspinall, Edward, Allen Hicken, Meredith L. Weiss and Michael W. Davidson. "Local Machines and Vote Brokerage in the Philippines", *Contemporary Southeast Asia* 38, 2 (2016): 191–6.

Aspinall, Edward, Noor Rohman, Ahmad Zainul Hamdi, Rubaidi and Zusiana Elly Triantini. "Vote Buying in Indonesia: Candidate Strategies, Market Logic and Effectiveness", *Journal of East Asian Studies* 17, 1 (2017): 1–27.

Avendano, Christine. "Know Your Candidates: Jejomar Binay 24 Hour Veteran of 60,000 Wakes", *Philippine Daily Inquirer*, 28 April 2016. Available at http://newsinfo. inquirer.net/782047/jejomar-binay-24-hour-veteran-of-60000-wakes [accessed 30 June 2016].

Balgos, Cecile C.A., Malou Mangahas and Ramon Casiple. "Campaign Finance Reader: Money Politics and the May 2010 Elections". Quezon City: Philippine Center for Investigative Journalism (PCIJ) and the Pera at Pulitika, 2010.

Ballaran, Jhoanna and Bonz Magsambol. "Who Were the Presidential Candidates' Top Donors?" ABS CBN Investigative Group, ABS CBN News, 14 April 2016. Available at http://news.abs-cbn.com/halalan2016/focus/04/14/16/who-were-the-presidential-candidates-top-donors [accessed 26 June 2016].

Bentley, Carter G. "Mohammad Ali Dimaporo: A Modern Maranao Datu", in *An Anarchy of Families: State and Family in the Philippines*, ed. Alfred McCoy, Kris Olds, Anderson Sutton and Thongchai Winichakul. Wisconsin: The University of Wisconsin Press, 1993, pp. 243–84.

Bikolandia: HISTORY 103: CAMARINES NORTE. Available at Bikolandia.blogspot. com/2010/06/history-103-camarines-norte_05.html Jun 5, 2010 (this site is no longer available).

Bikol Initiative: Camarines Norte Politics. Available at https://bikolinitiative.word press.com/bikol-wiki/bikol-politics/bikol-politicscamarines-norte-politics/ [accessed June 2016].

Borja-Slark, Aileen. "Reciprocity and The Concept of Filipino 'Utang na Loob'". Filipino-Western Relationships, 2008. Available at https://ipfs.io/ipfs/QmXoypizj W3WknFiJnKLwHCnL72vedxjQkDDP1mXWo6uco/wiki/Utang_na_loob.html [accessed 8 June 2016].

Cabyabyab, Mark Jayson. "Binay Woos Vote-rich Laguna", *Philippine Daily Inquirer Online*, 10 Feb. 2016. Available at http://newsinfo.inquirer.net/763591/binay-woos-vote-rich-laguna.

Caduaya, Editha. "LP Allies in Mindanao Jump Ship to Support Duterte", *Rappler*, 28 November 2015. Available at http://www.rappler.com/nation/politics/elections /2016/114298-liberal-party-allies-jump-ship-support-duterte.

Calimbahin, Cleo. *The Promise and Pathology of Democracy: The Commission on Elections of the Philippines*. Madison: University of Wisconsin, 2009.

Cardinoza, Gabriel. "Pangasinan City Councillor Found Dead", *Inquirer.Net*, 7 December 2015. Available at http://newsinfo.inquirer.net/745447/pangasinan-city-councilor-found-dead [accessed 3 January 2016].

Caronan, Rowena F. "In Last 8 Elections, 68 Families Victors in 6 Vote-rich Provinces", Philippine Center for Investigative Journalism, 7 May 2016. Available at https://pcij. org/blog/314/in-last-8-electionsbr68-families-victors-in-6-vote-rich-provinces.

Carson, Jamie L., Erik J. Engstrom and Jason M. Roberts. "Candidate Quality, the Personal Vote, and the Incumbency Advantage in Congress", *American Political Science Review* 101, 2 (2007): 289–300.

Carter Center. "Limited Election Observation Mission to the Philippines, June 2016 Statement". Available at https://www.cartercenter.org/resources/pdfs/news/peace _publications/election_reports/philippines-june-2016-election-statement.pdf.

Carvajal, Nancy. "AMLC: Binay's Own Firm Supplied Birthday Cakes in Makati", *Philippine Daily Inquirer*, 15 May 2015. Available at http://newsinfo.inquirer. net/691481/amlc-binays-own-firm-supplied-birthday-cakes-in-makati [accessed 25 April 2016].

Cepeda, Mara. "Abby Binay Running for Mayor a Big Sacrifice", *Rappler*, 29 October 2015. Available at http://www.rappler.com/nation/politics/elections/2016/110968-abby-binay-running-mayor-big-sacrifice [accessed 26 June 2016].

_____. "Binay Pre-campaign Spending a Non-issue", *Rappler*, 11 March 2016. Available at http://www.rappler.com/nation/politics/elections/2016/125470-binay-pre-campaign-spending-non-issue [accessed 12 May 2016].

Checa, S.L. "Antique Candidates Vow Peaceful and Honest Elections", *Panay News*, 3 March 2016. Available at http://www.panaynewsphilippines.com/2016/03/13/ antique-candidates-vow-peaceful-honest-polls/ (this site is no longer available).

Chua, Yvonne T. "The (Not So) Great Escapes", Philippine Center for Investigative Journalism, 2003.

CNN Philippines. "Three Cases of Election-related Violence Recorded on Second Day of Campaign Period", *CNN Philippines*, 10 February 2016. Available at http:// cnnphilippines.com/news/2016/02/10/election-violence-gun-ban.html [accessed 3 January 2017].

Co, Edna, Acram Latiph, Ramon Fernan, Maria Diola, Amina Rasul, Mehol Sadain, Rufa Guiam, Benedicto Bacani and Raphael Montes. *State of Local Democracy in the Autonomous Region in Muslim Mindanao (SoLD ARMM)*. Stockholm, Sweden: International Institute for Democracy and Electoral Assistance (IDEA), 2013.

COMELEC. "Election – Philippines 2016 – ELECTIONS 2016". Available at https:// www.pilipinaselectionresults2016.com/#/coc/0/4A/3400 (this site is no longer available).

_____. "Philippine 2016 Voters Profile by Province and City/Municipality Posted: 07 January 2016". Available at https://www.comelec.gov.ph/?r=2016NLE/Statistics/ Philippine2016VotersProfile/ByProvCity (this site is no longer available).

Commission on Elections, 2016. *Commission on Elections*. Available at www.comelec. gov.ph

Concepciòn, Sylvia. "Breaking the Links Between Economics and Conflict in Mindanao", Discussion paper. International Alert, 2003. Available at https://pdfs. semanticscholar.org/82fb/a4fec90db1d599dd44b1a37f40b75cde595f.pdf

Coronel, Sheila, ed. *Pork and Other Perks: Corruption and Governance in the Philippines*. Quezon City: PCIJ, Evelio Javier Foundation, Institute for Popular Democracy, 1998.

_____. "The Seven Ms of Dynasty Building", 2007. Online. Available at https://old. pcij.org/stories/the-seven-ms-of-dynasty-building/ [accessed 16 May 2016].

Coronel, Sheila S. and Cecile C.A. Balgos. *Pork and Other Perks: Corruption and Governance in the Philippines*. Philippine Center for Investigative Journalism, 1998.

Coronel, Sheila, Yvonne Chua, Luz Rimban and Booma Cruz. *The Rulemakers: How the Wealthy and Well-born Dominate Congress*. Quezon City: Philippine Center for Investigative Journalism, 2004.

Cruz, Cesi, Philip Keefer and Julien Labonne. "Incumbent Advantage, Voter Information and Vote Buying", *IDB Working Paper Series*. IDB-WP-711, 2016.

_____. "Social Networks and the Targeting of Vote Buying", presented at the Annual Meeting of the American Political Science Association, 2013.

Cudis, Christine. "PNP: 90% of Private Armies are in ARMM, Cotabato", *Sun Star Davao*, 2 April 2016. Available at http://www.sunstar.com.ph/article/66408/ [accessed 16 May 2016].

Cupin, Bea. "Inside Balay: Who's Who in the Roxas Campaign", *Rappler*, 4 March 2016. Available at www.rappler.com/newsbreak/in-depth/124403-mar-roxas-campaign-team [accessed 2 July 2016].

Diaz-Cayeros, Alberto, Federico Estévez and Beatriz Magaloni. *The Political Logic of Poverty Relief: Electoral Strategies and Social Policy in Mexico*. Cambridge Studies in Comparative Politics. Cambridge: Cambridge University Press, 2016.

Diaz, Patricio P. *Understanding Mindanao Conflict*. MindaNews Publication, Mindanao News and Information Cooperative Center, 2003.

Diola, Camille. "Dasmarinas Residents Commend Guards For Refusing Binay", *Philippine Star*, 24 December 2013. Available at http://www. philstar. com/news-feature/2013/12/24/1271774/dasmarinas-residents-commend-guards-refusing-binay (this site is no longer available).

Espina, Marchel P. "NUP Members 'Free' to Choose Presidential Bets in 2016 – Solon", *Rappler*, 30 Sept. 2015. Available at http://www.rappler.com/nation/politics/elections/2016/107603-nup-free-choose-presidential-candidates-2016.

Ferrer, Miriam C. "From Rebels to Governors: 'Patronage Autonomy' and Continuing Underdevelopment in Muslim Mindanao", in *Regional Minorities and Development in Asia*, ed. H. Cao and E. Morrell. London and New York: Routledge Contemporary Asia Series, 2010.

Finan Federico and Laura Schechter. "Vote-buying and Reciprocity", *Econometrica* 80, 2 (2012): 863–81.

Franco, Jennifer C. *Elections and Democratization in the Philippines*. New York: Routledge, 2001, pp. 1–200.

Friedman, Daniel and Donald Wittman. "Why Voters Vote for Incumbents but Against Incumbency", *Journal of Public Economics* 57, 1 (1995): 67–83.

Gans-Morse, Jordan, Sebastian Mazzuca and Simeon Nichter. "Varieties of Clientelism: Machine Politics during Elections", *American Journal of Political Science* 58, 2 (2014): 415–32.

Gloria, Glenda. "One City, Two Worlds", in *Boss: 5 Case Studies of Local Politics in the Philippines*, ed. J.F. Lacaba. Philippine Center for Investigative Journalism, 1995, p. 92.

Gumba, Bernadette. "Camarines Sur split: Economic Issues", 2011. Available at http://www.voxbikol.com/article/camarines-sur-split-economic-issues (this site is no longer available).

Gutierrez, Eric and Marites Vitug. "ARMM after the Peace Agreement", in *Rebels, Warriors and Ulama: A Reader in Muslim Separatism and the War in Southern Philippines*, ed. K. Gaerlan and Mara Stankovitch. Quezon City: Institute for Popular Democracy, Philippines, 1996.

Gutierrez, Eric U. *The Ties that Bind: A Guide to Family, Business, and Other Interests in the Ninth House of Representatives*. Philippine Center for Investigative Journalism, 1994.

Gutierrez, Eric U., Ildefonso C. Torrente and Noli G. Narca. *All in the Family: A Study of Elites and Power Relations in the Philippines*. Quezon City: Institute for Popular Democracy, 1992.

Gutierrez, Pia. "Binay Spent P463 million for Presidential Campaign: SOCE", *Manila Bulletin*, 8 June 2016. Available at http://news.abs-cbn.com/nation/06/08/16/binay-spent-p463m-for-presidential-campaign-soce [accessed 26 June 2016].

Hedman, Eva-Lotta E. *In the Name of Civil Society: From Free Election Movements to People Power in the Philippines*. Honolulu: University of Hawai'i Press, 2006.

_____. *Democratisation & New Voter Mobilisation in Southeast Asia: Beyond Machine Politics?: Reformism, Populism and Philippine Elections*. IDEAS reports – special reports, ed. Kitchen, Nicholas SR005. London, UK: LSE IDEAS, London School of Economics and Political Science, 2010.

_____. *In the Name of Civil Society: From Free Election Movements to People Power in the Philippines*. Honolulu: University of Hawai'i Press, 2006.

Hicken, Allen. "Electoral Design: Why it Matters for Development Outcomes", presented at the workshop, *Electoral System Redesign for Development* (Manila, 13–14 July 2016).

_____. "Party and Party System Institutionalization in the Philippines", in *Party System Institutionalization in Asia: Democracies, Autocracies and the Shadows of the Past*, ed. Allen Hicken and Erik Martinez Kuhonta. Cambridge: Cambridge University Press, 2014, pp. 307–27.

_____. "Clientelism", *Annual Review of Political Science* 14 (2011): 289–310.

_____. *Building Party Systems in Developing Democracies*. New York: Cambridge University Press, 2009.

Hicken, Allen, James Atkinson and Nico Ravanilla. "Pork & Typhoons: The Influence of Political Connections on Disaster Response in the Philippines", in *Building Inclusive Democracies in ASEAN*, ed. Ronald U. Mendoza, Edsel Beja, Jr., Julio Teehankee, Antonio La Vina and Maria Fe Villamejor-Mendoza. Mandaluyong City, Philippines: Anvil Publishing, 2015, pp. 74–96.

Hicken, Allen, Stephen Leider, Nico Ravanilla and Dean Yang. "Temptation in Vote Selling: Evidence from a Field Experiment in the Philippines", *Journal of Development Economics* 131 (2018): 1–14.

Hirsch, Philip and Carol Warren, eds. *The Politics of Environment in Southeast Asia*. New York: Psychology Press, 1998.

Hofilena, Chay F. "Fake Accounts, Manufactured Reality on Social Media", *Rappler*. 9 October 2016. Available at https://www.rappler.com/newsbreak/investigative/148347-fake-accounts-manufactured-reality-social-media [accessed 12 April 2016].

Human Development Network (HDN). *Philippine Human Development Report: Geography and Human Development in the Philippines.* World Bank Group Publication, Human Development Sector Unit East Asia and Pacific Region, Manila, 2013.

Human Rights Watch. *They Owned the People: The Ampatuans, State-Backed Militias, and the Killings in the Southern Philippines.* New York: Human Rights Watch, 2010. Available at http://www.hrw.org/sites/default/files/reports/philippines1110W_1.pdf [accessed 15 June 2016].

_____. *One Shot to the Head: Death Squad Killings in Tagum City, Philippines.* New York: Human Rights Watch, 2014. Available at https://www.hrw.org/report/2014/05/20/one-shot-head/death-squad-killings-tagum-city-philippines

_____. *"License to Kill": Philippine Police Killings in Duterte's "War on Drugs".* New York: Human Rights Watch, 2017. Available at https://www.hrw.org/sites/default/files/report_pdf/philippines0317_insert.pdf

Hutchcroft, Paul. "Linking Capital and Countryside: Patronage and Clientelism in Japan, Thailand, and the Philippines", in *Clientelism, Social Policy, and the Quality of Democracy*, ed. Diego Abente Brun and Larry Diamond. Baltimore: Johns Hopkins University Press, 2014a, pp. 174–203.

_____. "Dreams of Redemption: Localist Strategies of Political Reform in the Philippines", in *Social Difference and Constitutionalism in Pan-Asia*, ed. Susan H. Williams. New York: Cambridge University Press, 2014b, pp. 75–108.

_____. "Re-slicing the Pie of Patronage: The Politics of The Internal Revenue Allotment in the Philippines, 1991–2010", *Philippine Review of Economics* 49, 1 (2012): 109–34.

_____. "Dreams of Redemption: Localist Strategies of Political Reform in the Philippines", in *The Politics of Change in the Philippines*, ed. Yuko Kasuya and Nathan Gilbert Quimpo. Mandaluyong City, Philippines: Anvil Publishing, 2010, pp. 418–54.

_____. "Countries at the Crossroads: Philippines". Freedom House, *Countries at the Crossroads 2007*. Available at: http://www.refworld.org/docid/4738692964.html [accessed 27 June 2016].

_____. "Reviewed Work: Capital, Coercion, and Crime: Bossism in the Philippines", *Pacific Affairs* 76, 3 (2003): 505–7.

_____. *Booty Capitalism: The Politics of Banking.* Ithaca: Cornell University, 1998, pp. 20–234.

Hutchcroft, Paul and Joel Rocamora. "Patronage-Based Parties and the Democratic Deficit in the Philippines: Origins, Evolution, and the Imperatives of Reform", in *Routledge Handbook of Southeast Asian Politics*, ed. Richard Robison. Routledge, 2012.

_____. "Strong Demands and Weak Institutions: The Origins and Evolution of the Democratic Deficit in the Philippines", *Journal of East Asian Studies* 3, 2 (May–August 2003): 259–92.

Ilas, Joy. "Binay, Honasan Hold Sortie in Vote-rich Laguna", *CNN Philippines,* 10 Feb. 2016. Available at http://cnnphilippines.com/news/2016/02/10/Binay-Honasan-Laguna-campaign.html

Inquirer Archives. "In the Know: Who is Kid Pena?" *Philippine Daily Inquirer*, 17 March 2015. Available at http://newsinfo.inquirer.net/679282/in-the-know-who-is-kid-pena [accessed 26 June 2016].

Inquirer.net. "Bohol Province Top in Governance", 6 September 2011. Available at http://newsinfo.inquirer.net/53729/bohol-province-top-in-governance [accessed 14 October 2016].

International Crisis Group (ICG). "The Philippines: After the Maguindanao Massacre", *Asia Briefing* No. 98, 21 December 2009.

Jocano, F. Lando. *Slum as a Way of Life: A Study of Coping Behavior in an Urban Environment*. Quezon City: University of the Philippines Press, 1975.

_____. *Slum as a Way of Life: A Study of Coping Behavior in an Urban Environment*. Diliman, Quezon City: PUNLAD Research House, 2002, pp. 196–9.

Johnston, Michael. "Patrons and Clients, Jobs and Machines: A Case Study of the Uses of Patronage", *The American Political Science Review* 73, 2 (1979): 385–98.

Jubair, Salah. *Bangsamoro: A Nation under Endless Tyranny*. Kuala Lumpur: IQ Marin Sdn Bhd, 1985.

Kasuya, Yuko. *Presidential Bandwagon: Parties and Party Systems in the Philippines*. Mandaluyong City, Philippines: Anvil Publishing, 2009.

Kawanaka, Takeshi. *Power in a Philippine City*. Chiba: Institute of Developing Economies, Japan Trade Organization, 2002.

_____. "The Robredo Style: Philippine Local Politics in Transition", *Kasarinlan: The Philippine Journal of Third World Studies* 13, 3 (1998): 5–36.

Kerkvliet, Benedict. "Toward a More Comprehensive Analysis of Philippine Politics: Beyond the Patron-Client Factional Framework", *Journal of Southeast Asian Studies* 26, 2 (1995): 401–19.

Kerkvliet, Benedict J. and Resil B. Mojares. *From Marcos to Aquino: Local Perspectives on Political Transition in the Philippines*. Honolulu: University of Hawai'i Press, 1992.

Kimura, Masataka. "Changing Patterns of Leadership Recruitment and the Emergence of the Professional Politician in Philippine Local Politics Re-examined: An Aspect of Political Development and Decay", *Southeast Asian Studies* 36, 2 (1998): 206–29.

_____. *Elections and Politics Philippine Style: A Case in Lipa*. Manila: De La Salle University, 1997.

Kitschelt, Herbert and Steven I. Wilkinson. *Patrons, Clients and Policies: Patterns of Democratic Accountability and Political Competition*. Cambridge: Cambridge University Press, 2007.

Kuhonta, Erik Martinez. *The Institutional Imperative: The Politics of Equitable Development in Southeast Asia*. Redwood City, CA: Stanford University Press, 2012.

Labonne, Julien. "The Local Electoral Impacts of Conditional Cash Transfers: Evidence from a Field Experiment", *Journal of Development Economics* 104 (2013): 73–88.

Landé, Carl H. *Leaders, Factions, and Parties: The Structure of Philippine Politics*. New Haven: Southeast Asia Studies, Yale University, 1965.

_____. "Introduction: The Dyadic Basis of Clientelism", in *Friends, Followers and Factions: A Reader*, ed. Steffen W. Schmidt, James C. Scott, Carl Landé and Laura Guasti. Berkeley: University of California Press, 1977a, pp. xiii–xxxvii.

_____. "Networks and Groups in Southeast Asia: Some Observations of the Group Theory of Politics", in *Friends, Followers and Factions: A Reader*, ed. Steffen W. Schmidt, James C. Scott, Carl Landé and Laura Guasti. Berkeley: University of California Press, 1977b, pp. 75–99.

_____. *Post-Marcos Politics: A Geographical and Statistical Analysis of the 1992 Presidential Elections*. Singapore: Institute of Southeast Asian Studies, 1996.

Laquian, Aprodico A. "Isla de kokomo", *Philippine Journal of Public Administration* 8 (1996): 112–22.

Lara Jr., Francisco J. *Insurgents, Clans, and States: Political Legitimacy and Resurgent Conflict in Muslim Mindanao, Philippines*. Honolulu: University of Hawai'i Press, 2014.

Laylo, Pedro and Carijane Dagdag-Laylo. *The 1998 Philippine Presidential Elections: Candidate Images, Media Portrayals, and Vote Intentions*. Quezon City: Social Weather Stations, 1999.

Legislative Districts of Pangasinan (as of 5 June 2016). *Wikipedia, The Free Encyclopedia*. Available at en.wikipedia.org/wiki/Legislative_districts_of_Pangasinan [accessed 3 July 2016].

Leveriza, Jose P. *Public Administration "The Business of Government"*. Mandaluyong City: National Bookstore, 1983.

Lorber, Judith. *Paradoxes of Gender*. New Haven: Yale University Press, 1994.

Lucero, Vino. "Votes by the Bucket: Same Provinces Keep Vote-rich Status in 12 Years", Philippine Center for Investigative Journalism, 28 April 28 2016. Available at https://old.pcij.org/stories/latest-stories/same-provinces-keep-vote-rich-status-in-12-years/.

Machado, Kit G. "Changing Aspects of Factionalism in Philippine Local Politics", *Asian Survey* 11 (1971): 1183.

_____. "From Traditional Faction to Machine: Changing Patterns of Political Leadership and Organization in the Rural Philippines", *The Journal of Asian Studies* 33, 4 (1974): 523–47.

Macob, J.M. "In Pangasinan, Dynasties are Here to Stay", *Vera Files Vote 2013*, 12 May 2013. Available at http://vote2013.verafiles.org/in-pangasinan-dynasties-are-there-to-stay/ (this site is no longer available).

Mahmood, Saba. "Feminist Theory, Embodiment, and the Docile Agent: Some Reflections on the Egyptian Islamic Revival", *Cultural Anthropology* 16, 2 (2001). Available at https://www.jstor.org/stable/656537?seq=1#metadata_info_tab_contents [accessed 15 August 2017].

Mangada, Ladylyn L. "Grooming the Wards in Leyte-Samar Islands", in *What's New? Filipino Generations in a Changing Climate*, ed. Amaryllis T. Torres, Laura L. Samson and Manuel P. Diaz. Philippine Social Science Council, 2015, pp. 191–205.

Mares, Isabela and Lauren Young. "Buying, Expropriating, and Stealing Votes", *Annual Review of Political Science* 19 (2016): 1–15.

Martin, Lynn. "A Report on the Glass Ceiling Initiative." Washington: US Department of Labor, 1991.

McCoy, Alfred W., ed. *An Anarchy of Families: State and Family in the Philippines*. Madison: University of Wisconsin Press, 2009.

Mendoza, Ronald U. et al. "Inequality in Democracy: Insights from an Empirical Analysis of Political Dynasties in the 15th Philippine Congress", Munich Personal RePEc Archive, 17 July 2012. Available at https://mpra.ub.uni-muenchen. de/40104/ [accessed 15 August 2017].

Mendoza, Ronald U., Edsel Beja Jr., Victor Venida and I.I. David Yap. "Political Dynasties in the Philippine Congress", in *Building Inclusive Democracies in ASEAN*, ed. Ronald U. Mendoza, Edsel Beja, Jr., Julio Teehankee, Antonio La Vina and Maria Fe Villamejor-Mendoza. Mandaluyong City, Philippines: Anvil Publishing, 2015.

Millari Jr., Delfin T. "Binay: I Will Win by $4M Votes", *Philippine Daily Inquirer*, 8 April 2016. Available at http://newsinfo.inquirer.net/778439/binay-i-will-win-by-4m-votes.

Montiel, Cristina Jayme. "Philippine Political Culture and Governance", in *Philippine Political Culture: View from Inside the Halls of Power*, ed. Cristina Montiel, Lutgardo Barbo and J.R. Nereus Olaivar Acosta. Manila: Philippines Governance Forum, 2002, pp. 1–46.

Moss, Trefor. "Filipino Politician's Graft Probe Draws Shrug", *Wall Street Journal*, 27 November 2014. Available at https://www.wsj.com/articles/filipino-politicians-graft-probe-draws-shrugs-1417149507 [accessed 12 May 2016].

Northbound Philippines News Online. "Number of Towns in Pangasinan Under Election Watchlist Now Only 16 from Previous 20", *Northbound Philippines News Online*, 29 April 2016. Available at http://northboundasia.com/2016/04/29/ number-towns-pangasinan-election-watchlist-now-16-previous-20/#. WGz4cL0RXtJ [accessed 4 January 2017].

Op-Ed, Asian Journal. "Black Propaganda in Philippine Politics", *Asian Journal*, 6 May 2016. Available at http://asianjournal.com/editorial/black-propaganda-in-philippine-politics/ [accessed 30 June 2016].

Pascual, Jamaica Jane. "Special Report: Who is Gerry Limlingan?" GMA News Report, 25 May 2015. Available at http://www.gmanetwork.com/news/news/ specialreports/492862/special-report-who-is-gerry-limlingan/story/ [accessed 25 April 2016].

Perron, Louis. "Election Campaigns in the Philippines", in *Routledge Handbook of Political Management*, ed. Dennis W. Johnson. Routledge, 2009.

Philippine Statistics Authority. *The Countryside in Figures: Antique.* 2017. Available at http://nap.psa.gov.ph/countryside/showperregion.asp

_____. *The Countryside in Figures: Leyte.* 2017. Available at http://nap.psa.gov.ph/ countryside/showperregion.asp

Pitkin, Hanna F. *The Concept of Representation.* Berkeley and Los Angeles, CA: University of California Press, 1967.

Ponte, Romulo and Maricar Cinco. "In Laguna, 2 Ejercitos on Ballot Stir Confusion", *Philippine Daily Inquirer Online*, 6 May 2016. Available at http://newsinfo.inquirer. net/783478/in-laguna-2-ejercitos-on-ballot-stir-confusion

Porcalla, Delon. "It's Final: LP to be Minority", *The Philippine Star*, 20 July 2016. Available at http://www.philstar.com/headlines/2016/07/20/1604752/its-final-lp-be-minority [accessed 18 August 2017].

Province of Antique. *Provincial Development and Physical Framework Plan: Province of Antique: 2008–2013*. 2008. Available at https://www.scribd.com/doc/70627655/Antique-Provincial-Development-and-Physical-Framework-Plan-2008-2013

Querubin, Pablo. "Family and Politics: Dynastic Persistence in the Philippines", *Quarterly Journal of Political Science* 11, 2 (2015): 151–81.

Quimpo, Nathan. "Oligarchic Patrimonalism, Bossism, Electoral Clientelism and Contested Democracy in the Philippines", *Comparative Politics* 37, 2 (2005): 229–50.

_____. *Contested Democracy and the Left in the Philippines after Marcos*. New Haven: Yale University Southeast Asia Studies, 2008.

Quintas, Kristine B. et al. "One Cebu Cuts Ties with UNA", *The Freeman*, 22 March 2016. Available at https://www.pressreader.com/philippines/the-freeman/20160322/281479275536361.

Ramos, Malon. "Liberal Party Sure of Roxas Victory on May 9", *Philippine Daily Inquirer*, 15 April 2016. Available at http://newsinfo.inquirer.net/779616/liberal-party-sure-of-roxas-victory-on-may-9 [accessed 17 August 2017].

Rappler.com. PHVote 2013, *Rappler*, 2013a. Available at http://www.rappler.com/nation/politics/elections-2013 [accessed 16 January 2016].

_____. "Namfrel to Comelec: Act on Vote Buying", *Rappler*, 2013b. Available at http://www.rappler.com/nation/politics/elections-2013/28654-namfrel-comelec-vote-buying

_____. "Camarines Sur, Bicol Region Elections 2016", *Rappler*, 2016. Available at http://ph.rappler.com/local/region/Bicol-Region/Camarines-Sur (this site is no longer available).

Resabal, Cooper. "Concerned Citizens of Bohol Launch Campaign to Stop Vote Buying", 6 April 2016. Available at http://verafiles.org/concerned-citizens-of-bohol-launch-campaign-to-stop-vote-buying/#sthash.Kwtrzt3U.dpuf (this site is no longer available).

Ressa, Maria A. "Propaganda War: Weaponizing the Internet", *Rappler*. 3 October 2016. Available at https://www.rappler.com/nation/148007-propaganda-war-weaponizing-internet [accessed 12 April 2018].

Robredo, Jesse M. *Making Local Governance Work: The Naga City Model*. City Publications Group, City Development Information Office, Naga City, 2003.

Rodriguez, Fritzie. "Billions of Pesos Spent on Pre-campaign Ads", *Rappler*, 10 March 2016. Available at https://www.rappler.com/newsbreak/in-depth/125335-campaign-spending-2016-election [accessed 26 June 2016].

Roskin, Michael G. et al. *Political Science: An Introduction*. New Jersey: Pearson Education, 2008.

Rufo, Aries. "Binay's 'Dear Friend' got 1. 3B Contracts in 4 Years", *Rappler*, 26 October 2014. Available at http://www.rappler.com/newsbreak/investigative/71704-vp-binay-friend-billion-contracts [accessed 26 June 2016].

Rye, Ranjit. "PHVote: Interview with Political Analysts Ranjit Rye and Pulse Asia's Ronald Holmes", *Rappler*, 8 May 2016.

Salaverria, Leila B. "Binay Got 13% for Each Deal: Money Placed in Bags says Vice-Mayor", *Philippine Daily Inquirer*, 12 September 2014. Available at http://newsinfo.inquirer.net/637278/binay-got-13-for-each-deal [accessed 25 April 2016].

Samonte, Mauro Gia. "Trying to Make out the Binay Phenomenon in Makati", *Manila Times*, 1 July 2016. Available at http://www.manilatimes.net/trying-to-make-out-the-binay-phenomenon-in-makati/271186/ [accessed 1 July 2016].

Sauler, Erika. "30 Killed, 22 Hurt in Election Violence—CHR", *Philippine Daily Inquirer*, 12 May 2016. Available at http://newsinfo.inquirer.net/785237/30-killed-22-hurt-in-election-violence-chr [accessed 17 August 2017].

Schaffer, Frederic Charles, ed. *Elections for Sale: The Causes and Consequences of Vote Buying*. Boulder: Lynne Rienner, 2007.

_____. *The Hidden Costs of Clean Election Reform*. Ithaca: Cornell University Press, 2008.

_____. *Why Study Vote-buying. Elections for Sale*. Quezon City: Ateneo de Manila University Press, 2007, pp. 1–16.

Scharff, Michael. "Building trust and promoting accountability: Jesse Robredo and Naga City, Philippines, 1988–1998". Innovations for Successful Societies, Princeton University. Available at http://successfulsocieties.princeton.edu/publications/building-trust-and-promoting-accountability-jesse-robredo-and-naga-city-philippines [accessed 16 August 2017].

Scott, James. "Corruption. Machine Politics and Political Change", *The American Political Science Review* 63, 4 (1969): 1142–58.

_____. "Patron-Client Politics and Political Change in Southeast Asia", *American Political Science Review* 66, 1 (1972): 91–113.

Shefter, Martin. *Political Parties and the State: The American Historical Experience*. Princeton: Princeton University Press, 1994.

Sidel, John Thayer. *Capital, Coercion, and Crime: Bossism in the Philippines*. Redwood City, CA: Stanford University Press, 1999.

Sidel, John. "Big Men with Bolos, Bosses, Bullets, Bank Loans, and Bus Companies: Local Power in Philippine Politics", Cornell University (Typewritten), 1990.

_____. "Philippine Politics in Towns, District and Province", *Journal of Asian Studies* 56, 4 (1997): 947–66.

Soltes, Jonas Cabiles. "A Poor Man Sitting on a Pot of Gold", *Inquirer News*, 7 July 2011. Available at http://www.newsinfo.inquirer.net/21847/'a-poor-man-sitting-on-a-pot-of-gold' (this site is no longer available).

Stokes, Susan C., Thad Dunning, Marcelo Nazareno and Valeria Brusco. *Brokers, Voters, and Clientelism: The Puzzle of Distributive Politics*. New York: Cambridge University Press, 2013.

Stokes, Susan. "Perverse Accountability: A Formal Model of Machine Politics with Evidence from Argentina", *American Political Science Review* 99, 3 (2005): 315–24.

Sunday Punch. "Mother-and-daughter Arenas Tandem Enjoys People's Love and Trust", *Sunday Punch*, 24 January 2016. Available at https://punch.dagupan.com/articles/news/2016/01/mother-and-daughter-arenas-tandem-enjoys-peoples-love-and-trust/ [accessed 1 July 2016].

Tagum City at a Glance. 2016. Available at http://www.nscb.gov.ph/ (this site is no longer available).

Tan, Netina. "Are Gender Quotas Helping Female Politicians in Asia?", *East Asia Forum*, 24 June 2016. Available at http://www.eastasiaforum.org/2016/06/24/are-gender-quotas-helping-female-politicians-in-asia/.

Tan, Samuel. *A History of the Philippines*, 4th edition. Diliman, Quezon City: University of the Philippines Press, 2009.

Teehankee, Julio C. "Clientelism and Party Politics in the Philippines", in *Clientelism and Electoral Competition in Indonesia, Thailand and the Philippines*, ed. D. Tomas and A. Ufen. Oxford, UK: Routledge, 2012a, pp. 186–214.

_____. "The Philippines", in *Political Parties and Democracy: Western Europe, East and Southeast Asia 1990–2010*, ed. Jean Blondel and Takashi Inoguchi. Basingstoke, Hampshire: Palgrave Macmillan, 2012b, pp. 187–205.

_____. "Image, Issues and Machinery: Presidential Campaigns in Post-1986 Philippines", in *The Politics of Change in the Philippines*, ed. Y. Kasuya and N. Quimpo. Mandaluyong City, Philippines: Anvil Publishing, 2010, pp. 114–61.

_____. "Citizen-Party Linkages: Failure to Connect?" in *Reforming the Philippine Party System: Ideas and Initiatives, Debates and Dynamics*, ed. M. Herberg. Pasig: Friedrich Ebert Stiftung, 2009, pp. 23–44.

_____. "Electoral Politics in the Philippines", in *Electoral Politics in Southeast and East Asia*, ed. Aurel Croissant, Gabriele Bruns and Marei John. Singapore: Friedrich Ebert Stiftung, 2002, pp. 149–202.

_____. "Emerging Dynasties in the Post-Marcos House of Representatives", *Philippine Political Science Journal* 22, 45 (2001): 55–78.

The Bohol Chronicle. "Bohol Poll Poverty Rating Clarified", 2015. Available at http://boholchronicle.com.ph/2015/05/06/bohol-poll-poverty-rating-clarified/ [accessed 8 June 2016].

Thompson, Mark R. *The Anti-Marcos Struggle: Personalistic Rule and Democratic Transition in the Philippines*. New Haven: Yale University Press, 1995.

Torres III, Wilfredo M. ed. *Rido: Clan Feuding and Conflict Management in Mindanao*. Metro Manila: The Asia Foundation, 2007.

Udtohan, Leo. "Same Faces Running in Bohol in 2016", *The Bohol Chronicle*, 18 October 2015. Available at http://boholchronicle.com.ph/2015/10/18/same-faces-running-in-bohol-in-2016/ [accessed 9 June 2016].

Van de Walle, Nicolas. "Meet the New Boss, Same as the Old Boss? The Evolution of Political Clientelism in Africa", in *Patrons, Clients and Policies: Patterns of Democratic Accountability and Political Competition*, ed. Herbert Kitschelt and Steven I. Wilkinson. Cambridge University Press, 2007, pp. 50–67.

Vatikiotis, Michael J. *Political Change in Southeast Asia*. London, New York: Routledge, 1996.

Vilas-Alavaren, Ana Liza. "Makati Posts 14B in Revenues", *Manila Bulletin*, 17 January 2016. Available at http://www.mb.com.ph/makati-posts-p14b-in-revenues-for-2015/Inquirer.

Vitug, Marites Dañguilan. "The Scrum: Roxas, Binay, and the Political Machine", *Rappler*, 20 April 2016. Available at http://www.rappler.com/nation/politics/elections/2016/129982-roxas-binay-political-machine [accessed 17 August 2017].

Vitug, Marites. "Shadows Over Binay's Leadership of Boy Scouts", *Rappler*, 7 March 2015. Available at http://www.rappler.com/newsbreak/in-depth/85639-jojo-binay-leadership-boy-scouts-philippines [accessed 15 August 2017].

Wang, Chin-Shou and Charles Kurzman. "The Logistics: How to Buy Votes?", in *Elections for Sale*. Quezon City: Ateneo de Manila University Press, 2007, pp. 61–78.

Weiss, Meredith L. "Patronage Politics and Parties in the Philippines: Insights from the 2016 Elections", in *Strong Patronage, Weak Parties; The Case for Electoral Reform in the Philippines*, ed. Paul H. Hutchroft. Manila: Anvil Publishing, 2019.

Weiss, Meredith L. and Arnold Puyok, ed. *Electoral Dynamics in Sarawak: Contesting Developmentalism and Rights*. Malaysia/Singapore: SIRD/ISEAS, 2017.

Weiss, Meredith L., ed. *Electoral Dynamics in Malaysia: Findings from the Grassroots*. Malaysia/Singapore: SIRD/ISEAS, 2015.

Wolters, Willem. *Politics, Patronage and Class Conflict in Central Luzon*. Quezon City: New Day Publishers, 1984.

Wurfel, David. *Filipino Politics: Development and Decay*. Ithaca: Cornell University Press, 1988.

Yap, DJ and Gil C. Cabacungan. "Binay, Roxas Bank on Party Machinery", *Philippine Daily Inquirer*, 13 April 2016. Available at http://newsinfo.inquirer.net/779277/binay-roxas-bank-on-party-machinery.

Zaide, Sonia M. *Political Science*, 2nd edition. Quezon City: All-Nations Publishing, 1996.

Zamfirache, Irina. "Women and Politics – The Glass Ceiling", *Journal of Comparative Research in Anthropology and Sociology* 1, 1 (2010): 175–85.

Zucco, Cesar Jr. "When Payouts Pay Off: Conditional Cash Transfers and Voting Behaviour in Brazil 2002–10", *American Journal of Political Science* 57, 4 (2013): 810–22.

Contributors

Tetchie D. Aquino is an instructor at the Political Science Department, Ateneo de Davao University.

Edward Aspinall is a professor in the Department of Political and Social Change at the Coral Bell School of Asia Pacific Affairs, The Australian National University.

Mary Joyce Borromeo-Bulao is the chairperson of the Social Sciences Department, Ateneo de Naga University, Naga City.

Cleo Calimbahin is an associate professor of Political Science, De La Salle University.

Duke Thomas G. Dolorical is an independent researcher.

Juhn Chris P. Espia is an assistant professor at the University of the Philippines Visayas.

Gerardo V. Eusebio is a lecturer of Political Science, De La Salle University.

Allen Hicken is a professor in the Department of Political Science, University of Michigan.

Ronald Holmes is an assistant professor of Political Science, De La Salle University.

Paul D. Hutchcroft is a professor in the Department of Political and Social Change at the Coral Bell School of Asia Pacific Affairs, The Australian National University.

Acram Latiph is research coordinator and associate professor in Economics, Mindanao State University.

Regina E. Macalandag is a PhD student at the Crawford School of Public Policy, The Australian National University.

Ladylyn Lim Mangada is an associate professor at the University of the Philippines Visayas, Tacloban College.

Armida D. Miranda is a professor/lecturer, learning and development module developer and organizational behavior coach.

Margie A. Nolasco is an institutional research coordinator at BISCAST, Naga City.

Neil Pancho is a director at the Center of Politics and International Affairs, Ateneo de Davao University.

Jose Aims R. Rocina is a professor of Political Science, De La Salle University-Dasmarinas.

Michelle Sta. Romana is an assistant professorial lecturer of Political Science, De La Salle University.

Donabel S. Tumandao is an instructor at the University of the Philippines Visayas, Tacloban College.

Meredith Weiss is professor and chair in the Department of Political Science, Rockefeller College of Public Affairs and Policy, State University of New York, Albany.

Index

Page numbers in *italics* indicate figures; those in **bold** indicate tables.

347

Carigara, 225–6
case studies
  from Bohol, First District of, 250–4
  from Camarines Norte, Second
    District of, 91–3
  from Leyte, 217–20
Cataquiz, Calixto, 118
Cataquiz, Lourdez, 119
Cataquiz clan, 118
centralised control, 48
Chatto, Edgar, 244
City Social Welfare and Development
  (CSWD) office, 194
Civilian Affiliation Officer (CAFO), 305
clan-based politics, *see* family/clan-
  based politics
  in Lanao del Sur, 321–7
clientelism
  definition of, 4–5
  key elements of, 65
  local machine and, 29–34
  overview of, 11–17
  in Rinconada, Camarines Sur, 77–8
club goods, 9, 36
Combong Junior, 272
Commission on Elections
  (COMELEC), 99, 105, 264, 301,
  314, 316
Commission on Human Rights, 17
compartmentalisation, 48
Compostela Valley Province
  background of, 282–6
  campaign structure in, 286–91
  conclusions regarding, 295
  election results from, 295–6
  image and, 286–91
  introduction to, 281–2
  logistics in, 286–91
  patronage system in, 291–5
Condez, Victor, 269, 273
conditional cash transfers (CCTs), 50,
  180, 198
consultants, 34n31
contingency, 65
coordinators
  in Laguna, First District of, 127–32

role of, 126
Corro, Raul, 152, 162, 163, 165, 166
corruption, charges of, 68, 86–7, 142–3,
  144–6, 233–4
Couples for Christ, 159
"crawl, the" (*gapang*), 103
credit-claiming, 228

datu system, 321
Davao Death Squad (DDS), 307
de la Flor, Mayor, 264
de Venecia, Jose, 44
De Veyra, Marge, 140
death threats, 303
debt of gratitude (*utang na loob*), 27,
  66, 84, 87, 131–2, 164–5, 242,
  244, 306
Decena, Benjamin, 71
decentralisation, 23
Delfin, Robert, 272
Denosta, Edgar, 268, 269, 273
developmental machine, 168, 174–84
Diaz, Alexander, 158, 159
Dimpaoro clan, 321
Dioko, Vice-Mayor, 156
direct service, 100–1
Disoma, Gamal, 323
Domantays, 170
Duterte, Rodrigo
  Acuña and, 182
  Amatong and, 285–6
  Arenas (Baby) and, 181
  election of, 1, 43
  governing style of, 38–9
  local political machine and, 3
  PDP–Laban Party and, 298
  Remullas and, 49
  Roxas and, 180
  San Luises and, 110
  support for, 48
  term limits and, 19
  Uy and, 307
dyadic relationships, 65
dynastic expansion and contraction, in
  Makati, First District of, 144–8